CHILDREN OUT OF COURT

by

F. M. MARTIN,
SANFORD J. FOX and
KATHLEEN MURRAY

in collaboration with

PATRICIA ERICKSON,
BARBARA KELLY and
MICHELLE MYERS

1981

SCOTTISH ACADEMIC PRESS

Published by
Scottish Academic Press Ltd,
33 Montgomery Street
Edinburgh EH7 5JX

SBN 7073 0287 0

Printed in Great Britain by
Clark Constable Ltd, Edinburgh

CHILDREN OUT OF COURT

CONTENTS

LIST OF TABLES

ILLUSTRATIONS

THE AUTHORS

F. M. Martin is Professor of Social Administration, University of Glasgow.

Sanford J. Fox is Professor of Law, Boston College Law School, Massachusetts, U.S.A.

Kathleen Murray is Lecturer in charge, Panel Training Resource Centre, University of Glasgow.

COLLABORATORS

Patricia Erickson is Sociologist, Addiction Research Foundation, Toronto, Canada.

Barbara Kelly is Research Fellow, Department of Social Science and Communication, Queen's College, Glasgow.

Michelle Myers is Sociologist, Social Paediatric and Obstetric Research Unit, University of Glasgow.

INTRODUCTION

THE STUDIES REPORTED in this book grew out of a longstanding relationship between its American and its two Scottish authors. The exchange of knowledge and ideas about developments in juvenile justice in our respective countries led, early in 1977, to a shared awareness of the limitations of the research-based information then available on the Scottish system as it neared the end of its sixth year of operation. From this arose a decision to undertake a major enquiry, the findings of which would be of interest and relevance on both sides of the Atlantic.

The project was made possible by a grant from the National Institute of Juvenile Justice and Delinquency Prevention, Law Enforcement Assistance Administration, United States Department of Justice. This was awarded as LEAA Grant No. 77JN -99 -0014 to Boston College Law School, with Sanford Fox as Project Director. The grant included an experiment in the application of a form of path analysis to the provisions of the Social Work (Scotland) Act, Part III, to be conducted by Professor Fox in collaboration with Professor Jeffrey A. Meldman of the Massachusetts Institute of Technology. That part of the project is not reported in the present volume. Responsibility for planning and carrying out a variety of field studies in Scotland was sub-contracted to Glasgow University, and was in the hands of F. M. Martin and Kathleen Murray. Observations and interviews were carried out by Patricia Erickson, Barbara Kelly and Michelle Myers.

It is a pleasure to acknowledge our indebtedness to many colleagues and collaborators. We have in mind particularly David Goda, who as statistical adviser gave valuable help in matters relating to sampling, the design and layout of field instruments and a variety of other statistical and related questions; Peter Boyle, who on the basis of personal interest developed what became an indispensable role as our computer analyst; Ella Dunbar, project secretary, organizer, progress-chaser and devoted friend; and Anne Kelly, for her help with both coding and typing.

Our unnamed collaborators run to several hundred: panel members, reporters, social workers, children and their parents, who gave us their permission to observe and to question; our gratitude is no less sincere for being addressed anonymously.

F. M. M.
S. J. F.
K. M.

Glasgow and Boston, September 1980.

I

NEW DIRECTIONS

The Kilbrandon Report

Scotland, although an integral part of the United Kingdom, has maintained since the Act of Union of 1707[1] a judicial system which in criminal matters is entirely self-contained, and which formally links with that of England and Wales as far as civil proceedings are concerned, only at the supreme level of the House of Lords.[2] There are differences in substantive law as well as in procedure. In spite of the growth of United Kingdom legislation during the past century, there remain a number of areas in which legislation for Scotland must be separately enacted; these include education, health services, criminal justice and personal social services.[3] There was therefore a well-understood legal context for the coming into effect in 1971 of a new system for dealing with children in Scotland who had committed offences or who were for other reasons deemed to be 'in need of compulsory measures of care' – a system which differed quite sharply from that prevailing in England as well as from the arrangements that had previously been in force in Scotland.

These new provisions emerged, as is common in British practice, from the recommendations of a committee appointed by a Secretary of State – in this case, the Secretary of State for Scotland.[4] Whether that committee had been expected, at the time of its appointment, to propose radical changes is questionable. It had been established in 1961 with the following remit:

> 'To consider the provisions of the law of Scotland relating to the treatment of juvenile delinquents and juveniles in need of care or protection or beyond parental control and, in particular, the constitution, powers and procedure of the courts dealing with such juveniles, and to report.'[5]

The existing arrangements were certainly not uniform, and had been slow to respond to recent trends in thought. Although powers to establish separate juvenile courts had been available since 1932,[6] only four districts – Ayr, Renfrew and Fife Counties and Aberdeen City – had in fact set up such a service.[7] These four courts handled about one-sixth of all juvenile offenders, with the remainder appearing before the ordinary Sheriff Courts and Burgh Courts.[8] In the early nineteen-sixties, well over 20,000 youngsters aged eight or over but under 17 were dealt with annually by one or other of these bodies. The Kilbrandon Committee (as it has come to be known, after the title of the judge who chaired it) did not however recommend any simplification or tidying-up of the prevailing pattern, but rather its abolition and replacement by an entirely new set of provisions.

The committee recognized that the existing courts did not restrict themselves to the determination of guilt and the imposition of punishment; they argued however that although the courts had to an increasing extent come to accept a measure of responsibility for the welfare of the children who came before them, they were handicapped in any attempt to give full weight to the needs of the individual child by the necessary concern of a judicial system to emphasize responsibility for criminal acts and to impose punishments. The committee proposed therefore – and it was a proposal without precedent in either Scots or English law – that the responsibility for deciding on the measure appropriate for any given child should be separated from the responsibility for reaching decisions on guilt or innocence.

For the former purpose they proposed the establishment of wholly new bodies – juvenile panels, made up of laymen recruited in each local authority area.[9] Three members of the panel would sit on any given occasion, and to them would be referred children who were believed to be 'in need of compulsory measures of care'. If the child and parents accepted the 'grounds of referral', the panel would proceed to consider what measures were called for. If the grounds were denied, it would be for the sheriff[10] to decide in a private hearing whether the denial was soundly based – unless of course the panel members were sufficiently impressed by the denial to discharge the case; otherwise, the jurisdiction of the panel would not be resumed unless the denial of grounds was rejected by the sheriff.

A new official, the reporter to the juvenile panel, was to provide the means by which primary referrals would reach the panel. The reporter, whose background and qualifications were not prescribed but were expected to be most commonly in law or administration, would receive referrals from the police, the education authority or indeed from any agency or private individual. In each case he would be free to decide whether to bring the child and his parents before the panel, or to arrange for informal supervision by a social worker, or to take no action at all. In making his decision, the reporter would take into account not only the nature and quality of the information placed before him by the referring agent but also reports from school and social worker. In addition to his role as intake official, the reporter would be responsible for advising the panel on questions of procedure and for the administrative side of the work of the panel. The concept of an official who is notified of offences but makes an independent decision as to whether or not to take further action was greatly influenced by the ancient office of procurator fiscal.[11] In Scotland, unlike England, the police do not prosecute offenders but refer cases to the procurator fiscal for evaluation and, if deemed appropriate, subsequent prosecution. The reporter was not seen however as a replica of the procurator fiscal. The latter is in practice invariably legally qualified, though this does not appear to be required by statute. And although independent of the police authorities, the procurator fiscal forms part of a Scotland-wide service, subject to the oversight of a senior civil servant known as the Crown Agent who in his turn is responsible to the Lord Advocate, a Government minister.[12] No comparable mode of accountability was proposed for the reporter.

It was not intended that the new juvenile panels would deal with all offences by young people. Kilbrandon recommended that there should be no change in the common law power of the Lord Advocate to direct that a particular case should be heard in the Sheriff Court or even in the High Court of Justiciary. In practice, said the report, directions affecting juveniles had been almost entirely confined to the gravest crimes such as murder, attempt to murder, culpable homicide, wounding with attempt to cause grievous bodily harm, and rape; it was assumed that under the new dispensation the direction of young people to the adult courts would continue to be restricted to exceptional cases.

The juvenile panels before which would appear the large majority of young offenders and of other children judged to be in need of compulsory measures of care should, the report recommended, have a number of powers. They might of course think it appropriate to take no further action. More positively, they might assume 'supervisory jurisdiction over the child', either while he continued to live at home or requiring him to live in a residential school; or they might admonish the child, with or without a supervision order; or require attendance during leisure hours at an 'attendance centre'; or make a finding of caution[13] by the parents for their child's good behaviour, normally combined with a supervision order on the child. There should be a right of appeal to the sheriff against decisions made by the panel, but there was no suggestion that the duration of supervision orders should be restricted. Whatever the panel's decision, the over-riding criterion should be the welfare of the child. How that objective was to be identified was not a matter on which the report gave any guidance.

Kilbrandon saw the new panels as closely linked with the work of the local education authority. It was the latter that would provide lists of persons suitable for panel membership, though the final choice and the actual appointments should be made by the sheriff. In addition, and more importantly, the education department would provide the 'executive arm' of the panels. A 'social education department' should be established under the control of the Director of Education, and the staff of this department (experienced social workers) would be responsible for providing social background reports on children entering the system, making recommendations to the panels, and carrying out the supervision orders that the panels might impose.

The Kilbrandon Report is almost as interesting for its omissions as for its contents. It might have been expected that a committee whose collective view of delinquency management emphasized intervention and prevention would scan with some care the very considerable body of theory and research about the nature and causes of delinquency that had been assembled by psychologists, psychiatrists and sociologists.[14] There is nothing in the report however to suggest even the most superficial flirtation with these ideas. The theory of delinquency that underlies the report's recommendations is rooted in a kind of liberal common sense. Delinquents are for the most part children in whose case something has gone wrong in the bringing-up process. Sometimes a 'quite minor delinquency was simply a symptom of personal or environmental difficulties' (para. 13), but there is no suggestion that for the most part pathological processes are assumed to be at work. In general, delinquency arises because for whatever reason parents have been unable or unwilling to ensure that their children develop a firm sense of social responsibility. The consequent need is for the 'application of training measures appropriate to the child's needs' (para. 72), the 'application of a process of social education, which in the great majority of cases will be carried on while the child remains within the home, but which will sometimes involve his removal from home for temporary periods for more specialised and intensive residential training' (para. 140). The principal instrument for putting the principles of education and training into effect is seen to be social case-work, though the latter is never defined nor its principles and their relevance examined.

The emphasis on education and training throughout the Kilbrandon Report is striking. The few references to delinquency as sometimes stemming from an underlying maladjustment are superficial and not worked out in any detail. There are indeed numerous references to 'treatment', but it is obvious from the context (including the fact that the term is used equally to refer to the decisions of the old juvenile courts) that it is employed in the most neutral sense of 'management' or 'doing something about.' The concern with systematic education and training on the other hand, based on a rather mechanistic conception of child development, seems central to the committee's thinking. It is not easy therefore to understand why a number of commentators have claimed that the report reflects a 'medical model' of delinquency.[15] The patronizing explanations of the sociological differences between becoming delinquent and breaking a leg seem to be entirely misplaced. Even when Kilbrandon uses specifically medical analogies, as in justifying indeterminate supervision orders on the grounds that a doctor does not specify in advance the appropriate length of a treatment programme (para. 54), it is evident that the use is merely illustrative; one might equally well refer to the uncertain length of a programme for teaching literacy. Unless one subscribes to the view that any theories and practices should be defined as 'medical' if they imply that purposive intervention can bring about change in some facet of human living – a view which in our opinion robs words of meaning – there seems to be no justification for the argument that Kilbrandon's model of delinquency was a 'medical' one, apart from the effortlessness with which that model can be demolished by its critics.

The changing climate

The Kilbrandon Committee's recommendations may well have been more far-reaching than had been expected at the time of its establishment, but the context in which they were re-shaped and, in their final form, brought into effect, was one which few could have anticipated. Some of the committee's witnesses had suggested that the time was ripe for the development of a comprehensive welfare service for families, but the committee itself had never pursued such ideas, regarding them as falling well beyond its terms of reference. But the victory of the Labour Party in the General Election of 1964 brought a new group of Ministers into the Scottish Office and led to the incorporation of a specialized if imaginative set of proposals for the reform of juvenile justice into a wide-ranging reorganization of the personal social services.

During the late nineteen-fifties and early nineteen-sixties the most powerful trend in social work was the growing emphasis on those elements of theory and practice that were deemed to be common to all social work activities, irrespective of the particular client group to which they were directed or of the setting in which the work was done. Professional social work remained fragmented, carried out by small groups of specialists with circumscribed responsibilities and distinctive training; but increasingly the notion of common principles, methods and objectives in all work with individuals and families gained ground. Professional training courses, especially those based in the universities, began to shift towards a new generic pattern. Qualified social workers in Scotland, though relatively few in number, were not isolated from the mainstream of ideas and practice in their profession, and indeed made notable contributions to its development.

It could not be said that the reform of personal social services ranked high on the Labour Party's list of priorities; nor was there within the Scottish Office an influential group of social workers occupying Civil Service positions who might have exerted strong pressure for change more radical than Kilbrandon had recommended. But Mrs. Judith Hart, the energetic Under-Secretary whose responsibility it was to deal with the Kilbrandon Report, was conscious not only of the growing sense of unity among social workers but also of the many criticisms that had been expressed – though not specifically in a Scottish context – of the wasteful and possibly even harmful effects of dividing responsibility for family care between different specialists. She was also aware of the absence of preventive social work when existing social services were geared to dealing with crisis and breakdown. She recognized the possibility of carrying through a very far-reaching piece of reform within Scotland and argued therefore that, instead of implementing the Kilbrandon proposals in isolation, the opportunity should be taken to re-structure quite fundamentally the personal social services of Scottish local authorities. The comprehensive social work departments that emerged from these new moves would take on responsibility for the provision of supportive services to the proposed juvenile panels, together with a wide range of other duties hitherto carried out separately by the staff of children's departments, welfare departments, public health departments and the probation service.

The movement towards unification of the personal social services was now considerably ahead of that in England and Wales, where consideration of the future of the juvenile courts had not been linked up with any other issues and where the structure of central government – with two powerful departments sharing responsibility for the oversight of services – was less favourable to radical reform than in Scotland where only one department was involved.[16] By the end of 1965, when the Seebohm Committee on local authority social services was appointed in England, the Secretary of State for Scotland had already indicated his commitment to a new comprehensive social work service, as well as to the establishment of a reformed system of juvenile justice.

Towards implementation

The Government's intentions for Scotland were set out in the White Paper *Social Work and the Community* (Cmnd. 3065) published in October 1966. Most of the essential features of the structure outlined by Kilbrandon were retained, but a number of significant changes in nomenclature and procedure were introduced. 'Juvenile panels' became 'children's panels', and although it seemed that the local authority was still held to be the appropriate recommending body, the actual method of confirming appointments was kept open for further consideration. The concept of panel membership was considerably broadened. Kilbrandon had intended this lay body to be made up of 'persons who either by knowledge or experience were considered to be specially qualified to consider children's problems'. The White Paper advocated drawing members from a wide variety of occupation, neighbourhood, age and income groups as well as those whose 'occupations or circumstances had hitherto prevented them from taking a formal part in helping and advising young people'. The range of disposals to be available to a children's hearing – as a group of three panel members convened to consider the cases of children believed to be in need of compulsory measures of care came later to be called – appeared to be narrowed; apart from the discharge of the referral, only two alternatives were now mentioned, an order requiring supervision with the child remaining in the community, and a supervision order with a residential requirement. The flavour of indeterminacy which Kilbrandon had given to supervision orders was considerably attenuated. All supervision orders must be reviewed within a year; and they could be reviewed at any time after three months if requested by the child's parents.

The final change, and perhaps in the long run a particularly influential one, was the proposal that the 'matching fieldwork organization' should be provided by the new comprehensive social work departments, and not by the local education authorities. The Minister was no admirer of Scottish education, which in her personal opinion had too many illiberal features to be an appropriate source of supportive services for the new hearings system. In giving her allegiance to the still embryonic social work departments which were to take over *inter alia* the duties of the former probation service, she created a functional link which was likely to have important consequences for the new juvenile justice system; whatever the future vicissitudes of the social work service now outlined, they could not fail to have repercussions for the new hearings system.

In England and Wales the point of departure for reform was very different, as was the sequence of proposals, reactions and decision.[17] The admittedly poorly argued proposals for the abolition of juvenile courts which were contained in the 1965 White Paper encountered fierce opposition from the Magistrates' Association, from lawyers, and from the Probation Service, and were in due course withdrawn. There is some evidence that the incoming Home Secretary was unimpressed by the White Paper, and that civil service opinion was distinctly divided. Its successor, the 1968 White Paper *Children in Trouble* was also criticized by the same groups, but was able to muster sufficient support to find its way, fundamentally unaltered, into the following year's Children and Young Persons Act. Much of the resistance was blunted by the retention of the juvenile courts, even though the traditional functions of the court were greatly circumscribed and its underlying philosophy significantly shifted through the emphasis on such concepts as care proceedings and voluntary agreements, as well as through the transfer to social workers of important discretionary powers in respect of care orders and supervision orders. It seems probable that the comparative backwardness of the Scottish juvenile justice system in the mid-sixties, and in particular the absence of a substantial and articulate lay magistracy, made it a good deal easier to carry through strikingly innovative measures.

Nevertheless, certain similar basic assumptions underlay the proposals for reform in both Scotland and England, independently of the different historical and institutional contexts in which they were formulated. Both moved a long way from a traditional 'crime and punishment' approach to the young offender, in the direction of an essentially welfare-oriented approach. Both took the view that delinquent conduct was often symptomatic, a reflection of some maladjustment or failure of development.

Another common feature of English and Scottish reforms of the sixties was the belief that involvement in a formally constituted judicial process was in itself likely to be harmful and potentially stigmatizing to a young person. There is no reason to suppose that the Kilbrandon Committee showed the slightest interest in emerging trends in American sociology, and it may safely be assumed that its foreshadowing of labelling theory emerged spontaneously from its own deliberations. In Scotland at any rate the move towards a less formal system was also thought of as having major positive advantages. The children's hearing was seen as a forum in which panel members, referred child, parents and social worker would be able to talk freely about the problems that had led to the child's appearance and, ideally, communicate sufficiently openly and honestly that even an unpleasant decision could be accepted as in the best interests of the child.

Finally, a common characteristic of both English and Scottish reforms was the heavy responsibility given to social service departments both for advising decision-makers by the provision of background reports, and for giving effect to many of the decisions actually made. Nevertheless, although the social worker carrying out a supervision order in Scotland would enjoy great freedom in deciding on the style and content of the supervision process, he would not have complete control over it. He would have the power neither to determine the duration of the supervision order nor to convert a home supervision order to one with a residential requirement.

The Social Work (Scotland) Bill that followed the White Paper and was enacted in 1968 is rarely held up by Scots lawyers as a model of elegant draftsmanship. But although unclear on some points and ambiguous on others, it remains a document of considerable historical importance. Those parts of the Act which established and defined the duties and powers of the new social work authorities came into effect in November 1969. Part III, dealing with the children's hearings system, was not implemented until April 1971.

Several interesting alterations were introduced in these last stages of preparation for the new system, though it cannot be said that any of them involved major changes of principle. The recruitment of members of children's panels was to be in the hands of new bodies, the Children's Panel Advisory Committees, though the formal appointment of members was to be by the Secretary of State. The right to require a review of a supervision order was extended to the child as well as the parent; and any supervision order, if it had not been reviewed and extended, would automatically lapse at the end of one year. For the most part however the relevant sections of the Act gave specific and detailed form to the recommendations contained in earlier documents.

The system in outline

Part III of the 1968 Act has remained the principal legal foundation of the children's hearings system, though augmented by detailed rules regulating the work of reporters and the conduct of hearings, and modified in some particulars by subsequent legislation.[18] The formal functions and responsibilities of the different components of the hearings system and the way in which those components articulate in practice, are set out in the following paragraphs. These describe the position at the time our field studies were carried out (1978–1980), and therefore take account of recent modifications as well as of the continuing provisions of the 1968 Act.

Children are brought before a hearing by a reporter if he considers them to be in need of compulsory measures of care; for the purpose of the Act 'a child' is defined as a child under the age of 16 years or a child over 16 years but under 18 years in respect of whom a supervision requirement is in force. The Act leaves the age of criminal responsibility unchanged at eight years (Children and Young Persons (Scotland) Act 1937, S.55).

A child may be in need of compulsory measures of care (which include protection, control, guidance and treatment) if:

(a) he is beyond the control of his parent; or
(b) he is falling into bad associations or is exposed to moral danger; or
(c) lack of parental care is likely to cause him unnecessary suffering or seriously to impair his health or development; or
(d) any of the offences mentioned in Schedule 1 to the Criminal Procedure (Scotland) Act 1975 has been committed in respect of

him or in respect of a child who is a member of the same household;[19] or

(dd) the child is, or is likely to become, a member of the same household as a person who has committed any of the offences mentioned in Schedule 1 to the Criminal Procedure (Scotland) Act 1975; or

(e) the child, being a female, is a member of the same household as a female in respect of whom an offence which constitutes the crime of incest has been committed by a member of that household; or

(f) he has failed to attend school regularly without reasonable excuse; or

(g) he has committed an offence; or

(h) he is a child whose case has been referred to a children's hearing in pursuance of Part V of the Act. (Children moving to Scotland referred to a reporter by a juvenile court in England, Wales or Northern Ireland, by a local authority in England and Wales or by a welfare authority in Northern Ireland.)

Any person who has reasonable cause to believe that a child may be in need of compulsory measures of care may give to the reporter such information about the child as he may have been able to discover (1968 Act, S.37(1)). Such a notification may reach the reporter from a number of sources; for example from a social worker, a doctor, a friend or neighbour concerned about a child, his parents or the police. In practice most cases are notified to the reporter by the police. The police do not however refer to the reporter all children who are known to have committed offences; first offenders and those committing minor offences may at the discretion of the police be given an informal warning, or a formal warning before a senior officer.

At the other end of the spectrum a variety of more serious cases also do not come within the scope of the children's hearings system at this stage. The 1968 Act provided that children could be prosecuted in the sheriff court or in the High Court on the instructions of the Lord Advocate. Procurators fiscal have been directed to consider such prosecution in serious cases involving offences against the person, in cases where forfeiture of weapons or of a driving licence may be necessary and where technically necessary for proof, as in some cases where offences have been committed jointly with adults. However the court may and, where the child is already subject to a supervision order, must remit the case to the children's hearing for advice; and may also remit the case for disposal (Criminal Procedure (Scotland) Act 1975, S.372).

A reporter to the children's panel is employed by each of the twelve regional and island authorities. Most of these appointments are full-time, and in all but the smallest areas the reporter will have a number of assistants. In the whole of Scotland there are about 85 reporters, deputies and assistants. The reporter may not be removed from office by a regional authority nor be required to resign, nor be employed in any other capacity without the consent of the Secretary of State. The backgrounds of reporters are varied, some having qualifications in law and some in social work, but no official requirements are laid down. The Secretary of State is empowered to prescribe the qualifications necessary for reporters but has not so far chosen to do so.

Once the reporter has been informed of a child who may be in need of compulsory measures of care it is his function to assess (a) whether one of the preconditions laid down by the 1968 Act for intervention by the State in the child's life is satisfied, (S.32(2)), and (b) whether the child appears to be in need of compulsory measures of care (S.39(1), (2) and (3)). In the course of his investigation the reporter may obtain information from the social work department, the child's school, the police, the medical services or from any other person or agency to whom the child might be known. The reporter has three main courses he may follow:

1. to take no further action;
2. to ask the social work department to advise, guide and assist the child and his family on a voluntary basis; or
3. to bring the child before a children's hearing
   (i) if he is satisfied that there is sufficient evidence of at least one ground for referral; *and*
   (ii) if it appears to him that the child is in need of compulsory measures of care.

When the reporter has decided to refer a child to a children's hearing he has to make various arrangements. The date, time and place of the hearing are arranged in consultation with the local authority which has to provide suitable accommodation (S.34(3)); with the chairman of the children's panel, whose duty it is to arrange for members of the children's panel to be available to hear the case (Rule 5); and with the social work department which has to provide a social background report (S.39(4)). In most areas there are standing arrangements for hearings to be held at certain times and places and for rosters of panel members to be drawn up.

The child and his parents receive from the reporter seven clear days before the hearing written notification of the time and place of the hearing together with the grounds of referral (Rules 7, 8, 14, 15 and 27).

The reporter must also make available to members of the hearing at least three clear days before the hearing the relevant documents, including the grounds for referral and the social enquiry report (Rule 6(1)). If he receives any other information or document which is material to the consideration of the child's case, he must make it available to the hearing members before the hearing (Rule 6(2)). The members of the hearing are responsible for keeping secure any documents made available by the reporter, and for their immediate return to him at the conclusion of a hearing.

As a general rule there should be present at the hearing of a case the three panel members, the reporter, the child, both his parents and a representative of the social work department. The child is under an obligation to attend a hearing when he has been notified that his case has been referred to it (S.40(1)). A case may however be considered in the absence of the child if the hearing believes that his attendance is unnecessary or is likely to be detrimental to the child's interests (S.40(2)). This permits the exclusion of a child when, for example, details are given of a sexual offence or an offence involving cruelty to the child or for other intimate matters relating to his parents.

A parent has a duty to attend at all stages of a hearing at which his child's case is being considered, unless the children's hearing is satisfied that it would be unreasonable to require his attendance or that his attendance would be unnecessary to the consideration of the case (S.41(2)). Apart from this duty a parent has a *right* to attend at all stages of a children's hearing which is considering the case of his child (S.41(1)). A parent who fails to attend a hearing of his child's case when he is under a duty to do so is guilty of an offence and, if convicted, would be liable to a fine not exceeding £50 (S.41(3)). A child and his parents may be accompanied at a hearing by a representative who may be anyone chosen by the child or parent. A lawyer may act as a representative but since a hearing does not have the status of a court there is no entitlement to legal aid.

Persons apart from those already mentioned may be present. Members of the Council on Tribunals and of the Scottish Committee of that Council have a right to attend any children's hearing (S.35(3)). Press representatives are also entitled to be present but no report may reveal the name, address or school or include any particulars calculated to lead to the identification of any child in any way concerned with a hearing unless the Secretary of State allows publication because he is satisfied that this is in the interests of justice (S.58(3)). Other persons who may attend hearings at the discretion of the chairman are potential members of children's panels, panel members in training, members of the Children's Panel Advisory Committee, social workers in training and persons studying the system of the children's hearings (S.35(1) and (2)). The chairman must take all reasonable steps to ensure that the number of persons present at any one time is kept to a minimum: the purpose is to ensure as far as possible that the hearing takes the form of a confidential discussion and not a public enquiry.

In each region and islands area members of the children's panel are appointed by the Secretary of State from a list of applicants nominated by the Children's Panel Advisory Committee (CPAC), a committee created for the main purpose of recruiting and selecting members. The committee consists of two members appointed by the local authority and three, including the chairman, by the Secretary of State. In the large region of Strathclyde the composition is four local authority representatives and six appointed by the Secretary of State. Most CPACs have exercised their power to set up sub-committees to serve areas within the region.

The CPACs were also given the task of advising the Secretary of State on certain matters relating to the general administration of panels. These include

1. the number of members to be appointed to the panel;
2. the action to be taken in any circumstances which may cast doubt on the fitness of a panel member to serve;

3. the extent to which further training for panel members may be needed.[20]

Apart from their obligation to advise the Secretary of State on questions he may refer to them, it is open to the CPACs to consider other matters relating to the work of the hearings: for example, relations with the general public, proposals for research or general questions on which the chairman of the panel wishes consultation. Consideration of the cases of individual children is of course completely the responsibility of the hearings and not the function of CPACs.

A children's hearing may consider the case only if the child and his parents accept the grounds of referral. Should the child be incapable of understanding the grounds, as in many cases of non-accidental injury to young children, or be unwilling to accept the grounds or the parents be unwilling to accept the grounds, the hearing may consider the child's case only if the sheriff finds the grounds established after hearing evidence (S.42(2)(a), (b) and (c)). The sheriff deals with such cases in chambers and not in open court. The procedure does not correspond either to that of criminal trial or to that of civil proof, and has been described by a distinguished legal commentator as a procedure *sui generis* (Gordon, 1976).[21]

If the family accept the grounds, or the sheriff finds the grounds established, the hearing goes on to discuss the whole circumstances of the child and his social background. The grounds of referral must be discussed (S.43(1)) but so also may such matters as relationships within the home, the child's school attendance and progress, and any medical or psychiatric factors as may be relevant.

In order that the hearing takes account of only such facts as are made known to the family, the chairman of the hearing is obliged to inform the family of the substance of all reports laid before the hearing (Rule 17(3)). After a full discussion of the case the hearing has to come to a decision on whether the child requires compulsory measures of care and, if so, what measures are appropriate (S.44(1)). In reaching this decision the hearing is obliged by the Act to have regard only to the 'best interests of the child' (S.43(1)): no mention is made in the statute of the hearing being in any way concerned with retribution, the protection of society or deterrence. 'Best interests' are not however defined either in the Act or in any supporting statutory documents. The range of decisions open to a hearing is limited. It may discharge the referral; or it may make a supervision order which allows the child to remain at home but requires him to remain under the supervision of a social worker; or it may require a child to reside in a residential establishment[22] (S.44(1)(a) and (b)).

One of the essential features of the children's hearings system is that children under supervision (at home, or under a residential requirement) have their cases kept under review. A supervision requirement lasts for a year and a child under supervision must appear before a hearing at least every year (S.48(3)). The family may ask for a review three months after the initial decision (where a hearing has renewed a previous requirement, without alteration, that period is extended to six months) (S.48(4)). The social work department may call for a review at any time (S.48(2)).

The child or parents who are unhappy about the decision of the hearing, either because they think that the disposal is inappropriate or because of some procedural defect in the conduct of the case before the hearing, may appeal against the hearing's decision to the sheriff (S.49(1)). The sheriff is enjoined to support the appeal only if he is satisfied that the decision of the hearing is not justified 'in all the circumstances of the case' and not otherwise (S.49(5)). In allowing the appeal the sheriff may either discharge the child from further proceedings or remit the case to a hearing for reconsideration of the original decision (S.49(5)(b)). Further appeal lies, on a point of law only, to the Court of Session (S.50).

Legal advice and assistance are available to the child and his parents free or at a reduced cost in accordance with income. Advice may be sought about, for example, acceptance of grounds for referral or the procedure of the hearing. The legal aid system by which the fees of defence counsel may be met from Government funds does not extend to the provision of a lawyer to speak for the child or his parents at the hearing. Legal aid is however available for proceedings before the sheriff or in appeals to the Court of Session.

Getting off the ground

Contrary to some earlier expectations, it did not prove difficult to recruit members of children's panels. During 1970 between three and four thousand men and women applied for not much more than a thousand places. The Secretary of State provided the committees with guidance on the desirable characteristics of panel members (Social Work Services Group, Circular No. SW7/1969).

> 'Essential to the success of children's hearings is the finding of sufficient suitable members of the community to serve in them. They should have knowledge and experience in dealing with children and families and should be drawn from a wide range of neighbourhood, age group and income group. They require the right personal qualities, including the absence of bias and prejudice, and a genuine interest in the needs of children in trouble and their relationship to the community. Moreover the success of the children's hearings will depend to a large extent on the ability of their members to get through to the children and their parents; and a capacity to communicate with them, and an understanding of their feelings and reactions so that they gain their confidence will be of great importance. It is hoped that the new system will attract suitable people whose occupations or circumstances have hitherto prevented them from taking a formal

> part in helping and advising young people or who might not have previously thought of themselves as candidates for public service'.

At the same time the committees were given the following advice about selection procedure:

> 'Persons who appear to be eligible for consideration should generally be invited to attend an initial interview, with the dual purpose of giving information about what panel membership involves and of enabling a preliminary view to be obtained of persons' capabilities. A single interview would not normally be sufficient for this purpose, however, and it is therefore important that the persons considered appropriate by the Children's Panel Advisory Committee should thereafter attend a fuller session of interviews and group discussions designed to give a clearer picture of the implications of panel membership and of the suitability of individuals for it. Generally speaking the Secretary of State would intend to appoint as panel members only those who have been recommended by the Advisory Committee after going through a procedure broadly of this kind.'

Selection procedures of varying degrees of sophistication were established in the hope of ensuring that those recruited would be people with a genuine concern for the welfare of children, yet free from extreme attitudes either of punitiveness or of permissiveness, and at the same time of achieving a wide representation of different social groups. The compatibility of these objectives, the varying degrees of success with which they have been achieved, and in particular their implications for the actual practice of children's hearings have been extensively discussed since the hearings system came into effect;[23] some of the issues involved are examined in later chapters.

The introduction of children's hearings in 1971 involved the recently established social work departments in new responsibilities which were both exacting and large in scale. These new demands cannot be said to have created welcome tasks for idle hands. An early but recurrent problem of the new social work authorities had been that of an unforeseen level of demand for personal social services. In the urban-industrial districts in particular, the new provisions brought to light areas of need not previously recognized, which placed very heavy demands on departments that soon came to be seen as seriously understaffed. Much of the new demand stemmed from problems in which financial and environmental factors played a large part. Whether social work solutions are the most appropriate response to such problems is, to say the least, arguable; but the open-ended commitment of the 1968 Act gave no ready-made protection, and the operational philosophy that emerged tended to be an uneasy compromise between the generous aspirations of professional social work and the day-to-day exigencies of local authority practice. The almost inevitable consequence was a heavy emphasis on work with crisis situations as they arose, rather than the carefully planned long-term preventive work to which the White Paper had looked forward. The additional work load generated by children's hearings was a heavy one: in a typical year there would be some 15,000 referrals by reporters to hearings, and some 7,000 orders made for social work supervision in the community. The priority necessarily – if sometimes reluctantly – accorded to these statutory responsibilities inevitably reduced still further the scope for that careful assessment and long-term intensive work with vulnerable individuals and families that had been seen as a major objective of the unification of personal social services.

A new dimension of uncertainty was added when it became clear that existing social work departments were soon to be amalgamated as a consequence of the proposed reorganization of local government. Following the recommendations of the Wheatley Commission, it was decided to create two tiers of local government in Scotland.[24] The location of social work was seriously debated but the arguments of those who saw it as essentially a community-based service, responsive to local needs, and wanted it to be given to the smaller district authorities, were outweighed by the claim that the amalgamation of resources at the regional level would make for a more comprehensive range of provision and access to more high-powered specialist services. As far as the regional pattern itself was concerned, the principal subject of debate was the proposal to establish the Strathclyde Region, covering half the population of Scotland and a good deal more than half of its industrial, social and delinquency problems. In the end the Local Government (Scotland) Act, 1973 created nine mainland regions, including Strathclyde with a population of 2·5 millions and Lothian with 0·76 million. The three all-purpose island authorities also became responsible for social work. Thus within five years of coming into existence 50 social work departments and reporter's departments – and 50 reporters and directors of social work – were each reduced to 12. Those social work directors who were unsuccessful in the competition for the new regional directorships were with few exceptions incorporated into the larger new departments as second- or third-tier officers. The newly formed regional reporters' departments, on the other hand, were not large enough to offer attractive opportunities to all the able men and women who had headed small but independent city or county units, now disbanded; the regional reporter of the largest region controlled a smaller staff than the director of social work of the smallest region. As a result, there were some qualitatively important losses to the reporters' profession. Legally qualified reporters in particular were tempetd to seek alternative outlets for their skills, in local government administration, in the procurator fiscal service, or in private practice.

County, city and burgh panels too were merged to form regional groupings, not without considerable initial regrets at the loss of local identities. Regional panels subsequent to reorganization ranged in size from 900 in Strathclyde to

30 in Borders; the island authorities had their own children's panels, as small as 11 and 9 in Shetland and Orkney. A potentially important step was taken when in 1977 the Scottish Association of Children's Panels came into existence, with the prospect of providing a single voice for the lay participants in the system and the hope of counteracting an already marked tendency to regional introversion.

NOTES

1. Prior to 1603, Scotland was an independent kingdom, and even after the Union of the English and Scottish Crowns in that year retained its own parliament for another hundred years. The *Act of Union* of 1707 allowed each country to retain its own laws and its own Church. While the united parliament is the sole source of legislation, Scotland continues to maintain an independent legal system. For a detailed account of the historical events, *see* J. D. Mackie, *A History of Scotland*. Penguin, Harmondsworth, 1964.
2. *House of Lords*. In a general sense, the second (non-elected) chamber of parliament, consisting of hereditary and life peers, senior bishops of the Anglican Church and the Lords of Appeal in Ordinary. In the present context the House of Lords is the supreme judicial authority of the United Kingdom consisting of the Lord Chancellor and the Lords of Appeal in Ordinary.
3. *For example*, the Mental Health Act, 1959 and the Mental Health (Scotland) Act, 1960; the Local Government Act, 1974 and the Local Government (Scotland) Act, 1973.
4. The *Secretary of State for Scotland* is one of two government ministers with particular responsibility for Scottish affairs, the other being the Lord Advocate (see note 12). By tradition the Secretary of State is always a member of the House of Commons and has responsibility for a wide range of administration including health, education, housing, roads, etc. His duties include the administration of the courts, and in particular the sheriff court, but in this sphere he works in close consultation with the Lord Advocate.
5. The findings were published in 1964 in the Report of the Committee on Children and Young Persons (Scotland), Cmnd. 2306, HMSO (Kilbrandon Report).
6. Section 1 of the Children and Young Persons (Scotland) Act, 1932 which was subsequently consolidated in the Children and Young Persons (Scotland) Act, 1937.
7. There are no obvious reasons for the development of special juvenile courts in these areas. It was certainly not due to increasing crime rates.
8. The *burgh courts* dealt with minor offences and were presided over by lay magistrates who were normally senior elected members of the local authority. In May 1975 they were replaced by new *district courts* which were set up in each district and islands area staffed by part-time lay justices of the peace. Most justices are appointed by the Secretary of State but district and islands councils may appoint up to one quarter of their members to be *ex officio* justices.
   The *sheriff courts* deal with the greater part of all civil and criminal proceedings in Scotland. The most serious crimes such as murder, rape, incest and treason are reserved for the High Court. Appeals lie to the High Court sitting as a court of appeal. The sheriff – the equivalent of a judge in most other countries – is an experienced legal practitioner who holds a permanent appointment under the Crown.
   The *High Court of Justiciary* is Scotland's supreme criminal court and is both a court of first instance and a court of appeal. The judges of the High Court when dealing with civil matters, sit as the Court of Session.
9. In addition to the central government, Scotland has a system of local government which was reorganized in 1975. Prior to that date Scotland was divided into counties governed as regards local issues by an elected council. The larger towns and cities also had their own elected councils. In 1975 all these bodies ceased to exist, and

instead, Scotland is now divided into nine mainland regions, the territory of each of which is sub-divided into a number of districts, and three all-purpose island authorities. Each regional and district authority has its own elected council.

10. See Note 8.
11. The *procurator fiscal* is the prosecutor in the sheriff court, although his duties range much further. The office of procurator fiscal was known in the 16th century when he was an officer employed by the sheriff with the duty of collecting fines imposed by the court. The prosecuting duties passed from the sheriff to the procurator fiscal who by the middle of the 19th century became responsible to the Lord Advocate. In 1927 the appointment of procurators fiscal was placed in the hands of the Lord Advocate and since then all procurators fiscal and their deputes have been whole time civil servants. Today the procurator fiscal is completely independent of the sheriff.
12. The *Lord Advocate* is the Government's senior law officer for Scotland. Although his is a political appointment, he is not necessarily a Member of Parliament. He is always however a practising advocate of high standing. The Lord Advocate has a permanent staff, known as the Crown Office, which is headed by the Crown Agent. All these officials are permanent civil servants with the same conditions of service as other branches of the British civil service. Appointments to the Crown Office are made from the procurator fiscal service which the Lord Advocate has the responsibility for administering as well as directing.
13. *Caution* is a sum of money lodged as a surety for the child's good behaviour over a stated period of time. Should the child be of good behaviour the money would be refunded to the parent at the end of the period, but if he gets into further trouble during the period the parents would forfeit the caution.
14. *For example*, John Bowlby, *Forty Four Juvenile Thieves*. Baillière, London, 1947. *Child Care and the Growth of Love*. Penguin, Harmondsworth, 1953.
 Albert K. Cohen, *Delinquent Boys: The Culture of the Gang*. Free Press, Chicago, 1955.
 Richard Cloward and Lloyd Ohlin, *Delinquency and Opportunity: A Theory of Delinquent Gangs*. Free Press, Chicago, 1960.
 Gordon Trasler, *The Explanation of Criminality*. Routledge and Kegan Paul, London, 1962.
 H. S. Becker, *Outsiders*. Free Press, New York, 1963.
 H. J. Eysenck, *Crime and Personality*. Routledge and Kegan Paul, London, 1964.
 D. Matza, *Delinquency and Drift*. Wiley, New York, 1964.
 L. Wilkins, *Social Deviance*. Tavistock, London, 1964.
15. David May, 'Delinquency control and the treatment model: some implications of recent legislation', *British Journal of Criminology*, 1971, 11(4).
 Allison Morris in collaboration with Mary McIsaac, *Juvenile Justice?*. Cambridge Studies in Criminology, Heinemann, 1978.
 Paul D. Brown and Terry Bloomfield (eds.), *Legality and Community*. Aberdeen Peoples Press, 1979.
16. The two departments in England and Wales are the Home Office which was responsible for child care services as well as probation and after care; and the Department of Health and Social Security which was responsible for personal social services associated with local authority health and welfare departments.
17. The English reform was preceded by:
 (i) *Report of the Committee on Children and Young Persons* (Ingleby Committee), Cmnd. 1191, HMSO, 1960.
 Set up in 1956 to inquire into the operation of the juvenile court and to make recommendations for its improvement; it was also invited to consider the powers and duties of local authorities in the prevention of child neglect. The committee recognized the conflict between the court's judicial and welfare functions but still argued in favour of its retention. It recommended raising the age of criminal responsibility from 8 to 12 and below that age replacing criminal proceedings with care and protection proceedings. These recom-

mendations did not become law (except that the age of criminal responsibility was raised to 10 in England and Wales).

(ii) Labour Party Study Group, *Crime – A Challenge to Us All.* Transport House, 1964.
As an alternative to the juvenile court this suggested a 'family service' in which the child, family and social worker would discuss the treatment of the child and only where agreement could not be reached or where the facts of the case were disputed would the child be referred to a new 'family court'.

(iii) *The Child the Family and the Young Offender.* Cmnd. 2742, HMSO, 1965.
The proposals in (ii) were endorsed except that a 'family council' consisting of social workers and other persons selected for their understanding and experience of children replaced the 'family service'. It aroused considerable opposition.

(iv) *Children in Trouble.* Cmnd. 3601, HMSO, 1968.
This abandoned the family council concept and retained the juvenile court. Children between the ages of 14 and 17 could be subject to criminal proceedings but only after mandatory consultation between police and social workers and after application to a magistrate for a warrant to prosecute. Social workers were also given the power to vary as well as implement the disposition orders made by the courts. Magistrates were no longer to be involved in detailed decisions about the kind of treatment appropriate for the child. Thus, although the composition and constitution of the juvenile court was virtually unchanged, its jurisdiction was radically altered. This formed the basis of the Children and Young Persons Act, 1969.

18. The main statutory instruments are:
The Social Work (Scotland) Act 1968 subsequently referred to as *1968 Act.*
A few amendments have been incorporated by the Children and Young Persons Act 1969, the Local Government (Scotland) Act 1973 and the Children Act 1975.
The Children's Hearings (Scotland) Rules 1971 No. 492 (S.60) subsequently referred to as *Rule(s)*.
The Reporter's Duties Rules 1971 No. 525 (S.72).

19. Schedule 1 to the Criminal Procedure (Scotland) Act 1975 broadly deals with sexual offences and offences of assault and neglect against a child.

20. On appointment panel members are required to attend a short course of part time training and subsequently they are encouraged though not obliged to take part in courses of in-service training. For discussion of current trends in panel member training *see* Kathleen Murray, 'Representing the community', *Times Educational Supplement*, 25 July 1980.

21. Gerald Gordon, 'The role of the courts' in: F. M. Martin and K. Murray (eds.), *Children's Hearings*, Scottish Academic Press, 1976.

22. The range of residential establishments to which hearings have power to send children includes children's homes and hostels and List D schools, formerly known as 'approved schools'. Hearings cannot send children to borstal, detention centre or attendance centre. The term *List D* is derived from the classification on the Scottish Education Department lists. There are 25 List D schools in Scotland of which six are for girls.

23. David May and Gilbert Smith, 'Policy interpretation and the children's panels – a case study in social administration', *Journal of Applied Social Studies*, 1970, 2.
'The appointment of the Aberdeen city children's panel', *British Journal of Social Work* 1971, 1(1).
Andrew Rowe, *Initial selection for children's panels in Scotland.* Bookstall Publications, London, 1972.
Elizabeth Mapstone, 'The selection of the children's panel for the county of Fife', *British Journal of Social Work*, 1973, 2(4).

24. The Report of the Royal Commission on Local Government in Scotland, Cmnd. 4150, HMSO, 1969.

2

AREAS OF DEBATE

The man and woman in the street

The absence of certain institutional obstacles to juvenile justice reform in Scotland in the late nineteen-sixties should not be taken to imply the presence of a uniformly favourable environment for the types of change that were planned. Indeed, Scotland was in some important respects an unlikely setting for a new development that placed a strong emphasis on the welfare of the individual child and did not employ the vocabulary of punishment. By comparison with most countries of Western Europe, or even with England and Wales, Scotland seemed to retain many illiberal and even punitive features in its social life – a greater emphasis on formal discipline and an acceptance of corporal punishment in schools, a failure to reform either the law of divorce or the law relating to homosexuality in line with changes already accepted in England. The response to social problems often seemed to emphasize segregative residential solutions. The populations of the prisons, the psychiatric hospitals, the institutions for the mentally handicapped, the residential establishments for deprived children were all proportionately larger in Scotland than south of the Border.

Given these strands in the cultural context, it is scarcely surprising that the children's hearings system gave rise, especially in its early years, to a good deal of adverse criticism. This was reflected in and possibly encouraged by the popular press.[1] It seemed that any local authority councillor, police spokesman or member of the general public who expressed himself forcefully about the rising tide of crime and violence, derisively about the 'toothlessness' of the panel system or sneeringly about the impotence of 'do-gooders' was assured generous press publicity, with headlines that emphasized thuggery and hooliganism and the failure of the hearings system to control them. Any reported increase in the number of children referred to reporters was likely to be interpreted as further evidence of the system's failure.

Bruce (1978),[2] referring to what he calls 'critics of "the right"', says that those who expressed such views had either never understood or never accepted the principles on which the new system was based. He further suggests that it has been difficult to know whether the real target was intended to be the extent of the hearing's powers or the available resources or the decision-making of the panel members. But it would be irrelevant to fault criticisms of this kind for their lack of closely reasoned argument. They both expressed and appealed to emotionally-based attitudes, and were none the less effective for that.

No one, as far as we know, has ever made a systematic study of attitudes towards the hearings system and towards delinquency in general in different sectors of the Scottish public. We might reasonably speculate however that in the early seventies, it was not just a very small but vocal minority that had an imperfect understanding of the new system, was cynical about its aims and methods and continued to hold to a belief in the value of punishment for the erring young. Yet even if conservative and punitive attitudes were widespread, it would be misleading to assume that they were universal. The motives of those who joined children's panels were no doubt sometimes mixed, but, as our own later evidence shows, the large majority of the considerable numbers who volunteered for that demanding task were closely identified with the formal aims of the new system.

Panel members in particular, anxious for social approval,[3] were deeply pained by what they saw as ill-informed and sensationalist criticism, and outraged by the difficulties of promoting rational discussion in the mass media. Forced into a defensive position, they often found themselves responding to attacks in ways which implicitly accepted the underlying assumptions of their critics – maintaining for example that it was unfair to condemn children's hearings as a 'soft option', because just as many if not more children were being sent to residential establishments than before the introduction of the new system. Most commonly however they argued that their good work was being undermined by a lack of the resources necessary to implement their decisions. There were not enough social workers available, and most of those in post were inexperienced; what was the point, they asked, of making supervision orders if they were going to be carried out so perfunctorily as to discredit the whole system? There was a serious shortage of places in List D schools[4] (the former 'approved schools'); why should panel members be blamed if, having decided that admission to a residential establishment was essential in a particular case, it then became necessary to wait for weeks or even months before a place became available? If only more – and perhaps better – resources were available, panel members argued, the virtues of the new system would soon become apparent to its critics.

In fact, by the time our own research got under way significant quantitative changes were already taking place. The number of children referred to reporters was declining annually. The problem of the List D schools had been dramatically reversed; instead of a shortage of places there was now a surfeit, and there was serious discussion of possible closures. At the same time the availability of social workers was improving rapidly. Between 1974 and 1978 the fieldwork staff of Scottish local authority social work departments doubled. Inevitably, the growth was principally in newly qualified practitioners, though it seemed likely that the turnover rate of field staff was lower than it had been in the early seventies. It is also worthy of note that after about the first five years of the system's operation strident expressions of criticism seemed to appear markedly less often. The files of newspaper cuttings grew perceptibly thinner. No doubt there was a continuing discrepancy between the theoretical principles of the hearings system and the lowest common denominator of public opinion; but it seemed that the system in practice had come to be accepted as an integral part of the Scottish scene. It is unlikely that the reservations felt by the police were ever fully overcome, but their spokesmen's condemnations became comparatively muted, and in an institutional sense at any rate they came fully to terms with the hearings system – which would indeed soon have come to a halt without their day-to-day co-operation.

On the fringe of Academe

The preoccupations of academic critics of the hearings system were very different from those of the man in the street – or at any rate the self-appointed exponents of his views. In considering the former, it is important to recall some of the changes in the climate of discussion that were characteristic of the second half of the nineteen-sixties and the first half of the following decade. The changes in question were complex, and it is not possible here to do more than outline them in rather broad terms. The key features seem to be certain shifts in thinking that were more readily diffused as a result of the expansion of higher education in Britain: first, a move towards 'sociological' rather than 'psychological' modes of conceptualization and explanation; and within sociology itself a reaction against the positivist tradition, a reluctance to take for granted 'official' categories and definitions as non-problematic, a new emphasis on the role of social agencies in creating or at least amplifying social problems, and an upsurge of political radicalism.

All of these trends had major implications for the fields of criminology and penology. In many ways they created a framework for discussion which could not easily contain the assumptions, expressed and implicit, of the Kilbrandon Committee. That committee had done singularly little to review current ideas of the nature and causation of delinquency; certainly it had made no attempt to place its own recommendations in a specific theoretical context. Knowing who was and was not a delinquent was not seen as presenting any particular problems. Delinquency stemmed from some failure or weakness in upbringing; the belief that the root causes of crime were to be found in bad housing, unemployment and material deprivation was explicitly rejected. (Kilbrandon Report, para. 77).[5] And the most appropriate response to delinquency was essentially that of re-education, with the object of aiding the child's social and emotional development. Involvement in a formal judicial process was to be avoided, as likely to do more damage than good.

Academic commentary on and criticism of the Kilbrandon Report and of the children's hearings system has not been voluminous, nor have all those who have contributed to it worked within a common frame of reference. With the possible exception of one collection of essays (Brown & Bloomfield, 1979),[6] there is no coherent critique of the theory and practice of children's hearings from a clearly defined theoretical standpoint. Several strands of argument can be identified, and these occur in different combinations in different pieces of writing. Our present attempt is not to review the literature article by article in a systematic fashion, but rather to indicate the types of concept employed and propositions advanced.

The long search for the distinguishing characteristics of young delinquents had yielded, over the years, disappointingly few clear-cut and unambiguous findings. Interest was tending to shift away from the question 'Who are the delinquents?' towards the question 'What is involved in becoming a delinquent?'.[7] Some studies of self-reported offences gave the impression that some recourse to law-breaking was a very common experience; yet only a minority of those who committed offences became formally identified as 'delinquents'. What was the nature of the selective processes at work?

One common finding of statistical studies of juvenile delinquents was that they tended to be drawn with disproportionate frequency from the least privileged socio-economic groups.[8] No one has carried out a comparable study of the origins of children entering the hearings system (though some information is presented in *Chapter 5*), but the impressions of observers appear to agree that the social distribution is much the same. The surface relationship is open to a wide range of explanations, including crude environmental determinism, response to blockage of legitimate opportunities, and class antagonism. But in the light of the newly-awakened interest in the role of social agencies in 'constructing' delinquency,[9] it now seemed plausible that the socio-economic distribution of offenders might reflect nothing more fundamental than the selective response of law enforcement agencies to lower class delinquents.

The significance attached to this assumed selectivity was immeasurably enhanced by the introduction of the set of ideas generically referred to as labelling theory.[10] Some variations of labelling theory are more subtle than others, but the alternative versions all have in common an incrimination of the justice system itself as a major – if not the major – factor in the making of delinquents. The processes of arrest, trial and punishment, the argument ran, tended powerfully to reinforce a delinquent sense of identity. Tentative, minimal lawbreaking, which if ignored might well have petered out with no further consequences, could be converted as a result of police and judicial intervention into a career of long term delinquency.

The principles of labelling theory came to be applied not only to crime and delinquency but to almost all modes of deviant behaviour, and in one form or another came to be quite widely accepted, particularly in the professions and semi-professions associated with the personal social services. This acceptance was comparatively uncritical, and wholly out of proportion to the volume and quality of the evidence that was actually available in corroboration of the theory. In the eyes of those who accepted labelling theory, any judicial or correctional system was likely to be suspect. The Kilbrandon Committee, working without any explicit reference to such ideas, had expressed the opinion that involvement in a formally constituted judicial process was likely to prove detrimental to children and had produced a lay system with an explicit emphasis on the welfare of the child in the belief that this would at the very least avoid damage and in most cases prove positively beneficial. The adherent of labelling theory, however, was more sceptical. The supposed advantages of the hearings system might be largely illusory. The damage inflicted by a lay panel and a supervising social worker might be no less than that caused by an old-style juvenile court and probation officer.

The prevailing climate of ideas among those who wrote about deviance in the late sixties and seventies – and to a large extent also among social work practitioners – was not merely generously optimistic in its view of human nature but also quite strongly libertarian. The term 'social control' came to be used pejoratively. Traditionally, sociologists had employed the concept quite neutrally to refer to a large range of processes by which all societies maintain a degree of stability and continuity. Even such influential contemporary writers as Berger and Luckman (1967) comment:

> 'Institutions also, by the very fact of their existence, control human conduct by setting up predefined patterns of conduct, which would channel it in one direction as against the many other directions that would theoretically be possible. It is important to stress that this controlling character is inherent in institutionalization as such, prior to or apart from any mechanisms of sanctions specifically set up to support an institution. These mechanisms (the sum of which constitute what is generally called a system of social control) do, of course, exist in many institutions and in the agglomerations of institutions that we call societies.'[11]

Nevertheless, the phrase came increasingly to be used in the sense of 'enforced – and therefore unarguably undesirable – conformity to certain arbitrary norms of behaviour'. From this perspective (the implications of which seem never fully to have been examined) any form of intervention with delinquents comes under critical scrutiny with respect to its objectives. Protestations that a given system is dedicated to promoting the welfare of the individual children passing through it tend to be received with some scepticism as long as compulsory powers are exercised in order to bring about changes in behaviour in the direction of greater obedience to laws and social conventions. The incompatibility of 'welfare' and 'social control' tends, from this standpoint, to be assumed rather than demonstrated.

The concept of class differences in value systems plays an important linking role, and recurs in a number of discussions of the children's hearings system. A sharp contrast is postulated between the values of (predominantly working class) delinquents and those of the (predominantly middle class) panel members who sit in judgment on them. This leads, the argument runs, to a lack of understanding and of empathy, to an assumption that 'middle class' values are universally applicable, and to the imposition of measures of control (such as social work supervision) which aim to achieve a shift from supposedly less desirable to more desirable social values. This particular argument, which takes it for granted that delinquents reflect a class-typed value system, is difficult to reconcile with the notion that delinquent acts occur indiscriminately in all social classes and that it is only the selective activities of law enforcement agencies that explain the social distribution of those who become 'cases'. More importantly, the theory includes a number of generalizations whose accuracy is not self-evident. The presumption of a simple dichotomy of value-systems may be more romantic than realistic. Some values may transcend class boundaries, while in respect of others the variations within social classes may be no less significant than the differences between them. Specifically, to assume that the values of young delinquents are easily compatible with those of the manual working class as a whole, or that the dominant working class values in respect of property violations or of physical aggression are sharply at variance with the corresponding middle class values may or may not be justified. In the absence of detailed empirical evidence, the confident generalizations may amount to little more than fashionable prejudices. It is unfortunate that ideas about class and conformity, like so many of the themes that recur in discussions of delinquency and related issues during the period under review, were never carried beyond the level of casual assertion.

An American argument

Central to the American experience has been the realization that traditional juvenile court theory has provided a wholly inadequate account of what juvenile courts were in fact doing, and had been doing from their initial creation in Illinois in 1899. That theory postulated that juvenile courts – and the special juvenile correction institutions that had preceded them three-quarters of a century earlier – functioned to advance the welfare of the children who came before them, and that there was a near perfect match between these children's interests and the welfare of the community as a whole. All of this was predicated on rehabilitative and treatment programmes that would save children from future careers in crime and for the present, preserve them from the demoralizing experience of the criminal court and the dehumanizing and brutalizing experience of adult imprisonment.

It was no secret, however, that both the knowledge and the resources needed for the rehabilitative programmes were in perpetual short supply and that there was all too often very little to distinguish the inhumanity of a reform school from that of the state penitentiary. Nearly all of 19th-century juvenile justice reform had been a round of trial and error determined by the stubborn persistence of these realities. Nor was there any novelty in the realization that juvenile court intake was premised on the occurrence of misbehaviour sufficiently serious to warrant an official response, and not on the diagnosis of a pathological condition in the child for which the court could administer a remedy. The brief period of association with psychiatric facilities, exemplified by the delinquency prevention efforts jointly undertaken in the nineteen-thirties by the Boston Juvenile Court and the Judge Baker Guidance Center under the direction of Drs. William Healy and Augusta Bronner, had amply demonstrated that access to even eminently skilled services produced little in the way of delinquency control or benefit to children. But unlike a clinic, which traditional child welfare theory took the court closely to resemble, the court could not and did not turn away children whose welfare it could not advance and whose problems it could not solve. Like the correctional institutions of the preceding century whose philosophy they inherited and which found themselves required to receive children from the courts even when their programmes were only remotely related to those children's needs, juvenile courts found themselves with unavoidable responsibilities. It remained for the court to reiterate the norms that had been traversed and to incapacitate, by a variety of freedom-depriving measures, children who, for whatever reason, either could not or would not accord minimal respect to the rights of others. But that it did this in the name of child welfare, denying that it was in the law enforcement business, permitted the juvenile court to act free of the usual constraints Anglo-American legal and political values place on judicial agencies that administer punishments.

Why, in the past twenty years, these features of juvenile justice have been 'discovered' can admit only of speculation. One factor must have been the dynamics of the civil rights movement and its concern for the alienated black youths who became the clientele of major urban juvenile courts following the large-scale northward migration of blacks during and after the Second World War. The development of egalitarian ideals in this same period also served to highlight the discrepancy between what happened to children processed through the justice system and those whose families were affluent enough to utilize private treatment resources when they were apprehended for breaking the law. In addition, the War on Poverty and other Great Society programmes designed to upgrade education, housing, employment and other weaknesses in the ecology of the classes whose children were grist for the justice mill served to support a renaissance of environmental theories of delinquency causation. These theories not only emphasized that rehabilitative efforts with individual delinquents were largely unsuccessful, they also provided theoretical arguments for why they *could* not be successful and ought, therefore, to be abandoned. If the genesis of a child's delinquency is in his environment, there is little justification for keeping him in prolonged custody in order to neutralize his personal contribution to the misbehaviour. Juvenile court informalities in the name of a largely illusory commitment to child welfare, as well as the unwarranted correctional programmes thus became the natural targets of the latest round of juvenile justice reforms. The criminal court and its jurisprudential principles designed to control overreaching in the enforcement of the law no longer appeared as the nemesis of children but rather, in Christopher Lasche's[12] phrase, as a haven in a heartless world.

A major contributor to this development was the Supreme Court of the United States. While it could not bring children to the criminal court in any direct sense of relocating jurisdiction to hear their cases, it could bring the criminal court to them in the juvenile court. In the landmark case of *In re Gault* (1967)[13] the Court held that major safeguards of criminal procedure had to be observed in delinquency proceedings. Of central importance, it mandated the opportunity of having the assistance of a lawyer to defend against the state and to ensure fidelity to the procedural rules. Other major Supreme Court pronouncements emphasized the law enforcement focus of juvenile court litigation – that the offence had to be proved beyond a reasonable doubt (*In re Winship* (1970))[14] and that protection against being twice placed in jeopardy applied to children (*Breed* v. *Jones* (1975))[15] – although the Court refused to accord the right to trial by jury in the view that this would constitute a definitive renunciation of all child welfare purposes.

Juvenile court legislation in the states is being rewritten to flesh out the Supreme Court initiatives. Detailed procedural prescriptions and a great narrowing of judicial and administrative discretion have come to replace the exhortation to provide such parental care for child offenders as seems fit in particular cases. The trend is toward limiting the duration of sanctions that may be imposed, to no longer than could be included in an adult criminal sentence for the same offence, or to construct a special set of sanction limits which, although significantly less severe than comparable adult sentences, adhere to the ethic of proportioning their possible duration to the seriousness of the misconduct.

There is in these developments an awakening of retributivist principles in the juvenile court, not in the Kantian sense that punishment must be inflicted for its own sake and regardless of any utilitarian ends that may be served or disserved, but rather in recognition that the general justifying aim for having a system of juvenile justice is the social need to control criminal behaviour and that pursuit of this utilitarian goal must itself be limited and controlled by retributivist principles that prevent benign purposes from becoming cruel injustice.

Yet, there is a risk of lapsing into absurdity by a wholesale importing of criminal jurisprudence into the juvenile court. The value of these principles in cases of serious misbehaviour where the state is likely to impose severe sanctions cannot obscure that criminal jurisprudence is not a rational response to the problems presented by what have been called 'juvenile nuisances', the minor offenders or those such as status offenders who violate no criminal prohibition at all. It has been estimated that only 5 to 10 per cent of all police-juvenile encounters involve serious crime, and large numbers of children brought to juvenile court are status offenders. To impose the full panoply of legal procedures here is to have the tail wag the dog. In light of this, consideration of a strongly bifurcated system becomes highly relevant, with the 'criminalized' juvenile court dealing with children charged with serious offences while the others would come under the jurisdiction of a more simple and informal body, possibly a lay community-based panel. This, however, raises a number of sensitive issues concerning the work and powers of such a body: how much power over children can and should it be given; how will its intake be controlled; how will the discretion granted its officials be exercised; to what extent must lawyers be involved? The possible advantages of an examination of the *modus operandi* of the lay panels in Scotland – where a closely related degree of bifurcation already operates – soon become apparent.

Systematic research

Although there has been no shortage of discussion and argument about the children's hearings system, the volume of serious research has remained fairly small. The system is not in this respect unique or even unusual. One has only to compare the poverty of research into the English juvenile courts, which in recent years have been no less controversial than children's hearings. Quite commonly, major new initiatives in social policy lead to a feeling that research is desirable, even necessary, but without any clear sense of how such research should be focused. The idea of evaluative research often seems particularly attractive. Here a given policy is weighed in the balance; its measured achievements are compared with its stated objectives, and the discrepancies are assessed. But there is less scope for this kind of investigation than one might wish, notably because policy objectives are rarely formulated with the clarity and precision which are prerequisites for a systematic evaluation of performance. Because complete breaks with the past are rare, because new developments may depend on the goodwill or at least the tolerance of many different groups, each with its own values and goals, because there is not a strong tradition of systematically setting out assumptions about behaviour and how it may be influenced, many changes in social policy have a shield of ambiguity which defies the penetration of evaluative research. The layman may understandably wish to know whether the children's hearings system 'has worked' or 'has been a success', but these are not questions to which the research worker can give a direct answer. This is not because evasiveness holds any attractions but because there is no explicit or self-evident criterion of success; even if a criterion can be tentatively identified 'for the sake of argument' – for example, the reduction of delinquency – changes over time in the relevant measurements may be related to factors quite other than the operation of the justice system. Recorded delinquency rose sharply in the early years of the children's hearings system, and those associated with it resisted assertions in the popular press and elsewhere that this increase was attributable to the weakness of the system; in the last four years recorded juvenile delinquency in Scotland has fallen steeply, and it would be equally unjustifiable simply to assume that the hearings system should be given the credit for this decline.

To take the complex mass of interactions that constitutes a juvenile justice system in operation, and to separate out specific questions to which research is capable of providing reliable and objective answers – and which are worth asking – requires persistence and some imagination. A further dimension of difficulty is added by the private and opaque nature of the decision-making processes that play an important, often a central, role in any system that requires the exercise of discretion. The temptation to concentrate research attention on the more readily accessible aspects of the system is understandably strong.

In his comprehensive review of research into the children's hearings system – a review that incorporates unpublished higher degree theses, work in progress, and a number of discursive papers unencumbered by any empirical evidence, as well as research publications proper – Curran (1977, 1979)[16] draws attention to the markedly uneven distribution of research interest between different aspects of the system. It is also worthy of note that the greater part of such research as has been carried out was undertaken in the first year or two of the system's operation, when little practical experience had been accumulated, and that virtually all publications are based on work carried out in one or at most two districts and are therefore of uncertain representativeness.

The most wide-ranging study is that of Morris (1978).[17] The fieldwork was carried out in the first three months of 1972 and the corresponding quarter of 1973, and was confined to two areas, a city and a 'mainly rural' county. It covers some 1,600 children who were referred to the two reporters during the periods in question. The researchers were concerned to identify the distinguishing characteristics of those children who entered the system, of those who were dealt with in different ways by the reporter, and of those who were dealt with in different ways by the hearings. They note the predominance of offence criteria in police decisions to refer to the reporter, and note the influence of particular descriptive comments in social background reports, as well as family size and paternal unemployment, in increasing the likelihood that a given child will be referred by the reporter to a hearing. There are however a number of ambiguities in their analysis of the reporter's discretion, and they describe their findings as 'inevitably impressionistic'. Their general conclusion is that the system is not operating wholly according to the philosophy of the Kilbrandon Report, but is 'an empirical amalgam of welfare, due process and control'. They suggest that detention is used in the hearings system in much the same way that it was used in the juvenile courts – that is, as a last resort. Children sent to a hearing are, they argue, largely pre-defined as 'troublesome' rather than in need of compulsory care and education; middle-class definitions of social conformity tend to be substituted for criteria of need. It should be emphasized however that these conclusions are in the nature of personal interpretations and do not arise from any concrete study of the actual as distinct from the presumed values of the decision-makers; any such study might of course corroborate Morris's interpretations but could equally well lead to alternative explanations.

A competent if specialized study of an aspect of 'sifting mechanisms' is Rushforth's (1976)[18] comparison of boys committed to 'List D' schools through two different routes – by children's hearings and after prosecution in the courts. She found, contrary to expectations, that there were no significant differences between the two groups of boys in respect of family and home background and of previous offence patterns. Those who had been sent to court had only rarely (4 per cent of all court cases) committed one of the offences formally listed as sufficiently serious to make court prosecution obligatory; more commonly the grounds were technical, in that the 'child' was co-accused together with an 'adult' (commonly someone only a year older) or because a driving offence had been committed and a hearing could not require the surrender of a driving licence. It seemed likely however that in spite of similarities of background and offence history, boys who had been prosecuted in the courts rather than referred to hearings might come to be seen as more seriously delinquent.

A few studies have examined the processes by which the original children's panels were selected (Smith and May, 1971; Mapstone, 1972),[19] the social characteristics of panel members (Rowe, 1972; Moody, 1976)[20] and their psychological features (Higgins, 1972).[21] In the context of more general discussions of such alternative notions as 'community representativeness' and 'personal suitability', these studies have all demonstrated the relatively high proportion of panel members drawn from white-collar occupations in general and from teaching in particular. It was further shown that this statistical imbalance results primarily from self-selection of applicants for panel membership, marginally amplified by the original selection processes. Higgins also demonstrated a high degree of upward social mobility among the original members of the Glasgow panel, as well as a tendency to 'seek approval' and to describe themselves in 'socially desirable' ways. No study has so far examined the success or otherwise of the deliberate attempts made more recently in some areas to attract working-class applicants for panel membership. More important, no one has yet made any attempt to determine what attitudes and values relevant to questions of delinquency, punishment, treatment and child care are actually characteristic of panel members; how if at all these vary according to age, sex and social status; nor to what extent such personal characteristics influence panel members' perceptions of children and their problems and their judgments as to alternative courses of action.

The reporters to children's panels are universally recognized as key figures in the processing of children referred by various agencies, but so far there has been no examination of their backgrounds, previous experience, personal attitudes or views of their own functions. Inevitably therefore nothing is known about the part if any played by such factors in handling referrals or in giving greater or lesser weight to different elements in the child's history and background when deciding on a course of action.

Reporters in their turn receive the overwhelming majority of their referrals from the police, and are therefore highly dependent on the discretionary processes operated by police officers. This latter also remains almost wholly unexamined. Ritchie & Mack (1975)[22] studied the practice of police warnings in six districts before and after 1971, but their material, though interesting, throws little light on the way in which cases are referred or not referred to reporters.

The dynamics of the hearing situation itself have never been analysed, and it is clear that a study on these lines is essential in order to ensure a rounded understanding of the psychological processes that intervene between referral and disposal. How far decisions are influenced by different factual statements, interpretations and recommendations in professional reports, how far by specific aspects of the hearing itself, has never previously been examined, presumably because of difficulties of access and the complex problems of research method involved.

Very little is known about the consequences of disposals in terms of subsequent history, though one would have supposed such information to be of critical interest in a system with a markedly consequentialist view of intervention. The skeletal data presented in *Chapter 3*, derived from linkage of the routine returns made by reporters to the Scottish Office, represent the only longitudinal information so far available. Studies of the 'careers' of those passing through the hearings system need however to be supplemented by a closer examination of the implications of various 'disposals'. If hearings decide to take positive action, it is in the form of either social work supervision or admission to residential treatment in a List D school. What these experiences mean for the various participants, and for the children in particular, is significantly under-researched. Anstey[23] has studied some of the adjustment problems of girls in List D schools, but there has been only one piece of participant observation of staff-pupil relations and attitudes (Walter, 1975),[24] and no systematic attempt to characterize the regimes, psychological climates and day-to-day practices across the whole range of List D schools, although appropriate instruments could be adapted with comparatively little difficulty. One recent study (Vernon, work in progress) has examined the supervision process in the community, in terms of the perceptions and expectations of social workers, panel members, children and parents, and in terms of the actual contracts between child and supervising social worker. In view of the critical part played by social workers in providing background reports and making recommendations as well as in giving effect to supervision orders, a further study of the attitudes of social workers to these components of their generic case-loads would be of great interest.

How children and parents perceive social work supervision is perhaps only one aspect of the wider question of how the whole hearing process is seen and evaluated by its involuntary participants. Willock (1975)[25] interviewed a sample of parents and reported a relatively low level of criticism and complaint; in general, children's hearings were compared favourably with juvenile courts by those with experience of both systems. Neither Willock's sampling methods however nor his interviewing technique provide substantial grounds for confidence in his findings, and there is a strong case for a larger-scale and more sensitive examination of this complex area.

Curran's conclusion that at the time of writing (1977) the children's hearings system was 'an under-researched subject in general' seems to have been fully justified. In *Chapter 4* we outline some new topics for investigation identified in that year, and discuss the problems of obtaining relevant research material. Before that however, and before setting out any of the findings of such studies, it may be useful to consider what information about the operation of the hearings system is available from published sources. This is the theme of the chapter which follows.

NOTES

1. For example, 'Reform that is making heavy going', *The Press and Journal*, 10 May 1972.
   'Young crime panels blasted', *Daily Record*, 16 September 1974.
   'Children's panels – a costly failure', *Glasgow Herald*, 8 March 1975.
   'Police boss hits at panel powers', *Evening Times*, 28 April 1976.
2. Nigel Bruce, 'The Scottish children's panels and their critics', *Journal of Adolescence*, 1978, 1(3).
3. Louise Higgins, 'Personality characteristics of children's panel members and members of other voluntary organizations', Ph.D. Thesis, University of Glasgow, 1979.
4. *'List D' schools* are those schools classified on the Scottish Education Department lists as specialist schools formerly known as 'approved schools' for young delinquents. There are 25 List D schools in Scotland of which six are for girls. On 30 June 1979 there were 1,247 children in List D schools (13·7 per cent of all children under a current supervision requirement on that date).
5. The Report of the Committee on Children and Young Persons (Scotland), Cmnd. 2306, HMSO, 1964 (Kilbrandon Report).
6. Paul D. Brown and Terry Bloomfield (eds.), *Legality and Community: the Politics of Juvenile Justice in Scotland.* Aberdeen Peoples Press, 1979.
7. *See*, for example, D. Matza, *Delinquency and Drift.* John Wiley, New York, 1964; *Becoming Deviant.* Prentice-Hall, 1969.
   H. S. Becker, *Outsiders: Studies in the Sociology of Deviance.* Free Press, New York, 1963.
8. *See*, for example, Sir Cyril Burt, *The Young Delinquent.* University of London Press, London, 1925.
   T. Ferguson, *The Young Delinquent in his Social Setting.* Oxford University Press, London, 1952.
   D. J. West and D. P. Farrington, *Who Becomes Delinquent?.* Heinemann Educational Books, London, 1973.
9. *See*, for example, A. Cicourel, *The Social Organization of Juvenile Justice.* 2nd ed., Heinemann, London, 1977.
10. *See*, for example, H. S. Becker, op. cit.
    Edwin M. Lemert, *Human Deviance, Social Problems and Social Control.* Prentice-Hall, Englewood Cliffs, 1972.
11. P. L. Berger and T. Luckman, *The Social Construction of Reality.* Allen Lane, The Penguin Press, London, 1967.
12. Christopher Lasch, *Haven in a Heartless World.* Basic Books, New York, 1977.
13. In *re* Gault 387 U.S. 1 (1967).
14. In *re* Winship 397 U.S. 358 (1970).
15. Breed *v.* Jones 421 U.S. 519 (1975).
16. J. H. Curran, *The Children's Hearing System: A Review of Research.* HMSO, 1977 (supplementary mimeo 1979).
17. Allison Morris in collaboration with Mary McIsaac, *Juvenile Justice?.* Heinemann, London, 1978.
18. Monica Rushforth, *Committal to Residential Care: A Case Study in Juvenile Justice.* A Scottish Office Social Research Study, HMSO, 1976.
19. Gilbert Smith and David May, 'The appointment of the Aberdeen City children's panel', *British Journal of Social Work*, 1971, 1(1).
    Elizabeth Mapstone, 'The selection of the children's panel for the county of Fife', *British Journal of Social Work*, 1972, 2(4).
20. Andrew Rowe, *Initial Selection for Children's Panels in Scotland.* Bookstall Publications, London, 1972.
    Susan R. Moody, 'Survey of the background of current panel members', Scottish Home and Health Department (mimeo), 1976.
21. See note 3.

22. Margaret Ritchie and John Mack, *Police Warnings*. University of Glasgow, Glasgow, 1974.
23. S. C. F. Anstey, 'A study of List D schools for girls, their modes of treatment and some effects upon girls', unpublished Ph.D. Thesis, University of Edinburgh, Department of Social Administration, 1976.
24. J. A. Walter, *Sent Away: A Study of Young Offenders in Care*. Saxon House, 1978.
25. I. D. Willock, 'An inquiry into parental involvement in the work of children's hearings', University of Dundee, Department of Jurisprudence, (mimeo), 1975.

3

STATISTICAL PATTERNS

FROM THE VEHEMENCE with which the use of the official statistics of crime and delinquency has been attacked by phenomenologists and radical criminologists, it might be thought that 'conventional' criminologists have always interpreted such data as precise measures of the level of criminal behaviour. In fact, as Radzinowicz and King point out,[1] the limitations of such statistics, reflecting as they do unknown and largely unknowable variations in the reporting of crimes and the efficiency and policies of law enforcement agencies, have long been recognized. But to know that there are serious constraints on the inferences that may legitimately be drawn from the figures contained in official publications does not oblige us to abandon all such material as totally uninformative. To assume that a small increase from one year to the next in, say, the number of young people charged with theft or assault is necessarily an accurate measure of change in the actual frequency of the type of criminal action concerned by members of the age-group in question is naive beyond justification. But to reject as wholly worthless the evidence of large-scale, long-term and internationally comparable trends may be no less misguided. When Radzinowicz and King, looking particularly at the period from the middle nineteen-fifties to the mid-seventies, say that the outstanding feature of '. . . crime on the world scale is a pervasive and persistent increase everywhere', it is difficult to brush aside the weight of the generalization by reference to the undoubted flaws in individual pieces of statistical data. Nor is it easy to dismiss as a mere artefact the international evidence, over the same decades, for the particularly rapid growth of law-breaking among young people.

There was no reason why Scotland should have been any exception to this general trend. During the decade between the appointment of the Kilbrandon Committee and the bringing into operation of the system of children's hearings, the number of juveniles prosecuted in the Scottish courts increased every year, with only one exception. The trend seemed inexorable, with an average increase in the number of juvenile offenders reaching the courts, over the 10 years preceding the implementation of the new system, amounting to 3·2 per cent per annum. The first year in which proceedings were taken against more than 20,000 juveniles (aged 16 and under) was 1960. The 21,441 cases of that year increased to more than 25,000 by 1965 and to 29,496 in the last complete year of the old system.[2] Differences in age limits and in the implications of the statutes make it difficult to compare in detail the statistics of referrals to reporters since 15 April 1971, with the figures for children proceeded against in the courts before that date. Nevertheless, it is clear that the orders of magnitude are broadly similar.[3]

Table 3.1 sets out the number of referrals to reporters in each region of Scotland from 1972 to 1979. ('Regions' as such did not come into existence until 15 May 1975; figures prior to that date relate to the old local authority areas, aggregated to approximate the regions created by reorganization of local government. The statistical system was changed at the same time, but the effect on the figures quoted in this chapter is small.) The overall number of referrals increased steeply over the first three or four years of the new system's operation but then began to fall steadily; referrals in 1979 were 19 per cent lower than in

TABLE 3.1

REFERRALS TO REPORTERS, BY REGION, 1972–79[1]

Region[2]	1972	1973	1974	1975[3]	1976	1977	1978[4]	1979
Borders	307	343	507	389	402	360	337	304
Central	1,231	1,517	1,991	1,718	1,633	1,729	1,540	1,590
Dumfries & Galloway	345	536	441	421	513	509	487	341
Fife	1,365	1,984	1,769	1,745	1,947	1,864	1,550	1,480
Grampian	1,371	1,380	1,802	1,576	1,327	1,429	1,264	1,352
Highland	602	736	749	877	887	883	893	811
Lothian	3,664	4,270	4,842	4,156	3,658	3,627	3,444	3,515
Strathclyde	13,628	16,874	17,682	16,945	17,367	16,414	15,073	14,509
Tayside	1,676	1,888	2,002	2,064	1,637	1,613	1,848	1,822
Orkney	14	13	26	35	38	44	49	51
Shetland	15	25	53	41	47	37	40	29
Western Isles[5]	—	—	—	45	58	42	58	38
Outwith Scotland	1	1	12	10	—	—	—	—
Total referrals	24,219	29,566	31,876	30,022	29,514	28,551	26,583	25,842

Notes

1. A referral may allege any number of separate offences, or derive from facts relevant to more than one of the 'care and protection' grounds; a child may be referred a number of times in a year. Excludes reviews (unless fresh grounds are involved), and references and remits from Courts.
2. Returns up to 15 May 1975 related to the former local authority areas (counties of cities, large burghs and counties) and have been aggregated to give approximate figures for the present regions and islands authorities.
3. Figures for 1975 are known to be less reliable than for other years, with some under-recording immediately prior to the reorganization of local government.
4. The figures for 1978 and 1979 relate to referrals disposed of during the calendar year, rather than (as in previous years) referrals received by reporters.
5. There are no separate figures for Western Isles prior to local government reorganization; referrals there are included in the totals for Highland.

1974. Variations from region to region in the trend over time are not large. Highland is the one region in which referrals have moved consistently, it sometimes slowly, upwards. Fife's peak year was 1973, with a decline in the next two years being followed by a rise in 1976, and after that another fall; the pattern in Dumfries and Galloway is similar. The general trend is however unmistakably in a downward direction.

A child may be referred to the reporter on more than one occasion in a given year. The numbers of individual children involved in each year are shown in the middle column of Table 3.2. This suggests a peak in 1975 – when however the statistics may have been particularly unreliable, as a direct consequence of reorganization – rather than the previous year, and a somewhat more rapid rate of decline than the fall in referrals. The number of children referred in 1979 was 24 per cent lower than the corresponding figure for 1975, and 23 per cent smaller than the more reliable figure for 1974. This difference in the rates of fall implies a small increase in the average number of referrals per child in a calendar year.

The evidence of a reduction in the number of young people entering the hearings system on the basis of delinquency is strengthened by Table 3.3, which shows for each of the years discussed above the number of reports on each of the grounds for referral listed in the 1968 Act. Offences constitute in every year the overwhelmingly most common reason for referral. But as a percentage of all grounds of referral they fall from between 86 and 88 per cent in the period 1972–1975 to 80 per cent in 1979. The actual number of referrals on offence grounds drops from 28,164 in 1974 to 20,873 five years later, a fall of fully one quarter. This decline is to a small extent counter-balanced by an overall increase in referrals on non-offence grounds, though some of these, notably truancy, have fluctuated inconsistently from year to year. Referrals alleging that the child lacks parental care or has been the victim of an offence increase steadily through the nineteen-seventies, more than doubling over the period and finally accounting for a little more than 5 per cent of all referrals.

The Scottish system of juvenile justice is bifurcated. The hearings normally

TABLE 3.2

REFERRALS TO REPORTERS AND CHILDREN PROCEEDED AGAINST IN ALL COURTS, 1972–79

Year	*Total referrals to reporters*	*No. of children referred*	*Children* (under 16) *proceeded against*
1972	24,219	17,950	2,390
1973	29,566	21,017	3,192
1974	31,876	21,907	2,900
1975	30,022	22,207	2,262
1976	29,514	18,638	2,094
1977	28,551	18,537	1,727
1978	26,583	17,308	1,639
1979	25,842	16,924	1,055

deal with children under 16, together with children aged 16 but not yet 18 who are already subject to a supervision requirement. A child may however still be dealt with in the sheriff court or in the High Court, rather than referred to the reporter to the children's panel, if he is alleged to have committed an offence of particular seriousness; or if the alleged offence, whether or not particularly serious, also involved an adult and it is considered essential to deal with both (or all) the accused together. In addition, cases which may require disqualification from driving or the confiscation of a weapon (neither of which may be ordered by a hearing) are sometimes dealt with in court. The right-hand column of Table 3.2 shows the number of children proceeded against in the adult courts between 1972 and 1979, and indicates a steep decline since 1973. Court proceedings in 1979 were of only one-third the frequency that obtained six years previously. Whatever the precise significance of these figures – and it is possible that to some extent they reflect a reaction to public criticism of what appeared to be an over-ready recourse to formal judicial procedures – they do at least dispose of any suggestion that a decline in the rate of referral to the hearings system has been balanced by a more frequent use of the sheriff courts in juvenile cases.

Table 3.4 (derived from Table 19 in *Criminal Statistics Scotland, 1978*) indicates that three types of alleged offence predominate among both the children proceeded against in the courts and those referred by the police to reporters. These are housebreaking (which includes theft by opening lockfast places and attempted housebreaking), theft (including theft by shoplifting) and breach of the peace (which includes 'petty assaults'). Crimes against the person amount to 1·5 per cent of the cases referred directly to a reporter and just under 5 per cent of those reaching the courts. Half of each group are classified as 'other crimes against the person'; almost all of these probably involve carrying offensive weapons or firearms offences, rather than actual violence. Offences

TABLE 3.3

GROUNDS FOR REFERRAL TO REPORTER, 1972–79

Grounds[1]	1972	1973	1974	1975	1976	1977	1978	1979
(a) Beyond control	745	732	771	595	556	513	532	677
(b) Moral danger	191	195	176	101	132	90	131	177
(c) Parental neglect	506	538	738	775	879	891	941	1,061
(d) Cr. Proc.	{95	104	209	208	256	332	450	622
(dd) 1975 Act	—	—	—	8	14	24	20	48
(e)	9	4	3	—	3	—	5	8
(f) Truancy	1,469	2,053	2,345	1,960	2,870	3,387	3,010	2,514
(g) Offence	21,594	26,418	28,184	26,495	24,823	23,340	21,533	20,873
(h) Transfers	47	58	49	33	37	35	37	31
Total grounds	24,656	30,102	32,475	30,175	29,540	28,612	26,659	26,011

Note 1. Grounds for referral are set out in full on pages 8–9.

relating to motor vehicles, including taking a vehicle without the consent of the owner, amount to over 20 per cent of the cases dealt with by the courts but only 2 per cent of those referred directly to reporters.

The pattern of crimes has changed relatively little in recent years. The commentary in the Criminal Statistics for 1970 notes that of all the crimes (as technically distinguished from offences) proved committed by juveniles (under 17) in that year, 43 per cent were housebreaking and 44·7 per cent theft; of the offences 44 per cent were breach of the peace. The corresponding figures for 1978 are 35·3, 52·7 and 45·2 per cent. Relative to the overall level, therefore, housebreaking has declined and theft (largely, no doubt, theft from shops and supermarkets) has increased; the two together have altered only from 87·7 per cent to 88 per cent of crimes. The kinds of offences alleged against children brought to the notice of the reporter are considered more fully in *Chapter 5*.

Table 3.5 relates the numbers of boys and girls referred to reporters in 1978 to the size of the relevant age-groups.[4] Over all, 78 per cent of the children referred (once or more frequently) during the calendar year were boys: 27 per cent were 15 years of age and 78 per cent between 12 and 15. Of the 47,000 boys aged 15 living in Scotland, almost one in twelve was brought to the notice

---

TABLE 3.4

CHILDREN (UNDER 16) REFERRED BY POLICE TO REPORTERS AND PROCURATORS FISCAL, AND PROCEEDED AGAINST IN ALL COURTS, BY TYPE OF CRIME OR OFFENCE, 1978

Crime or offence	*Referred to reporter*[1]	*Referred to P.F.*[2]	*Proceeded against*[3]
Crimes against the person	258	403	79
Housebreaking	4,822	1,858	373
Theft	6,224	1,699	316
All other 'crimes'	1,190	355	95
Breach of the peace	2,234	1,493	312
Police acts, bye-laws, etc.	439	768	9
Taking motor vehicle	143	565	164
Malicious mischief[4]	747	176	29
Motor vehicle offences	245	451	176
All other 'offences'	502	364	86
Total crimes and offences	16,804	8,132	1,639

Notes

1. Excludes cases referred to reporters by procurators fiscal.
2. Includes cases subsequently referred to reporters and cases proceeded against.
3. Children shown as originally referred by the police to procurators fiscal.
4. Comprises damage to property under £20 value and false fire alarms.

of a reporter during that year. Analysis of the numbers of children referred at least once between May 1975 and December 1979 suggest moreover that, of all the boys in Scotland, about one in every seven is reported at some time before reaching the age of 16. The corresponding proportion for girls is one in 20. The referred rate varied from region to region, though not very dramatically. The highest mainland figure was almost 50 per cent higher than the lowest, and nearly twice as high as in the islands. Similarities between the larger regions are more striking than the differences. There are of course very substantial variations within regions; the cities of Aberdeen, Dundee, Edinburgh and Glasgow tend to have significantly higher referral rates than the smaller towns and rural areas that make up the remainder of their regions. The tendency for offences to predominate among grounds of referral is common to all regions, and the ratio for Scotland as a whole varies only marginally from one area to the next.

Before the reorganization of local government, reporters to the children's panels of the then burghs and counties differed markedly in their propensity to refer cases to a children's hearing. The formation of the larger regional units – and, no doubt, discussions among reporters themselves – have done much to narrow the range of variation. Even so, Table 3.6 does not suggest that uniformity now prevails. The proportion referred to a hearing in 1978 ranged from 35 per cent in Borders and 36 per cent in Grampian to 57 per cent in Highland and 58 per cent in Strathclyde. And the general pattern was that the higher the rate of referral to the reporter (in proportion to the relevant population), the more are referred to a hearing. Overall, 53 per cent of referrals to reporters were referred by them to a hearing, 5 per cent were referred to the social work department for voluntary care and 5 per cent were referred back

TABLE 3.5

CHILDREN REFERRED TO REPORTERS, 1978, BY SEX AND AGE

Age (at first referral in 1978)	*Children referred*			*Rate per 1,000 population*[1]	
	Boys	*Girls*	*Total*	*Boys*	*Girls*
0–7	485	452	937	1·7	1·7
8	256	79	335	5·9	1·9
9	415	102	517	9·2	2·4
10	662	125	787	14·7	2·9
11	908	165	1,073	19·4	3·8
12	1,399	325	1,724	30·4	7·5
13	2,310	585	2,895	48·3	12·9
14	3,299	882	4,181	69·2	19·3
15	3,691	999	4,690	78·4	22·2
16+	141	28	169		
Total	13,566	3,742	17,308		

Note 1. Estimated population aged 15 and under at 30 June 1978.

to the police for a formal warning or admission to a juvenile liaison scheme. In the remaining cases, the reporter decided that no formal action was necessary. These proportions however varied greatly between offence referrals and the remainder. Three-quarters of non-offence referrals, but only 48 per cent of those alleging offences, were referred to a hearing; the corresponding figures for referral to the social work department were 9 per cent and 4 per cent. Reporters took no formal action on 41 per cent of offences but only 16 per cent of other referrals.

To some extent, the hearings themselves seem to counteract variations in the practices of their reporters. Where proportionately fewer reports come to a hearing, as in Borders and Grampian, the proportion of hearings leading to a supervision order tends to be higher; Strathclyde, above average on the former index, ranks low on the second. The generalization that roughly one-third of all referrals to reporters lead to supervision requirements has only one significant exception, Central Region, where the proportion is only 22 per cent. (Two of the islands areas also seem to be unusual, though the total number of cases involved is small: Western Isles 21 per cent, Orkney 45 per cent; in all other areas, the percentage is between 29 and 38.)

TABLE 3.6

CONSEQUENCES OF REFERRAL TO REPORTERS, BY REGION, 1978

	Age 0–15	*All ages*			
Region	*Children referred to reporter per 1,000 population.*[1]	*Alleged offences as per cent of all grounds for referral*[2]	*Per cent refs. to hearing*	*Per cent refs. to hearing leading to SR*[3]	*Per cent refs. to reporter leading to SR*[3]
Borders	11·3	85	35	85	29
Central	13·7	84	47	46	22
Dumfries & Galloway	10·0	91	46	79	37
Fife	13·1	69	51	68	35
Grampian	9·7	84	36	79	29
Highland	15·2	83	57	67	38
Lothian	14·6	77	48	76	37
Strathclyde	14·1	82	58	59	34
Tayside	12·7	81	46	73	33
Orkney	9·7	68	51	88	45
Shetland	6·7	75	40	88	35
Western Isles	7·1	91	38	55	21
SCOTLAND	13·4	80·9	53·4	63·1	33·7

Notes
1. Estimated population aged 15 and under at 30 June 1978.
2. Excluding ground (h) – transfers – 0·1 per cent of all grounds.
3. Supervision requirement made, varied or continued.

The simple statistics of the hearings system presented above are derived ultimately from the returns made routinely by reporters to the Social Work Services Group of the Scottish Office.[5] A standard card is completed for each case dealt with – whether referral on new grounds, review, or reference or remit from a court – and valuable statistical summaries of the data gathered in this way are produced annually. Because of the large scale of the exercise, there are inevitably limits to the range of information that can be submitted for each case, and limits to the kind of statistical treatment that can be undertaken as a matter of routine. Each year's referrals, for example, are necessarily analysed as a discrete series, and there is consequently no means of knowing the extent to which children who have once been in the hearings system are likely to re-enter it, and at what intervals. To fill this gap in our knowledge of the subsequent history of referred children, a longitudinal study was planned jointly with the Statistics Branch of Social Work Services Group.

The methods and findings of the longitudinal enquiry are discussed in detail elsewhere, but a brief summary has a place here as an essential complement to the preceding analysis of annual trends. The study involved the selection of two cohorts of children entering the hearings system for the first time in two separate periods, and following their subsequent progress. This was done by linking the statistical records relating to each referral of the same child. Some errors in the data are inevitable. In particular, it is known that some children referred both before and after the reorganization of local government in 1975 were allocated fresh reference numbers, so that the later records could not be linked to the earlier.

Table 3.7 shows the extent to which boys first referred in the first three months of 1973 and 1976 were again referred, for further alleged offences, by 31 March in each subsequent year, up to 1978. The next two tables analyse, by the age of the boy (at the date of the first referral) and by the disposal of that first referral, the proportions re-referred within two years – that is, by 31 March 1975 for those first referred during the period 1 January to 31 March 1973, or by 31 March 1978 for the 1976 cohort.

Of the earlier cohort, one-third offended again within a year and two in

TABLE 3.7

CRUDE RE-OFFENDING RATES (%) AFTER FIRST OFFENCE REFERRAL (BOYS)

Period of follow-up	Cohort 1973	Cohort 1976
1 year	33·3	27·6
2 years	41·4	34·7
3 years	44·4	—
4 years	45·3	—
5 years	45·7	—
No. of boys	2,638	1,675

five within two years. Follow-up over a longer period brings to light very few additional lapses; it seems that the passage of two years without a new referral implies a good prognosis, though faulty data may exaggerate this effect. For the later cohort, re-offending rates were lower: little over one in four in the first year and one in three after two years. Because however of the age distribution of first referrals – over half in each cohort were 14 years or over when first referred – a substantial proportion of the boys concerned moved outside the purview of the hearings system before the end of the follow-up period. It would be of great interest to know at what rate boys referred to the reporter subsequently appear before the adult courts. At present there is no means of effecting the necessary data linkage: the problems of confidentiality would be severe.

Table 3.8 confirms that, of boys aged 15 when first referred, only a small minority were again referred to reporters before ceasing to be, in this regard, statutorily children. For boys aged 13 and under when first referred, who spent the two years wholly within the ambit of the system, the re-offending rates vary within fairly narrow limits, being mostly just under 50 per cent with no consistent pattern either between or within the cohorts.

Table 3.9 indicates that, in both cohorts, boys referred back to the police for a formal warning, or for admission to a juvenile liaison scheme, were least likely to be referred again within two years; boys referred to a hearing, and especially those made subject to compulsory supervision, were much more likely to re-offend. In the later cohort, those whose first referral ended in no formal action by the reporter were little more likely to re-offend than those warned by the police. It should however be clear that these crude percentages must not be interpreted as measures of the success of the original disposal. The reporter's decision with regard to the first referral obviously reflected the depth of the child's problems at the time and any previous history not involving the

TABLE 3.8

TWO-YEAR RE-OFFENDING RATES (%) BY AGE AT FIRST REFERRAL (BOYS)

Age at first referral	*Cohort* 1973	1976
8	52·3	36·0
9	37·5	52·5
10	46·1	44·3
11	46·6	41·6
12	46·6	53·6
13	50·7	44·0
14	45·4	36·9
15	25·9	14·9
Total[1]	41·4	34·7

Note 1. Includes a small no. of boys (19 in the 1973 cohort, 6 in the 1976) aged 16+ at first offence referral, very few of whom were again referred to reporters.

reporter. Thus, for example, those first offenders immediately placed on supervision (23 per cent of the earlier cohort, some of whom may earlier have been dealt with under the previous legislation, and 14 per cent of the later) must already have been thought to be in more serious difficulty than those against whom no formal action was taken (41 per cent in 1973, 52 per cent in 1976).

The overall impression then is of a system that deals principally with offences, to a lesser but increasing extent with truancy, and to a small but growing extent with neglect or damage by parents. Referrals on offence grounds appear to be falling quite sharply; how far this reflects any real change in the level of delinquent conduct and how far differences in police practice cannot be determined in the course of a study limited to the inner workings of the hearings system. About one-third of referrals to reporters lead to compulsory supervision requirements (supervision within the community outnumbering residential requirements by between two and three to one). Approximately three-fifths of all children referred come to the notice of the system only once. How their treatment within the system affects their subsequent history is a matter for exploration at a later date.

TABLE 3.9

TWO-YEAR RE-OFFENDING RATES (%) BY DISPOSAL OF FIRST REFERRAL (BOYS)

Disposal of first referral	*Cohort* 1973	1976
No formal action	35·7	27·7
Referred to SWD	41·9	32·3
Police warning/JLO	22·1	26·0
Hearing – no SR	38·6	43·8
– non-residential SR	62·0	61·6
– residential SR[1]	65·9	71·4
Total	41·4	34·7

Note 1. The numbers of boys placed on residential supervision requirement as a result of their first referrals were small: 41 in the 1973 cohort, 14 in the 1976. Some of those in the 1973 cohort may earlier have been dealt with under the previous legislation.

NOTES

1. Sir L. Radzinowicz and Joan King, *The Growth of Crime*. Hamish Hamilton, 1977.
2. Scottish Home and Health Department, *Criminal Statistics Scotland*, 1970. Cmnd. 4707, HMSO, Edinburgh, 1971.
3. Scottish Home and Health Department, *Criminal Statistics Scotland*, 1972. Cmnd. 5464, HMSO, Edinburgh, 1973.
4. Registrar General for Scotland, Annual Estimates of the Population of Scotland as at 30 June 1978.
5. The statistics of children's hearings were included in the annual report, *Scottish Social Work Statistics* until 1974. Since then Social Work Services Group have produced annual bulletins, *Children's Hearings Statistics*.

4

METHODS OF ENQUIRY

Topics for investigation

Given the complexity of the children's hearings system and the relatively under-developed state of research when our own studies began, it was clear that there was a wide range of issues on which new research might be focussed. Ultimately, such a choice depends upon a variety of factors – a systematic consideration of gaps in knowledge, the possibility of designing and putting into effect appropriate research instruments given the time and manpower available, but perhaps most importantly (though frequently unacknowledged) the values and interests of the principal investigators. Our point of departure was the realization that neither formal descriptions of the system nor the statistical information derived from reporters' returns could possibly provide an adequate account of the way in which the hearings system actually operated. A systematic examination of a major social innovation would we believed be of value in its own right, the more so because of the comparatively large volume of dogmatic and unsubstantiated assertion that the thoughtful enquirer was likely to encounter. We hoped to provide a framework of empirical findings within which the case for developments in policy, practice and training could be argued, though we had no illusions that research-based knowledge would necessarily prevail over emotional convictions and ideological prejudice.

The kinds of research material needed for these domestic purposes would also provide, at least in part, relevant contributions to current American discussions. Students of the hearings system and American colleagues share a major interest, for example, in the study of discretionary decision-making. Consider first the case of the reporter to the children's panel. The choices open to him when children are brought to his notice as presumably 'in need of compulsory measures of care' have been described in *Chapter 1*, but we know nothing of the criteria actually employed by the reporter in making decisions when he is functioning as an intake official. We know that overall about half of all the children brought to the notice of the reporter are referred by him to a hearing, but how far reporters' decisions are influenced by the seriousness of the alleged offence, by the number of previous offences or by knowledge of the child's background derived from school reports or preliminary social work reports, has never so far been ascertained. We did not suppose that there was one factor which had a dominating influence in the decision-making of reporters. Rather we assumed that a number of factors interacted; the statistical problem was therefore to identify the combination of elements which gave the best prediction of the path on which the child would be set.

The next stage at which discretion is exercised is of course the hearing itself. In broad terms, we know that about 50 per cent of the children who reach this stage are placed on supervision, that about 10 per cent are sent to a residential school, and that the remainder, approximately 40 per cent of the total, are in effect discharged. We know also that prior to any hearing the panel members concerned will have received and no doubt perused a file of papers on each child containing reports and recommendations and varying in size from the scanty to the voluminous; and that before reaching a decision they will have spent anything from 20 minutes to an hour-and-a-half in conversation with child and parents. What elements enter into the shaping of their decisions, and how are these elements patterned? In the study of justice systems generally, this tends to be an extremely difficult area to penetrate. However, a bona fide researcher may, at the discretion of the chairman, sit in at a hearing, and we were fortunate in receiving an extremely high level of co-operation from panel members, reporters and families. Our objective was to devise a means of analysing in detail what actually occurs in children's hearings – the level of participation by each actor, the content of discussion and the styles of discourse adopted. It was also necessary to design a standard form for a content analysis of the case papers relating to each of the hearings observed.

The material derived from observation at hearings can be examined in two ways. First, the complex of factors associated with specific decisions can be disentangled. In this case it is necessary to take account of two sets of data, those derived from the documentary material and those relating to the interaction processes of the hearing. We are conscious of a wish by many panel members to understand the nature of their own decision-making, and recognize also that this part of the project is likely to have significance for American observers interested in the deliberations of lay bodies. The same research findings can also be used to provide a basis for critical examination of the quality of practice in children's hearings. How often and in what circumstances are procedural requirements disregarded? How often can it truthfully be said that the child and parent participated fully in the discussion? How often do panel members threaten or deliver homilies or use sarcasm – or, for that matter, show understanding and concern and empathy? The model of 'a good hearing' is familiar to all participants in the system; we should be able to show to what degree that model is realized in actual practice, and perhaps identify the circumstances associated with varying qualities of performance. In a similar way, the content analysis of professional reports can be used to throw light on the facts and ideas that social workers believe to be relevant when framing recommendations in the context of juvenile justice.

Obviously, the way in which a hearing is conducted and the outcome of its discussions depend only in part on the information available and the interplay of personalities. Panel members bring into the hearing room not only the principles they have acquired in training, but their whole life histories and a body of personal values and attitudes that have developed over the years. We were not in a position to investigate these intensively, let alone to correlate them with behaviour in the hearing or with decisions reached; the fact that three panel members are involved, as distinct from a single judge in court practice, makes it virtually impossible to look for correlations between personal characteristics and decision-making. It did seem important however to examine the range of ideas prevailing among panel members about the causes of delinquency, the objectives of children's hearings, the characteristics deemed desirable in panel members, and the uses of alternative disposals. Because there are numerous suggestions that the views and beliefs held by social workers about juvenile delinquency and the justice process are in some respects at variance with those of the members of children's panels, a similar enquiry was directed at practising social workers.

Finally, it was essential to understand something of the reactions of the system's clients – in this case the children who are brought before a hearing, and to a lesser extent their parents. This was not because we believed that the client is the only valid arbiter of the quality of public services; reactions are influenced by prior experience and expectations, and there is a fair amount of evidence that British working class clients are not very exacting in their demands. But the children's hearings system in particular incorporates a number of explicit and implicit assumptions, the validity of which cannot be satisfactorily estimated unless the client's perspective is taken into account. Does the child have a clear understanding of what went on at the hearing? Does he see the panel members as helpful in their intentions or as punitive? Does he feel that he was able to contribute all that he had to say? Does he believe the proceedings were fair? Does he feel some sense of stigma as a result of the experience? An additional advantage of interviewing some of the children whose hearings had been observed was that the reactions they expressed could be related systematically to the characteristics of the hearings in which they were involved, as recorded independently by the members of the research team.

Before the processes involved in preparing and carrying out each of our various sub-studies are outlined, one general limitation should be made clear. Although the project included an examination of several important facets of the hearings system – on the whole, from our perspective, the most important – it cannot claim to be a fully comprehensive study. We have examined certain key aspects of the work of reporters, but have made no attempt to examine all of their functions. From our observational studies of hearings we have drawn various conclusions about the way in which panel members approach certain aspects of their responsibilities; but our sample of hearings was selected with the primary aim of illuminating decision-making, so that particular types of hearing were deliberately excluded and the way in which these were conducted could not be examined. Most importantly, the incompleteness of the study is defined by the points in the child's 'career' at which the study begins and ends. The starting-point for us has been a piece of paper landing on the reporter's desk; the discretionary practices of the police and to a lesser extent of other agencies which lead to the decision to bring one case but not another to the notice of the reporter did not form part of the study. Similarly, we did not proceed beyond the disposal made by the hearing. We believe we have learned a good deal about the way in which decisions to impose home supervision or residential supervision are made, and about the objectives of panel members in making such disposals; but how the orders are put into effect, how the child experiences supervision and what consequences it has for him have lain beyond the scope of our enquiries.

It seemed important to us in planning this study to avoid some of the more obvious methodological limitations of earlier research into the children's hearings system. We have already commented on the localized nature and limited scope of most published studies. In addition, data-collection has tended to be casual and impressionistic, and sometimes a splendid edifice of speculation and criticism has been built upon a very slight foundation of systematic knowledge. We aimed therefore to attain a number of methodological objectives.

First, representativeness. All enquiries should so far as possible cover all areas of Scotland, with regional weightings preferably reflecting the scale of the activities being studied; any failure to meet this criterion should be clearly acknowledged and its significance estimated.

A second consideration was methodological diversity. Rather than rely on a single technique for gathering data, we aimed to employ a variety of methods – systematic observation, content analysis of documents, personal interviews, questionnaires, as we judged appropriate.

Openness was a further prerequisite. Having criticized other investigators for, for example, quoting subjects' interview responses without setting out the questions that had evoked them, we thought it essential to make all our research operations explicit both by the description of procedures in this chapter and by making all the instruments that we employed for data-collection available to all bona fide research workers.

Finally, objectivity. In an area where value-judgments and ideologies inevitably loom large, the maintenance of complete scientific detachment might be an unattainable ideal; but this did not diminish the importance of trying so far as possible to minimize subjectivity and distortion. This involved, apart from the normal care in designing research instruments, an emphasis on explicitness and specificity, an avoidance to the best of our ability of subjective generalizations in favour of detailed observation, and a concern for fidelity in the presentation and interpretation of data. Complete success in the pursuit of these goals is no doubt beyond the possibility of achievement, but this did not in our opinion make the search less desirable.

The analysis of reporters' discretion

Our task was to throw light on the decisions made by reporters whether to bring a given referral to the attention of a children's hearing or to take some other action or to take no action at all. One way in which this might have been approached was through the analysis of manufactured cases. We might have constructed imaginary reports, in which the presence or absence of certain factors was carefully controlled, and asked reporters what decisions they would have made if presented with such cases. Although this method has the advantage of tidiness, it seemed to us that the findings derived from it would carry considerably less credibility than conclusions drawn from an analysis of decisions actually made in practice.

We aimed therefore to produce a data sheet which could be used to summarize all or virtually all of the major areas of information that are available to reporters when they exercise their discretion. The format of reports varies somewhat from region to region, but with the generous co-operation of Regional Reporters in Lothian, Strathclyde and Tayside Regions we were able to examine a variety of patterns, with a view to designing a summary sheet compatible with each of them. Successive versions were tested in order to eliminate ambiguities and simplify the process of completion.

In its final version this form was not restricted to those items of information which appeared invariably in the personal files held by reporters (such as age, sex, referral) but included a considerable number which were known to be recorded in only a proportion of all cases. Four distinct types of information were assembled for each case:

(i) the family background and personal characteristics of the child (such as age, sex, family size, with whom the child normally lives, economic activity of head of household, occupation of head of household if employed, known family problems, school attendance and attainment).

(ii) the formal characteristics of the referral (such as its source, the grounds of referral, number of offences if any alleged, the nature of those offences, the value of the goods involved if the offence involved theft or damage to property).

(iii) any previous record of delinquency (such as the number and intervals of earlier referrals to the reporter, police warnings, supervision orders).

(iv) a few personal characteristics of the reporter (age, sex, previous occupation).

It had originally been intended to invite all practising reporters to complete a form in respect of each of ten recent decisions. This plan was altered in order to safeguard against any possibility, however remote, that there might be some seasonal variation in the pattern of reporters' work. Two approaches were therefore planned, one for June 1978 and the other for December 1978. The opportunity was taken to increase slightly the scale of the sample; reporters were now to be asked to complete six forms on each of two occasions. After the project had received the approval of the Association of Reporters to Children's Panels, reporters were approached individually. Those known to be practising as reporters on a part-time basis were asked to select three cases, all others six. The cases selected were to be drawn from those on which the reporter in question had made a decision during the previous month, and simple instructions were provided for identifying cases for inclusion in the sample by means of a series of random numbers. Explanatory notes were also included for any items on the form which seemed likely to raise difficulties of interpretation.

It was soon brought to our notice that the sampling method proposed could not easily be applied in some of the larger divisional offices of Strathclyde Region. Here cases were registered in order of referral to the reporter; but for various reasons, principally delay in obtaining preliminary social work reports, the interval between initial referral and decision may vary from a few days to a few months. The decisions made in any given month therefore would apply to cases that had been referred over a considerable period of time. As the decision was logged against the entry made in the register at the time of referral, it might be necessary to scan several hundred entries in order to ensure that all those potentially eligible for inclusion in our small sample had in fact been identified. After discussion, a modified sampling procedure was developed. This involved calculating the overall ratio of cases referred to hearings to cases not referred, and providing for each reporter's office a separate random case selection procedure for each of the two groups. It proved possible to put this method into effect without any further serious difficulty.

The rate of response to the first stage of the enquiry was extremely high. A few of the reporters approached indicated that their duties were purely administrative and that they did not make decisions on individual cases. They were excluded from the sample, leaving 69 full-time and part-time reporters who were eligible to participate. Of the 396 forms that might have been returned by these practitioners we in fact received 384 (97 per cent). The second round, in December 1978, encountered no new methodological problems but understandably less enthusiasm for what had undoubtedly been a time-consuming task. The response rate on this occasion was 70 per cent. The fact that the summary forms had been completed by busy practising reporters and not by specially trained research staff meant that particularly careful checking was essential. Any case in which essential information was omitted or where there appeared to be some internal inconsistency was referred back to the reporter concerned with a request for further clarification. Of the total of 684 forms returned in the two rounds (an overall response rate of 84 per cent) it was finally necessary to eliminate six because the information provided was seriously and irremediably incomplete. All subsequent analyses were carried out with the remaining 678 completed questionnaires.

Observational and records studies

We carried out a series of linked studies designed to throw light on several related aspects of the work of children's hearings. Our leading initial interest was in the determinants of decision-making, and this greatly influenced our approach to the sampling of hearings. It became clear at an early stage however that we had an admirable opportunity to analyse a number of features of the quality of practice in hearings, as well as of the quality of professional reports. Our studies of client reactions to the experience of appearing before three panel members were also built around the same sample of hearings.

We began by deciding on the size of the sample of children's hearings at which we should aim. We judged that a series of about 300 was as large as we could handle in the time available for fieldwork, and that this should be quantitatively sufficient for the analyses we had in mind. Examination of the published national statistics of children's hearings indicated that a two per cent sample of all hearings would yield a total of 306. It should be added that when the sample was drawn there was no published material later than 1974 to refer to; when our fieldwork was carried out in 1978–1979, a sample of 306 represented, because of falling referrals, nearer to 3 per cent of all the hearings in that year. Using the national statistical returns as a guide, the overall target sample of 306 was divided between regions and the major component areas of each region in proportion to the numbers of cases dealt with annually (see Table 4.1). Regretfully, we decided to exclude Orkney, Shetland and the Western Isles from our field studies. Their proportionate contributions would have been

TABLE 4.1

DISTRIBUTION OF OBSERVATION SAMPLE BY ADMINISTRATIVE AREAS

Regions	*Initial sample of hearings*	*Number achieved*
Borders	3	3
Central	15	15
Dumfries and Galloway	5	3
Fife	19	18
Grampian		
Aberdeen	6	6
Remainder of region	4	4
Highland	10	8
Lothian		
Edinburgh	22	22
Remainder of region	12	12
Strathclyde		
Argyll	2	2
Ayr	27	27
Dumbarton	17	17
Glasgow North	50	50
Glasgow South	50	50
Lanark	24	24
Renfrew	25	25
Tayside		
Dundee	8	8
Remainder of region	7	7
	306	301

less than one case each, and the infrequency of hearings combined with the high cost of travel made their inclusion prohibitively expensive. All mainland regions were however included.

At an early stage in our planning we approached all the chairmen of regional panels, all chairmen of children's panel advisory committees, regional reporters, directors of social work and directors of education to advise them of our interests and plans, and to seek their consent to our having access to hearings, their records and their personnel. In almost every instance consent was readily given. In two regions it was necessary to respond to the anxieties of panel chairmen or reporters by a detailed exposition of our aims and method. After discussion, no barriers were placed in our way, apart from some restriction of interviewing in one region discussed further below. The decision whether or not we should be permitted to observe on any particular occasion was to remain the responsibility of the chairman of the hearing in question; in the event, consent was very rarely withheld. However much we resented any questioning of our motives or methods, or even a limited denial of access, we were obliged to admit that having regard to the sensitive nature of the field in which we were working the positive co-operation and goodwill that we encountered was in general of an impressively high level. At a later date detailed arrangements for fieldwork were negotiated with each reporter, and it was necessary then to set out clearly the precise types of hearing in which we were interested. Because of our concern with the decisions made by hearings to discharge a case or to impose a supervision order, we chose to study only those hearings in which there were grounds of referral. In particular, we would exclude review hearings unless they were precipitated by new grounds.

Meanwhile, work was in progress on the development of an instrument for recording the processes of children's hearings. This struck us as a particularly difficult task, for which – unlike the construction of data summary forms, mailed questionnaires or interview schedules – there were few exemplars. Our first inclination was to turn to the very substantial body of work on interaction process analysis that had been built up since the pioneering studies of Bales nearly 30 years earlier (Bales, 1950; Argyle, 1969).[1] It soon became obvious however that these techniques were not suitable for our purpose. They enable one to classify many kinds of behaviour in group situations according to generalized socio-psychological categories such as 'showing solidarity' or 'giving orientation'. But from our standpoint these approaches to the characterization of group processes did not appear to be particularly illuminating. We were concerned with the children's hearing as a legally and sociologically specific form of human encounter, and our objective was to depict as faithfully as possible the behaviour of those who participated in it. There was no alternative to designing an instrument explicitly and uniquely for this purpose.

Several areas of information were clearly relevant to our purpose:

(i) basic descriptive information, such as the persons present, the location, the setting, the duration of the hearing, the grounds

of referral, whether or not the child had previously appeared before a hearing;
(ii) the observance or disregard of certain formally identified rules of procedure;
(iii) the topics introduced into discussion;
(iv) the styles of discourse and attitudes adopted by the panel members;
(v) the mood and level of involvement of the child and his parent or parents;
(vi) the decision, the ways in which it was reached and communicated to the family.

We had no plan to make verbatim transcripts of hearings. Although a number of excerpts of dialogue were subsequently recorded in the course of the hearings observed, and are drawn upon in *Chapter 8*, these were thought of as merely illustrative and were not selected systematically according to any agreed principle. It was essential therefore that our coverage of the events of the hearing should be as comprehensive and as accurate as possible, as there could be no further checking once the hearing was at an end. Given the inevitable selectivity of human perception and the fact that all our observations would be carried out, so to speak, in real time, we could never be in a position to claim honestly that everything had been observed and that everything observed had been classified unambiguously and recorded accurately. We tried however to approximate to the ideal in two ways during a prolonged period of pilot studies. First, group discussion was used after each run of preliminary observations to identify what remained in the recollections of the observers as significant omissions, and to consider how far the areas of behaviour concerned could be incorporated into a revised version of the observation schedule. Secondly, two research workers independently recorded their observations of every hearing in the pilot stages. The degree of agreement between them was assessed for each successive version of the schedule developed during this trial period. The sources of unreliability were noted, and in the next draft an attempt was made to modify categories so as to reduce variations in judgment; this often involved the grouping together of categories which had been differentiated by over-refined criteria dependent on subjective interpretation.

Several months were spent in finalizing the observation schedule. During this time 100 hearings were observed and their proceedings recorded in eight successive drafts of the schedule. Inter-observer reliability, which in the first hearings observed was below 50 per cent, was gradually raised to more than 80 per cent by means of the internal changes referred to above and the gradual evolution of agreed criteria for the classification of problematic forms of speech and behaviour.

During the same period work was continuing on the design of a form for summarizing the contents of the case papers that are required to be in the hands of panel members at least three days before a hearing. Both the sheer volume and the quality of these files vary very greatly, and our task was to construct an analytical framework that would encompass the diversity of the material put before panel members. We decided upon the following major areas for the classification of the information contained in case papers:

(i) the sources of reports, the numbers of reports from each source, and the numbers that were 'recent' (defined as less than six months old);

(ii) the nature of comments on the child included in the reports – his personality, school attendance, performance and relationships, leisure interests, home behaviour and health, irrespective of the source of the reports in which the observations were included;

(iii) the nature of comments on parents, again irrespective of the source of comments – personality, relationships, reported co-operation with agencies, indications of pathological behaviour;

(iv) some general features of the reports, such as whether they were on balance optimistic or pessimistic, or whether they identified unmet needs;

(v) the recommendations made and the arguments put forward in support of them.

Six different versions of a schedule for the content analysis of case papers were tested out on files relating to hearings that we observed during the pilot stages before a final format was agreed upon as suitable for use in the fieldwork proper.

Fieldwork was carried out between September 1978 and June 1979, and covered all mainland areas of Scotland. Shortly before each area was visited, the panel members in that area received personal letters from the project co-ordinators introducing the field workers and inviting their co-operation. Although the letter made it clear that the field workers would observe a number of hearings, no indication was given of the scope of the observations. Our target of hearings to be observed was 306; we fell short of it by five. By June we were working in peripheral areas where numbers of cases are comparatively small, especially during the summer holiday period, and we judged that the delay to the entire programme that would be involved in collecting five additional hearings could not be justified in terms of the marginal improvement in representativeness that might thus be achieved. Table 4.1 sets out the intended distribution of the sample of hearings between regions, and compares this with the distribution of the 301 events actually observed. The characteristics of the children drawn into the sample are summarized in *Chapter 6*.

At each hearing the chairman introduced the research workers, explaining that they were carrying out a study of the panels and asked the family members if they had any objection to their presence. While some chairmen made it quite clear that the child and his parents had a full right to exercise choice in this matter, others, it must be admitted, tended to ask the question in such a way as virtually to take the family's consent for granted. In practice, only two families expressed any objection to the observers' presence.

Our concentration on hearings that ended with a formal disposal created a major practical problem. Routine reviews we had agreed to exclude from the beginning. But those hearings that were potentially eligible for inclusion in our sample because they involved grounds of referral would not necessarily end in a disposal. In some instances the grounds would not be accepted, and the case would be referred to the sheriff for proof. In others, the panel members would feel the need for additional information on the child or his circumstances, and the hearing would be 'continued' so that further reports could be obtained from, say, an assessment centre[2] or a child guidance clinic.[3] In fact, it proved necessary to begin the processes of observation at 426 hearings in order to extract the 301 cases that conformed to our criteria. Table 4.2 shows, month by month, the number of hearings observed and the number qualifying for inclusion in the series. The same Table also sets out the number of children eligible for interview, the number actually interviewed and the number of parents interviewed. Methodological aspects of the interview studies are considered in the next section of this chapter.

Interview studies

The decision to carry out personal interviews with a sub-sample of the children whose hearings had been observed arose from the conviction that an understanding of their responses to the experience was crucial to any assessment of the extent to which the hearings system achieves its own objectives. If children do not understand the essential features of the proceedings in which they have been involved, if they are not satisfied with the extent of their own participation in those proceedings, if they are left with a serious sense of unfairness or injustice or stigma, it is arguable that there are discrepancies,

TABLE 4.2

OBSERVATION AND INTERVIEW FIELD PERIOD

Month	*Total observed*	*Total qualifying*	*Total eligible for interview*	*Interviews completed*	
				Child	*Parent*
1978					
September	44	23	18	15	6
October	70	44	27	18	9
November	29	21	11	5	2
December	36	25	17	10	0
1979					
January	53	37	22	14	8
February	39	32	17	9	2
March	44	35	18	14	3
April	35	22	13	5	1
May	46	38	23	9	4
June	30	24	17	6	1
Total	426	301	183	105	36

perhaps significant discrepancies, between the image of the hearings system put forward by its protagonists and the human reality.

The criteria for the inclusion of a hearing in our observation sample have been outlined above. For the child in the case to be eligible for an interview, additional criteria were established: he or she should (i) have been referred on offence grounds, (ii) have no manifest psychiatric disorder, (iii) be of at least low normal intelligence and (iv) be between 12 and 15 years of age.

Non-offence cases were excluded because it was unlikely that sufficient would be obtained for valid comparisons and because there were ethical reservations about imposing any further strain in cases that characteristically involved very stressful problems. Where manifest psychiatric disorder was involved, it was also deemed unacceptable to risk aggravating an already known condition. Absence of mental retardation that would compromise the ability to communicate in an interview was an obvious requirement. Access to the reporter enabled us to assess the eligibility of the candidates on these conditions. The decision to restrict the sample to those aged 12 to 15 was based on the consideration that children in this age group have been found to be more able to concentrate, conceptualize, and communicate in an interview situation than younger children (Yarrow, 1960; Leon, 1978).[4] A number of studies have demonstrated that older juveniles can be interviewed successfully (Baum and Wheeler, 1968; Snyder, 1971; Morris and Giller, 1977).[5] Given these criteria, 183 cases qualified for inclusion, and interviews were completed with 105 children. The response rate for the sample of children interviewed was thus 57·4 per cent.

Interviews were completed with 95 boys and 10 girls, of whom 47 per cent were age 15, 25 per cent were 14 years old and 29 per cent were 12 or 13. While 55 per cent of the 105 were at their first hearing, 45 per cent had appeared at least once before on another referral, and 30 per cent of the total were already under supervision when the sample case was heard. In addition, ten of these children had been to court but only one of these cases had involved a separate prosecution; all the rest had appeared for proof following the non-acceptance of the grounds at a hearing. Forty per cent of cases contained one offence only. Among the serious charges laid, those involving theft (36 per cent) or house-breaking (39 per cent) predominated, followed by 9 per cent for offences against the person. Also included were breach of peace (7 per cent), malicious mischief (5 per cent), taking a vehicle and trivial public order occurrences (2 per cent each). Of the 105 children, 83 per cent were charged as 'acting along with others' and 17 per cent were charged with offences committed while alone.

Sixty-nine per cent of the sample were making a first appearance on the grounds of referral, 12 per cent had been continued from an earlier hearing for the purpose of obtaining reports and 19 per cent had been previously adjourned for some other reason. The most populous region, Strathclyde, provided 61 per cent of the cases while the balance was drawn from all other regions. The decision of the hearing was to impose custodial supervision in 12 per cent of cases, place the child under compulsory home supervision in

50 per cent, and discharge the grounds in 28 per cent. In one case where all grounds were discharged, the child was already under supervision and the order was continued in force. As is evident from our discussion of the observational data, there is no one 'typical' hearing, and the sample of children's interviews reflects the diversity of cases.

This raises the important question of whether those interviewed differ in any significant way from those who were eligible and could have been but were not. In other words, is our sample representative of all those eligible to be interviewed and therefore generalizable to children appearing before hearings generally, or has serious bias occurred? A completion rate of less than 60 per cent makes the consideration of such questions essential.

The characteristics of completed and non-completed interviews of eligible subjects on all the dimensions described above were compared, using the chi-square test. This showed the magnitude of differences to be almost invariably insignificant. One exception was on the measure of joint versus solo offending: those acting alone were *less* likely to be interviewed ($p < 0{\cdot}03$). However, greater recalcitrance of the 'loner' child does not seem seriously to threaten the validity of the findings. On all important measures theoretically related to the likelihood of stigma and sense of injustice (e.g. number of offences charged, nature of offence, prior record and sentence) as well as the more minor factors, the two groups were not significantly different.

How far the likelihood of a positive response to the request for an interview was affected by the actual conduct of the hearing was also a matter for consideration. Again, few differences emerged, but the exceptions were interesting. The styles adopted by panel members appeared to have some relationship to success in obtaining an interview. Children were *more* likely to be interviewed when we recorded a panel style of being encouraging/non-directive ($p < 0{\cdot}02$) and sympathetic/understanding ($p < 0{\cdot}03$), and *less* likely when a style of interruption was recorded ($p < 0{\cdot}03$). It must remain a moot point whether a less sympathetic hearing experience might have led children or parents to reject the interviewers as a part of the 'official' system, or perhaps just left parents in these eligible cases feeling eager to move off as soon as possible. What these differences do tentatively suggest is that the views that were recorded might reflect, especially in interviews with parents, a somewhat more positive view of the hearings than would have been shown if all eligible subjects had been included.

Unwillingness to take part in an interview was not the sole reason for failure to obtain an interview. Refusal by child or parent or both occurred in 31, or less than half, of the 78 eligible but uncompleted cases (Table 4.3). After refusal, the next most common reason (29 cases) was that the researcher decided not to approach the family for a variety of reasons, including the absence of private interview facilities, the child being visibly very upset, and time constraints when the hearing facility had to be closed due to the lateness of the hour. Interviewers had to exercise their discretion in these matters. Yet a third reason (11 cases) for non-response was that the researcher was not permitted to approach the child by the reporter, the panel member or the social worker. This difficulty occurred disproportionately in Edinburgh. A final reason for non-response (7 cases) was interviewer failure to approach an eligible child due to confusion over one of the criteria for inclusion; with the pressure of hearings and busy reporters, the clarification was not always achieved in time to approach the family before they left.

Thus, the refusal of the children and their parents to participate in the interview was a fairly minor contributing factor to lack of success. Even the figure of 31 'refusals' is somewhat misleading, as many of these families expressed interest but said they were unable to stay because of commitments elsewhere after the hearing. While the response rate is no doubt lower than would have been expected if all eligible children had been approached, it is nevertheless adequate given the absence of bias in the sample.

The interview method always requires careful attention to techniques that will ensure the validity of the data collected. When the subjects are children, this presents particular problems associated with their age, immaturity, level of verbal ability, social separation and general relative powerlessness in an adult world.

In making the initial contact with the child and parent, the interviewer introduced herself and told them her university affiliation, the purpose of the project, its confidential nature and the time required for the interview. She invariably made it clear that she was not connected with the panel members or any official, and that co-operation was entirely voluntary. When possible, this contact was made prior to the hearing, but often it did not occur until afterwards. The interviewer was usually the same person who had observed the hearing, so that the family had already heard confirmation of the researcher's status from the hearing chairman[6] when those present had been introduced. If the parents and child agreed, the interviews were conducted immediately after the hearing (with the exception of some hearings resulting in 'List D' placements, see below). In adopting this tactic, we followed the approach of the 'life-space interview' (Redl, 1959)[7] which aims to tap the child's affective involvement and recall of an event that has just occurred.

Once consent was obtained, the interviewer had the difficult task of

---

TABLE 4.3
REASONS FOR NON-RESPONSE IN INTERVIEW SURVEY

Reasons for non-response	*Frequency* %
Refusal by child and/or parent	17
Lack of suitable time or place, or child upset	16
Request of reporter or social worker or panel member	6
Interviewer's uncertainty about eligibility	4
Total non-response	43
N (sample of eligible children)	183

establishing rapport with the child, while under some time pressure to proceed with the interview fairly quickly in order to avoid further inconveniencing the parents who were usually waiting when not being interviewed themselves. The interviewer attempted to relieve any anxiety about the purpose of the interview at the outset by explicit clarification of her role and the nature of the study. She reiterated that her job was with the university and not in any way connected with the panel, and that everything was confidential and not available to anyone from the reporter's department, the panel or social work department. It was emphasized that the purpose was to hear the child's views about the experience he or she had just undergone. Since the child during the hearing had been in an unequal power relationship with adults who quite obviously had considerable authority over his or her life, it was thought important to establish a more egalitarian relationship in the interview context. The interviewers strove to convey a non-judgmental acceptance of the children's views, a genuine interest in their feelings and ideas, and respect for them as persons.

The setting of an interview may also affect rapport. We endeavoured to conduct each interview in a quiet, private room apart from parents, and while some interruptions did occur, they were kept to a minimum. Usually a vacant office near the hearing room was made available. Chairs were arranged near to each other in order to avoid intervening desks or tables and thereby to reduce feelings of social distance.

Interviews conducted at List D schools require special comment. Because of the procedures involved in sending children to these schools after a hearing, or their state of upset at the decision, or both, it was usually inappropriate to approach them immediately after the hearing. However, since it would have seriously biased the sample not to include interviews with those given the most severe available disposition, it was decided to make an effort to interview them later. Nine of the 13 children in our sample who received residential supervision were interviewed at these schools. No problems were encountered in contacting children via the List D headmaster or in arranging for interviews in private at the schools. Subjects were given a few days to settle in, and all were interviewed within one month of the hearing, a time deemed adequate for recall of the event (Baum and Wheeler, 1968).[8] Responses by the List D group tended to be more loquacious. Perhaps this was due to the lack of time pressures on the interview and the more distanced setting compared to those done soon after hearings, but these respondents were otherwise similar in co-operation and attention.

That considerable rapport was established seems evidenced by the fullness and apparent openness of most children's answers (even from those who had been uncommunicative in the hearing) and by our own best judgment that the children took the interview as a serious opportunity to express their personal views to an interested adult. The brief nature of the interview, its proximity to the hearing event and the nature of the questions (i.e. avoiding issues around the offence and relations with parents) may all have contributed to a high level of co-operation.

In designing the interview schedule, we wanted a standardized format that would permit comparability of responses but would none the less encourage an undirected 'free' response. The pattern was to start with the more straightforward questions about what had happened at the hearing, move to the projections involving stigma, then to the role perceptions and to close with the more general evaluative questions. Most questions about the hearing were open-ended, with no choice of response provided, leaving the child to answer in his or her own words. Great care was taken not to suggest a preferred response in the light of the susceptibility of children to adult cues (Maccoby and Maccoby, 1954).[9]

The decision to attempt some interviews with parents was made after the basic plan of the project as a whole had been determined. The sample was small and geographically biased and the findings can make no serious claim to representativeness. Given those provisos however the data derived from this study are of considerable interest.

The pattern of the interview followed fairly closely that administered to the children, with the exception of the sections on role perception and identification. These were omitted; although useful in assisting children to identify roles, their format was inappropriate for adult respondents. Some other questions were redrafted in a more adult style, but the essential similarity of the two instruments was retained.

In general, parents were interviewed only when both an additional interviewer and suitable accommodation were available. The former was easier to ensure in the vicinity of Glasgow and the necessary privacy was more difficult to obtain in rural areas. Making appointments to see families at home at a later date was considered as a possible solution but was rejected, partly because such a procedure was not compatible with our complex timetable and partly because we attached some importance to the relatively raw quality of the feelings and perceptions that could be gathered by an interviewer in the immediately post-hearing situation.

One further factor influencing the size and distribution of the parent sample should be mentioned here. Lothian Region did not permit us to approach parents and we did not attempt any of these interviews in Central Region, where an independent research worker was carrying out a separate study of parental reactions to children's hearings. Of the 36 parent interviews carried out, 23 were in Glasgow and five elsewhere in Strathclyde Region, two in Grampian, three in Fife, one in Highland and two in Borders.

The parents of 31 boys and five girls were interviewed. The age range of the children included all ages in the sample range. Parents of two 12-year-olds, nine 14-year-olds, and fifteen 15-year-olds participated in the sample. Exactly half the sample were attending their first hearing. The grounds of referral included the commonest categories of offence – theft, theft by shoplifting, housebreaking, breach of the peace, malicious mischief, obstruction. There were no unusual grounds of referral in terms of quality or quantity apart from one child referred on fourteen separate grounds of theft, all committed within a two-week period and involving almost the entire stock of one shop on each occasion. Three children were simultaneously referred for truancy as well as offences. Twenty-seven of the cases were initial hearings and nine were precipitated reviews. The decisions reached by the hearing were as follows: 18 home supervision orders, 14 discharges and four residential supervision orders including one child received into care. In all identifiable features other than regional distribution, this small sub-sample of interviews was very similar to that of the sample as a whole. The findings, nevertheless, should be seen as indicative rather than definitive.

Opinion studies

Conscious of the key role of children's panel members as decision-makers, and having strong subjective impressions of both common elements and variations in their attitudes to delinquency and the work of the hearings system, we hoped from the beginning of the project to include some study of the personal characteristics of these centrally located lay participants. We were at first attracted by the possibilities of the techniques that have been developed on the basis of personal construct theory (Kelly, 1955).[10] These seemed to open up the prospect of a sensitive exploration of conceptions of delinquency and related issues, without the imposition on the subject of the investigator's own categories and criteria. After some preliminary work however we decided not to pursue this line of enquiry. Personal construct techniques, it seemed to us, were essentially idiographic, potentially valuable for use in clinical situations where the emphasis was upon the unique individual and perhaps the assessment of change within the individual; but they were not adaptable to use in fairly large-scale research enquiries, where the resulting data would be expressed in terms of averages, frequency distributions and cross-tabulations, except at the cost of modifications so far-reaching as to undermine the underlying theory's most basic assumptions. We subsequently carried out trials with the use of a variety of instruments: semantic differentials, sentence completion tests and scales designed to measure such generalized attitudes as conservatism and punitiveness. None of these appeared to meet the combined criteria of suitability for large-scale application and manifest relevance. We believed that any study of the beliefs and values that panel members bring to their task would be of very limited value unless it embraced a substantial fraction of all panel members. This almost inevitably pointed to some form of postal enquiry, with the attendant risk of a low level of participation. That risk we thought would be minimized if the people who were approached could see the questions that were being asked as clearly relevant to their activities as panel members.

These considerations led us to conclude that our aim should be to study quite explicitly the opinions and beliefs held by panel members concerning the work of the hearings system, without attempting to identify other than inferentially any possible underlying structures, whether of generalized attitudes or of personality traits. With the co-operation of a fairly small group of panel members who were quite well known to us, we began to develop an instrument suitable for use on a large scale. This was a self-completion questionnaire, covering several different areas of information:

(i) characteristics seen as desirable in panel members and in the conduct of children's hearings;
(ii) areas of difficulty encountered, and satisfaction with the working of the system;
(iii) possible changes in the powers and jurisdiction of children's hearings;
(iv) supposed causes of delinquency;
(v) views on the objectives of different 'treatment' measures, and the types of children for whom they are appropriate;
(vi) limited personal data – age, sex, occupation and number of years' service as a panel member.

While a considerable number of questions were pre-coded, using such categories as 'in favour/not in favour' and 'important/not important' a number of key questions were left open-ended. These included views on the objectives of supervision and residential commitment, and ideas about the causes of delinquency; in reply to the latter question, panel members were invited to write not more than four brief statements.

A final version of the questionnaire was ready at about the time that our observations of hearings began. As we thought it important to reassure panel members that we had no plans in any way to check their expressed opinions against their actual behaviour in hearings, we decided on two measures which seemed likely to reduce any anxiety even though both would inevitably create inconvenience for us. First, we ensured that all returns would be genuinely anonymous; the only serial number on the questionnaire was that which identified the region. Secondly, we phased the distribution of questionnaires over a period of six months (from September 1978 to March 1979) so that the panel members of each area received their forms some months before or after the visits by field workers. Each questionnaire was accompanied by a covering letter which explained our interests and stressed anonymity, and by a reply-paid envelope.

Distribution was by direct mail to all persons listed as members of children's panels in the most up-to-date lists available to us. A total of 1570 questionnaires was mailed. Some six to eight weeks after the original distribution, a reminder was despatched. Since we had no means of knowing who had or had not replied, the reminder was sent (with an appropriate explanation and apology) to all panel members.

A total of 44 questionnaires was returned to us, either by the postal authorities because the subject was no longer at the listed address and had made no forwarding arrangements, or by the respondent with an explanation that he or she had given up panel membership since the compilation of the lists that we had used. Of the remaining 1526, 921 returned completed questionnaires, corresponding to a response rate of slightly over 60 per cent. Response rates in mailed questionnaire surveys are notoriously variable, ranging between perhaps 25 per cent and 80 per cent. The response we actually achieved was fairly close to the level that we expected; we believed that we had the advantage of addressing members of an identifiable group on a subject of direct concern to them, countered by the drawback of a questionnaire that was long and demanded considerable time and intellectual effort. As Table 4.4 shows, the response rate varied from region to region, tending to be lower in Strathclyde than elsewhere, while the highest returns were achieved by Highland (76 per cent). Orkney's impressive 78 per cent refers in fact to the return of seven questionnaires by a total of nine panel members.

At a fairly late stage in the life of this research project, we decided to undertake a small-scale survey of the opinions of social workers. Some commentators on the hearings system had emphasized its dependence on 'social work principles' and had seen both the selection and the training of panel members as attempts to build up a body of laymen who would be highly sympathetic to the aims and methods of the social work profession – whatever those were assumed to be.[11] Whether this was ever a valid observation is arguable; but certainly in recent years we have had strong subjective impressions of quite marked ideological divergence between panel members and social workers. How profound or how extensive such differences are could be determined only by direct comparison.

The questionnaire designed for this comparative study fell into two parts. Half the items were identical with the questions about delinquency, its causes and management that had been asked of panel members. Questions relating to the role and attributes of panel members were omitted, and replaced by a

TABLE 4.4

QUESTIONNAIRE RESPONSE RATES, BY REGION

	Panel members questionnaires			*Social workers questionnaires*		
	Mailed	*Returned*	%	*Mailed*	*Returned*	%
Borders	31	19	61	5	5	(100)
Central	68	45	66	16	11	69
Dumfries and Galloway	37	23	62	7	5	(71)
Fife	81	48	59	15	11	73
Grampian	103	68	66	26	15	58
Highland	80	61	76	9	7	(78)
Lothian	179	120	67	62	30	48
Strathclyde (Glasgow)	396	210	53	58	34	59
Strathclyde (Other divisions)	435	253	58	72	41	57
Tayside	83	49	59	28	11	39
Orkney	9	7	(78)	1	1	(100)
Shetland	11	6	54	1	1	(100)
Western Isles	13	9	69	2	2	(100)
	1,526	921[1]	60	302	174	58

Percentages are given in brackets when based on ten or fewer cases.

Note 1. Region code removed in three cases.

number of items concerning the functions of social workers in the children's hearings system.

We decided, somewhat arbitrarily, on a target sample size of 300. This corresponded to almost exactly one-sixth of the main-grade and senior social workers in the service of Scottish local authorities, according to a staffing census carried out in the previous year. All directors of social work in Scotland kindly agreed to help in drawing a one in six sample of staff in the grades concerned – those whose everyday responsibilities included the preparation of social background reports, attendance at children's hearings and the carrying-out of supervision orders. Some directors of social work preferred to arrange for the direct distribution of our questionnaires to members of their staff, while others provided us with a list of names and office addresses to which we sent the schedules by mail. Three hundred and two questionnaires were in fact sent out, and 174 were returned completed. The response rate of 58 per cent was marginally lower than that of panel members. There appeared to be some quite marked inter-regional variations, but the small numbers involved in most regional samples make for unreliable percentages.

In concluding this chapter on methods of enquiry, it is appropriate to draw attention to the emphasis placed on the maintenance of confidentiality. The anonymity of the questionnaires returned by panel members and social workers has already been mentioned. The referrals in respect of whom reporters completed case summary forms were never personally identified to us; each form carried a unique serial number, but only the reporter concerned knew the names corresponding to the serial numbers. The issue was however a more urgent one where material relating to children appearing before hearings was concerned, because of both the Law Enforcement Assistance Administration's rules relating to privacy and our own insistence on high standards of data protection. All children in the category had at least two research documents, an observation schedule and a records summary. Some also had an interview schedule, and in a small proportion of cases a parent interview in addition. A cover slip showed the child's name and identifying number, the latter indicating region, district and personal serial number. Individual documents showed the identifying number only. On completion of each phase of fieldwork, the information on the cover slips was transferred to a master register. The latter was kept under secure conditions and located away from all other documents.

It is perhaps worth adding that throughout the period of fieldwork no complaint was received by the project co-ordinators, or to the best of our knowledge by any local authority official or panel member, either about any breach of confidence or any invasion of privacy, or indeed about any aspect of the activities of the field staff of the project.

NOTES

1. R. D. Bales, *Interaction Process Analysis*. Addison-Wesley, Cambridge, Mass., 1950. Michael Argyle, *Social Interaction*. Tavistock, 1969.

2. There are 17 *assessment centres* in Scotland. Some were formerly remand homes but others have been purpose built. Their function is both to detain children on a short term basis and to offer assessment by the members of the centre staff as well as consultation with medical and educational specialists. A full account of the work of assessment centres is expected to emerge from current research at the University of Dundee.

3. *Child guidance* in Scotland is an educational service providing advice on the management of handicapped, backward and difficult children as well as specialist remedial help. Based in local clinics psychologists with teaching experience form the majority of staff: social workers are engaged to a lesser extent and medical personnel visit on a part time basis. The Education (Scotland) Act, 1969 gave child guidance services a specific remit to provide advice as requested on the needs of any child under the provisions of the Social Work (Scotland) Act, 1968.

4. L. J. Yarrow, 'Interviewing Children'. Chapter 14, in: P. H. Mussen, ed., *Handbook of Research Methods in Child Development*. Wiley, New York, 1960.
   J. S. Leon, 'Recent developments in legal representation for children: a growing concern with the concept of capacity', *Canadian Journal of Family Law*, 1978, 1(3).

5. M. Baum and S. Wheeler, 'Becoming an inmate', Chapter 7, in: S. Wheeler, ed., *Controlling Delinquents*. Wiley, New York, 1968.
   E. C. Snyder, 'The impact of the juvenile court hearing on the child', *Crime and Delinquency*, 1971, 17 April.
   Allison Morris and Henri Giller, 'The client's perspective', *The Criminal Law Review*, 1977.

6. The term *chairman* is used in the 1968 Act and the Rules irrespective of the sex of the person appointed and we are following that usage.

7. F. Redl, 'Strategy and techniques of the life space interview', *American Journal of Orthopsychiatry*, 1959, 29.

8. *See* note 5.

9. E. E. Maccoby and N. Maccoby, 'The interview as a tool of social science', in: G. Lindzey, ed., *Handbook of Social Psychology*. Addison-Wesley, Cambridge, 1954.

10. George A. Kelly, *The Psychology of Personal Constructs*. Vols. 1 and 2, Norton, New York, 1955.

11. *See*, for example, Gilbert Smith, ' "Little Kiddies" and "criminal" acts: the role of social work in the children's hearings', *British Journal of Social Work*, 1978, 7(4).

5

REPORTERS' DISCRETION

Entering the system

The reporter to the children's panel is, as our earlier discussion makes clear, the single portal of entry to the hearings system. He receives all referrals, and he alone decides what steps should next be taken. The essence of his activities in respect of referrals is the exercise of discretion, not in the range of options available, for these are few and precisely defined, but in his interpretation and assessment of the meaning of the information available to him. His initial information is itself the end-product of a process of interpretation by the person or agency instigating the referral. We have no direct information on the nature of the discretionary practices actually operated by Scottish police forces, but it is quite clear that juveniles believed by the police to have committed offences are not invariably and automatically referred to the reporter. The use of police warnings is widely recognized; whether the decision to issue a warning as an alternative to referral depends solely on the perceived seriousness of the offence or the familiarity of the culprit, or whether other considerations affect the choice, has never been systematically examined. American evidence, which suggests that becoming defined as delinquent depends on the interaction between the offender and the arresting officer, with the outcome of the encounter being crucially influenced by the nature of the interaction (Piliavin and Briar, 1964),[1] may or may not be relevant in a Scottish context.

Having considered the information provided by the referring agent, the reporter may conclude that no further action is required because there is insufficient supporting evidence, and may therefore decide not to request any further reports. In most cases however he will ask for a social background report from the social work department and a school report where relevant; less frequently reports may be sought from more specialized sources.

In trying to determine an appropriate course of action on the basis of information that others have gathered, the reporter is not guided by any centrally established formal rules or criteria for decision-making. In their absence he is likely to be influenced by his personal convictions, however founded; by informal group norms, evolved from the shared experience of colleagues; and by such rule-of-thumb principles as may have been incorporated into departmental practice. We know that prior to the formation of regional reporters' departments there was wide variation from district to district in the proportion of cases referred to hearings, suggesting that there were considerable differences in the criteria employed by reporters. Regionalization appears markedly to have narrowed but not eliminated this variation; differences between individual reporters or teams of reporters within regions may also still be quite significant. All that can be said with certainty is that there is little justification for assuming from the outset that reporters share a common set of beliefs concerning the specific factors and combinations of factors that indicate a need for compulsory measures of care.

Those children who were brought to the notice of reporters in our two study periods were referred from a variety of sources and for a number of different reasons. Tables 5.1 and 5.2 respectively summarize the sources and the grounds of referral.

TABLE 5.1

SOURCES OF REFERRAL TO REPORTERS

	First source of referral %	*Second source of referral* %	*Third source of referral* %
Police	65	—	—
Procurator fiscal	13	2	—
Court	1	—	—
Education department	13	2	—
Social work department	6	1	*
RSSPCC	1	—	—
Parent/relative	1	*	*
Medical	*	—	—
(N = 100%)	678		

TABLE 5.2

GROUNDS OF REFERRAL TO REPORTERS

		First grounds of referral %	*Second grounds of referral* %	*Third grounds of referral* %
Beyond control	(a)	6	—	—
Moral danger	(b)	*	*	—
Parental neglect	(c)	3	*	—
Crim. Proc. 1975	(d)	2	*	—
Act	(dd)	*	—	—
Truancy	(f)	16	*	*
Offence	(g)	73	3	*
(N = 100%)		678		

* Less than 1 per cent.

As we know from earlier discussion, any agency or any private individual may direct the attention of the reporter to a given child. Our findings in this series of cases are broadly in line with the national statistics reviewed in *Chapter 3*. The police remain by a very considerable margin the largest source of referral, accounting for nearly two-thirds of all cases. The 90 instances in which the procurator fiscal was the first source of referral are in a sense police referrals at one remove, the procurator fiscal having decided that the case would be more appropriately dealt with within the hearings system than by prosecution in court. The education authorities generate as many referrals as the procurator fiscal, and are in practice the almost exclusive means by which truancy cases are brought into the hearings system. Care proceedings generally emanate from the social work department of the local authority or from a voluntary body;[2] it should be emphasized however that a social work department concerned about, say, non-accidental injury to a child may have recourse to other powers to take children into care without necessarily involving the reporter and the children's panel.[3]

Cases may of course be referred from more than one source, and reporters were asked to indicate up to three sources of referral. Only 6 per cent of the children in the sample came to the reporter's attention on this occasion from more than one agency, and in two of the 41 instances three referring sources were involved. The education department of the local authority and the procurator fiscal were in absolute terms the most likely to appear as second sources.

Nearly three-quarters of all referrals were on offence grounds (Table 5.2), and almost one-sixth on grounds of truancy. The numerical predominance of offences, although entirely in line with the national trends reported in an earlier chapter, deserves nevertheless to be stressed. Many panel members are anxious to see an increase in that part of their workload concerned with 'care and protection' cases and would welcome changes in their jurisdiction which would give them the opportunity to deliberate on a wider range of problems in the child care field; but there is in some quarters perhaps something of a tendency to over-estimate the part currently being played in the business of children's hearings by non-offence referrals. Without disputing either the importance of such cases or the thoroughness with which they are considered, it remains beyond question that the bulk of children's hearings are concerned with offenders, and that any evaluation of the work of reporters or of panel members must assign particular importance to the management of children alleged to have committed offences.

The growth area in recent years has of course been truancy;[4] not an offence within the meaning of the 1968 Act, but certainly an area of behaviour where the man and woman in the street are less likely to think of the child as sinned against than as sinning. The high degree of concern that panel members constantly express over school attendance (*Chapter 8*) might suggest that truancy would be for them a welcome sphere of activity; yet doubts about the wisdom of a policy of treating truancy simply as individual deviance are not unknown.[5]

The remaining first grounds of referral were almost evenly divided between allegations that a child was beyond parental control – also not an offence in terms of the Scottish legislation, although held to be a 'status offence' in some other jurisdictions – and other cases, particularly cases of parental neglect. The quantitatively limited contribution of care and protection cases to the reporter's caseload reflects of course not merely the existence of alternative modes of processing such cases but the relative rarity of publicly recognized offences committed by adults against children as compared to delinquent acts in which young people have engaged. To say that such cases are not very common does not detract in any way from the significance rightly attached and the time devoted to them by reporters and panel members alike when they do arise.

Thirty-seven of the children in this series (5 per cent) were referred on two separate grounds, and four on three grounds. Non-offence reasons were relatively more common among second than among first grounds (approximately half of the former); in particular, being in moral danger is unique in appearing more often as a second ground of referral than as a first.

Because of the anticipated scale of the 'offence' category, more detailed information was gathered in such cases so as to permit a fuller analysis of factors in decision-making. In this general characterization of the sample we note variation both in the number of offences alleged and in their seriousness. Slightly more than two-thirds of all the referrals involved only one offence, with the remainder being roughly evenly divided between those with two offences (15 per cent) and those with three or more (17 per cent). Seriousness is largely a matter of subjective judgment though one on which there is a reasonably high degree of agreement in most communities.[6] We examined

TABLE 5.3

SERIOUSNESS OF OFFENCES ALLEGED

	Most serious offence %	*Second most serious offence* %
Illegal consumption of alcohol	*	*
Local bye-laws	6	*
Public order	10	3
Property damage	7	3
Taking and driving away a motor vehicle and Road Traffic Act offences	3	2
Theft	40	5
Housebreaking	19	*
Violence	3	—
Other, unclassifiable offences (e.g. malicious 'phone calls, failure to keep an animal under control)	2	—
(N = 100%)	514	

* Less than 1 per cent.

various classifications of offences, and developed eight broad categories which may be seen as representing a scale of increasing seriousness and into which all but ten of the reported individual offences could be fitted. Table 5.3 shows the distribution of the most serious offence reported (including of course the sole offence where there was only one) and of the second most serious offence. Four offences out of 10 involved theft, including shoplifting and reset (receiving goods knowing them to have been stolen). This was by far the largest category of offences and was fully twice as common as offences involving entry into locked premises. In one referral in eight, the most serious offence alleged involved the use or the threat of violence. At the other end of the scale, about 6 per cent of those referred were not alleged to have committed anything more serious than an offence against local bye-laws – which in Glasgow at any rate may mean in practice playing football in the street. Offences against public order, including drunkenness and various forms of 'breach of the peace' were responsible for one referral in 10. Charges of damage to property were not very common and motor vehicle offences quite unusual. In short, a very varied range of offences, including some that were of a comparatively trifling nature but others that no community could be expected to ignore.

The offenders who came to the notice of the reporter were, as is invariably the case in studies of reported delinquency, mainly boys, outnumbering girls in this instance by more than seven to one (452 and 62 referrals respectively). Girls accounted however for a substantial majority of referrals on non-offence grounds (95, compared to 69 boys). Non-offence grounds were responsible for three-fifths of all girls referred to reporters but for only little more than one-eighth of all boys. In terms of age we find a marked concentration towards the upper limit of eligibility. Distinctly more than half of those referred were aged 14 or 15 (367, or more than 54 per cent), with only five aged 16 or more. Just over one in nine (78, or 12 per cent) was aged 10 or less, with comparatively small numbers at or nearing transition from primary to secondary school (110 in all) and a marked increase to 17 per cent of all referrals (118 children) at the age of 13.

Reporters' decisions

In just over half the cases in this series (52 per cent) the reporter's decision was to refer the child to a hearing (Table 5.4). In more than three quarters of the remaining cases the decision was to take no formal action. One child in 14 was referred to the local authority social work department with the intention of achieving some form of voluntary supervision, while the other 31 children (5 per cent of the total) were referred to the police for a formal warning. In the remainder of this chapter we examine the influence of a variety of factors on reporters' decision-making. The analyses offered will for the most part be in terms of comparison between only two categories – those referred to children's hearings and those dealt with otherwise. The use of voluntary supervision is not very common, and tends to reflect the reporter's recognition that such a service is in fact obtainable rather than a set of distinctive features on the part of the child; there is little doubt that many reporters would make greater use of voluntary supervision if it were possible, and that some children currently referred to hearings and possibly even some in respect of whom no formal action is now taken would be brought to the notice of the social work department for voluntary measures if resources could be made voluntarily available. Those referred for police warnings, though potentially an interesting group, are too few in number to stand up to much statistical analysis.

In these analyses we consider first the inter-related influences of the age and sex of the child, the grounds of referral and the existence or otherwise of a record of a previous referral; then some characteristics of the present offence or offences, where these constituted all or part of the grounds of referral; then some aspects of the child's earlier history within the hearings system; and the influence of indications in the reports provided for the reporter of certain problems in the child's background. Finally, this chapter examines something of the combined influence of a group of identified factors as well as the reasons given by reporters in support of their decisions.

Age, sex and referrals present and past

Table 5.5 relates the disposals made by reporters to the first ground of referral recorded. It expresses vividly the striking difference between the management of non-offence cases, the large majority of which are referred to hearings, and offence referrals, of which nearly half are dismissed with no formal action being taken. The marked propensity to retain non-offence referrals within the hearings system applies not only to care and protection cases but also to those alleged to be beyond parental control and very strikingly to truants. Only one truancy case in nine leads to no formal action. The small numbers involved in almost all the non-offence categories, and the extremely small numbers dealt with other than by referral to a children's hearing, mean that opportunities for the study of discretionary processes in relation to non-offence grounds are very restricted. In many of the tabulations that follow the principal emphasis will be on the processing of offence referrals, where the discretion of reporters can be seen to operate on a substantial scale.

TABLE 5.4

REPORTERS' DISPOSALS OF REFERRED CHILDREN

	Disposal %
No formal action	36
Referral to hearing	52
Referral to social work dept. for voluntary measures	7
Referral to police for warning	5
(N = 100%)	678

Age of the child appears to influence the decision of reporters, to judge from Table 5.6, which indicates a high rate of referral to hearings in the youngest age-group, and a concentration of referrals for voluntary supervision and police warnings among the 12-year-olds. When dealing with children aged 13, 14 or 15, the reporter's reduced use of the latter two agencies is balanced by an increased tendency to take no formal action, while younger children are instead more likely to be referred to a hearing. The age-groups are not however

TABLE 5.5

DECISION IN RELATION TO FIRST GROUNDS OF REFERRAL

	Grounds of referral						
	a	*b*	*c*	*d*	*dd*	*f*	*g*
Decision	%	%	%	%	%	%	%
No formal action	13	(33)	18	(10)	—	11	45
Refer to hearing	77	(33)	82	(80)	(100)	84	41
Refer to SWD	10	(33)	—	(10)	—	5	8
Refer to police	—	—	—	—	—	—	6
(N = 100%)	39	3	22	10	3	109	492

TABLE 5.6

DECISION IN RELATION TO AGE OF CHILD

	Age						
	10 *or under*	11	12	13	14	15	16+
Decision	%	%	%	%	%	%	%
No formal action	24	30	21	35	41	43	(80)
Refer to hearing	64	55	53	53	52	46	(20)
Refer to SWD	8	9	12	7	5	7	—
Refer to police	4	6	14	5	2	4	—
(N = 100%)	78	53	57	118	173	194	5

TABLE 5.7

DECISION IN RELATION TO AGE AND GROUNDS OF REFERRAL

	Referred to a hearing						
	10 *or under*	11	12	13	14	15	16+
	%	%	%	%	%	%	%
Offence grounds	46	51	38	45	46	40	(20)
Non-offence grounds	84	70	88	82	74	77	—

Percentages are given in brackets when based on ten or fewer cases.

directly comparable in terms of the grounds of referral. Almost half those under the age of 11 are referred on non-offence grounds, while this is true of less than one quarter of the older children. If we divide the children in each age category into two broad groups according to grounds of referral, we find that most of the age-related differences really reflect the varying contributions of offence and non-offence grounds respectively. We note that in most age-groups just less than half of all referrals on offence grounds are dealt with by further referral to a children's hearing, while something close to 80 per cent of all non-offence cases are disposed of by reporters in this way. The low rate of referral to hearings for 12-year-old offenders should be seen in conjunction with the relatively generous use of informal supervision and police warnings for this age group mentioned above. Children aged 12 who come to the notice of the reporters are in fact less likely to have no action taken than those of any other age.

Referral decisions for the two sexes are also affected by a differential distribution of grounds of referral. On the face of it, boys are more likely than girls to have no formal action taken or to be referred for a police warning and distinctly less likely to be referred to a children's hearing (49 per cent compared to 62 per cent). Holding grounds of referral constant however has something of the effect of reversing that pattern. Boys referred on offence grounds are rather more likely than girls to be referred to a hearing, while so far as non-offence grounds are concerned there is no difference in the propensity of reporters to refer those of either sex for further consideration by panel members.

It seems unlikely that reporters would be wholly uninfluenced by the knowledge that a given child had been referred to them on some previous

TABLE 5.8

DECISION IN RELATION TO SEX OF CHILD

Decision	*Boys* %	*Girls* %
No formal action	39	29
Referral to hearing	49	62
Referral to social work dept.	7	8
Referral to police	6	1
(N = 100%)	521	157

TABLE 5.9

DECISION IN RELATION TO SEX AND GROUNDS OF REFERRAL

	Referred to a hearing	
	Boys %	*Girls* %
Offence grounds	45	36
Non-offence grounds	78	80

occasion. May the apparent difference in the treatment of male and female offenders be attributable to differences in the proportions of recidivists? Table 5.10 does not lend support to this hypothesis. When previous offence history is held constant, it is clear that referral rates for the two sexes are virtually identical when they come to the attention of the reporter for the first time. The chances of a boy being referred to a hearing when he is brought to the notice of the reporter on a subsequent occasion are increased by about 75 per cent; the possibility of a recidivist girl being dealt with in this way seems to be increased only marginally. The number of girls involved in repeated offending is however small enough to discourage speculation about possible causes.

Aspects of the offence

A number of characteristics of the offence which in the light of earlier studies[7] might presumably be expected to influence discretionary decision-making were identified in the study. These included the actual number of offences alleged on this occasion, the type of offences, classified according to a rough scale of seriousness, and the value of goods where the offence involved theft or damage. Table 5.11, which relates source of referral to reporter 's decision, does not add a great deal to the information derived from the earlier analysis of grounds of referral; some grounds are for all practical purposes source-specific. The most interesting and perhaps surprising feature of this table is the higher proportion of cases in which no formal action was taken among those referred by the procurator fiscal than among direct police referrals. It seems unlikely that this is due to an uneven distribution of new and recurrent offenders between the two referral groups; Table 5.12 confirms that there is indeed a greater likelihood that a police referral will proceed from the reporter to a children's hearing than will a procurator fiscal's referral, irrespective of whether or not earlier offence referrals are on the record.

On the face of it, this is a puzzling finding. On balance one might expect to find a *higher* rate of referral to hearings for fiscal's cases, since these will have been submitted in the first place with a view to possible prosecution in the courts and are likely to include a higher than average proportion of the more serious offences. The explanation is presumably to be sought in terms of some

TABLE 5.10

DECISION IN RELATION TO SEX AND PREVIOUS REFERRAL ON OFFENCE GROUNDS (CURRENT OFFENCE REFERRAL ONLY)

	Referred to a hearing	
	Boys %	*Girls* %
No previous offence referral	32	34
One or more previous offence referral(s)	55	38

aspects of police discretion and fiscal's discretion that are not at present properly understood.

Three different ways of estimating the seriousness of the offence alleged are examined in Table 5.13 with reference to their influence on the reporter's decision-making. It is clear that the number of separate offences covered by the referral in question plays an important part in the judgment of the reporter, especially when considered in conjunction with the existence of a history of earlier referrals. Only one-quarter of those who on their first referral to a reporter are charged with a single offence are subsequently dealt with by a children's hearing, while for those who have come to the reporter's notice at least once before and on this occasion have as many as three offences against them, the corresponding proportion is three-quarters. The recidivist with a single offence alleged on the present occasion is about as likely to be brought before a children's hearing as a first offender with two or three current charges against him.

The type of offence alleged also plays a significant part, though its influence is a little less clear-cut than that of number of offences. In order to obtain reasonable numbers for analysis several small offence categories have been combined in this table to form a group loosely designated 'minor offences'. This includes breach of the peace, offences against the local bye-laws, taking and driving away a motor vehicle and offences under the Road Traffic Acts as

TABLE 5.11

DECISION IN RELATION TO SOURCE OF REFERRAL

	Source of referral							
Decision	*Police* %	*Fiscal* %	*Court* %	*School* %	*SWD* %	*RSSPCC* %	*Parent* %	*Medical* %
No formal action	40	57	(25)	12	13	(20)	(20)	—
Refer to hearing	45	39	(75)	83	82	(80)	(70)	(100)
Refer to SWD	9	2	—	6	5	—	(10)	—
Refer to police	7	2	—	—	—	—	—	—
(N = 100%)	439	90	8	86	38	5	10	2

TABLE 5.12

DECISION IN RELATION TO SOURCE OF REFERRAL AND PREVIOUS REFERRAL ON OFFENCE GROUNDS

	Referred to hearing	
	Police cases %	*Fiscal cases* %
No previous offence referral	31	24
One or more previous offence referral(s)	56	40

well as a small 'miscellaneous and unclassifiable' group. Among the first offenders, damage to property is slightly more often dealt with by referral to a children's hearing than is theft, while house-breaking and personal violence are markedly more frequently handled in this way; it is noteworthy however that even offences in the two latter groups are referred to a hearing in less than half of all first referrals. Once again, the influence of a previous history is striking. The young person charged with a 'minor' offence who is already known to the reporter has the same chance of being referred to a hearing as one who is alleged to have committed an offence involving violence, but has no previous history of referral. For any given type of offence, the probability of coming before a hearing is substantially increased when there is a history of prior referral.

This table finally considers the part played by the value of goods involved, where the offence was one of stealing or damaging property. It is sometimes suggested that decisions to invoke legal procedures against young delinquents depend on some simple informal rule involving property value. Morris (1978)[8] indicates value of goods as a significant influence on reporters' decision-making. Of the cases in the present sample 373 involved offences against property, but in 63 of these the extent of the loss or damage was not clearly identified. In the

TABLE 5.13

DECISION IN RELATION TO CHARACTERISTICS OF THE OFFENCE AND PREVIOUS REFERRAL ON OFFENCE GROUNDS

Number of offences alleged

	Referred to hearing		
	One offence %	*Two offences* %	*Three+ offences* %
No previous offence referral	26	45	47
One or more previous offence referral(s)	45	60	76

Seriousness of offence

	Referred to hearing				
	Minor offences %	*Property damage* %	*Theft* %	*House-breaking* %	*Violence* %
No previous offence referral	22	33	38	46	41
One or more previous offence referral(s)	40	42	54	62	63

Value of goods involved

	Referred to hearing		
	Value not more than £20 %	*Value £21–£100* %	*Value £101+* %
No previous offence referral	27	36	47
One or more previous offence referral(s)	53	46	84

remaining 310 instances the value of the goods involved ranged from a few pence to many hundreds of pounds. These were grouped into three value categories – not more than £20, £21–£100 and over £100. On first referrals, the probability of referral to a hearing rose steadily with increasing value of the goods damaged or stolen. Where one or more referrals had occurred in the past, the value of the property did not increase the chances of referral at values under £100, but above that level there was a very sharp increase in the referral rate. The influence of property value is not unexpected, given the demonstrated relationship between referral and number of offences alleged at this referral, and the probability that the greater the number of separate offences, the greater the value of the goods concerned. However, this influence is not nearly strong enough to outweigh the significance of recidivism in itself. The young person who has damaged or stolen property of only minimal value is rather more likely to be referred to a hearing if he is already known to the reporter from an earlier referral than one whose first offence involves goods of substantial value.

Previous offence history

As is evident from the foregoing pages, the fact of an earlier referral exercises a strong and independent influence on reporters' decisions. Certain limited other aspects of prior involvement with police or with the hearings

TABLE 5.14
DECISION IN RELATION TO PRIOR RECORD

Supervision order in force

	Referred to hearing		
	No current supervision order %	*Home supervision order* %	*Residential order* %
No previous offence referral	32	—	—
One or more previous offence referral(s)	57	59	24

Interval since last referral

	Less than 6 months %	*6 months–1 year* %	*1–2 years* %	*2 years+* %
One or more previous offence referral(s)	49	52	59	68

Police warnings issued

	Referred to hearing	
	No police warning %	*Police warning(s) issued* %
No previous offence referral	27	53
One or more previous offence referral(s)	55	57

system were also examined, and the resulting frequencies summarised in Table 5.14.

A child with a history of previous referral may or may not be currently under home or residential supervision as a result of an earlier disposal by a children's hearing. All children who are the subject of a supervision order must be brought before a children's hearing for review within twelve months, but it is possible for that review to be precipitated by the entry of new grounds of referral. One in five of the children in the present series of reporters' cases was at that time the subject of a supervision order, 99 of them living at home and 40 being under residential supervision; children in List D schools may be allowed week-end leave and sometimes commit further offences while in the community. We see however that the child currently on home supervision is no more likely to be referred to a hearing than one with a previous history of referral on offence grounds but with no supervision order in force. Those who are under residential supervision at the time of the referral have a very low probability of onward referral for a precipitated review at a children's hearing – lower even than those who are completely new entrants to the system. Reporters no doubt reason that, given new grounds of referral, a children's hearing is scarcely likely to order discharge or home supervision, and that it is simplest to allow the present period of residential supervision to continue until a routine review is scheduled. Indeed, so far from a recent referral (likely to be associated with a current supervision order) increasing the likelihood of referral to a hearing, it is the more remote encounters with the hearings system that are inclined to have that consequence; more than two-thirds of those who were last referred more than two years previously were referred by reporters to a hearing, compared to slightly less than one-half who had been referred within the previous six months.

Information about the child's contact with police juvenile liaison officers was sketchy, but whether or not the child had previously been the subject of a formal police warning was more consistently recorded. Police warnings are obviously an important differentiating feature where first referrals to reporters are concerned, being associated with a two-fold increase in the chances of referral to a hearing. Where a child is already known to the reporter however the fact that he has or has not received a police warning has no measurable effect upon the reporter's decision as to how next to proceed.

We conclude that when a child is referred to the reporter on offence grounds some but not all aspects of his prior involvement with the police and with the hearings system have an effect on the reporter's decision-making, but that these effects are neither as clear-cut nor as powerful as the apparent severity of the present offence – with the exception of course of the basic fact of an earlier referral to the reporter; this variable, as discussed earlier, is of critical importance in decision-making.

Domestic and educational circumstances

In assessing the child's needs for compulsory measures of care, reporters will normally gather in information on his home background and school situation from the relevant departments. In cases where the reporter has some doubt as to the adequacy of the evidence relating to the grounds of referral, or where he is already in possession of a recent report, he may decide that he is not justified in requesting further information. In 176 cases in our sample (26 per cent) initial investigation reports were not requested of the social work department. There were 37 other instances in which reports, though requested, had not yet reached the reporter at the time he decided what to do about the case. In 100 of these 213 cases the reporter held earlier social background reports to which he could refer. Allowing for those instances in which reporters did not reply to the relevant question, we know that there were at least 110 cases (16 per cent of the sample) in which no social background reports were either available or requested. Reporters referred 21 of these cases to a hearing.

A social history report is submitted to the reporter by the police in some areas in addition to any legal evidence that they provide and independently of any information presented by social workers. In almost half of all cases (327) a social history was submitted by police officers, including 11 non-offence referrals. Such police reports tend to be less detailed than those produced by social workers, but may routinely include some observations on the child, on housing circumstances and on any known criminal history in the family. Our analysis did not however indicate that the provision of a social history report by the police significantly affected the decision to refer to a hearing; such reports are or are not routine features of the local pattern, and seem to have no exceptional influence.

Although social work, school and police are the commonest sources of the reporter's information, he not infrequently requests reports from other sources. As Table 5.15 indicates, extra reports were requested in about one-fifth of all cases in the series; in 35 of these cases two additional reports were called for.

While school and police reports within a given area tend to follow a standard format, this is rarely if ever the case with social work reports. For

TABLE 5.15

ADDITIONAL REPORTS REQUESTED AND RECEIVED BY REPORTERS

	%
Assessment	6
Educational welfare	14
Child guidance	28
Psychiatric	14
Medical	9
RSSPCC	10
Additional social work reports	2
Other sources	7
Requested but not available	11
(N = 100%)	131

certain basic items of information, generally regarded as essential for obtaining the simplest profile of the child, data were available from one source or another in all but a very small proportion of instances. Thus, information on the make-up of the child's household, on family size, on the activity of the head of household and on school attendance were all present in at least 90 per cent of cases. There were rather more gaps in the available information on educational achievement and on the head of household's specific occupation. Tables 5.16, 5.17 and 5.18 set out the relationships between these factors and the decision to refer or not in offence cases.

Some three-fifths of the children in the series lived with both parents, and a further one-fifth with the mother alone. Morris (1978)[9] had observed a greater tendency to refer to a hearing when a child came from a broken home. There is a comparable indication in the present data of a tendency for children in unusual family situations to be referred more frequently, but the pattern is not entirely clear-cut, especially in instances where the child has a history of previous referrals.

Family size, which is commonly found to be associated with a variety of social and environmental problems is an important discriminating factor when a child comes to the reporter's notice for the first time. The referral rate for those with five or more brothers and sisters is getting on for double that of children from small families. Among repeaters, on the other hand, there are only extremely small differences in referrals associated with size of sibship.

Information was sought on type of housing tenure and on household income. Under the former heading, the sample was too nearly homogeneous for any useful analysis to be possible. For more than 78 per cent of the sample, reporters indicated that the child lived in a local authority house. This is a high figure, even by Scottish standards; 54 per cent of all Scottish households occupy homes rented from public authorities (Department of the Environment, 1977).[10] But since no information was available in one case in 10, the numbers falling into any other category (owner-occupier, privately rented) are too small to support any comparative analysis. Household income, on the other hand, was recorded relatively infrequently, and relevant data were available in less than one-quarter of all cases. The employment status of the head of the household was however recorded rather more fully.

As far as children not previously referred are concerned, there is a clear contrast in terms of referral rates between those from a household headed by someone in full-time employment and all others. Even so, not all the non-employed categories receive the same treatment; those with a parent who was unemployed and looking for work had a rate of referral only slightly higher than those with a fully employed parent, while those from a household with a 'not economically active' head had a considerably higher rate. The latter category overlaps but is not identical with that of fatherless households. The pattern was not maintained among recidivists. Again, the children from homes headed by a non-employed housewife or other not economically active head have a high referral rate, but otherwise there are no consistent variations associated with employment status. Slightly more children with parents in

TABLE 5.16

DECISION IN RELATION TO DOMESTIC CIRCUMSTANCES AND PREVIOUS REFERRAL ON OFFENCE GROUNDS

Who is responsible for child

	Referred to hearing	
	No previous offence referrals %	*One or more previous offence referral(s)* %
Both parents	28	50
Mother alone	38	65
Father alone	40	60
Mother with other(s)	63	46
Father with other(s)	57	67
Other (e.g. relatives, grandparents)	57	43
Not known	17	100

Number of siblings

	Referred to hearing			
	0–2 *siblings* %	3–4 *siblings* %	5–8 *siblings* %	*Not known* %
No previous offence referrals	32	37	58	3
One or more previous offence referral(s)	52	54	55	22

Activity of head of household

	No previous offence referrals %	*One or more previous offence referral(s)* %
In full-time education or training	33	50
Employed full-time	29	56
Employed part-time	60	38
Not economically active (inc. retired, housewife)	56	77
Unemployed, seeking work	37	52
Other unemployed (inc. sick)	47	37
In hospital/prison/other institution	0	0
Unknown	9	24

Social class of head of household

	Referred to hearing					
	Class I–III (non-manual) %	*Class III (manual)* %	*Class IV* %	*Class V* %	*N/A (housewife, etc.)* %	*N/K* %
No previous offence referral	21	34	30	38	53	24
One or more previous offence referral(s)	77	55	37	62	70	34

full-time employment go on from the reporter to a hearing than of those with unemployed fathers.

Social class is a variable frequently identified in studies of the processing of delinquents, usually with the suggestion that children from the least privileged end of the social scale are the most likely to be handled punitively.[11] Where adequate information on the head of household's occupation was available, this was coded to one of the standard categories of the Registrar General's classification.[12] Some sub-classes were examined separately, in order to test a hypothesis that reporters might tend to refer more often to a hearing children whose fathers were often away from home, abroad or at sea. Lorry drivers, oil rig workers and sailors were coded separately, but failed to show any distinctive referral characteristics. Eventually, a very simple classification was utilized. Once again, a distinct contrast between first and subsequent referrals is apparent. In cases not previously known to the reporter, children from white-collar households clearly had the lowest rate of referral to hearings. As far as children from manual worker families are concerned, there is not a simple linear relationship between status and referral rate. Those whose parents are unskilled manual workers have the highest referral rate, but the children of semi-skilled workers are less likely to go on to a hearing than those from skilled working class families. Quite the sharpest contrast however is between all of these 'employed' groups and the quite large category of children whose families could not be classified in these terms because the head of the household was not gainfully employed, as might have been expected from the earlier analysis of referral rates in relation to parents' economic activity. When a child has been referred at least once before the class pattern is markedly altered. It is children from non-manual families who now have the highest rate of referral to hearings, higher even than the children of unemployed parents. Referral is rather more likely when the parent is unskilled than skilled, but once again the relatively low referral rate when a parent falls into the intermediate semi-skilled category undermines any suggestion of a straightforward occupational status gradient.

Reporters taking part in the enquiry were asked in each instance whether they were aware of the existence of family problems. This was one of the few questions which did not require the direct transfer of information but rather a broad summary and evaluation of a varied body of material. Reporters indicated that family problems were known to exist in 398 (59 per cent). In non-offence cases problems were identified in a high proportion of the families involved; where such problems were known, 82 per cent of non-offence children were referred to hearings, as were 70 per cent of the children referred on non-offence grounds where there was no knowledge of a family problem. Among offence cases, as Table 5.17 indicates, the influence of known problems was very powerful at the first referral. Children in whose background there are known to be difficulties were nearly four times as likely to be brought before a hearing as those for whom no such difficulties were identified. Where there had been an earlier referral, the influence of known family problems, though real, was a good deal weaker, increasing the possibility of onward referral from 41 per cent to 59 per cent.

The 398 cases in which problems were identified were divided in the ratio of approximately 2 : 1 between those where two problems were indicated (255) and those where only a single problem was listed. The specific problem areas covered a wide range. Divorce or separation of parents was mentioned in 118 instances and marital relationships – with conflict presumably not leading to formal separation – about as often (107 cases). Financial, housing or employment problems were cited with a similar frequency (111 instances, or nearly 28 per cent of all those with problems) and were more often listed first than any other issue. Problems of physical or mental health were identified in nearly one-fifth of the 'problems' group, but alcohol or drug abuse was referred to a good deal less frequently (slightly more than one case in eight). However, there is little to suggest that the particular type of family problem of which the reporter is aware produces significant variations in the propensity to refer children to hearings. Awareness that there are difficulties in the home situation triggers the decision, and not one type of difficulty rather than another.

The level and pattern of influence of school attendance are quite similar to those of recognized domestic problems. Of those children who were of school age 44 per cent were classified as regular attenders and 54 per cent as irregular attenders, while 3 per cent had been excluded from school – the latter on the whole a measure of behaviour rather than of attendance, but clearly making a classification by attendance inappropriate. Table 5.18 considers only offence

TABLE 5.17

DECISION IN RELATION TO FAMILY PROBLEMS AND PREVIOUS REFERRAL ON OFFENCE GROUNDS

Whether family problems were known	*Referred to hearing*	
	Family problems known %	*Family problems not known* %
No previous offence referrals	61	17
One or more previous offence referral(s)	59	41

Nature of family problems	*No previous offence referral* %	*One or more previous offence referrals* %
Traumatic events	100	33
Divorce, separation	50	55
Physical or mental health	63	77
Alcohol or drug problems	60	50
Care or control of child	60	56
Marital relationship	73	60
Finance, employment, housing	67	67
Anti-social behaviour	36	67

referrals, excluding the truancy cases where irregular attendance was the ground of referral. In the 'no previous offence referral' group, children with irregular school attendance had two-and-a-half times as high a rate of referral to hearings as those with a record of regular attendance; the few who had been excluded from school altogether were without exception brought before a children's hearing. As in the case of domestic problems, attendance record discriminated less sharply where there had been at least one previous referral, though it still had a notable association with decision-making.

Nearly half the children in the series were classified by their schools as having a poor level of educational attainment in relation to age; three in ten were graded as average and only 5 per cent as 'good'. Educational attainment was clearly correlated with the decision to refer or not refer a child to a hearing, with the referral rate twice as high among those of 'poor' attainment than those judged to have a 'good' level of achievement, at any rate among those who had come to the reporter's notice for the first time. It did not discriminate as powerfully as level of school attendance however, and had no capacity to differentiate referred from non-referred cases where there had been earlier referrals on offence grounds.

TABLE 5.18

DECISION IN RELATION TO EDUCATIONAL CIRCUMSTANCES AND PREVIOUS REFERRAL ON OFFENCE GROUNDS

Nature of school attendance	*Referred to hearing*		
	Attendance regular %	*Attendance irregular* %	*Excluded from school* %
No previous offence referral	25	61	100
One or more previous offence referral(s)	47	64	69

Educational attainment for age	*Referred to hearing*		
	'Good' attainment for age %	*'Average' attainment for age* %	*'Poor' attainment for age* %
No previous offence referrals	20	32	48
One or more previous offence referral(s)	50	58	53

Whether school behaviour problems were known	*Referred to hearing*	
	School problems known %	*School problems not known* %
No previous offence referrals	67	31
One or more previous offence referral(s)	68	50

A question about the existence of problems of behaviour at school elicited a positive response in 246 cases, a little over one-third of the sample. The problems referred to here most commonly involved disobedience and unruliness, though by no means invariably. Related to decisions, it is clear that children reported as presenting behavioural difficulties at school had a very much greater chance of appearing before a hearing; if they have a history of previous offences the influence of school behaviour problems is somewhat diminished but by no means eliminated.

The very considerable part played by information about factors other than those directly related to offences is emphasized by the foregoing analysis. The employment status of the head of the child's household, the existence of 'problems' in the family and school situations, the level of school attendance and to a somewhat lesser extent the level of achievement in school are all closely associated with the decision whether or not to refer a child to a hearing. All of these influences are particularly powerful in first referrals, however, while in cases with a history of earlier referrals their weight is reduced and in some instances eliminated.

Factors in decisions

Although this study was planned principally to throw light on the strength of the relationships between a large number of reported items and the decisions made by reporters to children's panels, it seemed important also to invite those who made the decisions to set out their own reasons for the actions they had taken. In 346 cases, 36 per cent of the series, no specific reasons were listed, the reporters concerned presumably regarding the formal criteria for decision-making as self-evident explanations. We did not of course dispute that reporters decided on a particular course of action because they were convinced that the child in question was or was not in need of compulsory measures of care, and because they were satisfied (or not, as the case may be) that the evidence was adequate; our concern was rather to ascertain what specific aspects of the child's behaviour and personality entered into the conception of 'being in need of compulsory measures of care'. Those reporters who responded positively gave between one and three reasons in each case. Among first reasons given, 'the referral itself' was by far the largest category amounting to one-third of all first reasons. 'The child's history', including no doubt his history of previous offences was the second most common 'first reason' and is cited in one-seventh of cases where a first reason was given. References in various forms to the child's family and school circumstances are all a good deal less common when specific first reasons are considered; however, they occur with greater frequency as second or third reasons, and are collectively responsible for more than 600 statements in respect of the 432 decisions where a reason was given.

The variety of explanations put forward by reporters is not inconsistent with the wide range of factors that our analysis of records has demonstrated to be associated with the decision whether or not to refer. From either standpoint, we confront the problem of understanding the determinants of discretionary decision-making. This issue has been of great concern to some commentators on juvenile justice systems; in particular, the question of whether decisions can be predicted in any consistent fashion within a particular system has resulted in several important recent studies.

Some American studies have focussed upon juvenile court decision-making in general and have produced varied results. Meade (1973), Arnold (1974) and Thornberry (1973)[13] suggested that such personal characteristics of the child as race, socio-economic status and place of residence were most significant in terms of predicting severity of outcome. Terry (1967)[14] on the other hand found the age of the juvenile, seriousness of offence and prior record to be more significant. A study specifically of detention by Cohen (1975)[15] found that the number of previous referrals was the single most important indicator of the detention decision; furthermore there were indications in Cohen's study that different types of offence were treated differentially by the Court. In his study of the pre-hearing detention decision Dungworth (1977)[16] found that, regardless of the type of offence committed, referral history and school problems were the two most significant indicators of severity of outcome. In addition he found that where status offences are concerned home factors were important but in the case of juveniles committing 'adult' offences home factors were of minor significance.

The Scottish system of children's hearings is unusual in allocating a central role to an official who may receive referrals from any source and has unfettered discretion to decide whether to retain the referral within the hearings system or to proceed no further. It has been evident since the first statistics on the system appeared that reporters do not merely pass on police and other referrals, but in fact exercise their discretion quite liberally, diverting from the system about as

TABLE 5.19

REPORTERS' REASONS FOR DECISIONS

	First reason %	*Second reason* %	*Third reason* %
None	36	41	53
Referral itself	20	7	4
Child's history	9	4	4
Behaviour and attitude	5	9	4
Care and control of child	4	7	6
Parental attitude	3	6	5
Home circumstances	8	9	7
School circumstances	4	9	6
Success/failure of existing arrangements	6	6	7
Other	3	3	3
(N = 100%)	678	678	678

many children as they keep within it. The only earlier study of the reporter's role of which we are aware is that of Morris (1978).[17] Her findings and ours are not directly comparable, because she describes her method as an impressionistic one and makes no attempt to quantify the various elements in reporters' discretionary decision-making. Her observations are of interest none the less. She concludes that the child's prior record, the value of the property involved where relevant, the number of offences involved in the current referral and, in the city, the nature of the offence were significant influences upon the decision whether to take or not take formal action. All of these factors recur in our own study, which confirms their continuing significance. Non-offence considerations also loom large in our analysis; Morris is conscious of the considerable volume of personal information that the reporter often has at his disposal and of its possible contribution to his thinking, but hesitates to assess the weight of that contribution. Our findings tend to suggest that a number of aspects of the child's home and school circumstances are no less influential than are features of the present offence and rather more so than most identifiable characteristics of his previous offence history, with the exception of the very existence of such a history.

The many factors discussed above overlap and interact with one another in varying degrees, and it is not possible to judge the strength of their independent influence by simple inspection of measures of association. In an attempt to isolate some of the relevant variables we have used the technique of multiple classification analysis.[18] Tables 5.20 and 5.21 consider respectively the decisions made concerning children when referred to the reporter on offence grounds for the first time, and those relating to children who had been referred on offence grounds on at least one prior occasion. The tables indicate the extent to which the presence of each of a number of factors contributes to increasing or reducing the likelihood of referral to a hearing. The 'adjusted' column shows the contribution of each factor after allowance has been made for any influence arising from the interactions of all other factors.

Three measures of offence seriousness are included. It is clear that although in first referrals each of these has an independent influence on the reporter's decision, the total number of offences alleged on this occasion carries considerably more weight than the value of the property involved. The sex of the child has no significant independent effect on decisions, and the more substantial influence of age at referral appears to stem mainly from the low referral rate, discussed earlier in this chapter, of children aged 12. In cases where the child is already known to the reporter the overall likelihood of referral by the reporter to a hearing is of course strikingly higher. The specific influence of offence-related factors is not very different from that in first referrals, with seriousness of offence having a slightly more weighty impact than the number of offences alleged and distinctly more so than the value of the property involved. Girls, though few in number, are less likely than boys to be referred to a hearing; and if there is a bias associated with age at second or subsequent referrals, it is in the direction of a lower referral rate for children at the upper end of the 'juvenile' age range.

TABLE 5.20

MULTIPLE CLASSIFICATION ANALYSIS OF INFLUENCES ON REPORTERS' DECISIONS IN OFFENCE REFERRALS

(Children not previously referred)

Decision: refer to hearing/not refer
Grand mean = 0·32 (P (refer) = 0·32)

	Deviations from grand mean				
Independent variable	*Unadjusted*		*Adjusted*		N
Value of goods involved					
None	−0·04		0·03		64
£1–£20	−0·05		−0·05		89
£21–£100	0·04		−0·02		44
£101+	0·12		0·07		45
effect		0·14		0·10	
Total offences alleged					
One	−0·06		−0·06		166
Two	0·13		0·11		38
Three+	0·15		0·16		38
effect (p < 0·02)		0·20		0·20	
Most serious offence alleged					
Miscellaneous	−0·10		−0·21		18
Local bye-laws	−0·09		−0·09		13
Public order	−0·12		−0·12		20
Property damage	0·01		0·07		24
Theft	−0·04		−0·01		92
Housebreaking	0·14		0·12		41
Violence	0·09		0·05		34
effect		0·19		0·19	
Age when referral received					
10 or under	0·09		0·09		29
11	0·06		0·06		21
12	−0·23		−0·23		21
13	0·01		−0·01		45
14	0·07		0·07		53
15	−0·03		−0·04		73
effect		0·18		0·18	
Sex					
Boy	−0·01		−0·01		201
Girl	0·03		0·03		14
effect		0·03		0·03	
Social class					
Not known	0·02		−0·03		77
Non-manual	−0·12		−0·10		29
Skilled manual	0·02		0·06		70
Semi-skilled manual	−0·03		−0·02		37
Unskilled	0·06		0·06		29
effect		0·10		0·12	

When other factors are held constant, parental social class is significantly associated with reporters' decisions in relation to recidivists, but not in first referrals. A slight tendency, below the level of statistical significance, to decide against referring children from white collar households the first time they come to the notice of the reporter, is transformed into a marked propensity to bring them before a hearing if they appear on a subsequent occasion. Children from semi-skilled manual backgrounds have a less than average chance of referral to a hearing on second or later referrals. The numbers in some social class categories

TABLE 5.20—*contd.*

	Deviations from grand mean				
Independent variable	*Unadjusted*		*Adjusted*		N
Child lives with					
Both parents	−0·05		−0·03		167
Other	0·10		0·06		75
effect		0·15		0·09	
Activity of head of household					
Not known	−0·23		−0·10		32
Employed	−0·02		0·03		144
Unemployed	0·15		−0·01		66
effect		0·24		0·09	
Family problems					
Not known	−0·16		−0·15		157
Known	0·29		0·29		85
effect ($p < 0·001$)		0·46		0·45	
Educational attainment for age					
Not known	−0·22		−0·08		50
Good	−0·12		−0·02		20
Average	0·00		0·00		82
Poor	0·15		0·05		90
effect		0·31		0·10	
Nature of school attendance					
Not known	−0·25		−0·16		39
Regular	−0·08		−0·07		134
Irregular	0·29		0·22		67
effect ($p < 0·001$)		0·42		0·31	
Behaviour problems at school					
Not known	−0·12		−0·09		171
Known	0·30		0·23		70
effect ($p < 0·001$)		0·42		0·31	

N = 242
Multiple R = 0·275
R^2 = 0·525

TABLE 5.21

MULTIPLE CLASSIFICATION ANALYSIS OF INFLUENCES ON REPORTERS' DECISIONS IN OFFENCE REFERRALS

(Children previously referred)

Decision: refer to hearing/not refer
Grand mean = 0·53 (P (refer) = 0·53)

Independent variable		*Deviations from grand mean*				
		Unadjusted		*Adjusted*		N
Value of goods involved						
None		−0·11		−0·06		77
£1–£20		0·00		0·01		85
£21–£100		−0·07		−0·10		41
£101+		0·17		0·11		69
effect			0·21		0·15	
Total offences alleged						
One		−0·08		−0·06		183
Two		0·07		0·07		40
Three+		0·23		0·17		49
effect	(p< 0·02)		0·24		0·19	
Most serious offence alleged						
Miscellaneous		0·02		0·01		11
Local bye-laws		−0·35		−0·30		17
Public order		−0·06		−0·08		32
Property damage		−0·11		−0·12		12
Theft		0·01		0·01		112
Housebreaking		0·10		0·10		56
Violence		0·10		0·08		32
effect	(p< 0·01)		0·22		0·22	
Age when referral received						
10 or under		0·05		0·06		12
11		0·11		0·10		22
12		0·15		0·16		19
13		0·06		0·06		46
14		−0·03		−0·02		82
15		−0·05		−0·06		86
effect			0·16		0·17	
Sex						
Boy		0·01		0·01		246
Girl		−0·15		−0·18		21
effect			0·09		0·10	
Social class						
Not known		−0·02		−0·05		100
Non-manual		0·24		0·23		13
Skilled manual		0·02		0·05		53
Semi-skilled manual		−0·16		−0·15		46
Unskilled manual		0·09		0·11		60
effect	(p< 0·05)		0·19		0·21	

are small, and one is struck by the contrast between the first referrals and the 'recidivists'. We see in the latter group a marked shift towards the least skilled end of the social spectrum. First referrals to reporters on offence grounds include as many children from white collar as from unskilled households, but among second or subsequent referrals the latter outnumber the former by more than four to one.

Children not living with both parents account for a relatively high proportion of first referrals to reporters on offence grounds and a markedly higher

TABLE 5.21—*contd.*

	Deviation from grand mean				
Independent variable	*Unadjusted*		*Adjusted*		N
Child lives with					
Both parents	−0·03		−0·04		164
Other	0·04		0·06		103
effect		0·07		0·10	
Activity of head of household					
Employed	0·01		0·00		125
Unemployed	0·02		0·04		130
effect		0·05		0·05	
Family problems					
Not known	−0·12		−0·10		90
Known	0·06		0·05		182
effect ($p<0·05$)		0·17		0·14	
Educational attainment for age					
Not known	−0·13		0·09		30
Good	−0·03		−0·02		8
Average	0·05		0·09		81
Poor	0·00		−0·07		148
effect		0·10		0·16	
Nature of school attendance					
Not known	−0·25		−0·22		42
Regular	−0·06		−0·06		89
Irregular	0·11		0·11		123
Excluded	0·16		0·08		13
effect ($p<0·005$)		0·27		0·25	
Behaviour problems at school					
Not known	−0·12		−0·09		142
Known	0·13		0·10		125
effect ($p<0·005$)		0·25		0·20	

N = 272
Multiple R = 0·152
R^2 = 0·390

proportion of 'recidivists'. The family structure in itself however has only a very slight influence on the action taken by the reporter at either level of delinquency – when all other factors are held constant. Children from non-conventional family situations are indeed marginally more likely to be brought before a children's hearing, but the difference is not statistically significant. The employment status of the head of the household, which in first referrals at any rate also appears to differentiate between referred and non-referred cases, is also shown to have no bearing on reporters' decisions when the influence of other factors is removed from the calculation.

What *does* influence reporters' decisions, massively in first referrals but on a very much slighter scale on subsequent occasions, is the belief that the child is exposed to or involved in family problems. Obviously, such problems are identified more readily when the child is a member of a single parent household and contribute to what is on the face of it a distinct tendency to assume that children in such households are in need of compulsory measures of care. But when single parent families are not seen as presenting significant problems, their children, if referred to a reporter on offence grounds are more likely to have no formal action taken than children from two-parent households where problems *have* been recognized. Among those children with a history of earlier referral, the proportion with known family problems is higher than among 'new' cases, as are the proportions of children from single parent families and from families where the head of household is unemployed; but although the recognition of problems still discriminates significantly between those referred and those not referred to a hearing, the level of significance is very much lower than in relation to children never previously referred.

School-related variables are also of considerable importance in shaping reporters' decisions. The level of educational attainment is not a significant discriminant, but both irregularity of school attendance and known behaviour problems at school strongly and independently of other influences encourage reporters to judge that compulsory measures of care may be desirable. As in the case of family problems, these factors continue to affect decisions in relation to recidivists, but at a somewhat lower level of intensity.

Morris (1978)[19] refers to the reporter as being required in effect to make a prediction – to distinguish the child who runs the risk of a career of serious delinquency from one who though he has committed an offence has sufficient positive influence in his background for compulsory measures of care to be dispensed with. In making these judgments reporters are inevitably conscious of their vulnerability to criticism. If they appear to divert young offenders from the hearings on a generous scale, they are liable to be charged with a casual and negligent attitude to juvenile crime; such views were in fact forcefully expressed by police spokesmen in the early years of the hearings system. If they decide to minimize such risks by maintaining a high rate of referral to hearings they may come under fire from a numerically smaller but articulate group of critics who argue for minimal intervention both on libertarian grounds and because they believe this to be the most effective means of aborting the development of delinquent careers. Between these irreconcilable positions, the reporter tries to chart a *via media* which he sees as consistent with the principles of the children's hearings system.

What emerges clearly from our analysis is his constant attempt to balance, in offence cases, the seriousness of the offence or offences committed against an inevitably subjective and indirect estimate of the strengths and weaknesses of the child's home and school situation. Neither set of considerations has an overall dominance, though it is very striking that the marked influence of personal and social factors at first referrals is substantially reduced when a child comes back on a second or subsequent occasion. Interestingly, the weight of offence-seriousness, however assessed, does not seem to be proportionately increased at second referrals; decisions in respect of recidivists seem to be more subjective and more difficult for the observer to predict.

When decisions such as those of reporters are made on a discretionary basis, there is always a danger that prejudices and simple stereotypes may become in effect the criteria for decision-making. Some studies of justice systems have claimed that such factors as race and low socio-economic status clearly predict outcomes. It is encouraging to find that the judgments of reporters are not as crudely based. Social status level does not, in this sample of cases, tell us what will happen to a child. Even the fact of living with a single parent does not in itself, contrary to the impression given by our initial findings, produce a large increase in the probability that an offending child will be deemed to be in need of compulsory measures. Incomplete and unstandardized though the information at their disposal undoubtedly is, reporters are concerned to derive from it the best estimate possible of both stresses and supports in the child's background as an essential component of their decisions.

NOTES

1. I. Piliavin and S. Briar, 'Police encounters with juveniles', *American Journal of Sociology*, 1964, 70.
2. In practice the relevant voluntary body is the Royal Scottish Society for the Prevention of Cruelty to Children (RSSPCC).
3. Under *section* 15 of the Social Work (Scotland) Act 1968 local authorities have a duty to receive into care any child who has no parent or guardian, or who is abandoned or lost, or whose parents or guardian are for any reason prevented from caring for him and where such action is necessary in the interests of the welfare of the child. In such cases it provides a service free of compulsion, except that the local authority may obtain parental rights over children in their care where it is shown that they have no parents or guardian, or that the parents or guardian are unfit to have the care of the children (*section* 16 of the 1968 Act).
4. The school leaving age was raised by one year to 16 in 1972–1973. This could account for some of the increase in truancy referrals subsequent to that date.
5. *See* for example F. M. Martin and K. Murray (eds.), *Children's Hearings*. Scottish Academic Press, 1976, p. 237.
6. Monica A. Walker, 'Measuring the seriousness of crimes', *British Journal of Criminology*, 1978, 18(4).
7. Lawrence E. Cohen, 'Delinquency dispositions: an empirical analysis of processing decisions in three juvenile courts', U.S. Dept. of Justice Law Enforcement Assistance Administration, 1975, Analytic Report No. 9.

Allison Morris in collaboration with Mary McIsaac, *Juvenile Justice?*. Heinemann, 1978, p. 103.
8. ibid., p. 103.
9. ibid., p. 106.
10. Department of the Environment, *Housing and Construction Statistics*, No. 25, 1977.
11. Edwin Schur, *Radical non-intervention: rethinking the delinquency problem*. Prentice-Hall, 1973.
Timothy Carter and Donald Clelland, 'A Neo-Marxian critique, formulation and test of juvenile dispositions as a function of social class', *Social Problems*, 1979, 27(1).
12. Office of Population Censuses and Surveys, *Classification of Occupations*, HMSO, 1970.
13. Anthony Meade, 'Seriousness of delinquency, the adjudicative decision and recidivism – a longitudinal configuration analysis', *Journal of Criminal Law, Criminology and Police Science*, 1973, 64(4).
W. R. Arnold, 'Race and ethnicity relative to other factors in juvenile court dispositions', *American Journal of Sociology*, 1974, 77(2).
Terence P. Thornberry, 'Race, socioeconomic status and sentencing in the juvenile justice system', *Journal of Criminal Law, Criminology and Police Science*, 1973, 64(1).
14. Robert M. Terry, 'The screening of juvenile offenders', *Journal of Criminal Law, Criminology and Police Science*, 1967, 58(2).
15. Lawrence E. Cohen, 'Who gets detained? An empirical analysis of the pre-adjudicatory detention of juveniles in Denver', U.S. Dept. of Justice Law Enforcement Assistance Administration, 1975, Analytic Report No. 3.
16. Terence Dungworth, 'Discretion in the juvenile justice system: the impact of case characteristics on pre-hearing detention'. Paper presented at the annual meeting of the American Society of Criminology, Tucson, Arizona, November 1976.
17. Allison Morris, op. cit.
18. Multiple Classification Analysis (MCA) is a statistical technique which examines the relationship between several independent (predictor) variables and a dependent variable under the assumption of an additive model. A form of Least Squares analysis, MCA can handle variables with no more than a nominal scale (e.g. sex, social class) and when the dependent variable is binary, MCA works best if the two frequencies are not greatly different. In presenting the results in terms of 'deviation from the grand mean' it is possible, under the additive model, to add deviations for several features to the grand mean and arrive at an overall probability. For a fuller description *see* F. M. Andrews, J. N. Morgan, J. A. Sonquist and Laura Klem, *Multiple Classification Analysis* (2nd ed.), Institute for Social Research, University of Michigan, Ann Arbor, U.S.A., 1973.
19. Allison Morris, op. cit., p. 102.

6

PLACES, TIMES, PERSONS

IN THE FIVE CHAPTERS that follow this we describe and analyse a wide range of features of the hearings observed in 1978–1979 – their dialogue, the involvement of various participants, their decision-making. By way of preface, we note in the present chapter some characteristics of the physical settings in which hearings take place, as in the course of our work we attended at nearly all the hearings centres in Scotland. We note also in this chapter the frequency with which different members of the dramatis personae are present, and summarize our information on the intervals that have elapsed between the offence or other event that gave rise to the hearing and the hearing itself and on variations in the duration of that event.

Local authorities are under a statutory obligation (1968 Act, S.34(3)) 'to provide suitable accommodation and facilities dissociated from criminal courts and police stations for children's hearings for their area'. The children's hearings system has as one of its objectives to provide an informal setting where children and their families are enabled to participate in the proceedings without feeling intimidated or overawed by their surroundings. Another objective is the provision of local centres in the community which are easily accessible, particularly in rural areas. Thus it was anticipated at the outset that use would be made of village halls, community centres and other similar premises on a regular but probably infrequent basis, and that in large urban areas premises would be allocated on a permanent basis to meet the needs of a large volume of cases. Before the implementation of the Act, the unofficial 'Rowntree' Working Party commented:

> 'Careful consideration should be given to the location of the children's hearings and to the time when they are held. It is essential that they be easily accessible to the public and housed in comfortable and cheerful premises. The actual room where the hearing sits should not be too large, as it is important that the child (and his parents) should not be too remote from those making vital decisions about his future. There should be a small adjacent anteroom so that the child may be asked to leave at any stage during

> the hearing when it is felt appropriate to allow private discussion with parents. The waiting area must provide adequate seating, toilet facilities and suitable reading material.'[1]
>
> (*Rowntree Report*, para. 422)

The way that these objectives are interpreted throughout Scotland varies a great deal, with hearings centres ranging from excellent to wholly inadequate in their facilities. The six major regional capitals – Glasgow, Edinburgh, Dundee, Aberdeen, Inverness and Stirling – as well as some of the smaller towns have permanent centres in regular use. Almost exactly one-third of all hearings in Scotland take place in the city of Glasgow where there are two centres, for the north and the south of the city respectively. The North Glasgow centre serves three different areas of the city and has three hearings rooms in constant use. These rooms are panelled in wood and carpeted, and are reminiscent of an informal English juvenile court. In the South Glasgow centre two hearings rooms operate on a rotating basis for each of the three areas of the city to the south. The rooms here are large and windowless. Fairly adequate waiting facilities for families are provided in both centres and one rather small room for the use of panel members in the Glasgow North offices. In the Glasgow North offices traffic noise tended to be a hindrance to discussions.

The most carefully planned centre of the six is in Edinburgh. A large two storey building near the centre of town is divided into two self-contained units – the lower floor serving Edinburgh West and the upper floor serving Edinburgh East. There are offices with telephone facilities for the use of social workers here as well as anterooms for panel members which adjoin the main hearings rooms. The reporters indicated that the social workers' rooms were used when necessary to interview families after hearings so that they would not have to return to the waiting rooms where they might encounter other families.

Dundee hearings are held in a large tenement flat in the centre of town. The hearings room is fairly spacious and – an innovation here – the reporter uses an intercom to communicate to the administrative staff when the hearing commences and finishes. Here too there are adequate facilities for families to use as a waiting room.

Generally all of the urban areas provide good facilities but some rural areas at the time of our visits left a lot to be desired. Confidentiality was a problem in some of these areas, the worst example being provided by an office in Lanark sub-region of Strathclyde. This centre shared its facilities with the registrar of births, deaths and marriages. There were no waiting rooms for families except in the public area of the registrar's office, and the hearings room was not very discreetly situated so that any passer-by who put his ear to the crack in the swing door could overhear all that was going on.

Dumbarton sub-region, on the other hand, makes available very varied settings ranging from a well-planned centre in Cumbernauld which provides interview rooms for social workers in addition to a good sized waiting room, to a Boy's Brigade Hall in Vale of Leven, with what must be the smallest hearings room in the country. Hearings at Bishopbriggs are held in the War Memorial Hall. Here families wait in the lavatories for their hearings to commence, and we thought that it must be at least a little unnerving for the families with various individuals sidling past to use the urinals. The rather *ad hoc* arrangements found in some parts of the country sometimes produce unexpected settings for hearings. In Macduff, which serves part of Grampian Region, there is a palatial council chamber containing a huge french-polished table and chairs and decorated with ornate wallpaper – a more formal setting than the most sumptuous juvenile court. Similarly in Ayr, hearings were held in the council members' lounge of the County Buildings, also a very elegant room.

The furnishings inside the hearings room itself appear to be subject to local conditions and the reporter's imagination. Most areas used a table of some kind, although a few centres used armchairs and coffee tables. We noted as a matter of interest that 84 per cent of all the hearings we observed were conducted across a square or rectangular table, with a further 11 per cent using a round or oval table. Inevitably, the table has something of a segregating and perhaps protective function, but it has practical uses too. Given the considerable importance of documentation in the work of the hearing (see *Chapter 10*) it is perhaps surprising that even 14 of the 301 observed hearings were carried out with no table at all. The presence of the box of tissues on the table was almost universal in the observed hearings, sometimes supplemented by a decanter of water. One peripatetic reporter carried round a purple bedspread which, laid on top of trestle tables, reminded us rather irresistibly of a high school dramatic society attempting to portray a juvenile court without sufficient funds for props.

Reporters in some areas complained quite volubly and justifiably about conditions in which hearings were held. The principal problem would seem to be that in many instances facilities are shared with other agencies and are only used rarely as hearings centres – a price paid for the use of community buildings. The most serious deficiency created by shared facilities appeared to be the lack of privacy, which in some cases was very serious. There were urban areas which also encountered this problem, most notably in Paisley, where one large room was divided by head-high partitions to form a waiting room for families on one side and for clerical functions on the other, thus running the risk of making confidential interviews between social workers and families the business of the administrative staff as well.

The children who appear before hearings have already passed through at least two selective processes. Their initial referring agents – most commonly but by no means exclusively the police – had decided to bring them to the notice of the reporter, using criteria of which we have no systematic knowledge. Reporters in their turn had exercised their discretion to bring these but not other children before a hearing. The children whose processing by reporters is discussed in *Chapter 5* constitute a separate sample (though there may well be some children who fortuitously appear in both), but we know from that analysis that those who are retained in the system differ in many ways from those screened out at the referral stage. We know that their chances of being required to attend a hearing are very much greater if they have been referred on truancy or care and protection than on offence grounds, and that if they are offenders the decision to bring them before three members of the children's panel depends on the interplay of a variety of factors – their previous known offence history, some characteristics of the most recent offence or offences, and the reporter's judgment of the presence of certain problems in the child's background. The application of our own sampling criteria, by excluding routine reviews, is also likely to produce a sample with a very slightly higher ratio of older to younger children and of offence cases to care and protection cases than we should have found if our sample had been one of all hearings rather than one of hearings where grounds of referral were considered.

Some key features of the cases in question are summarized in Table 6.1. Boys in this series outnumbered girls in the ratio of nine to two. Only six of the 301 children were aged seven years or less – all of them, of course, referred on non-offence grounds; a further 43 had reached their eighth but not yet their twelfth birthday. Just under 23 per cent were aged 12 or 13, but considerably more than half the total (173, or 57 per cent) were in the last two years of the period of compulsory education. A total of 10 had reached their sixteenth birthday, falling within the jurisdiction of the hearings system because they were already on supervision when the present offence was committed. These were not of course the only children in respect of whom a supervision order was currently in force. A total of 72 of the hearings observed were reviews which had been precipitated by the entry of new grounds of referral, although 42 of the remaining 229 children, though not currently on supervision had come before a hearing on at least one occasion in the past. In as many as 31 instances the hearing was being re-convened after a reference to the sheriff, the grounds having initially been denied and subsequently upheld.

Offences were by far the commonest ground of referral, figuring in more than three-fourths of all the hearings observed. Two hundred and nine, or just under 70 per cent, had offence grounds only while in a further 24 there was a combination of offences and truancy or, very exceptionally, of offence and care and protection grounds. As many as one-sixth of all the children (50) were referred because of truancy alone, and in 18 instances the children concerned were held to be suffering from lack of care, to be in physical or moral danger, or to be beyond parental control. The mean number of offences charged (where offences figure in the grounds of referral) was 2·245 and the median (probably a more appropriate measure) was 1·695. Just under half of all children charged with offences had only one offence cited, and seven out of 10 had one or two offences. Some offences were denied, and the denial accepted. A total of 523 offences were alleged, but only 430 were established; the mean was thus reduced to 1·920 and the median to 1·418. Multiple offences were reduced in number more often than single offences were eliminated.

Offences, where these were involved, varied from the relatively trivial to some of unquestionable seriousness. As in the study of reporters' discretion, we used a very rough scale of seriousness for classifying offences. Table 6.2 sets out the frequencies with which offences of varying degrees of seriousness

1. Children's panel hearing rooms, Alloway Place, Ayr, Strathclyde Region.

(By courtesy of Strathclyde Regional Council)

Plate 2. Children's panel hearing rooms, Howden House, Livingston, Lothian Region.

(By courtesy of Lothian Regional Council)

were both charged and established, showing only the most serious where more than one offence was involved. Property offences predominate, accounting for more than four-fifths of the entries in each column; it is noteworthy that offences involving some form of forced entry into premises are not very much less common than shoplifting and other forms of stealing not involving force. Offences involving violence or the threat of violence against persons were established in eight per cent of offence-based hearings; serious charges of assault would generally be dealt with in the sheriff courts.

The distribution of decisions reached at the observed hearings was very similar indeed to the pattern recorded in national statistics. Home supervision

TABLE 6.1

SOME CHARACTERISTICS OF A SAMPLE OF 301 HEARINGS

Type of hearing	
Initial	198
After proof	31
Precipitated review	72
Grounds of referral	
Offence(s)	209
Truancy	50
Offence(s) + truancy	24
Other	18
Sex of child	
Boy	246
Girl	55
Age of child	
Under 8	6
8	5
9	10
10	8
11	20
12	27
13	41
14	75
15	99
16 or over	10
Prior record at hearings	
First hearing	187
'Repeater'	114
Outcome	
Discharge	94
Supervision	171
Residential supervision	29
Children's home	7

orders were made in more than half of all cases, while almost one in three was discharged. A residential supervision order (List D) was the outcome in almost exactly one-tenth of the hearings, and seven children, just over two per cent of the total, were taken into local authority care and admitted to a children's home.

A number of events must occur before a child comes before a hearing, and all of them are likely to give rise to some delay. The police or other referring agency will have made their own enquiries and decided to bring the case to the notice of the reporter. The reporter will have assessed the evidence, decided whether to request a preliminary social background report and possibly other reports, and perhaps been obliged to wait some weeks for them to be submitted. He may well have consulted colleagues in his own department before deciding to frame grounds of referral. Finally, the case must have been slotted into the timetable of hearings for that area and the participants notified. As events recede into the past, most people find it more difficult to discuss them and the circumstances associated with them in a realistic fashion, and there would appear to be sound reasons for keeping the delay to the minimum compatible with the gathering of essential information and the careful consideration of relevant aspects of the case. In fact, the median time from the incident that began the process to the hearing was 14·27 weeks, with half of all the cases being heard after an interval of between nine and 18 weeks. There was however a small but not insignificant 'tail' of cases where the interval was six months or more.

At four hearings in every five (81 per cent), the child was accompanied by his or her mother. Fathers were present, either instead of or together with

TABLE 6.2

SERIOUSNESS OF OFFENCES CHARGED AND ESTABLISHED

	Most serious offence	
	Charged %	*Established* %
Type of offence		
Illegal consumption of alcohol	—	—
Against public order –		
local acts and bye-laws (loitering)	2	1
drunkenness, breach of peace	6	8
Against property –		
damage	5	4
vehicle theft and related R.T.A.	3	5
stealing (theft, shoplifting)	40	42
housebreaking	33	31
Against person –		
assault, robbery	10	8
Miscellaneous	1	1
(N = 100%)	233	228

their wives, at slightly more than one-half (55 per cent) of all the hearings that we attended, and another member of the family – most commonly a grandparent or an older sibling – was present at 11 per cent. The extent to which parents are actively involved in the dialogue of the hearing is examined in *Chapter 9*. Although legal aid is not available in respect of appearances before children's hearings, families are permitted if they so wish to be accompanied by a friend or other representative. Contrary to some early expectations, this opportunity is comparatively rarely used, only eight of the families present at the observed hearings being represented in this way.

The presence of a social worker is usually taken to be as indispensable a feature of a children's hearing as the attendance of a member of the reporter's department. There were in fact only 19 hearings out of 301 which were carried out in the absence of a social worker. Although it is customary for the attending social worker to be the author of the social background report, it is not unknown in some urban areas with hard-pressed social work departments for the representative to be someone with little or no previous connection with the case. No other persons were present (apart from our own observer of course) at three hearings in four. One other person, most commonly a guidance teacher,[2] appeared at 20·9 per cent of hearings; two other participants or observers were present at eight hearings and three at four of those that we attended.

A hearing is required to include at least one man and at least one woman (1968 Act, S.34(2)). In practice therefore only two sex compositions are possible – two women, one man and two men, one woman. A hearing must also appoint a chairman. Struck by the fact that 55 per cent of the hearings in our sample were chaired by a man, while only 42 per cent of the other participating panel members were male, we looked at the propensity to appoint male rather than female chairmen in the two types of hearing. All other things being equal, men would of course chair two-thirds of the hearings in which they provide two of the members and one-third of those hearings which include two women. In our sample there were 116 hearings which were numerically predominantly male; in 90 of these (78 per cent) a man was appointed chairman. One hundred and eighty-five hearings included one man and two women, and a male chairman was appointed on 76 or 41 per cent of these occasions. It is clear that there is a significant tendency for male panel members to be over-represented among those taking the chair at children's hearings. This has some consequences for the style and content of discussions, but not very far-reaching ones.

One variable that is not affected by the sex composition of the hearing is its punctuality. Families are given appointments, and although some waiting is unavoidable prolonged delays are unusual. Sixty-five per cent of the hearings that we observed began at or before the scheduled time or within fifteen minutes of it. Delays in excess of a quarter-hour were recorded in very slightly more than one-third of all cases.

The duration of the hearing was also recorded, and used as a variable in some of the analyses discussed in later chapters. An ordinary wristwatch was used for this measurement, not a stopwatch, and when the distribution of durations was tabulated by single minutes we were aware of a distinct tendency for time to be rounded up or down to the nearest five minutes. The grouped distribution used in Table 6.3 probably minimizes distortion. Mean duration is 28·81 minutes with a standard deviation of 12·01; median duration is 26·33 minutes. Some hearings are in their second phase, and these tend to be of shorter duration. Only 34 per cent of the hearings that had been continued for further reports lasted half an hour or longer, as did 43 per cent of those that had been adjourned for proof. Hearings that were carried through to a formal disposal at the one sitting ran to 30 minutes or longer on 57 per cent of occasions. The grounds of referral made a marked difference to the duration of the hearing. Truancy hearings tended to be the briefest, with only 28 per cent lasting 30 minutes or more; care and protection referrals were also dealt with fairly expeditiously, with nearly two-thirds (63 per cent) being over within the half-hour. Hearings on offence grounds on average took a little longer, 42 per cent lasting for a half-hour or longer, while those that involved both truancy and offence grounds were quite the longest; as many as 55 per cent of these went on for 30 minutes or more.

How that time was used and how the various participants interacted with one another are examined in the next few chapters.

TABLE 6.3

DURATION OF HEARINGS

	Proportion of all hearings %
Duration	
Under 18 minutes	16
18–22 minutes	16
23–27 minutes	19
28–32 minutes	16
33–37 minutes	12
38–42 minutes	9
43–47 minutes	4
48 minutes or more	7
(N = 100%)	301

NOTES

1. Working Party on the Social Work (Scotland) Act, 1968, *Social Work in Scotland.* University of Edinburgh, 1969 (Rowntree Report).
2. In Scottish secondary schools, attended by children of 12–16 years or over, *guidance teachers* have as well as their teaching duties specific responsibility for co-ordinating the personal, vocational and leisure interests of the pupils. Guidance in schools is quite different from child guidance (*Chapter 4, Note 3*). *See* F. Martin and K. Murray (eds.), *Children's Hearings.* Scottish Academic Press, 1976, Chs. 15, 16.

7

ACCORDING TO THE RULES

CRIMINAL TRIALS IN COURTS OF LAW are conducted within a complex framework of rules governing almost every aspect of procedure. Lawyers, virtually without exception, see these bodies of rules as of fundamental importance in ensuring fair treatment of the accused person. Radical critics, on the other hand, have sometimes suggested that less reputable purposes are served by the complexities of court procedure; but although they might argue for simplification, it is very doubtful whether they would prefer to see justice dispensed casually or arbitrarily. Children's hearings, committed to ideals of open communication, the use of plain language and the honest exchange of ideas, face a major difficulty in attempting to reconcile the pursuit of these objectives with the observance of formal procedural requirements. The need for rules of procedure is rarely questioned, and indeed in a period of increased concern over the definition and protection of the legal rights of children, suggestions of procedural laxity have been obvious targets for criticism.

Grant (1976)[1] insists that difficulties, if any, lie only in the observance of rules, not in their existence. He emphasizes that violation of the rights of the child '. . . can arise only through imperfect appreciation or application of the procedural standards set by the Act and the Rules'. He points out that although Rule 9(1) stipulates that 'Except as otherwise provided by these rules and any other enactment, the procedure at any children's hearing shall be such as the chairman shall in his discretion determine', this apparent discretion in procedural matters is fettered by a number of specific statutory requirements. To quote Grant:[2]

> 'He (the chairman) must identify the child and ascertain the child's age (Act, S.55); he must ensure that the number of people present is kept to a minimum, while at the same time permitting the presence of those who have a right to attend (Act, S.35(2) and (3) and Rule 12), and he must explain the purpose of the hearing to the family (Rules 17 (1) and 19(2)). Further he must explain the grounds of referral to the child (Act, S.42(1)); he must

> ascertain whether they are understood and accepted by the child (Act, S.42(2) and (7)); he must ascertain whether the grounds are accepted by one of the parents (Act, S.42(2)). He must chair the discussion on the merits of the case, and the children's hearing must, under his direction, consider the grounds of referral (Act, S.43(1)) and any report made available to the hearing (Act, S.43(1) and Rules 17(2) and 19 (3)), discuss the case with the child, his parents and any representative (Rules 17(2) and 19(3)), and endeavour to obtain the view of the child and the parents on the best disposal of the case (Rules 17(2) and 19(3)). The chairman must inform the family of the substance of any reports before the hearing (Rules 17(3) and 19(4)); he must inform the family and any representative of the decision of the hearing (Rule 17(4)), and the reasons for that decision (Rule 17(4)); he must inform the family and any representative of the right to appeal to the Sheriff (Rule 17 (4)), and of their right to receive a written copy of the reasons for the hearing's decision (Rule 17(4)). As these matters afford no discretion, and as they exhaust the situations in which the rights of the child are most at risk, it is fair to say that the Act and the Rules afford adequate protection in the hearing situation'.

Given the existence of a substantial body of statutory requirements concerning the conduct of children's hearings, one of our interests in observing and recording the actual events of 301 hearings was to assess the quality of practice so far as procedure was concerned. We selected a number of rules, applicable at different stages of the hearing, and ascertained the frequency with which each was complied with or disobeyed. We also took the opportunity to record the observance or otherwise of certain precepts which, while lacking the status of rules *strictu senso*, have come to be widely accepted among panel members as elements of 'good practice'. In this chapter we set out the overall frequencies, consider whether there are any particular types or circumstances of hearings that are associated with significant variations in the compliance rates, and finally discuss the construction and application of a simple index that aggregates discrete items to give an overall measure of procedural conformity.

Table 7.1 shows the frequency with which certain aspects of procedure were in fact adhered to in the series of hearings observed. In 94 per cent of all cases, the child was identified by name and age (Act, S.55). There were a few instances in which he or she was identified by name only or by age only, and only four cases in which there appears to have been no identification at all.

These four children however were all appearing before hearings which had been either continued or adjourned from an earlier occasion, and it is reasonable to assume that they were already known to the panel members concerned. Of the 201 children who were making their first appearance (on that particular referral, at any rate), 197 were identified by name and age, three by name only and one by age only.

Surprisingly however there was a failure to explain the purpose of the hearing in slightly more than one-third of all the cases observed (Rules 17(1) and 19(2)). 'Failure' in this sense does not mean that an attempt to explain the purpose was judged to have been unsuccessful, but that no attempt was made. An explanation of the purpose of the hearing was given marginally less frequently when the case had been continued for reports (43 per cent) and when the child had been referred to a hearing on some previous occasion (41 per cent); but fully one-third of the children who were appearing before a hearing for the first time in their lives were offered no explanation of the hearing's purpose. Explanations were more often overlooked in truancy referrals and least often when the ground of referral was a fairly serious offence, but variations of this kind were not very striking. A deficiency on the part of the chairman seems very rarely to have been made good by another participant; a reporter provided an explanation of the purpose of the hearing in two cases, and a panel member other than the chairman in one instance.

Explanations given of the purpose of the hearing were classified according to whether their orientation was primarily legal or procedural, or principally in terms of the decision that had to be reached and its objective. Two explanations in three fell into the former category and one in six into the latter; the final one-sixth of explanations balanced both procedural and disposition aspects.

TABLE 7.1

FREQUENCY OF COMPLIANCE WITH CERTAIN PROCEDURAL REQUIREMENTS

	Per cent of hearings
Formal rules	
Child identified by name and age	94
Purpose of hearing explained	63
Social background report referred to	35
School report referred to	60
Reasons for decision stated	58
Right to receive written reasons indicated	44
Right to appeal indicated	74
'Good practices'	
Right to legal aid indicated	6
Child asked if agrees/understands decision	37
Parent asked if agrees/understands decision	31
(N = 100%)	301

Wholly procedural explanations were least common among those offered to two small groups of children – perhaps predictably, those referred on care and protection rather than offence grounds, and rather less obviously, those referred for distinctly serious offences.

The grounds of referral were not put to the child and parent in exactly one-quarter of the hearings observed (Act, S.42). What appears to be a quite serious level of omission is however attributable to the inclusion in the sample of 58 hearings that had been continued from a previous occasion, for reports or for some other reason, and 42 hearings that had previously been adjourned to go for proof. The grounds of referral were put in only a small minority of these cases (19 per cent and 29 per cent respectively of the two groups), but in those instances where the child was making his first appearance there was no failure to put the grounds of referral. The child was asked at some hearings whether he had or had not done the act in question, at others whether he accepted or denied the grounds of referral, at yet others whether he agreed or disagreed with the statement; in four instances the chairman followed his reading of the grounds of referral with a simple interrogatory 'Well?'. Complete denial of the offences or truancy alleged was rare, though a significant minority of children accepted some grounds while denying others. It must be emphasized however that ours is not a suitable sample from which to draw conclusions about the frequency of denial and its consequences; designed as a sample of hearings that terminated in a disposal, it inevitably excludes cases in which the grounds were wholly denied, except in those instances where the denial had occurred in a previous hearing and the child was now re-appearing after a sheriff had held that the grounds were valid. It is worth adding however that it was distinctly unusual (15 per cent of relevant occasions) for the chairman's statement of the grounds of referral to be preceded or followed by any explanation of what might be expected if the grounds were denied.

The distinction that is made in this report between 'procedure' and 'participation' is artificial in one sense, since the involvement of parent and child in discussion is itself a formal obligation upon the chairman of a hearing (Rules 17(2) and 19(3)), and not merely a theoretically desirable feature with no statutory basis. The distinction is justified however by the complexity of the issue of participation and the many qualitative problems that it raises; it would be easy to satisfy the formal requirement without ever achieving more than a minimal level of participation by parent and child, and for that reason we embark in *Chapter 9* on a detailed examination of the dimensions of involvement. Yet there are one or two specific topics which emerge from an analysis of areas of discussion that are relevant also to the present examination of conformity to procedural requirements. Foremost among these is the use made in the hearing of professional reports.

The chairman of the hearing is expected to disclose the essential features of any reports that have been made available to the panel members present, unless he has reason to believe that disclosure would be detrimental to the interests of the child (Rules 17(3) and 19(4)). On the face of it, this obligation is overlooked fairly frequently. Social background reports were available in all but three of the hearings studied, and school reports in all but 34, yet there was no explicit reference to the former in two-thirds of all hearings and no explicit mention of the latter in two hearings in every five. No report was ever shown to the family, and a formal summary of the contents of a school report was given at only one hearing. A partial account of the contents of the social background report was given to the family at slightly more than 5 per cent of hearings, while an extract from the school report was conveyed about three times as frequently. Most of the references that were made to reports were in the nature of allusions: 'I can see the social worker says you're more settled at home'. The social background report was referred to in this way at three hearings in every ten, and the school report at four in every ten hearings. Social background reports were mentioned more frequently in initial than in continued or adjourned hearings, more often in cases where the child had never previously appeared before a hearing, but in no category did the frequency of mention exceed 40 per cent. A similar pattern is found in the frequency with which school reports were mentioned, the proportion reaching as high as 70 per cent in the case of initial appearances.

The contrast between the use openly made of the two types of report is striking, and is presumably related to the tendency of social work reports to contain a higher proportion of sensitive and potentially embarrassing material. Nevertheless, the frequency with which aspects of the child's family situation were discussed in hearings considerably exceeds the rate at which reference was made to the report or reports that must have been a major source of the panel members' information; and although school reports were more often alluded to than social work reports, the frequency with which they were mentioned still falls short of the almost invariable introduction of school matters as topics of conversation in the hearing. Clearly, there is room for differences of interpretation. It might be held that if information derived from reports is brought under discussion in the hearing the rule requiring disclosure is satisfied, even though the source of the information is not explicitly indicated. While the precise significance of the rule in question has never been tested in the courts, we would be inclined to doubt whether such a liberal interpretation is justified.

If a strict interpretation was not intended when Rules 17(3) and 19(4) were framed, it is not clear what purpose they were designed to serve. Since Rules 17(2) and 19(3) require the hearing to consider all relevant reports and to discuss the case with the child, parent and representative, Rule 17(3) and 19(4) would appear to be superfluous unless the phrase '. . . shall inform the child and his parent of the substance of any reports . . .' is to be interpreted fairly literally. The matter should in any case be viewed in a wider context than that of the hearings system alone. Recent years have seen increasing criticism of the practice of compiling reports which, however well intentioned, almost inevitably combine factual statements with an admixture of impressions, opinions, interpretations and judgments – and which are then withheld from the very persons who are the subjects of the reports. The recommendation by the Committee on Data Protection[3] to the effect that social work clients should normally have access to computerized personal data concerning them is an important recent step in the direction of greater openness. If we are in general to move towards subject access as a guiding principle for social work and many other records, the rule governing disclosure of the content of records in the children's hearings system with its central commitment to open communication, should *a fortiori* be interpreted with some strictness.

The chairman of the hearing is expected to try to obtain the views of child and parent as to the disposal most likely to be in the child's interests (Rules 17(2) and 19(3)). In nine-tenths of the hearings in our series there was in fact some discussion of the decision. Most commonly – at two hearings in three – discussion centred on the supervision process, with panel members attempting to explain its nature or emphasize its advantages. In almost every other hearing, the family members were asked for their opinion as to what should be done – asked sometimes hopefully, sometimes despairingly. It was a good deal less common – and here we move from a formal obligation to what we would judge to be good practice – for child or parent to be asked whether they agreed with the decision actually reached by the hearing. Only 16 per cent of children and 25 per cent of parents were asked whether they agreed with the decision, and nearly 30 per cent of children and 16 per cent of parents whether they understood it. The categories overlap, with some being asked both about agreement and about understanding; but three children in every five and two parents in every three were not questioned under either head. It should be emphasized however that this is not a statutory requirement.

When a hearing reaches a decision, the chairman has a duty to announce the nature of the decision, to give the family orally reasons for that decision, and to advise the family that they have a right to receive a written statement of reasons (Rule 17(4)). The obligation to formulate reasons at the conclusion of the hearing was overlooked in 42 per cent of the cases observed. The requirement was less frequently neglected in those cases that had been proved before a sheriff – reasons were stated in three-quarters of such cases, compared to one-half of all the others – and slightly less often forgotten when the child had no prior record of appearance before a hearing than when he was something of a recidivist. Parents were notified of their right to receive a written statement of reasons at slightly less than one-half of all hearings. Precipitated reviews and hearings where the grounds of referral were truancy were associated with rather greater laxity in this respect; the more serious types of offence referral tended more often to elicit an indication that written reasons would be provided.

Appeals against the decisions of children's hearings are rare – perhaps twenty are raised every year – but it is essential for all families to be notified of their right to appeal. There was however a failure to adhere to this requirement at one hearing in every four.

It is important to consider what were the decisions that had been reached at those hearings where no right of appeal had been notified. The letter of the law is perfectly clear. Rule 17(4) requires that '. . . the chairman shall inform the child, his parent, and any representative, if attending the hearing, of . . . (c) the right of the child and of the parent under section 49(1) of the Act to appeal to the sheriff against the decision'. Nevertheless, some might agree that when a hearing has decided on a discharge, a failure to notify child and parents of their right to appeal against this decision could be regarded as among the more venial sins of omission. The actual distribution of this particular procedural fault is interesting. Straightforward discharges accounted for 45 of the 76 instances in which the right to appeal was not notified; these amount to 48 per cent of all the hearings at which this decision was reached. Similarly, the eight hearings where jurisdiction had been established by a prior supervision order and where the decision had been to discharge the new grounds and to retain the existing supervision requirement were equally divided between those in which a right to appeal was and was not notified to parent and child. Of the seven hearings which decided that the child should be taken into the care of the local authority, none was at fault in failing to refer to the right of appeal. But there were 163 decisions to impose a supervision order without a residential requirement, at 21 of which (13 per cent) there was no notification of the right of appeal; the requirement was correctly discharged by the panel chairman in connection with seven out of ten such decisions (115 instances), while the reporter alone carried out the task in 24 cases and the reporter and chairman combined forces twice. Finally, there were 29 hearings which ended in an order for residential supervision. At 19 of these the hearing chairman indicated that there existed a right of appeal to the sheriff and at a further four the reporter provided the necessary information. But at six hearings a residential order was made without any right of appeal being notified. Even if a more lenient view is taken of this procedural failure when discharge was the outcome of the hearing, it is impossible to respond with any complacency to the neglect of Rule 17(4) in cases where a supervision order was imposed. Fortunately, these omissions occurred in only about one-seventh of such hearings, but anything that falls short of 100 per cent compliance must be taken extremely seriously. Prospective appellants may be entitled to receive legal aid. There is not however a formal obligation to remind families of this fact, and there were only twenty hearings where legal aid was mentioned either by the chairman or by the reporter.

It is clear from the foregoing account that some clearly defined rules of procedure are not infrequently neglected. It is scarcely surprising in the circumstances that certain canons of good practice which do not have the standing of procedural regulations should be neglected at an equal if not greater rate. Yet these facts do not tell us a great deal about the conduct of hearings as a whole. Do procedural oversights and omissions tend to be concentrated in a limited number of hearings, so that hearings in general might be divisible into two broad categories, those with a high degree of conformity to procedural requirements, and those with a large number of faults? Alternatively, is the distribution of procedural faults such that the majority of hearings have a few errors, with both very high and very low degrees of compliance being in the minority? We approached these questions by constructing a very simple overall measure of procedural conformity. This involved aggregating eight of the items listed in Table 7.1, and allocating to each hearing a score between 0 and 8 depending on the number of elements of procedure adhered to. The maximum score would be obtained by a hearing in which the purpose was explained, the social background report mentioned, the school report mentioned, the reasons for the decision stated, the right to receive written reasons advised, the right of appeal advised, the child asked whether he agreed/understood, and the parent asked whether he agreed/understood. The identification of the child was excluded from this index because it was correctly performed in virtually every hearing, and advice about legal aid was excluded from the index because it was omitted in almost every hearing. The resulting distribution of scores between 301 hearings is shown in Table 7.2.

The distribution of scores clearly indicates that it is quite unrealistic to assume that hearings may be simply dichotomized into those that are competent and those that are incompetent procedurally. Scores in the middle of the range – say four and five – are a great deal more common than extremely high or extremely low scores. Very few hearings were abysmally bad in a procedural sense, but only slightly more were outstandingly good in this respect. The nature of the distribution curve makes it unlikely that we shall find any over-riding criterion that clearly differentiates between hearings which conform closely to the rules of procedure and those which are characterized by procedural laxity. Nevertheless, there are potentially interesting if undramatic relationships to be sought between the types and circumstances of hearings on the one hand and their degree of rule-observance on the other. In order to simplify the search, the 301 hearings observed have been allocated to three groups by condensing the nine possible scores on the index of procedure described above. These are as follows:

82 below average hearings (27 per cent of the total), made up of those scoring 0, 1, 2 or 3;
132 average hearings (44 per cent of the total), made up of those scoring 4 or 5;
and 87 above average hearings (29 per cent of the total), made up of those scoring 6, 7 or 8.

The procedural quality of hearings tended to vary as between hearings of different types and with different characteristics, but there is clearly no single factor that is very strikingly associated with particularly impressive – or particularly casual – standards of performance. Thus, we find a lower proportion of 'above average' precipitated reviews than of initial hearings, as well as a lower proportion among continued hearings and those that have been sent for proof. When a child has been referred on offence grounds the standard of procedure tends to be higher than when truancy is the ground of referral, but neither the number of offences charged nor the number of offences established is related to the quality of procedure. There is however a tendency for the degree of compliance with procedural rules to increase with offences of greater seriousness; 34 per cent of the hearings where the most serious offence established was theft or shoplifting fell into the 'above average' category with respect to procedure, as did 39 per cent where the most serious established charge was housebreaking, compared with only 22 per cent of all other offence hearings.

It is perhaps worth recording that hearings which began late were somewhat more lax procedurally than those which commenced punctually, though as with most of the other relationships cited the difference was fairly slight – 24 per cent of the delayed hearings being graded above average, as against 32 per cent of those starting on time. The presence of the child's mother was not associated with any difference in the procedural quality of hearings, but of the hearings in which the father participated only 22 per cent were 'below average' procedurally, compared with 34 per cent of hearings where the father was absent. On the other hand, we note a surprisingly sharp decline in rule-observance in the small sample of hearings where another family member or a representative of the family was present; of the 32 hearings in this category only two came into the 'above average' group, contrasted with 32 per cent of all other hearings. Standards of procedure were also poor in the very small group of hearings (19) where no social worker was present.

It might be expected that particular attention is paid to the details of procedure when there is a greater likelihood that the hearings will terminate in a decision requiring the child to reside in a List D school. Some of the statistical associations referred to above seem to point in that direction – for example, the suggestion of greater procedural care in the most serious offence cases – while the greater laxity in precipitated reviews as well as in the general run of cases where the child had a prior record of appearance before a hearing does *not* imply closer observance of rules when a residential disposal appears to be more likely. In fact, the relationships between our measure of procedural compliance and the decisions actually reached at the 301 hearings observed are not clear-cut. Those hearings terminating in a discharge were as a group the least satisfactory in terms of procedure; nearly 40 per cent fell into the

TABLE 7.2

INDEX OF PROCEDURE: DISTRIBUTION OF SCORES

Score	*Frequency*	*Per cent of hearings*
0	2	*
1	12	4
2	31	10
3	37	12
4	68	23
5	64	21
6	57	19
7	20	7
8	10	3
	301	

* = Less than 1 per cent.

'below average' category. They contrasted quite sharply with the 163 hearings which led to an order requiring supervision in the community; 37 per cent of these scored 'above average' marks, and only 19 per cent had a large number of procedural omissions. Residential orders were made in only 29 cases. One would not wish to attach excessive weight to frequency distributions within a comparatively small sub-sample, but it must be said that the procedural standards in this important group appeared disquietingly low, considering the significance of the decision that was being made. Only at four of the 29 hearings were procedural requirements observed on a sufficient scale to justify inclusion in the 'above average' category. This was not balanced, fortunately, by an exceptionally large number of hearings observing very few rules, but rather by an unusually high proportion in the 'average' category.

Two other features of the hearings studied have an interesting relationship to the level of procedural observance. One of these is the duration of the hearing. To put it simply and perhaps obviously – hurried hearings cut corners. Those hearings which did not last more than 30 minutes were above average procedurally in only one instance in five, and below average in one-third of all cases; nearly half of those which took longer than half an hour observed all or most of the requirements that are listed, while only one in seven observed none or very few. The style of chairmanship seems also to be a discriminating factor. It was only in 28 instances that the chairman of the hearing simply assumed agreement with his decision rather than ask the other panel members, but it is worthy of note that there were only five of these hearings in which an excessively confident chairman was also punctilious in his observance of the rules of procedure.

We began this chapter by recognizing the difficulties inherent in a system which puts a premium on ease of communication but at the same time erects a framework of formality as a safeguard against arbitrariness, however well-intentioned. Almost all members of children's panels place a heavy emphasis on the importance of open discussion, but few if any would question the justification for a body of rules governing procedure. There may be some who feel the latter to be, on occasion, unduly restrictive, and would argue that 'the letter killeth'. We have some evidence on this point, and in a later chapter consider the relations between varying degrees of faithfulness in adhering to the rules of procedure and differing levels of success in involving child and parents in discussion. Without anticipating the arguments in any detail, it is relevant to note at this point that children's hearings are often successful, sometimes very successful, in creating an atmosphere in which their clients feel that they can speak freely and be heard sympathetically; but that there is nothing in our data to suggest that the two principles are necessarily in conflict, that open communication can be achieved only at the cost of casualness in procedure. Indeed, data already presented seem likely to point away from such a conclusion; a hearing which is over in less than half an hour (and which we know is relatively more likely to be 'below average' procedurally) does not appear ideal for a full exchange of views. We would argue therefore that a disregard for the rules of procedure in the interests of participation cannot be justified empirically and is in any event contrary to the principles of natural justice. If this is accepted, it follows that the standards of procedural compliance indicated by our evidence both can and should be improved upon.

A particularly onerous responsibility rests upon those panel members who act as chairmen of hearings, and are under a specific obligation to carry out most of the procedures laid down. The problem is not simply one of ensuring that the rules of procedure and principles of good practice are known – few if any panel members are unaware of these, and indeed some have difficulty in accepting that there are sometimes gaps in their performance. There is, too, an obligation on reporters. In the studies reported in this volume we have concentrated on the role of the reporter as an intake official with wide discretionary powers. He has other important responsibilities, however. *Inter alia* he must, in Finlayson's words, 'be present at each session of the children's hearing . . . where he acts in some quasi-legal advisory role to the hearing members and also in a clerical role to record the minutes of proceedings of the actual hearing'.[4] The precise nature of this 'quasi-legal advisory role' is not defined statutorily, but it is generally accepted among reporters that he should provide guidance as necessary on all matters of law and procedure. So far as uncorrected flaws in hearings are concerned, there can be no question of lack of relevant knowledge on the reporter's part being a contributory factor; yet it seems equally beyond dispute that errors, some of them by no means insignificant, are neither prevented nor rectified by the hearing's adviser. The problem seems rather to be one of attitude, and of the human skills necessary to contribute to the proceedings appropriately, without obtrusiveness and without creating embarrassment. The implications for policy and practice of these undoubted flaws in the work of children's hearings are considered in a later chapter.

NOTES

1. John P. Grant, 'Protecting the rights of the child' in: F. M. Martin and K. Murray (eds.), *Children's Hearings*. Scottish Academic Press, 1976.
2. Ibid.
3. *Report of the Committee on Data Protection*, Cmnd. 7341, HMSO, London, 1976.
4. A. Finlayson, 'The Reporter' in: F. M. Martin and K. Murray (eds.), *Children's Hearings*. Scottish Academic Press.

8

THE DIALOGUE OF CHILDREN'S HEARINGS

THE DIALOGUE of a children's hearing is not subject to the constraints of relevance that apply to the processes of examination and cross-examination in a court of law; none the less, it is a far cry from the casual, random conversation of a tea-party. If there is to be a decision that accords with the interests of the child, it is necessary to identify those interests. Professional reports provide pertinent information of varying amount and quality, but this information must be clarified and evaluated through discussion with the family. The disposal should neither be nor appear arbitrary, but should have been considered openly by the panel members together with the family. The dialogue, in short, has objectives with a clear statutory basis. In addition, most panel members see the hearing as an opportunity to pursue certain informal goals. They may wish to convey a sense of moral disapproval of the behaviour that has resulted in the child's presence at the hearing, to bring home to the child an awareness of the dangers of a delinquent way of life or to communicate to the parents the importance of their exercising certain influences on the child's conduct and development. From our point of view therefore it is necessary to analyse both the subject-matter of the dialogue and the styles adopted by panel members, in order to understand more fully the means by which they pursue these various objectives.

Our observation of the actual events of 301 hearings included the careful recording of the topics introduced into the discussion, of the styles of discourse and attitudes adopted by panel members. While we did not make verbatim transcripts a number of excerpts of dialogue were noted in the course of the hearings observed and these are quoted here as illustrative of the dialogue. We look at the relationship where one exists between the topics raised and between the styles of the panel members in the hearing. To what extent the topics raised in discussion reflect the items appearing in professional reports available to the hearing is another important consideration.

Content of discussion

We found during pilot studies that almost all topics discussed in the course of children's hearings could be classified into 10 broad categories. To these we

ate 3. Interior of the Edinburgh hearing room. *(By courtesy of Lothian Regional Council)*

Plate 4. Children's hearing in progress. *(By courtesy of Strathclyde Regional C*

added a miscellaneous category into which all residual items fell. The frequency with which these topics were discussed is set out in Table 8.1. An average of five themes was discussed at any one hearing.

An emphasis on school was a very striking feature of the discussion in our sample of hearings, arising in 91 per cent of the cases. Given that eleven of the children (4 per cent) were either below or beyond school age, there were only 15 children (5 per cent) for whom this theme could possibly have been relevant where it was not in fact discussed.

The discussion of the child at school focussed overwhelmingly on the regularity of school attendance but reference was also made to educational progress, to patterns of behaviour within the class room and to the quality of relationships with teachers and other children. The importance that panel members attached to school matters was recognized by the children in our sample; of those interviewed 31 per cent thought that 'school' was the most important factor to panel members in their decision-making (*Chapter 12*).

These matters may arouse the interest of panel members for a number of reasons. They may well be aware of the association between truancy and delinquency and they may share the widely held belief that they are causally related; they may be conscious also of the evidence linking troublesome behaviour in school with later delinquency (West and Farrington, 1973).[1] In addition, their anxiety is likely to stem from their position as laymen, voicing a general community concern that public education is failing to benefit a substantial proportion of children, and indeed in some cases even failing to reach them. The dialogue is replete with references to the value of education, with efforts to instil feelings of guilt about not taking advantage of the educational opportunities offered, and with reminders that the hearings possess powers to compel school attendance by making residential orders.

TABLE 8.1

FREQUENCY OF CONTENT ITEMS DISCUSSED IN HEARINGS

	%
The child at school	91
Grounds of referral and motivation	81
Family's attitude to child	68
Relationship with the peer group, leisure activities	68
Contact, co-operation with social worker and other professional agencies	58
The child at home	51
Prior record	36
Family stresses, health	34
Future plans	34
Miscellaneous	30
Use of drugs and alcohol	16
Mean number of items discussed at each hearing	5
(N = 100%)	301

The following are examples of the discussion which took place on this theme:

Member – Why don't you like going to school?
Child – I don't know.
Member – Can you read?
Child – Yes.
Member – Read this then, son.
(Child reads)
Chairman – Do you realise you have got to go to school?
(Child nods)
Chairman – We all have commitments in life, you know. If you cannot attend school you may end up in a List D school.

⋆ ⋆ ⋆

Chairman – How do you get on at school?
Child – Alright.
Member – It says in the report that you are a known truant.
Member – Do you ever skip off for the odd day?
Mother – I've been down to school. The teacher told me he took days off.
Child – I don't do it.
Member – But it says so in the report.

⋆ ⋆ ⋆

Chairman – Why don't you attend?
Child – Don't like it.
Chairman – That's not a reason. Why are you punishing your mother and father? Your father's been in prison. They've paid £100 in fines for you and your sisters. Are you going to go to school?
Child – Don't know.
Chairman – That's not an answer.
Mother and Father – Give them another chance, and if they don't take it take them away.

⋆ ⋆ ⋆

While grounds of referral were associated with each case in our sample these were discussed in little more than 8 out of 10 instances (81 per cent). Panel members were very largely interested in the details of the incidents reported and often seemed to expect the child to recall with accuracy the particulars of the event. The child's motivation and involvement with others were frequently explored as were his and the parents' reactions to the referral.

The issue of responsibility was frequently in the minds of panel members when the grounds of referral were discussed. In some instances they were searching for extenuating factors, circumstances which appeared to minimise the degree of responsibility that could properly be imputed to the child before them. On many other occasions however their concern was rather to emphasize the child's responsibility for the delinquent acts and to bring home to him a greater awareness of their moral implications.

Chairman – Did you not think at all that you had to pay for these things? How did you feel when you were caught?
Child – Terrible.
Member – Now, did you give any of these things away?
Mother – She takes things out of the house and gives them away.

★ ★ ★

Chairman – Tell me about the shop-lifting.
(Child describes)
Chairman – And did the police come to you?
Mother – Yes, really he had no need to steal. He wants for nothing.
Chairman – And what about the second offence?
(Child describes)
Chairman – And somebody caught you?
Child – Yes.
Chairman – Are you normally so easily led?
Child – No.

★ ★ ★

Chairman – How on earth did you get involved in all this?
Child – Got led into it.
Chairman – How did you get all this away from the shops?
Child – In cars.
Chairman – So you were with adults?
Child – Yes, one or more adults each time.
Mother – One of them is a cousin of mine.
Chairman – This was planned then?
Father – Yes, I think so; the things were recovered.
Chairman – So this was organized crime?
Father – Yes, he was using the boys as a kind of Fagin.
Member – What did you get out of it?
Child – Nothing.
Member – Has this man got some hold over you?
Child – I suppose he has.
Member – Did he know you had been truanting from school and threatened to tell?
Child – No.
Member – So you did it of your own free will?
Member – Did you think it was exciting?
Child – Yes.
Member – Do you think so now?
Child – No.
Member – I've been a panel member for many years and I've never seen anything like it. How would you like it if someone did it to you? This is very serious! You have a caring mother and father.

Chairman – Were you paid by this man?

Child – No.

Member – You were set up.

* * *

Family attitudes came up in the discussion at 68 per cent of the observed hearings. This theme of enquiry explored the nature of the parental reactions to the particular incident and also whether adequate measures were taken by the parents to control the behaviour of their children. The dialogue rarely included discussion of attitudes to broader issues of family life.

Member to Father – What did you say to her when you found out?

Father – I told her she might get put away.

Member – For stealing a box of cheese?

Father – Quite possible.

Chairman – Was she punished?

Father – Yes, but I don't hit her.

Member to Mother – Do you feel you need more outside help with her?

Mother – No, she's settled down now.

* * *

Member – He looks tired. Does he go to bed early enough?

Chairman – The school thinks he's allowed to stay up too late.

Father – He runs about something terrible.

Chairman – Is he spoiled?

Father – Aye, he gets everything he wants.

Member – That's not good for the child.

* * *

Spare-time activities and relationships with peers were discussed in 68 per cent of cases. The panel members were primarily interested in identifying the range of the child's leisure activities, and the influence of the peer group on the child's behaviour.

Member to Parents – I see she works on Friday and Saturday.

Mother – Yes.

Member – You know you are breaking the law.

Mother – She has a permit from school.

Chairman to Child – Do you go to discos?

Child – Yes.

Chairman – Do you have boy friends?

Child – No.

* * *

Member – Have you had impulses to steal when you've been out with friends? What are your hobbies?
Child – Sports.
Mother – She is a very sports-minded girl.
Chairman – Are you associating with the wrong type?
Child – Well, I know one of them is at List D.
Mother – I've nipped that in the bud. She hasn't been up to that area for some time.

★ ★ ★

Member – Do you have any hobbies?
Child – Yes, playing football.
Member – Do you have friends?
Child – Yes.
Mother – He can't really avoid these friends. They are the only boys of his age, and they also get into trouble.

★ ★ ★

References to the family's contact and co-operation with social work and other professional agencies were made in 58 per cent of our sample. These tended to emphasize the efforts that had been made by various agencies in their attempts to provide help of one kind or another, and often drew attention to failure to respond on the part of the family with some questioning of possible reasons for this.

Member to Mother – Now, can you tell me why you never replied to the letters sent by the school?
Mother – I never received them; his sister was protecting him. She tore them up.
Member – I think you should go along to see the headmaster. He seems very worried. Maybe the school knows something he (the child) won't tell.

★ ★ ★

Member – Any more appointments with the psychiatrist?
Social Worker – Not at the moment.
Chairman – The report says she didn't keep appointments.
Member – Didn't you go to the shrink at all?
Child – No.
Member – But there was transport laid on from your house.
Child – I just stayed in the house.
Member – I still want to know why you didn't go back to Dr X. The Red Cross put themselves out for you. Don't you feel ashamed?
Social Worker – I think social work support is more important at this time.
Chairman – Well, I think all this has been going on too long.

★ ★ ★

Chairman – Both doctors think a supervision requirement with John remaining at home. Both reports say that John and family have come a long way.
Father – Yes, I feel better about a lot of this.
Chairman – Both reports are a bit wary of your being too optimistic.
Father – There's hope. I was unhappy about contact with panels. I thought them a lot of do-gooders. But I have changed my views.

* * *

The child's behaviour at home was discussed in 51 per cent of our sample of hearings. The panel members were attempting to assess the standard of the child's conduct within the home and the capacity of the parents to handle any difficulties. Here as well as elsewhere the panel members would pick up any suggestion that the parents might be worried or embarrassed by the child's behaviour. They would often seize the opportunity to try to create feelings of guilt, arguing in effect that causing distress to 'good' parents added a new dimension to the offence, and attempting to use the child's presumed affection for his parents as a lever for effecting change in behaviour.

Member to Mother – How has he been behaving at home?
Mother – Very well, he hasn't run away again.
Member to Child – Do you help at home?
Child – Yes.
Mother – He did the dishes for a while when he came home.

* * *

Chairman – What's bothering you?
(Child is silent)
Mother to Child – Speak up.
Child – Shut up you. I am not answering anyone's questions.
Chairman to Mother – Is there some animosity between you and your daughter?
Mother – No.
Chairman to Mother – Is she like this, on a knife edge, at home?
Mother – Sometimes.

* * *

Member – What do you do all day?
Child – I lie in my bed.
Chairman – All day?
Child – No, not all day.
Member – Don't you find that time drags?
(Child nods)

Member – How will you manage to get up at 8 o'clock in the morning, eh?
(Child smiles)
Chairman – He'll do it to get his wages.
Chairman to Father – How have you found him at home?
Father – Very good. He's really been no bother.

★ ★ ★

The child's prior record was discussed in little more than one-third of all cases in the sample (36 per cent). The panel members questioned the child about previous 'trouble', particularly contact with the police through informal or formal warnings. The child was also asked about previous referrals to the hearings system and about his behaviour record since the expiry of any compulsory supervision requirement earlier in force.

Chairman – You've also had a police warning. Were there any other incidents?
Member – Now, have you done anything of this kind before?
Child – Yes.
Chairman – Oh you have, have you?

★ ★ ★

Chairman – Have you been committing offences for years and not been caught?
Child – No, just started.
Chairman – This seems a bit amateur. Have you not had any practice at this sort of thing?
Child – Once, when I was eleven; but the police just warned me because I never took anything.

★ ★ ★

Member – This has been going on for some time. You've really made no attempt to send them to school.
Mother – I was going to send them to school on Monday.
Chairman to Social Worker – Their attendance used to be quite good when they were at primary school.
Social Worker – Yes.

★ ★ ★

Family stresses or health were discussed in 34 per cent of the sample. References were made to unsatisfactory living conditions, to stressful life events such as the illness and death of family members and to the separation or divorce of the parents.

Chairman – I think he should have pocket money.
Father – I cannot afford it. I'm out of work. I get £33 per week. Anyway, he gambles it.

Chairman	– What?
Father	– Pitch and toss.
Member	– I think he should have it anyway.
Father	– Well, I don't agree.

* * *

Chairman	– How is her father?
Mother	– One step forward sort of thing. But he's a little better.
Chairman	– It's pressure on you.
Mother	– It's a strain but all the children have been very good.

* * *

Teacher to Chairman	– A lot of changes have come about at David's home. Things are really a lot more stable now.
Father	– Oh yes, things are better at home now.
Member to Father	– Has there been any hope of accommodation?
Father	– No, we get some offers but nothing so far. We really need an extra room. We are living on top of each other.

* * *

Chairman	– Did you go to hospital?
Child	– Yes, I am going to have an operation.
Chairman	– Does it worry you?
Child	– No. (Child cries)

* * *

Plans for the future were discussed in one-third of the observed hearings (34 per cent). Much of the dialogue took the form of reminding the child that the prospect of employment might be seriously diminished if troublesome behaviour continued. In our sample of interviews with children 77 per cent projected that future employers would hold having been to a hearing against them. There seems every reason to believe that the discourse of the hearing did more to heighten than to minimise that expectation.

Member	– Your Dad has a business. It's not an easy job, you know. What are you going to do?
Child	– I like animals.
Member	– Well, if you are working with animals it's important to know that you are trustworthy, because they can tell, you know, who's been dishonest.

* * *

Member	– What will you do when you leave school?
Child	– Well, I don't know. The teacher said she'd talk to me about it.
Member	– Well, the school says that you could do quite well if you worked a bit harder.

Child – I would like to do a secretarial course.
Member – Oh, good!
Chairman – Well, you'd better stop missing school and going in late.

* * *

Member – What do you intend to do?
Child – I used to want to be a nurse.
Member – You realise that unless this stops you'll have a hard job getting employment.

* * *

Member – What do you want to do?
Child – Long distance lorry driver.
Chairman – Well, no one will give you a lorry if you are going to disappear with all the stuff, will they?

* * *

Hearings discussed the use of drugs or alcohol in 16 per cent of the cases. Their enquiries focussed largely on the child's habit of glue sniffing and the attendant risks, occasionally on the child's drinking pattern and only very rarely on the parents' alcohol abuse despite this being known as a feature of family life through the reports.

Member to Mother – I see there may be glue sniffing.
Mother – Yes, that's true.
Member to Child – Have you sniffed glue recently?
Child – No, not for one month.
Chairman to Social Worker – Has he stopped?
Social Worker – It's very bad in the area. I think he has stopped now.
Member – It's very dangerous. It could kill you, you know.

* * *

Chairman – I see you've been sniffing glue again.
Child – I was frightened into it by a boy.
Member – What kind of glue?
Child – Bostick.
Chairman – I find this hard to accept. Why does he want you to do it?
Child – Because he doesn't want to do it by himself.
Chairman – The reason for our concern is not that we want to be more punitive but we're worried.

* * *

Chairman – Had you been drinking?
Child – Two cans of beer. I wasn't drunk.

Chairman – Do you take a lot of drink?
Member – Do you feel that you have to have a drink?
Chairman – How about glue?
Child – No. I have stopped that.
Member – I think he's got a drink problem.
Father – I don't think a can of lager is a drink problem.

★ ★ ★

Chairman to Mother – Now, Mrs X, I must say you can't afford to drink when you have as little money as you do.
Mother – No, I know, but I've not been drunk since they (the children) were taken away.

★ ★ ★

Member – Is this habitual with you?
Father – Oh, many's the time I'm drunk.

★ ★ ★

Other topics arose in the discussion in 30 per cent of the cases. These focussed mainly on the financial circumstances of the family and the child's use of pocket money; on the difficulties created by poor housing and run-down neighbourhoods; on the child's personality and attitude to family life; on the range of alternative resources available to the hearing; on the possibility of inviting the child to participate in voluntary restitution.

The extent to which different content items occurred together in hearings is reported in Table 8.2, which shows those correlation coefficients between pairs of content items which are significant at the 0·01 level. Only 10 of a total of 55 correlation coefficients are significantly positive and even those are strikingly small. This seems to indicate a degree of specificity in the content of hearings, with an attempt to relate the choice of topics to the particular and unique circumstances of individual children.

TABLE 8.2

INTER-CORRELATIONS OF CONTENT ITEMS

Positive correlations significant at 0·01 levels:

	r
grounds × prior record	0·17
grounds × peers, spare time	0·18
prior record × the child at home	0·14
prior record × peers, spare time	0·20
prior record × family attitudes to child	0·17
prior record × future prospects	0·14
the child at school × peers, spare time	0·17
the child at school × family attitude to child	0·17
peers, spare time × the child at home	0·24
family attitude to child × contact with social worker	0·21

No *negative* correlations significant at 0·01 level.

Reports as sources of content items

The social background and other reports made available to panel members seemed to us of potentially great importance in influencing the selection of topics for discussion. We were therefore interested to know whether the frequency with which the subjects were talked about at hearings did in fact vary according to the contents of the reports submitted.

Table 8.3 sets out the report items affecting discussion of school-related topics. While discussion of school matters was in general very widespread this topic was more likely to be discussed if already the subject of reports. References to regular attendance and satisfactory behaviour at school were less likely to stimulate discussion of 'school' matters than references to irregular attendance and difficult behaviour. High intelligence and above average educational

TABLE 8.3

REPORT ITEMS AFFECTING THE DISCUSSION OF 'SCHOOL'

	Hearings in which 'school' is discussed %
Reports indicate:	
irregular attendance	94
satisfactory attendance	85
no comment on school behaviour	90
satisfactory school behaviour	85
lying	92
bullying	98
quick tempered	96
disruptive	91
restless	100
easily led	100
apathetic	100
no comment on relation with teachers	90
satisfactory relations	93
unsatisfactory relations	94
no comment on intellectual level	81
below average	93
average	94
above average	96
no comment on educational achievement	85
below average	94
average	90
above average	100

attainment were items in reports which attracted the attention of panel members and ensured some discussion of school at hearings.

Table 8.4 gives the report items affecting the discussion of 'home'. Hearings were more likely to discuss 'home' when the reports indicated unsatisfactory behaviour at home and least likely when the reports included no comment on this theme. Reports of deteriorating behaviour were more likely to be associated with discussion of home circumstances than improvement or no change and very much more than reports of any unevenness in the change in behaviour.

Report items affecting the discussion of 'peers' and 'leisure interests' are given in Table 8.5. When the child was described as 'easily led' in his relations with other children the hearing was more likely to raise for discussion the topics

TABLE 8.4

REPORT ITEMS AFFECTING THE DISCUSSION OF 'HOME'

	Hearings in which 'home' discussed %
Reports indicate:	
no comment on behaviour at home	50
satisfactory behaviour	57
unsatisfactory behaviour	63
no change over time	51
improved	50
deteriorated	60
some improvement, some deterioration	33

TABLE 8.5

REPORT ITEMS AFFECTING THE DISCUSSION OF 'PEERS' AND 'LEISURE INTERESTS'

	Hearings in which 'peers' discussed %
Reports indicate:	
no comment on leisure interests	56
some leisure interests	76
no information on relations with other children	58
positive relations	70
easily led	92
anti-social	66

of 'peers' and 'leisure interests'. Again *any* reference in reports was likely to increase the chances that these subjects would be discussed.

The report items affecting discussion in the hearing of 'family stress' are given in Table 8.6. An important change of direction is noted here. While the topics so far considered have been brought into discussion more frequently when they appear in available reports, we now find that mention of certain sensitive areas in background reports acts if anything as a signal to avoid what could prove to be an emotionally disturbing subject of conversation. Even when hearings received information on family circumstances likely to create great stress for the children, reference was made to this for the most part in less than 50 per cent of the cases. The chances of family stress being a topic of discussion decreased with reports of increasing severity of conflict between the parents. Indeed, reference in reports to severe parental conflict were *less* likely to be followed by discussion of family stress than reports making no reference to this topic. Similarly reports of violence between parents were marginally *less* likely to be followed by discussion of 'family stress' than no reports on this theme. Violence between parent and child was reported to the hearing in 17 cases but only eight of these discussed 'family stress'. Heavy drinking in the parent was reported in 54 cases but less than half of the hearings (23 cases) referred

TABLE 8.6

REPORT ITEMS AFFECTING DISCUSSION OF 'FAMILY STRESS'

	Hearings in which 'family stress' discussed %
Reports indicate:	
no reference to parental conflict	32
some parental conflict	45
severe parental conflict	27
separation of parents	38
no reference to violence between parents	35
violence between parents	33
no reference to violence between parents and child	34
violence between parents and child	47
no reference to heavy drinking in parent	33
heavy drinking in parent at present	47
heavy drinking in parent in past	32
no reference to family relationships in general	28
good family relationships	27
some family relationship problems	33
very poor family relationships	56
currently stable but history of poor family relationships	64

to 'family stress'. References in reports to family relationships in general were more likely to lead to discussion of 'family stress' if these relationships were reported to be very poor either currently or in the past.

Table 8.7 refers to those report items which initiated discussion of 'family attitudes' in the hearing. Reports describing the mother as 'caring and concerned' were more likely to lead to discussion of family attitudes than those where mother was described as 'anxious, inadequate, withdrawn' or 'dominant, aggressive'. References in reports to mother's criminal history were outstandingly weak as stimulants of discussion of family attitudes.

The influence of comments in reports on father's personality were similar to those for mother although when father was described as 'anxious, inadequate, withdrawn', the hearings were likely to discuss family attitudes just as frequently as when he was described as 'caring and concerned'. None the less any reference in reports to father's criminal history tended to inhibit discussion of family attitudes. Discussion on this theme was also less likely to arise if the reports referred to any delinquent history in the child's siblings.

References in reports to parental conflict increased the chances of discussion of family attitudes in the hearing and the frequency of such discussion increased according to the severity of the conflict reported. However 'violence between parents', 'violence between parent and child', 'mental illness of the parent', 'heavy drinking in the parent' were each less likely to lead to discussion of family attitudes if reference was made to each of these items in reports. Mention of relationships in general did lead to discussion of family attitudes in proportion to the severity of the problem although when difficulties lay in the past panel members tended to ignore discussion on family attitudes.

These findings strongly suggest, first, that for subjects that are emotionally relatively neutral, such as school matters and behaviour at home, the reports act as a springboard for discussion; but that where more emotionally charged issues are concerned there is a distinction between generalized references to 'poor relationships' or 'family difficulties' and the identification of very specific problems such as violence, heavy drinking or mental illness. The former are taken up readily by panel members while the latter tend to block discussion of family affairs.

Opening up very personal and sensitive matters with the family in the hearing is a difficult task and it is scarcely surprising that panel members appear to have little confidence in their ability to conduct discussion of highly personal and at times deeply distressing experiences. Our study of the views of panel members leaves little doubt that they attach a great deal of importance to the quality of family life and they identify parental inadequacy as a major factor in the etiology of delinquency (*Chapter 14*). From our study of the factors influencing the decisions of hearings (*Chapter 11*), we know that family circumstances weighed heavily, particularly at a first appearance. Panel members might well argue that their avoidance of highly emotive topics was justified in the interests of the child. Later in this chapter we refer to those occasions where hearings asked either the child or parent to leave, presumably to allow greater freedom for discussion of difficult or embarrassing topics.

TABLE 8.7

REPORT ITEMS AFFECTING DISCUSSION OF 'FAMILY ATTITUDES'

	Hearings in which 'family attitudes' are discussed %
Reports indicate:	
no comment on mother's personality	72
mother is dominant, aggressive	56
mother is anxious, inadequate, withdrawn	59
mother is caring, concerned	72
mother has a criminal history	33
no comment on father's personality	68
father is dominant, aggressive	68
father is anxious, inadequate, withdrawn	73
father is caring, concerned	72
father has a criminal history	50
no comment on personality of siblings or normal behaviour in siblings	69
delinquency of siblings	65
no comment on parents as disciplinarians	70
inadequate parental discipline	70
strict parental discipline	63
normal parental discipline	61
no reference to parental conflict	67
severe parental conflict	73
separation of parents	72
some parental conflict	68
no reference to violence between parents	69
some violence between parents	61
no reference to violence between parent and child	69
some violence between parent and child	59
no reference to mental illness in parent	69
mental illness in parent	63
no reference to heavy drinking in parent	71
heavy drinking in parent at present	61
heavy drinking in parent in past	53
no reference to family relationships in general	62
good family relationships	67
some family relationship problems	71
very poor family relationships	80
currently stable but history of poor family relationships	64

Aspects of style at children's hearings

In addition to noting the topics discussed at our sample of hearings we tried to identify certain styles of speaking or of relating to the child and parent. These styles were inferred from the words spoken and from the tone of voice.

At the pilot stage we were able to identify eight different styles which among them covered most of the interaction; they were also reasonably differentiating, minimized the amount of interpretation and obtained an inter-observer reliability of above 80 per cent. An average of three styles occurred in any one hearing. The frequency of some aspects of style in our sample of 301 hearings are given in Table 8.8.

Panel members regularly acknowledge that a central feature of the hearing is the open participation of the child and his family. In almost all the hearings observed a conscious effort was made to evoke this participation by using an encouraging and non-directive style. This does not mean to say that panel members were consistently non-judgmental or non-directive. It is clear from our evidence that the style we have called 'encouraging' often co-existed with approaches that were potentially more inhibiting. The encouraging, non-directive style was however observed at one stage or another at 91 per cent of all hearings. The following excerpts illustrate this particular style:

Chairman – Tell us what happened.
Child – Boy kept jabbing me with a pencil so I kicked and punched him.
Chairman – How did the police get involved?
Child – Teacher called them.
Father – They didn't tell us about it until much later. I met the boy's mother and she said he was in hospital.
Member – How do you get on at school otherwise?
Child – O.K. Sometimes I like arithmetic.

TABLE 8.8

FREQUENCY OF SOME ASPECTS OF STYLE

	%
Encouraging, non-directive, evokes participation	91
Sympathetic, understanding, listens carefully	48
Interrogating, demanding	44
Shocked, indignant, tries to elicit guilt, shame, remorse	36
Exhorts to shape up, threatens with legal consequences	35
Makes reference to positive aspects of the child	23
Sarcastic, contemptuous, suggests child guilty of other misdeeds	22
Advises parent on how to handle child	14
Mean number of styles in each hearing	3
(N = 100%)	301

Father – He has lost a lot of time through ill-health.
Chairman – Do you have a particular pal? Do you get into trouble?
Child – Got into a couple of fights.
Chairman – That's nice of you to say that because the school thinks that too.

★ ★ ★

Chairman – Why weren't you at school?
Child – I was ill some of the time and also I didn't want to go. I don't learn anything in that class. No one learns anything.
Member – What is a day at school like?
Child – Sometimes we just carry on. We get taught science properly. English is one of the worst.
Father – I think he is just truanting like his brother.
Chairman – The report says that you work hard when you are there.
Child – I do when I get peace, which is rare.

★ ★ ★

Chairman – Did you not think at all that you had to pay for these things? How did you feel when you were caught?
Child – Terrible.
Member – Now did you give any of these things away?
Mother – She takes things out of the house and gives them away.
Member – Why do you give things to your friends?
Child – To make friendship.
Mother – She doesn't have any friends of her own age.

★ ★ ★

Member – How did you come to be involved?
Child – I just broke a window. I wanted cigarettes.
Member – Have you ever done this before?
Child – No.
Member – What do you think about this?
Child – It's bad, isn't it?
Member – You don't seem to care very much.
Child – I do care about some things.
Member – What?
Child – (Shouts) My family.

★ ★ ★

Member – Why again, Kenny? Why the parking meters?
Child – Don't know.
Member – People at school are encouraging – it's a pity about this.
Child – I wanted the money.
Member – But you get caught. Why do you do it?
Child – Because it's a sin to be poor.
Member – Do you think you're poor?
Child – Aye.

★ ★ ★

A type of approach by panel members that we characterized as 'sympathetic, understanding' was observed at fractionally less than one half of all the hearings in our sample (48 per cent). Panel members listened very carefully and tried to convey their awareness of the family difficulties, and their own good intentions. It is perhaps worth noting that sympathy and understanding tended to be directed by hearings more often to the mother than to the erring child, sometimes even creating a sense of alliance among adults against him. Our interviews with clients confirmed that the helping motives of panel members were clearly recognized and appreciated, and that in spite of the 'parent to parent' orientation that we discern the children interviewed were no less positive in their assessment of the panel members' helpful intentions.

Member to Mother – Does your father give you a hand with him?
Mother – Oh, yes. I have nine children and my husband has left. My father is always willing to help with him and the others.
Member – Have you got control of him? Do you feel that you can stop him drinking wine?
Mother – Oh, yes.

★ ★ ★

Chairman to Mother – How did you feel about him?
Mother – He has been upset, perhaps by his father's visit.
Chairman – Was he close to his father?
Mother – He could answer that.
Member – Are you unhappy that you don't have a Dad at home just now?
Child – Yes.

★ ★ ★

Chairman to Mother – How on earth do you manage, living in a room and kitchen with you and the children?
Mother – I really don't know how we manage. I am to get a new house soon.
Member – She doesn't have any health problems?
Mother – Well, just her periods. They are very painful on the first day.
Chairman – Does she see the doctor?
Member – He could help.

★ ★ ★

Chairman to Mother – What did you think about all this?
Mother – Well, I warned him. I told him never to go down there.
Chairman – Do you think we are here to punish Robert?
Mother – Oh no! I know that you want to help him.
Chairman – Yes, we are very concerned to help him out of trouble.
Chairman to Mother – How do you feel about this? It's very hard to cope with five children on your own.

Mother – Well, I can cope when they are in the house but I don't know what they are doing when they are out.

★ ★ ★

Less frequent than hearings in which a sympathetic manner was apparent were those in which panel members brought into the discussion some reference to positive features of the child. We observed this at 70 hearings, or 23 per cent of the total. This approach seemed to us of considerable potential value as a means of encouraging positive participation by family members.

Member to Child – What will you do when you leave school?
Child – Well, I don't know. The teacher said she would talk to me about it.
Member – The school says that you could do quite well if you worked a bit harder.
Child – I would like to do a secretarial course.
Member – Oh, good!

★ ★ ★

Chairman to Child – Your school report is very good. No trouble there?
Child – No. I like school.
Father to Chairman – Oh, she goes to school every day.

★ ★ ★

Member to Child – Did you want to say something?
Child – Yes, I did this by myself; nobody told me to do it. He (father) is talking rubbish. I know I did wrong, it was just a notion.
Member to Child – You seem to be a very sensible boy. You've thought things through.
Social Worker – He relates very well, he is very honest.

★ ★ ★

Member to Child – You can't read. Have you ever thought of practising on your own?
Child – No.
Member to Child – How do you get on at school? What do you like?
Child – Cookery.
Member – Does the school help you?
Child – Yes, two periods a week.
Chairman – Well, it says in the report that you do make an effort at school, and you do go to school regularly. That has to be said in your favour.

★ ★ ★

Slightly less than one-half of the hearings in our sample (44 per cent) were 'interrogating and demanding' in their approach. The panel members were pushing hard to clarify and sometimes verify the information in reports, emphasizing in particular the present and earlier offences and the disadvantage to the child of continuing in a delinquent way of life.

Member – Now, can you tell me why you have decided to become a criminal?
Child – I don't know. I'm not guilty.
Member – But you are. The sheriff court proved it.
Member – What's the school attendance like?
Father – It's better. It's pretty average now.
Member – Your school record could be better, but you still haven't said whether you are going to stop becoming a criminal.

⋆ ⋆ ⋆

Chairman – How many other people were there (at the offence)?
Chairman – Do you usually go about with them? How did the offence come about? You are being set up, aren't you?
Member – Do you know what being a look-out is?
Member – Was all this planned?
Member – How did the police catch up with you?
Member to Father – Do you know about this?

⋆ ⋆ ⋆

Chairman to Child – Can you remember getting into trouble for trespassing in a garage? Come on Robert!
Child – No, I don't remember.
Reporter – There is no record of this.

⋆ ⋆ ⋆

Member to Child – Will your friends think more of you now that you've been away?
Child – No.
Member – Have you felt disgraced?
Child – No.
Member – Sin is fun is that it? You get a lot of kicks out of it, don't you? That's terrible.

⋆ ⋆ ⋆

Member – 1975 was the firearms, 1977 was the theft and now 1979.
Mother – He was cleared of the theft.
Member – Oh yes, no action.

⋆ ⋆ ⋆

Less common than an interrogating style at hearings was the expression of shock by panel members. This was noted at 36 per cent of our sample. Panel members were trying here to elicit guilt, shame or remorse in the hope that the child would modify his behaviour.

Member – I think she's mad. It's quite obvious she doesn't think much about this system.
Child – (Silent)
Member – We've come to the end of the road with you.

* * *

Member to Child – Were you on your own?
Child – Yes.
Member to Child – Why did you only steal some of the things?
Child – (No answer)
Mother – I don't know why she took the fat; I always have fat and she had enough money to pay for it.
Chairman – Do you know the difference between right and wrong?
Child – Yes.
Chairman – You hurt your Mum and Dad; did you like that?

* * *

Chairman – Well, what about this cheque then?
Child – We just did it for a lark.
Chairman – Well, think of it in these terms: that was someone's money for the week, someone's living, their bread and butter. What if someone stole your watch? How awful – especially if you have saved for it yourself.

* * *

Member – Your father is having a hard time. He's a widower. Do you realise what he's trying to do – keep the family together?

* * *

Chairman – What about your mates, or is that a sore point?
Child – (No answer)
Chairman – Do they come from the same type of home as you?
Child – Yes.
Chairman – Oh no, they don't. They come from homes where their parents don't care. Come on, you can pick your friends.

* * *

The use of threats came into 35 per cent of our sample of hearings. Here panel members advised the youngster to mend his ways and warned him about the legal consequences of failure to conform to society's standards.

Member – What about the theft of the bikes?
Child – I don't remember what happened.
Member – Try!

Father – I think it was just joyriding.
Member – Oh, you're not on!
Member – Yes, stop giving us a load of junk. We're not stupid you know. You've got to stop all this Al Capone stuff – you think it's funny. You'll be in court next time.
Chairman – Why did you do it?

* * *

Child – I just went up to town and thought I'd lift them. Got caught.
Member – What do you feel about it?
Member – Now, I see you laughing. It's not funny at all. You are a thief, you know.
Child – Mum hit me when I came home.
Member – Thou shall not steal! Don't laugh about it.
Chairman – You've got to pull up your socks.

* * *

Chairman – Now you have sampled List D. You could have walked right into it again. How would you feel about that?
Child – I wouldn't want that.

* * *

A sarcastic, contemptuous approach was observed at 22 per cent of the hearings in our sample. This usually involved casting doubt on the child's sincerity and hinting heavily at the possibility of other, undisclosed misdeeds. The objectives of this approach are not self-evident; we assume it to be in part an attempt to intensify feelings of guilt and shame and in part to be merely punitive.

Mother – A teacher struck her in the face. She had a bad black eye.
Member – You must have done something. Were you cheeky?
Child – No. He called me a tramp.
Member – Well, he must have had a reason for it.

* * *

Chairman to Child – I hope you weren't out getting into more trouble with friends this morning.
Child – No.

* * *

Chairman – Have you ever been involved in shoplifting?
Child – No.
Chairman – Well, you wouldn't admit it, would you?

* * *

Chairman – This seems a bit amateur. Have you not had any practice at this sort of thing?
Child – Once, when I was eleven, but the police just warned me because I never took anything.

* * *

Chairman to Child – Are these your friends from school?
Child – Yes.
Chairman – And in fact there are other things you have been doing: other things, is that right?
Child – (No reply)

* * *

Member to Child – I suppose you've stolen more.
Child – No.
Member – Why not? The police don't bother you.
Child – I just haven't been in town.
Member – Well, I thought you might at least have said because you knew it was wrong.

* * *

In view of the importance that panel members attach to parental responsibility, it is surprising that the opportunity to offer advice to parents was taken in only 14 per cent of hearings that we observed. This often took the form of suggesting to the parent how the child should be handled, drawing mainly from their own personal experience of bringing up a family.

Member – Do you think she's improved?
Father – Oh yes.
Member – How would you cope with her at home if she told lies?
Father – I'd put her straight to bed.
Member – But you can't do that with a 12 year old.
Mother – I'd like to have her home. I know you're trying to help, but she'd be better at home.
Member – What could you do to help if she came home?
Father – Oh, I'd keep her in.
Member – You can't keep her in all the time.
Father – I could take her swimming.

* * *

Chairman – Are you still friends with the other boy?
Child – Yes.
Mother – They are in the same class at school.
Member – You seem to get a fair amount of pocket money. What do you do with it?
Child – Football and pictures.
Chairman to Parents – You will have to watch him with his friends, you know.

* * *

Social Worker – Her mother was so afraid to let her stay off even although she has had a badly sprained ankle.

Chairman to Mother – You really shouldn't back away from problems. You should find out what's happening in this sort of situation.

* * *

Chairman to Mother – Don't you think this is a pattern starting here?

Mother – I don't know.

Chairman to Mother – How do you feel about this? It is very hard to cope on your own.

Mother – I can cope when they are in the house, but I don't know what they are doing when they are out.

Member to Mother – They are very uncommunicative. I think you should start talking things out with them. They seem afraid to talk.

* * *

Member to Mother – I am sure Aileen thinks a lot of what you have to say. You should give her encouragement to do well at school. I am sure she would do well.

* * *

In addition to those aspects of panel members' style which were recorded during hearings, we also took account of the presence or absence of certain modes of speech or questioning. Whether or not open questions were asked seemed to us important. We observed such questions at 89 per cent of all hearings, a basic measure of good practice which was well-nigh universal. However, we also found that closed questions were employed in 73 per cent of hearings, suggesting that linguistic devices likely to discourage discussion as well as those intended to stimulate it co-exist in the majority of hearings. Three other types of speech were noted, on the grounds that however motivated, they seemed distinctly unlikely to encourage the child or his parents to participate freely in the discussion. We recorded those occasions on which one panel member whispered to another in the course of the hearing, or made some attempt to conceal what he was saying; this occurred in exactly one-sixth of all the hearings observed. The second speech practice recorded was the use of the imperative mood, as in 'Now, pay attention!' or 'Listen to me!'; this was employed in slightly more than one in four of all hearings. Finally we noted that panel members interrupted and blocked the response of child and parent in 11 per cent of our sample.

When aspects of style are inter-correlated only a handful display statistically significant associations (Table 8.9). Hearings that are encouraging and sympathetic tend not to be characterized by styles that are interrogating, sarcastic or shocked in their approach. These negative styles tend to accompany one another.

We know from our observation of hearings that they leave undiscussed many of the sensitive and potentially stressful circumstances described in the professional reports. If these matters are material to the decision and non-disclosure cannot be justified on grounds that disclosure would be detrimental to the interests of the child, panel members are in breach of one of the main tenets of natural justice embodied in the Children's Hearings Rules (Rules 17(3) and 19(4)).

It is commonly believed by panel members that hearings are best conducted with all family members present and that because the child will be so familiar with the family problems, discussion is unlikely to be inhibited by his presence. This was reflected in our sample of 301 hearings: the child was asked to leave in six cases and the parent in only two. Both parents have a right to be present at all stages of the hearing (1968 Act, S.41(1)) but this does not prohibit inviting parents to leave; there are no corresponding rights accorded to the child.

In those cases occurring in our sample where the child was asked to leave, the panel members discussed with the parents their marital problems, their heavy drinking and features of the child's difficult behaviour.

In interviews with children without the parents being present the panel members posed questions about family relationships: in one case the girl was alleged to have been seduced by mother's 'friend' and in the second instance the boy was said to be on very bad terms with mother's 'friend' who was present at the hearing.

The circumstances of these eight cases were unusual but not unique. Issues no less emotive lay in the background of many hearings but were never brought to the fore. There is some reason to believe that other hearings might have benefited from discussion with child or parent alone. Instead many were characterized by the evasion of sensitive problems and a concentration on topics deemed 'safe' and 'manageable' but often of limited relevance to the needs of the child in the case.

TABLE 8.9

INTER-CORRELATION OF STYLE ITEMS

	r
Positive correlations significant at 0·01 level:	
encouraging × sympathetic	0·13
interrogating × sarcastic	0·30
interrogating × shocked	0·24
interrogating × threatens	0·15
interrogating × interrupts	0·15
interrogating × advises parent	0·14
sarcastic × shocked	0·16
shocked × threatens	0·19
Negative correlations significant at 0·01 level:	
encouraging × interrogating	−0·18
sympathetic × interrogating	−0·28
sympathetic × sarcastic	−0·18
sympathetic × shocked	−0·14

Conclusion

Children's hearings are private events where panel members are required to observe strictly the rule of confidentiality (Rules 6(3) and (4)). We were therefore highly privileged to be given access by the hearing chairmen and to be permitted to record sufficient of the dialogue to allow some clear impressions of the way hearings carry out their task. While inferences can be drawn from this study it is important to bear in mind that our sample of 301 hearings was only 3 per cent of the total held annually and that the recorded dialogue was made up of excerpts selected impromptu by the observers. Although for these reasons our account cannot be fully comprehensive the findings may be taken to signify a number of trends and patterns of practice.

Given the rich content and variety of stylistic devices discussed above, it is now our intention to look at the way in which these were employed in the fulfilment of both formal and informal objectives outlined at the beginning of this chapter.

In order to identify the child's interests, one of the key statutory requirements, panel members focused on a number of obvious areas of enquiry that are usually included in the reports, such as attendance record and behaviour at school, and behaviour at home and in the community. They seemed to look for formal and informal responsibilities of children and parents in respect of these areas of life and sometimes to offer suggestions about ways of approaching these that might be more constructive. A good deal of the dialogue did not appear to reflect any systematic searching for the specific etiology of the child's behaviour nor did it reasonably indicate any consideration of the implications of various possible dispositions. Panel members, like the authors of reports, did not appear to make use of a coherent framework of ideas concerning the causes of delinquency. What is more surprising, they rarely in the course of the hearing applied the theories of delinquency to which we know they adhere. In *Chapter 11* we discuss the importance panel members attach to parental inadequacy as a factor in the etiology of delinquency; yet in the hearing the dialogue gave little hint of this and parents themselves did not leave with the impression that their influence was believed to be crucial.

To attain the formal objectives implies a model derived from an ideal of professional practice in the child care field – one in which assessment of the child's interests and choice of the most appropriate course of action are based on a framework of knowledge about the developmental process. It would be very optimistic to assume that professional practice itself always conforms to this ideal, and if laymen with limited training sometimes fall short of this standard, the observer should be neither surprised nor in the long term unduly dismayed.

The informal goals adopted by panel members were in large measure fulfilled. The dialogue was rich in examples of moral disapproval of the behaviour that resulted in the child's presence at the hearing and panel members were observed regularly to be warning the child about the dangers of a delinquent way of life. They were observed to communicate to the parents the importance of their exercising certain influences on the child's conduct but this tended to be done in a more indirect fashion avoiding any possible confrontation with the parents.

What panel members strikingly did not do in the language of hearings was echo the terminology and thought processes of any professional group. Morris (1978)[2] remarks: 'Not only were hearing members *selected* primarily on the advice of social workers, but they were also *trained* by them.' Whatever the accuracy of this statement so far as the particular places and times to which it refers are concerned, it bears no resemblance to anything that has happened in selection or training throughout Scotland during at least the past five years. The imperviousness of panel members to social work or any other professional language and ideology is manifest in our study of the dialogue of hearings. The richness of the discussion lies in the variety and intensity with which the common man responds to the life style of others and tries where possible to locate points at which some pressure for change can be applied.

NOTES

1. D. J. West and D. P. Farrington, *Who Becomes Delinquent?* Heinemann Educational Books, 1973.
2. Allison Morris in collaboration with Mary McIsaac, *Juvenile Justice?* Heinemann, 1978, p. 116.

9

PARTICIPATION

THE HEARING'S SELF-IMPOSED TASK of involving child and parents in frank and open discussion, of encouraging them to confront their difficulties and perhaps find some new paths forward, is in reality a dauntingly difficult one. Panel members and family members will almost certainly be strangers to one another; and in the cities at any rate even the panel members may perhaps never have worked together before. The two sides do not meet as equals, and would not do so even if there were less dissimilarity of social background than is at present generally the case. Although the hearing is not a court of law and does not have punishment as its aim, the child is present under compulsion and both he and his parents are likely to take it for granted that he is there principally because he is alleged to have committed an offence. Given also the limited time available even in a relatively extended hearing and given a national character that tends towards the reserved and taciturn rather than the outgoing and loquacious, the obstacles in the way of achieving even an approximation to an ideal hearing are clearly formidable. Yet panel members themselves are convinced, as the findings reported in *Chapter 11* indicate, that informality and ease of communication are the hallmarks of the good hearing and the good panel member.

The skills required for successful performance in this part of the panel member's role are not easy to define in precise psychological terms. Children's Panel Advisory Committees would claim that the search for an ability to put people at their ease and to engage them in discussion plays a major part in the selection of new panel members, while usually acknowledging that this criterion must sometimes be balanced against considerations of community representativeness. However, the actual processes of selection are rarely described other than in the most general terms, and to the best of our knowledge no work has ever been done to validate any existing selection procedures against subsequent performance in practice. In the last three or four years it has also come increasingly to be recognized that training has a contribution to make, as well as selection, and there has been a marked growth of interest in the application of techniques for improving communications skills. But so far only a small proportion of serving members can have undergone training of this kind; while the development of training methods that are relevant and appropriate to this distinctive task is still at an extremely early stage.[1]

There is no single or uniquely accurate means of assessing the extent to which hearings are successful in actively involving the child and parents in their proceedings. Obviously, the ways in which the events are experienced by the young people and by the adults provide very important indications; we have examined these and obtained fairly clear-cut findings but do not see them as the only possible sources of relevant information. The feelings of satisfaction or disappointment of which panel members are conscious at the conclusion of a hearing might also contribute useful evidence, but we made no provision for gathering such information in our studies. Our principal data, apart from the interviews reported in later chapters, are derived from our observations of the actual events of 301 hearings. Our emphasis in these observations was not on generalized ratings of performance, which involve a high degree of subjectivity and are easily influenced by the values and prior assumptions of the observer, but rather on dispassionate recording of actions and reactions so far as that is possible. Of course, interpretation cannot be wholly avoided, and is implicit in the very act of classifying speech or posture. To classify statements or questions as 'sarcastic' or 'encouraging', or to describe someone as 'alert' or 'passive' is to draw inferences from what is seen and heard, with the attendant risk that intentions or underlying attitudes may sometimes be misinterpreted or the impact of words misjudged. As *Chapter 4* explains, we have recognized throughout this project that total objectivity is unattainable in any study of ongoing social processes, but have asserted nevertheless that it should be the goal of the research worker to reduce the risks of bias and subjective distortion to the lowest levels possible, particularly by means of an emphasis on specificity in observation and recording and the maintenance of a high degree of inter-observer agreement.

Two types of assessment of the responses of children and parents are summarized in Tables 9.1 and 9.2. One of these sums up the level of participation in the hearing by each family member and the other sets out our estimates of the overall mood of each during the course of the hearing. The former table is largely self-explanatory, the levels of participation ranging from complete silence to active questioning and direct expression of opinion. Mood is obviously more difficult to assess, and inevitably involves a major element of subjective judgment on our part. It is of course possible for more than one mood to be displayed by a participant in a given hearing, and our practice in the few such cases that arose was never to give the benefit of the doubt; if tears, anger or opposition were apparent, as well as a less stressed response at another stage of the hearing, it was the former and not the latter that was coded. The percentages in each column are based on the number of relevant observations, and not on the total sample size; the second and third columns in both tables refer to the number of hearings at which the child's mother and father respectively were present, and the very slight shortfall in the 'child' columns is brought about by a few instances when the child in question was too young for an assessment of mood or participation to be appropriate.

Bearing in mind our earlier discussion of the inescapable obstacles to open communication it can be argued that the data presented in these tables, though far from confirming that all hearings achieve an optimal level of family participation, indicate a degree of success that is by no means discreditable. Slightly less than one-quarter of all the children respond only minimally, and rather more than that participate actively in the discussion. Half of the mothers who attend and three-fifths of the fathers ask questions and/or express their own ideas. Active parental participation at this level, unlike that of children, is more frequent than the mere answering of questions – in the case of fathers, significantly more frequent. Only about one parent in every 12 goes through the hearing either in silence or replying monosyllabically to panel members' questions. As far as mood is concerned, it is the relatively high frequency of the category 'attentive, serious' that is perhaps the most striking feature of this table. It is between two and three times as common as 'comfortable, at ease'. In the case of children, negative or passive reactions are distinctly more common than 'comfortable' ones, though in aggregate a little less so than 'attentive' responses. Among mothers, nervous or anxious moods outweigh relaxed ones, though not very greatly, while 'attentive' or 'serious' moods are more than twice as common. Fathers are the most 'serious' of all, and are

TABLE 9.1

LEVEL OF PARTICIPATION BY CHILD AND PARENTS

	Child %	*Mother* %	*Father* %
Is silent throughout	1	6	4
Says 'Yes', 'No' or 'Don't know' only	21	3	3
Answers questions more fully	50	41	32
Asks questions, speaks out	28	50	61
(N = 100%)	295	254	173

TABLE 9.2

MOOD OF CHILD AND PARENTS

	Child %	*Mother* %	*Father* %
Cries	5	3	—
Shows anger	3	2	2
Expresses opposition	2	1	2
Combinations of above	2	2	—
Comfortable, at ease	22	19	23
Attentive, serious	40	54	62
Passive, withdrawn, blank	14	4	8
Anxious, nervous, ill at ease	12	14	4
(N = 100%)	295	154	173

described as 'at ease' more often than they are withdrawn, anxious or angry – the only participants of whom this is true. One child in twenty is in tears at some point, and one mother in thirty; but no fathers.

Level of participation and quality of mood are not, of course, unrelated to one another. Tables 9.3–9.5 show separately for children, mothers and fathers the degrees of participation associated with variations in mood, and

TABLE 9.3

CHILD'S PARTICIPATION IN RELATION TO CHILD'S MOOD

Mood	*Participation*				N
	Silent %	*Yes/No/DK* %	*Answers* %	*Asks, speaks* %	
Tears, anger, opposition	3	26	40	31	35
Comfortable, at ease	2	12	31	55	65
Attentive, serious	1	8	69	22	119
Passive, withdrawn	2	64	31	2	42
Anxious, nervous	—	21	53	27	34

TABLE 9.4

MOTHER'S PARTICIPATION IN RELATION TO MOTHER'S MOOD

Mood	*Participation*				N
	Silent %	*Yes/No/DK* %	*Answers* %	*Asks, speaks* %	
Tears, anger, opposition	—	5	27	68	22
Comfortable, at ease	—	—	16	84	49
Attentive, serious	4	1	49	44	138
Passive, withdrawn	(40)	(20)	(40)	—	10
Anxious, nervous	6	6	54	34	35

TABLE 9.5

FATHER'S PARTICIPATION IN RELATION TO FATHER'S MOOD

Mood	*Participation*				N
	Silent %	*Yes/No/DK* %	*Answers* %	*Asks, speaks* %	
Tears, anger, opposition	—	—	—	(100)	8
Comfortable, at ease	—	3	13	85	39
Attentive, serious	2	1	40	57	107
Passive, withdrawn	31	23	46	—	13
Anxious, nervous	(17)	—	(33)	(50)	6

indicate that the patterns of association, though broadly similar, are not identical for the different family members. Being 'comfortable' or 'at ease' is most likely to be associated with active participation in all three instances; but a negative or hostile mood is very nearly as likely to be linked with an active response in mothers and indeed more likely in the very small number of fathers for whom a mood of 'anger' or 'opposition' is reported, while children who are similarly affected are a good deal less likely to speak out or ask questions than those boys and girls who are at their ease. Children who are 'attentive, serious' are only one-third as likely to participate actively as they are to answer questions fully, but 'attentive, serious' mothers speak out and ask questions as often as they answer them, and fathers for whom this, the commonest mood, is recorded respond at the former level more frequently than at the latter. Very few parents are described as 'passive, withdrawn', with the low level of participation that that inevitably implies, though 42 children fall into this category, for the most part participating in hearings only minimally. Extremely few fathers are classed as 'anxious, nervous' but the not insignificant minorities of children and mothers who are thus characterized tend to have fairly low levels of participation.

The different styles adopted by panel members and the various topics raised for discussion in hearings have been described in *Chapter 8*, which summarized their relative frequencies and their inter-correlations. The same chapter also made it clear that the average hearing deals with at least five different topics and deploys at least three different styles, thus dismissing any suggestion that hearings can be characterized simply in terms of a dominant style or theme. Is there any relationship between, on the one hand, the subject-matter of children's hearings and the attitudes adopted by panel members and, on the other, the extent to which children and their parents participate in the proceedings? The short answer is that although some ways of conducting a hearing are rather more or rather less likely to evoke an active response from clients, there are no simple or clear-cut relationships. Conversational styles that are effective with children may have a negative effect upon parents, and vice versa; and none, it must be said, makes a really major impact on the extent to which family members contribute to the discussion.

A minimal level of participation on the part of the child – that is to say, silence or a monosyllabic response only – tends to be more common when panel members offer advice to his parents or issue orders or instructions, and are least apparent when his positive aspects are emphasized or when a sympathetic style is adopted. A comparatively high frequency of active participation – in the sense of the child asking questions or speaking out openly – is associated with panel members' reference to his positive features. Panel members' styles also influence the mood as well as the observed participation level of children. Interruption, and the use of the imperative are both disproportionately likely to evoke anger or opposition (coded together as 'negative'), though the use of sarcasm or exhortation has only a minute influence on the frequency of these reactions. Advice to parents generates nervousness in the child, as to a lesser extent does the use of sarcasm. Advice to parents, sarcasm and the use of the imperative have a greater than average chance of producing passivity or withdrawal. Children are clearly most often comfortable or at ease when their positive features are brought into the discussion, least often in the face of interruption, advice to parents or expressions of shock.

With one or two exceptions, the topics discussed at hearings seem to have less effect on the mood and participation level of the child than do the stylistic devices adopted by panel members. Silence or monosyllabic responses are most common when drugs or alcohol are brought into the discussion, least common when the child's future plans are discussed. No content item is associated with a notably low proportion of children speaking out openly or asking questions, and only references to the child's prior record or to his future plans seem to be capable of raising that proportion perceptibly above the average. On the other hand, the discussion of prior record has some tendency to produce a hostile or angry response in children, as does reference to the child's behaviour at home. References to prior record or future plans produce passive or withdrawn moods more often than do references to family stresses or to drugs and alcohol, but the differences are small. The discussion of future plans leads to more attentive or serious responses than do other content items, mention of drugs or alcohol leads to fewer.

Mothers, as noted previously, have in general a higher level of participation than their children, and only 1 in 12 is silent or monosyllabic throughout the hearing. That proportion rises when a panel member uses the imperative or expresses shock, but declines when a sympathetic or – surprisingly – a sarcastic tone is adopted. An above average tendency to ask questions or speak out is associated with the use of a sympathetic style, while this level of active participation is negatively correlated with expressions of shock or the use of the imperative by panel members, and with references to positive aspects of the child, balanced by less involvement on the part of the mother. The extent of mothers' active participation in hearings is rather more sensitive to variations in the topics discussed than is the level of children's participation. Consideration of family stresses leads to a marked increase in the percentage of mothers speaking freely, while mention of the child's behaviour at home is associated with a small increase. Active involvement on the part of mothers is at its lowest when the child's past (in the sense of his prior record) and his future (that is, his plans) are under discussion. This reduced level of participation presumably offsets the comparatively heavy involvement of the children themselves when these subjects arise.

Panel member styles affect some of the moods of mothers perhaps more strikingly than they influence levels of participation. The proportion of mothers judged to be 'serious' or 'attentive' drops when panel members are sarcastic and rises when panel members express shock or offer advice; but the variations are within fairly narrow limits. More strikingly, both advice and sarcasm double the percentage of 'nervous' or 'anxious' mothers, but produce little anger or antagonism. 'Nervous, anxious' reactions are also generated by the use of the imperative and, to a lesser extent, by an interrogating style. Few mothers are 'comfortable' or 'at ease' when at the receiving end of advice, and this mood is also relatively infrequent when shock is expressed or orders given. It is above rather than below average however in the face of both exhortation and interruption. Anger or opposition is not often expressed by mothers; when it occurs it is more commonly linked with references to contacts with the social worker or to family stresses.

Fewer fathers than mothers attend hearings, but the level of involvement of those who come is high. Silence or monosyllabic replies are rare, but the use of sarcasm by panel members doubles their frequency. Sarcasm does not however reduce the *average* level of participation; it reduces the number of fathers who 'answer questions fully', but increases the frequency of questioning and outspoken responses. As many fathers, in short, are stimulated by sarcasm to assert themselves as are reduced to silence. Asking questions or speaking out openly is the commonest response of fathers whatever styles panel members employ; it is only in those hearings where panel members express shock that the proportion of fathers participating actively falls even marginally below three-fifths.

The moods as well as the participation levels of fathers are influenced by panel members' styles. Both angry and opposed moods and nervous and anxious moods are less common in fathers than mothers. Both are expressed more frequently in the face of sarcasm, and negative reactions are particularly noticeable among fathers when advice is offered to the parents by panel members; advice does not however lead to any increase in nervous or anxious moods. The expression of sympathetic attitudes reduces both types of stressed reaction. Fathers' moods are assessed as 'comfortable, at ease' less often when panel members are sarcastic, are shocked, interrupt, offer advice or give orders. The last-named panel member style is also associated with an increase in the frequency of 'passive, withdrawn' moods.

Some of the contents of the hearing influence the reactions of fathers in ways similar to mothers, some produce rather different responses. For fathers as for mothers, references to family stresses are associated with a high level of participation, and discussion of the child's future plans with a distinctly low level. But consideration of the child's prior record raises the level of participation for fathers, though it has the reverse effect on mothers. This latter topic however seems to be associated with relatively more frequent 'nervous, anxious' moods among fathers, though the level of occurrence remains very low. That apart, there are extremely few indications of any relationships between the content of hearings and the moods attributed to fathers. Indeed, it must be emphasized that most of the differences discussed in the preceding pages, of mood and participation level in relation to both stylistic features of hearings and subject matter discussed, are of modest scale. Certainly there are no massive differences; nor would it be realistic to expect very clear-cut relationships, given the diversity of styles and discussion topics that is characteristic of the average hearing.

In analysing family participation in hearings, we have tended to use implicitly a rather simple model of the processes involved. That is to say, the styles adopted consciously or unconsciously by the hearing chairman and by the other panel members, and to a perhaps lesser extent the topics introduced into the conversation, have been discussed with the assumption that these were in effect the stimuli eliciting responses from the family members present, responses that we tried to identify in terms of both underlying mood and overt level of participation. Given the dominant position of the panel members within the hearing, this seems a reasonable working hypothesis. It is clear however that a large part of the observed variation in family involvement cannot be accounted for in this way.

Part of the unexplained residue may be attributable to aspects of 'style' that we have been unable to capture – personality traits or acquired skills which find expression in forms too subtle to be encapsulated in one or other of the categories that we have employed but which are capable of influencing the quality of response by child and parents. Again, we need ultimately to take account of the fact that three panel members are involved, often differing from one another in respect of many social and psychological dimensions; how the interaction between them affects the reactions of family participants raises methodological problems of great complexity, not so far explored. It would also be fallacious to assume that the child and his parents have merely the role of respondents, with a capacity for participation depending solely on the skills and temperaments of the panel members facing them. No less than the panel members, the child who is called before a hearing and the parents who accompany him bring into the situation their own life-histories, their own personalities and expectations. Some of these may militate against active participation in the hearing even if the panel members involved possess and deploy every conceivable skill. In other instances, even the most inept panel member may be unable to hinder family members in their expression of views.

One of the central if implicit assumptions of the hearings system is that full and open discussion is more likely to give rise to a decision appropriate to the child's needs as well as making that decision more readily acceptable to everyone concerned. What is not built into the system however is any theory that might serve to explain why one outcome rather than another should follow particularly commonly from a given level of involvement. Yet there are in fact striking relationships between particular decision outcomes and our measures of mood and of participation; these are set out and discussed in *Chapter 11*.

We asked in an earlier chapter whether competence in the procedural aspects of children's hearings might tend to run counter to skill in opening up and maintaining free discussion within the hearing. It is now possible to examine the inter-relations between the two dimensions. Table 9.6 clearly indicates that the ability to adhere to the rules of procedure does not entail a formal and legalistic approach which hampers ease of communication.

In this table hearings are classified into three categories, according to the overall quality of procedure, as explained in *Chapter 7*. The percentages indicate, for each of the three types of hearing, what proportion of children, mothers and fathers respectively communicated freely, to the extent of asking rather than merely answering questions or by speaking out openly. The figures in brackets indicate the numbers of participants on which the percentages are based. The relationships indicated are fairly complex, and it would be an exaggeration to conclude that good procedure and good communication invariably go hand in hand. There is certainly some suggestion of a positive association. In those hearings which were 'above average' with respect to procedure a higher proportion of family participants speak freely than in procedurally 'below average' hearings. In the case of mothers the difference is quite striking, though for fathers and children it is only marginal. Children however participate slightly more often when the procedural quality is only 'average', while parents in this large middle group do not communicate less freely than when procedural standards are low. It seems that the 'formal' and 'informal' skills of panel members have a slight positive association but are to a substantial extent uncorrelated with one another. Certainly there is no evidence such as might have been predicted on some hypotheses, of one type of ability contra-indicating the other.

In all our assessments of the performance of panel members in children's hearings, we are conscious of a wide range of variation. The apparent independence of many of the measures of participation, and the difficulty of identifying clear-cut constellations of 'good' and 'bad' except perhaps at the extremes of distributions is in one important sense reassuring. It at least implies that our judgments as observers have not been distorted by 'halo-effects' – a tendency for estimates of a particular feature to be influenced by over-riding judgments of general quality. But the difficulty of establishing well-defined lines of demarcation makes it equally difficult to estimate with any honesty how many hearings are of 'good' or 'bad' quality, even in terms of the criteria applied by panel members themselves. A small proportion seem by these standards to be beyond criticism, while at the other end of the distribution curve there are as many that have very few discernible virtues. Between these extremes lie the majority of children's hearings, blending different kinds of success and failure in varying proportions.

The data leave little doubt that there is, in the language of school reports, some room for improvement. But before we consider in a later chapter by

TABLE 9.6

LEVEL OF ACTIVE PARTICIPATION BY FAMILY IN RELATION TO INDEX OF PROCEDURE

	Family member asks questions, speaks out		
	Child %	*Mother* %	*Father* %
Index of procedure			
Below average	24 (79)	49 (66)	60 (37)
Average	31 (129)	46 (118)	59 (78)
Above average	28 (87)	60 (70)	64 (58)

what means this might be accomplished, any imperfections indicated by our study must be set in perspective. They must be seen, that is to say, against the background of the obstacles to communication outlined at the opening of this chapter, obstacles which must at times appear insurmountable even to the most admirably skilled and sensitive panel member. Intrinsic difficulties should be acknowledged, and achievement be given proper credit even though it often falls well short of the ideal. Yet if the ideal can only rarely be fully achieved, it makes us aware of discrepancies and shortcomings, and acts as a safeguard against complacency.

We are conscious of the fact that although we have examined in some detail the varying qualities of children's hearings, we have not compared our findings as a whole with any external standard. It would be a good deal easier to reach some comprehensive judgment if we could, for example, compare the quality of participation in children's hearings with the levels of communication that were characteristic of the courts in which similar cases were dealt with before 1971. But no systematic study of the *modus operandi* of the Scottish courts was ever carried out. There is anecdotal evidence, and it is not always to the credit of the courts, but there is nothing at all that could be used for serious comparative purposes. It might be of even greater interest if the work of English juvenile courts could be reviewed in parallel with our examination of Scottish hearings. Yet in spite of the quite large amount of discursive literature and in spite of the sharp controversies that have surrounded the work of the juvenile courts, especially since the passage of the Children and Young Persons Act, 1969, detailed studies of the ways in which the English juvenile justice system actually operates, are virtually non-existent.

As far as the specific issue of communication in the juvenile courts is concerned, we have been able to trace only one published paper reporting an even partially relevant study. Denise Fears (1977)[2] has carried out a linguistic analysis of the speech recorded in 203 transcripts of hearings in the juvenile courts of a city and a county in South West England in 1972–73. She took as her starting point a number of comments by thoughtful and experienced magistrates to the effect that children frequently fail to understand the proceedings in which they have been involved, and that magistrates are often unable to elicit essential information, and examined her data in two ways. The transcripts were analysed so as to show the number of sentences and the number of words contributed to the court hearings by four classes of participants – magistrates, clerks, children and other family members. Drawing in rather general terms on Bernstein's distinction[3] between restricted and elaborated codes, she also compared the levels of verbal complexity in the contributions of the different groups, calculating for the speech of each of them the number of verbal particles in relation to sentences and sentence elements. That the magistrates and clerks used more complex modes of speech than children or parents will not give rise to widespread astonishment; it is interesting to note however that the speech of parents is not very much less complex, as complexity is measured in this study, than that of justices' clerks, suggesting that the distinctive features of the children's speech patterns may stem as much from their immaturity as from their social class origins. A particularly striking finding is the purely quantitative one, that children contribute only 10 per cent of the sentences uttered and only 3 per cent of the words. Mothers, fathers and children together account for 25 per cent of the sentences and 15 per cent of the words. The speech contributions of clerks and magistrates together were at least three times as great. It is clear from Fears' discussion that children's contributions to the proceedings were almost always minimal. Our data on Scottish hearings were neither gathered nor analysed in a manner directly comparable to Denise Fears', but it is hard to believe that the overall level of family participation implied by the Bristol study is greater than or even equal to that indicated by the findings presented in this chapter. To say this however is emphatically neither to deny the hearings system's shortcomings in relation to its own ideals, nor to fail to recognize the need for a further raising of standards. How such changes might be achieved is considered in a later chapter.

NOTES

1. For discussion of the development of training and of current methods and objectives *see* K. Murray, 'Children's Panel Training: learning to change', *Scottish Journal of Adult Education*, 1974, 1(2). Also, 'Representing the Community', *Times Educationsl Supplement*, 25 July 1980.
2. Denise Fears, 'Communication in English juvenile courts', *Sociological Review*, 1977, 25.
3. B. Bernstein, *Class, codes and control*. Routledge and Kegan Paul, 1971.

10

THE SUM AND SUBSTANCE OF REPORTS

CHILDREN'S DRAWINGS of hearings in which they have taken part have invariably one feature in common, the impressive piles of papers that lie on the table in front of each participant, with the exception of the child himself and his parents. The background reports provided for panel members play a part in the hearings system that is not merely symbolic; indeed, some critics have claimed that panel members do little more than endorse the recommendations that the reports incorporate.[1] The provision of reports, by social workers in particular, stems from work that has long been carried out in the adult and juvenile courts. The practice began with the requirement for the probation officer to submit a social enquiry report in support of a claim that a probation order would be a particularly appropriate disposal in any specific case. This came to be extended to a wide range of offenders, as a guide to sentencing. The growth of social enquiry work, it has been argued (Davies, 1969),[2] has developed alongside the concept of individualized sentencing. This has not of course been the only concern of the courts, for whom the need to protect society and the need to deter potential offenders have remained powerful additional considerations. 'The cardinal principle' argued the Streatfeild Report of 1961, 'is that a sentence should be based on comprehensive and reliable information which is relevant to the objectives in the court's mind'.[3]

The more extensive use of social enquiry reports has been accompanied by increased discussion of their place in the penal process and by research into their influence upon sentencers. Some research studies have focused on the examination of the levels of agreement between probation officers' recommendations and sentences imposed (Jarvis, 1965; Ford, 1972; White, 1973; Thorpe and Pease, 1976; Mott, 1977).[4] A number of attempts have been made both in official publications and in professional and research documents to provide information on the appropriate content of the social enquiry report. How the task is actually accomplished has been the subject of recent study (Thorpe, 1979; Curran, 1981).[5]

Little attention has been given to the scope, content and objectives of social enquiry reports for juvenile courts, in spite of the fact that their distinctive need for the fullest possible information on the child was confirmed as long ago as 1933, when the Children and Young Persons Act made it an obligation to obtain reports on juveniles.

The children's hearings system introduced both a new form of decision making and a new set of objectives which places still greater emphasis on matching the disposition to the individual child. Reports by professionals are an integral part of the process and apart from the discussion at the hearing, represent the main source of understanding about the child and his circumstances. Responsibility for obtaining and collating information rests with the reporter. The local authority social work department has a statutory obligation to provide a report on the child and his social background but information may also be requested from educational, psychological, psychiatric and general practitioner sources, as well as from assessment services and voluntary organizations such as the Royal Scottish Society for the Prevention of Cruelty to Children (1968 Act, S.39(4)). In view of the central place of the reports it is surprising to find that virtually no guidance is available for professionals on the presentation and content of their reports. In 1974 the Social Work Services Group issued a commentary on the preparation and presentation of social work reports to courts, hearings and to associated agencies but the document is virtually unknown to practitioners, and unlike some jurisdictions no standard format prevails. No attempt has been made to offer guidance to the authors of school, child guidance and medical reports.

Sources of reports

At 300 of 301 observed hearings[6] the panel members had available a total of 1,113 reports. Their sources are given in Table 10.1. With the exception of

TABLE 10.1

SOURCES OF REPORTS

	One report available %	*More than one report available* %	*One or more recent reports available (less than 6/12)* %
Social work	67	32	97
School	67	21	82
Assessment	14	1	12
Child guidance	10	2	7
Psychiatric	5	1	4
List D	4	3	2
RSSPCC	1	—	1
Others (police, medical, psychological)	8	2	7
(N = 100%)			300

three cases the local authority social work department fulfilled their obligation to provide background reports; seven of these reports were more than six months old. For the great majority of school age children educational reports were provided to the hearing, and 21 of these were more than six months old. Reports from assessment teams or assessment centres were available for 15 per cent of the children, a proportion substantially lower than the 25 per cent forecast in 1971 by the Social Work Services Group.[7] The services of child guidance and child psychiatry clinics also figured less prominently than might have been anticipated in a system which is concerned with obtaining the fullest possible understanding of the child and his needs. The frequency with which specialist reports were provided might have been expected to vary according to the nature of the recommendation made. In fact however reports from child guidance and child psychiatric services were no more likely to be available for children who were being recommended for residential care than for those recommended for discharge or for termination of supervision. The great bulk of the information available for the consideration of panel members in those hearings that we observed was therefore derived from social work and school reports.

The content of reports

The reporter is required to send to the panel members at least three days before the hearing a copy of the social background report and other documents (Rule 6(1)). In practice difficulties sometimes arise in adhering to the timetable and it is not unknown for panel members to receive the reports on arrival at the hearing room: in such an event the hearing has the right to adjourn or continue the case (1968 Act, S.43(3)). Panel members obtain from the reports their first impression of the child in his family, school and social circumstances. The account given of those personal and family factors which might have contributed to the grounds of referral, references to strengths within the family, school and community life and the social worker's judgment as to why the situation has arisen and possibilities now open to the hearing, all help the panel members to form tentative views about the nature of the problems and the kinds of decisions that will have to be made. The reports are also potentially an aid to the encouragement of discussion during the hearing. It should be possible to identify from them significant questions which might help to open up fruitful discussion with the family.

Our concern here is not to identify supposedly causal factors within the child's background, but rather to define the areas seen as significant by the writers of reports. What facts and ideas do social workers believe to be relevant to the decision-making of children's hearings? The information contained in the reports examined has been classified according to its focus, and comments and opinions on the child and on the family are considered separately; we have also assessed the extent to which certain broad themes and comments arose in the reports as a whole.

Table 10.2 shows the frequency with which comments are made in reports on the characteristics of the child, and records such topics irrespective of the report or reports in which each occurs. References to the child's personality are included in the reports more often than any other single feature. Personality tends to be described in very broad, general and largely evaluative terms, with occasional forays into psychiatric terminology. In 15 per cent of cases the reports give different and apparently contradictory accounts of the child's personality so that the information most frequently introduced is by no means presented consistently to the hearing.

Attendance and behaviour at school are also very regularly recorded in reports (in 89 and 88 per cent of cases respectively). This is reflected in the content of discussion at hearings which in 91 per cent of cases included reference to the school (*Chapter 8*). Frequent comment is made also on the child's intellectual level and educational achievement. The descriptions used are on the whole very imprecise but they convey to the reader a notion of the child's potential ability and educational response. Apart from noting the child's record of school attendance, his level of educational ability and attainment and his standard of general behaviour, the school reports are either negative or incomplete. There may well be a tendency for the quality of the child's relationships with teachers and with other children to receive no mention in reports unless they are judged to be unsatisfactory.

References to the child's behaviour at home are noted in reports in less than half of the cases (48 per cent). The remaining areas of comment on the child, occurring in one-fifth or less of all case papers, are not necessarily applicable to the majority of children – serious illness, psychiatric symptoms

TABLE 10.2

CONTENT OF CASE PAPERS

Comments on the child

	Cases with some reference %
Personality make-up	89
School behaviour	89
School attendance	88
Intellectual level	80
Educational attainment	71
Relations with other children	61
Leisure interests	60
Behaviour at home	48
Relations with teachers	47
Unreported delinquency	21
Serious illness or accident	20
Psychiatric symptoms	7
(N = 100%)	300

and unreported delinquency. A number of possible interpretations are open in cases where no information is provided: either the characteristic simply did not apply to the child in question, or the social worker failed to discern it, or, having identified it, the social worker chose not to mention it in the report. There is no realistic way of establishing which of these possibilities is relevant.

Table 10.3 shows the frequency of reference to a number of parental characteristics. In less than half the cases reference is made to parental co-operation with the school and other agencies (49 per cent), to the parents as disciplinarians (45 per cent) and to the personality characteristics of the parents (52 per cent and 48 per cent).

Because specific behaviour patterns such as heavy drinking and family violence appear in only a small proportion of social workers' reports it is a matter of speculation whether these were reasonably accurate estimates of the frequency of such characteristics or whether they told us only what the social workers had noticed or had been told and thought relevant to the assessment of the child. Our interest, as indicated above, is only in defining those areas of information that were brought to the notice of the panel members.

In at least three out of four cases the reports refer to the quality of family relationships. This is described in evaluative terms: in 43 per cent the family relationships are described in terms such as 'good', 'well integrated', 'supportive', 'close knit', 'fairly happy'; 17 per cent are described as experiencing conflict which had led to family breakdown and separation; 14 per cent are said to be experiencing some friction although the family has remained intact; 4 per cent are said to have stable relationships currently in spite of an earlier history of instability.

TABLE 10.3

CONTENT OF CASE PAPERS

Comments on the parents

	Reports with some reference %
Family relationships in general	77
Father's personality	52
Parental co-operation with agencies/school	49
Mother's personality	48
Parents as disciplinarians	45
Conflict between parents	40
Family known to other agencies	29
Heavy drinking in parent	18
Violence between parents	11
Diagnosed mental illness in parent	6
Violence between parents and child	6
(N = 100%)	300

In Table 10.4 we consider the reports as wholes, and summarize the frequency with which certain important general issues are raised. The categories used in this table represent our attempt to identify what seem to us significant themes in a body of material that is extremely diverse and for the most part unsystematic. We find for example that an explanation of the child's behaviour is attempted in nearly two-thirds of the cases (62 per cent). More than half of these explanations refer to family and personal factors while environment and educational factors are the next most important group brought forward in an attempt to account for the child's behaviour.

Interestingly, a feeling of pessimism (31 per cent) pervades the reports less often than a sense of hope (43 per cent) and potential for development (40 per cent). Unmet needs are mentioned in just over one quarter of the cases (27 per cent); the largest single unmet need identified is financial, followed by a need for housing and social services.

From the content analysis of the case papers it would be reasonable to conclude that in more than half of all the cases examined, the reports did not provide the hearing with information on basic features of the child's growth and development which in terms of current professional opinion, might be held essential to any realistic discussion about his future.

There is considerable variation in the quality of reports. Overall however, the general impression conveyed is of a high frequency of rather piecemeal statements which in a substantial proportion of cases fails to organize and integrate the observations into a balanced whole.

Agreement between recommendations

In the great majority of hearings the panel members have reports only from the social work department and the child's school. In all but 42 of the 300 cases the social worker's report included a recommendation. The school

TABLE 10.4

CONTENT OF CASE PAPERS

General features of reports

	With some comment %
Reports attempting to explain the child's behaviour	62
Reports drawing attention to positive or hopeful family situations	43
Reports drawing attention to strength or potential for development	40
Reports with essentially pessimistic tenor	31
Reports commenting on unmet needs in the family	27
Reports which convey a sense of change over time	21
(N = 100%)	300

report is usually expressed according to a standard format which does not allow for a recommendation; some teachers also enclose additional notes on the child and may add a recommendation, but this is not encouraged. The reports which might be expected to convey advice about the appropriate course of action are those submitted by specialist agencies such as child guidance clinics, child psychiatry units, List D schools and assessment centres.

In 27 cases the hearing had available a child guidance report, but only 10 of these gave a specific recommendation. We should not expect to find, either in this group or among the children assessed by other specialist services, more than a minority of cases in which it is possible to compare two independent recommendations. The children referred to specialist agencies tended to be those where the social worker deliberately made no recommendation or asked for some further assessment. It is surprising however that such a substantial minority of these additional reports was limited to descriptive or 'diagnostic' comment, with no indications for action. Of the 112 reports received from sources other than social work and education, 67 (or almost exactly 60 per cent) provided the hearing with a recommendation. Child guidance clinics seem to have been the most reluctant to commit themselves in this way. For only 6 of their 10 recommendations was a social worker's recommendation also available, and the two suggestions were in agreement in five instances.

Twelve of the 18 psychiatric reports included a firm recommendation to the panel members, and this coincided with the social worker's proposal in six of the seven cases where both were available. The single disagreement was a recommendation of home supervision by the psychiatrist where the social worker had been in favour of a residential order. In the one case in which social work and child guidance differed in their views, the former opted for discharge and the latter for home supervision.

Just under half the reports received from List D schools advised the hearing on disposal; all of those which could be matched against a specific social work recommendation were in agreement. Composite reports from assessment teams, some based on assessment centres, make up the majority of those in the 'other

TABLE 10.5

CORRESPONDENCE BETWEEN RECOMMENDATIONS IN PROFESSIONAL REPORTS

	No. of Reports	*Recomm. made*	*Social work recomm. made*	*Specialist and social work recomm. made*	*Agreement*	*Dis-agreement*
Source						
Child guidance	27	10	16	6	5	1
Psychiatry	18	12	11	7	6	1
List D school	15	7	12	4	4	0
Other agencies	52	38	34	24	18	6

agencies' category, which also includes reports from miscellaneous medical sources. No recommendation was put forward in 14 of these 52 reports, while for 24 children both specialist and social work recommendations were before the hearing. These were in harmony three times out of four, and the nature of the six recorded disagreements did not suggest any consistent tendency for a particular solution to be preferred by either agency.

Our findings indicate that the degree of correspondence between professional recommendations is quite high, in that minority of cases where both agencies commit themselves to a proposed course of action. The high proportion of specialist reports in which no specific guidance to the hearing is offered raises interesting questions about the role of the agencies concerned in relation to the hearings system, as seen by the decision-making panel members and by the professionals concerned.

Factors associated with social workers' recommendations

One of the mysteries of social enquiry work is what information social workers consider to be important and what particular features of a child's background and history would be more likely to influence them in favour of one recommendation rather than another. The study identified those factors in the social background reports associated with a recommendation for discharge or termination of supervision, for home supervision or its continuation, for residential supervision or continuation. The study also identified the circumstances which might have led the social worker to give no recommendation. Our emphasis here is on the elements of the reports which are correlated with particular recommendations, and not on the reasons explicitly put forward by the social worker. Some of the important elements associated with alternative recommendations are summarized in Table 10.6.

Social workers recommended discharge or termination in 83 cases (28 per cent). The number of hearings previously attended influenced the social worker's recommendation quite dramatically. Only one in every eight children appearing at their second, third or fourth hearing had discharge recommended, compared with more than one-third of those attending for the first time. After a child's fourth hearing his chances of being recommended for discharge begin to increase; by this time he might be close to the upper age limit of the hearing's jurisdiction.

Children between 8 and 12 years of age and those over 16 years had a greater likelihood of being recommended for discharge than those in other age groups. These were likely to be either children attending their first hearing or 'old lags' whose supervision was due to be ended. Those least likely to have discharge recommended were children under eight years, a small group of only six children, all of them referred on non-offence grounds.

Discharge was recommended for one in three of those children living with both parents and in a family where the head of household was fully employed compared with only one in seven of the children living with one parent in the company of others and in a family where the head of household was unemployed.

TABLE 10.6

SOCIAL WORKERS' RECOMMENDATIONS IN RELATION TO CHARACTERISTICS OF THE CHILD

	Recommendation				
	Discharge/ Sup. terminated %	*Supervision/ Continued Sup.* %	*Residential Sup./Continued Res. Sup.* %	*Other** %	N
Sex of child					
Male	28	41	13	18	244
Female	25	43	9	23	56
Age of child					
Under 12	31	51	12	6	49
12–13	25	34	18	23	68
14 or over	28	41	10	21	183
No. of previous hearings					
None	36	47	5	12	191
One	14	28	21	37	143
Two and three	10	35	28	27	29
Four to eight	18	25	39	18	28
Employment status of head of household					
Employed	35	40	10	15	156
Housewife, not employed	27	40	14	19	52
Unemployed, sick, etc.	18	47	11	24	79
Social class					
Non-manual	23	36	27	14	22
Skilled	32	44	11	13	57
Semi-skilled	33	37	6	24	49
Unskilled	21	57	7	15	28
Child normally lives with					
Both parents	34	40	9	17	174
Other	19	44	17	20	124
Intelligence of child					
Below average	25	46	9	20	147
Average	28	41	13	18	71
Above average	26	30	30	14	23
School attendance					
Good	47	44	2	7	57
Irregular	23	41	14	22	206
Educational attainment					
Below average	24	40	12	24	122
Average	33	42	8	17	60
Above average	37	33	10	20	30

* Either no recommendation made or assessment recommended.

Children in this group of discharge recommendations were more likely to be described as polite, attractive and helpful at home; they were reported to have leisure interests, to attend school regularly and to have reached average and above average standards educationally. These children lived in families that were free of the stresses of mental illness, heavy drinking and violence, at any rate so far as these features are recorded in the reports. The parents of children recommended for discharge were more likely than those for whom supervision was recommended to be described as caring, warm and firm and capable of exercising effective discipline. The families of these children were unlikely to be known to the social work department or similar agencies.

The reports on the group of children recommended for discharge were less likely to reflect pessimism, to identify unmet needs or to record any change in the child's behaviour or attitude over time. The potential of these children was most frequently described in terms of their educational attainment.

The social worker recommended initiating or continuing home supervision in 123 cases (41 per cent of our sample). The important factors that appear to have led to this recommendation were the age of the child, the number of previous hearings attended, who the child lived with and whether anything was known about the social class and about the employment status of the head of household.

Children under 12 years of age and those attending their first hearing were nearly twice as likely to have supervision recommended as those over 16 years and those who had attended more than three previous hearings. Four out of every seven children who were reported to be living in families in which the head of household was an unskilled worker were recommended for supervision as compared with 4 out of every 11 children reported to be living in middle class families. Nine out of every 16 children who were reported to be living in families where the head of household was said to be unemployed and seeking work had supervision recommended by the social worker compared with 9 out of every 22 children living in families in which the head of household was in regular employment. Neither the social class difference nor that associated with employment status is however statistically significant.

The recorded personal and educational characteristics of the child had no association with the social worker's choice of recommendation although there were one or two features that made it unlikely that home supervision would be recommended. Children with high intelligence who were reported to display psychiatric symptoms and whose behaviour at home was said to be deteriorating were very much less likely to have home supervision recommended than children of dull intelligence who were free of psychiatric symptoms and whose behaviour at home was not reported to have changed over time.

In contrast, the social worker's knowledge of a family's criminal history is strongly associated with a particular recommendation being made. Supervision was recommended for 7 of the 10 children whose fathers were reported to have criminal records, for two of three children whose mothers were reported as criminal and for 10 of 17 children with siblings said to be delinquent.

When parental conflict was identified in the reports the social worker was inclined to recommend supervision but if the conflict was described as severe a supervision recommendation was much less likely to be made.

In one-third of the cases where home supervision was recommended the reports identified an unmet need in the family. When the family's need for better housing was recorded the social worker was nearly two and a half times more likely to recommend supervision than in those cases where marital stability and improved family relationships appeared to represent the greatest need.

When the reports pointed to an improvement in parental attitudes, in the child's behaviour at home and in his attitude, behaviour and attendance at school, the social worker was more inclined to recommend supervision than in a situation which appeared to be deteriorating.

From this analysis it would appear that a recommendation to initiate or continue supervision is more likely to be made for a child of primary school age, attending his first hearing, living in poor social and environmental circumstances and whose parents are in some conflict or are reported to have criminal histories.

In 37 cases (12 per cent) the recommendation made by the social worker was that a residential supervision order should be made or continued. The recorded factors most closely associated with this recommendation were the number of hearings at which the child had previously appeared and the regularity of school attendance. A child who enters the hearing room for at least the fourth time is eight times more likely to be recommended for residential care than a child making his first appearance. Irregular attendance at school is almost eight times more likely to lead the social worker to this choice than a report that a child is attending school regularly.

The age of the child was also influential. A child between 8 and 12 years was much less likely to be recommended for residential care than a child under eight years and a child between 12 and 14 years.

The social worker was also more likely to recommend residential care for children from families in which the head of household followed a middle class occupation (as defined by the Registrar-General's Classes I, II and III (non-manual)), for children with high intelligence, for those reported to have psychiatric symptoms and for those who were living in a household containing one of its parents (either father or mother) together with other adults.

Difficult behaviour at home was also more likely to be associated with the social worker recommending residential care, but on the other hand the child's behaviour at school and his relations with teachers and other children appear to have carried no weight. Certain family characteristics were however influential – especially references in the reports to parental conflict, to violence between parents or to their current pattern of heavy drinking.

Children recommended for residential care by the social worker were more likely than others to be described in reports as having good potential in their character and personality but to be living in families that were said to lack stability and hope for the future.

In 42 cases (14 per cent) the social worker's report did not include a specific recommendation. In some cases the absence of a recommendation was associated with reports containing only a limited range of information; in others however the social worker was not inhibited by the gaps in the information he had gathered from making a recommendation.

When information was lacking on the family structure – the number of siblings, whether the head of household was fully employed, who the child lived with – social workers were in general less likely to make any recommendation. This also tended to be the case if the reports included no reference to the child's school attendance, to his intellectual level and range of leisure interests, to his personality and the behaviour of his siblings.

Some specific factors appear to be associated with the absence of a recommendation, though the relevance of the connection is not always obvious. For example, the social worker was more likely to withhold a recommendation as the child grew older. His report was less likely to include a recommendation at the child's second hearing than at any other. Children living with both parents or with foster parents were also more likely to have no recommendation made by the social worker than children who were in the care of a single parent. In general the social worker had little confidence in making a recommendation when the reports referred to negative aspects of the child's personal development and to unfavourable parental characteristics.

Reasons for recommendations

So far we have looked at those items that appear in reports that seem to be correlated with particular recommendations to hearings. These are not necessarily identical with the reasons that social workers actually put forward in support of their recommendations. The great variety of reasons adduced by social workers are classified in Table 10.7. This table sets out the relative frequency with which different reasons were advanced to justify alternative recommendations.

Discharge or termination had the most clear-cut pattern of reasons. These recommendations were most commonly justified by reference to the child's good home background and personal history. Under this heading we included such items as 'good quality of care in the family', 'good attitude to school', 'uses leisure time constructively', 'realises the seriousness of the offence', 'out of character', 'general improvement in child, family or both'. The only other argument used with any frequency in favour of discharge or termination was the child's age – either very low or very high – or that adequate support was already available through alternative sources.

The recommendation to initiate or continue supervision was usually backed up by one of two major reasons. These we have called 'care' and 'positive control' which together accounted for more than four-fifths of all the reasons given for a recommendation of home supervision. By 'care' we refer to such arguments as 'to offer support for the family', 'encourage the child to discuss his problems', 'protect the child', 'to understand the child better', 'to pursue special help', 'to benefit the child'. Under 'positive control' we include such reasons as 'to prevent further trouble', 'to help avoid bad company', 'to reinforce the importance of school attendance', 'to provide a structured environment', 'to bring home the seriousness of the offence', 'to show that these actions will not be condoned by society', 'to give the situation time to improve', 'because it worked well in the past'.

The pattern of reasons for recommending residential supervision or its continuation was different and more diffuse. Three types of argument together accounted for 75 per cent of all reasons given. These were more or less evenly divided between 'care' (which was an argument much less commonly used in favour of residential care than supervision in the community), 'positive control' (which was also used to justify non-residential supervision but a good deal more frequently), and 'negative control' which accounted for 25 per cent of all these recommendations but hardly appeared when any other recommendation was sustained: 'negative control' included such reasons as 'total lack of co-operation', 'too soon to give up', 'constant absconding', 'not responding to other forms of supervision', 'no alternative'. There was also a small category of reasons which we called 'negative reasons'; this was made up mainly of comments on the child's failure to benefit from any other course of action.

TABLE 10.7

SOCIAL WORKERS' REASONS IN SUPPORT OF RECOMMENDATIONS

	Recommendation					
Reason put forward	*Discharge/ Terminate Supervision* %	*Supervision/ Continued Supervision* %	*Residential Supervision/ Continued Residential Supervision* %	*Assessment/ Other* %	*No Recommendation* %	*All cases* %
No reason given	2	3	8	7	86	15
Positive control	1	37	24	27	—	20
Negative control	2	2	24	7	—	5
Care	2	46	27	33	—	24
Good home background	58	6	3	—	—	19
Age	13	2	—	—	—	5
Negative reasons	8	2	11	7	10	6
Support already available	12	1	—	—	—	4
Other	—	2	3	20	5	3
Per cent of all recommendations	28	41	12	5	14	100
(N = 100%)	83	123	37	15	42	300

Summary and conclusions

The provision of professional reports for children's hearings is in an important sense a continuation of a long-established tradition. But whereas reports prepared for the courts by probation officers or social workers were intended to provide a guide to sentencing, those submitted to children's hearings have a dual function. They are expected to offer information which will help guide panel members to an appropriate decision, and indeed in most cases they will include a specific recommendation. In addition however they introduce a series of points of departure for the discussion between panel and family members. The current study of the reports available at 300 hearings does not justify us in relaxing into the complacent sense that they are adequate for these two demanding purposes. Important areas of information are often omitted, and they seem too often to have been constructed with an insufficient awareness of the needs of those who make use of them. There is too a prevailing impression of the lack of any coherent structure, arising at least in part from the absence of any general organizing theory.

For reports to be judged adequate for these purposes – and here we have in mind particularly social background reports – they would need to elicit each child's unique configuration of personal history, present circumstances and future needs. Individual items of information would be presented, not as isolated pieces of data but as elements in a whole. Overall however it is unusual to find reports that present an identifiable picture of an individual in his family and community setting. A comprehensive report would consider the alternative disposals available to the hearing and their implications against this personal backcloth, but such an approach is in fact rare.

The extent to which the decisions of hearings were influenced by the information contained in reports is discussed in a later chapter.

NOTES

1. Paul D. Brown, 'The hearing process: "telling like it is" ', in: P. D. Brown and T. Bloomfield (eds.) *Legality and Community*. Aberdeen Peoples Press, 1979.
2. M. B. Davies, 'Social inquiry for the courts', *British Journal of Criminology*, 1974, 14(1).
3. *Report of the Interdepartmental Committee on the Business of the Criminal Courts* (Streatfeild Committee), Cmnd. 1289, HMSO, 1961.
4. F. V. Jarvis, 'Inquiry before sentence': in T. Grygier, H. Jones and J. C. Spencer (eds.), *Criminology in Transition*. Tavistock, London, 1965.
   P. Ford, *Advising Sentencers*. Basil Blackwell, Oxford, 1972.
   S. White, 'The effect of social inquiry reports on sentencing offenders', *British Journal of Criminology*, 1973, Vol. 12.
   J. Thorpe and K. Pease, 'The relationship between recommendations made to the court and sentences passed', *British Journal of Criminology*, 1976, Vol. 16.
   Joy Mott, 'Decision making and social inquiry reports in one juvenile court', *British Journal of Social Work*, 1977, 7(4).
5. J. Thorpe, *Social Inquiry Reports: A Survey*. Home Office Research Study, No. 48, HMSO, London, 1979.
   J. Curran, *Social Inquiry Reports in Scotland*. HMSO, Edinburgh, 1981.

6. According to our notes, one hearing was conducted without reports being available. On subsequent enquiry this was denied by the reporter concerned, but we were unable to check with the original file. The case has been excluded from this part of the analysis.
7. In 1971 the Social Work Services Group recommended the setting up of multi-disciplinary assessment teams which would draw together the professional expertise of those concerned with the child. There are however very few areas where this principle of joint consultation has flourished.

II

SHAPING DECISIONS

Influences on decisions

Children's hearings serve more than one purpose. But however valuable their informal functions of improving understanding and awareness, the making of decisions is in a statutory sense their *raison d'être*. If a hearing is unable to reach a decision in a particular case because there is felt to be a need for additional information, it must re-convene at the earliest opportunity so that there can be a formal 'disposal'. Although the alternatives available are few, the decisions can have important and perhaps painful consequences for the persons concerned. How effective those decisions are – that is to say, to what extent they succeed in bringing about intended changes in behaviour or attitude – lies beyond the scope of this study; we have not carried any of our enquiries beyond the point of the decisions reached at hearings. How those decisions are arrived at is however a matter of great concern to us, and we have been conscious from the beginning of the extreme difficulty of understanding the processes involved in any systematic fashion. The most nearly relevant studies we have been able to find, relating to factors influencing judicial sentencing, have not on the whole encouraged us in the view that there was any simple or reliable means of illuminating the dynamics of decision-making.

Numerous investigations in both adult and juvenile courts in several countries have drawn attention to wide variations in sentencing practices, even when attempts were made to compare decisions reached in connection with apparently similar types of offence. These variations have generally been attributed to the operation of personal factors – values, attitudes, prejudices, personality traits – on the part of the judges or magistrates concerned; such factors however have provided residual explanations, and attempts to demonstrate systematic relationships between actual measures of such factors and patterns of judicial decisions have been rare. Hood and Sparks (1970)[1] have formulated a rather elaborate model of the sentencing process, which includes such components as the judge himself, defined in terms of both 'personal' variables and 'judicial role' variables which are jointly responsible for a set of attitudes towards sentencing; the information about the offence and the offender with which the judge is confronted in a particular case; and the categories employed in evaluating that evidence and defining its relevance, which they believe is most likely to explain disparities in sentencing. Hood and Sparks' principal concern is to contest the argument that variations in sentencing practice necessarily imply arbitrariness or irrationality; individual judges, they suggest, may perfectly well be operating quite consistently within the framework of their own values and priorities. The model cannot by itself explain or predict sentencing behaviour, and its validity can only be tested when it is fed with appropriate data. What we have found puzzling about Hood and Sparks' argument is their apparent belief that by demonstrating that judicial decisions make consistent sense when seen as the expression of an internally coherent body of beliefs, one may refute charges of irrationality. But a madman who executes summary justice on people who according to his private view of the world are representatives of the Devil may be totally consistent and at the same time utterly irrational. So too may authoritarian political regimes which systematically carry out judicial murder by the application of criteria that are internally consistent but quite without rationality when judged by any independent standards.

Studies which have actually tried to relate judicial decisions to specific personal or information factors have not been numerous. Wheeler *et al.* (1968)[2] in what is from our present point of view a particularly interesting study, showed that welfare-orientated juvenile court judges seemed particularly prone to send young offenders to institutions, reflecting their belief in the rehabilitative function of custodial care. Carter and Wilkins (1967)[3] demonstrated that variations between courts in the use made of probation were associated with differences in the frequency with which probation was recommended by the probation officers serving the courts, and that these in their turn stemmed from the latter's previous experience and qualifications.

An exceptionally sensitive and penetrating study is that of Hogarth (1971),[4] who explored factors associated with variations in sentencing practices among Ontario magistrates. Interviews and attitude scales were used to identify the penal philosophies consciously employed by magistrates as strategies for making decisions and the evaluative categories ('judicial attitudes') used by magistrates in assessing crime and determining the appropriate response to it. Five factorially-derived scales were constructed, the factors being designated 'justice', 'punishment corrects', 'intolerance', 'social defence' and 'modernism'. These attitudes were found to be capable of predicting sentencing behaviour for every offence considered, although the relationships between the two sets of variables were often complex. The legal and social constraints on sentencing of which magistrates were aware influenced their courtroom decisions, but their influence became most apparent when the magistrates' attitudes had been accounted for. The use made of information about the offence and about the offender was explored in considerable detail. It was concluded that magistrates tended to seek and evaluate the significance of different types of information very much in accordance with the priorities defined by their respective penal philosophies; information was used if it confirmed their preconceptions, avoided if it were in conflict with them. Pre-sentence reports submitted by probation officers did not necessarily lead to greater congruence in their views and those of magistrates; indeed, in urban areas they seemed to increase rather than narrow the gap. Selective interpretation of the information provided was seen as almost inevitable, and a wide range of antecedent factors was identified. Finally, several studies were carried out to throw light on the processes involved in using factual information; these were based on the concept of cognitive-complexity, involving the ability to discriminate, the volume of information taken into consideration and the amount of energy expended in reaching an appropriate decision. Cognitive-complexity, a factor closely allied to general intelligence, discriminated between magistrates with different penal philosophies. This crude summary cannot do justice to a subtle and complex study, which is unquestionably a landmark in the study of decision-making. Yet although it provided an invaluable source of ideas, we did not consider it possible for our work to follow similar lines.

Decisions in children's hearings present both opportunities and special problems for the investigator. One major problem as far as understanding personal factors in decisions is concerned is that the outcomes do not flow from individual judgments but from the collective view of three laymen. Even if it were possible to gather relevant information – about social attitudes or the perceived seriousness of offences or the goals of alternative 'treatments' – we should be faced with the virtually unmanageable task of predicting decisions from the interaction of three sets of personal data in each case. But we should still not have been prepared to undertake the task of relating personal data about panel members to their decisions concerning the children who appeared before them even if the technical problems had not seemed insoluble. We did in fact collect a very considerable amount of information from panel members on such matters as their theories of the causes of delinquency and the objectives of the disposals open to them; we also observed performance in three hundred hearings. But we believed it essential for the success of both enterprises that they should be clearly seen to be independent of each other. We were convinced that panel members would be extremely sensitive to any suggestion that we were in any way monitoring their performance on an individual basis, and we therefore both carefully separated the two enquiries in time and emphasized the anonymity of the opinion questionnaire.

There are however some compensating methodological advantages in the study of children's hearings. The number of possible disposals is extremely limited, very serious offences are excluded, and the virtually uniform duration of supervision orders further reduces the complexity of analysis. We know also (*Chapter 3*) that variations between areas of Scotland in the relative frequency of alternative disposals fall for the most part within narrow limits. (Most studies of sentencing begin as attempts to explain variability; it seemed to us that a fairly high degree of consistency is no less interesting.) Finally, the hearings system incorporates what is in effect a formal philosophy of decision-making which is at least nominally accepted by those who become panel members. This is not to say that the latter constitute a homogeneous group with respect to their approach to delinquency, rather that one might reasonably expect a certain body of values to be widely if not universally shared; material presented in *Chapter 14* makes it clear that there is indeed a very considerable measure of agreement among children's panel members in their views on the causes of delinquency and the hearings system. What none of these considerations tells us, however, is how principles are applied in practice; they do not enable us to predict accurately in what circumstances children will be discharged, or placed on supervision or consigned to a residential institution.

Our study of decisions draws upon two sets of data: the behaviour and interaction observed in a representative sample of hearings and the contents of the reports made available to the panel members concerned in advance of those hearings. Both bodies of material are discussed in earlier chapters; here we consider the extent to which the presence or absence of certain information in reports and the varying characteristics of the hearing appear to increase the likelihood of alternative decisions. The correlates of a large number of factors are first reviewed on an item-by-item basis; subsequently we isolate a series of factors, each of which seem to have a strong statistical relationship with decisions, and try to ascertain the independent influence of each when other factors are held constant.

The role of recorded information

It is clear that one factor very strikingly associated with the decision reached is simply the number of times that the child has previously appeared before a hearing. Table 11.1 summarizes the position. Of the 187 children who had never made a previous appearance, four out of ten were discharged, and well over one-half placed on supervision. Only three such children were required to enter a List D school, and another four were ordered to be placed in a local authority children's home.

In subsequent appearances the use of discharge drops steeply but not consistently, the use of social work supervision rises and then falls again. But it is in the use of residential orders that we see the most striking variation.

TABLE 11.1

FACTORS ASSOCIATED WITH DECISIONS

Number of previous hearings

	Decision				
Number of previous hearings	*Discharge* %	*Supervision* %	*List D* %	*In care* %	N
None	40	57	2	2	187
One	13	64	19	4	47
Two or three	17	55	24	3	29
Four or more	21	46	32	—	28
Not known	(33)	(56)	(11)	—	9
All children	31	57	10	2	300

When a child comes before a hearing for the second time his chances of being 'sent away' go up from one in 60 to almost one in five. The proportion increases to a maximum of one-third among children who have appeared on at least four previous occasions. Residential supervision remains nevertheless a minority disposal even for the most hardened recidivists. In theory of course panel members could regard List D schools as a treatment resource, to be employed whenever they might seem appropriate to the child's needs. In practice, one is impressed by the reluctance of panel members to use this power, and to retain it as in the nature of a last resort.

In view of the marked difference in the pattern of disposals between hearings at which the child is making his first appearance and those in which there is a history of one or more previous hearings, we first consider the 187 'first appearance' hearings, and examine the association between the decisions made and two sets of variables – those derived from the reports and those that describe the events of the hearing itself. There were so few residential orders that for all practical purposes the comparison is between discharge decisions and home supervision decisions.

The seriousness attached to truancy is immediately apparent. Among offenders, the number of offences established affected the decision far more strongly than their specific nature. Children who made their first hearings appearance while still of primary school age were much more often discharged than the majority who were aged 12 or over. Writers who argue for a therapeutic approach to delinquency might perhaps claim that an early entry

TABLE 11.2

FACTORS ASSOCIATED WITH DECISIONS
(*Children at their first hearing*)

	Decision				
	Discharge %	*Supervision* %	*List D* %	*In care* %	N
Grounds of referral					
Offence(s)	49	49	*	*	120
Truancy	27	68	3	3	37
Offence(s) + truancy	29	64	7	—	14
Others	6	81	—	13	16
Number of offences established					
1	55	43	3	—	73
2, 3	47	53	—	—	38
4+	24	71	—	5	21
Most serious offence established					
Theft	47	51	2	—	53
Housebreaking	40	58	—	2	45
Assault	43	57	—	—	14
Others	70	25	5	—	20

TABLE 11.2—*contd.*

	Decision				N
	Discharge %	*Supervision* %	*List D* %	*In care* %	
Age of child					
Under 12	46	46	3	5	39
12–13	31	62	4	2	45
14 or over	41	58	—	1	103
Number of siblings					
0, 1, 2	40	56	2	3	68
3, 4	41	58	2	—	64
5 or more	38	56	2	4	55
Child's behaviour at home					
Helpful	55	44	2	—	64
Difficult	22	70	5	3	37
Not mentioned	36	61	—	4	86
Child's leisure interests					
Mentioned	45	52	2	2	124
Not mentioned	29	67	2	3	63
School attendance					
Good/reasonable	59	39	2	—	46
Irregular	33	64	2	2	123
Not mentioned	33	50	—	17	18
Behaviour in school					
Normal	48	49	—	3	65
Anti-social	31	64	4	—	45
Easily led	56	44	—	—	29
Apathetic	31	66	—	3	29
Not mentioned	24	67	5	5	21
Relations with teachers					
Good	42	54	2	2	41
Poor	36	61	3	—	36
Not mentioned	40	57	*	3	110
Relations with peers					
Good/leader	40	57	1	3	81
Easily led	53	47	—	—	30
Unpopular	32	62	3	3	34
Not mentioned	36	60	2	2	42
Intelligence level					
Below average	37	61	1	1	87
Average	40	54	4	2	43
Above average	50	50	—	—	14
Not mentioned	42	54	—	5	43

TABLE 11.2—*contd.*

	Decision				
	Discharge %	*Supervision* %	*List D* %	*In care* %	N
Educational achievement					
Below average	35	62	3	—	69
Average	52	46	—	3	33
Above average	48	52	—	—	25
Not mentioned	35	58	2	5	60
History of serious illness					
Mentioned	34	58	2	5	44
Not mentioned	41	56	1	1	143
Psychiatric symptoms					
Mentioned	—	83	17	—	12
Not mentioned	42	55	*	2	175
Undetected delinquency					
Mentioned	32	66	3	—	38
Not mentioned	42	54	1	3	149
Child normally lives with					
Both parents	45	53	2	—	118
Mother alone	32	65	3	—	34
Other combinations	29	60	—	11	35
Employment status, head of household					
Employed	47	52	1	1	101
Housewife, not employed	32	62	3	3	34
Unemployed, sick	31	64	2	4	52
Social class					
Non-manual	33	67	—	—	15
Skilled	46	54	—	—	37
Semi-skilled	38	55	3	3	29
Unskilled	18	82	—	—	17
Not applicable, not known	43	52	2	3	89
Family known to agencies					
Mentioned	24	69	4	4	55
Not mentioned	46	52	1	2	132
Social worker's recommendation					
Discharge	82	17	—	—	68
Supervision	16	84	—	—	86
Residential	—	(56)	(22)	22	9
Assessment/other	—	(60)	—	(40)	5
No recommendation	21	74	5	—	19

* = Less than 1 per cent.

to a delinquent career indicates a particular need for guidance, and such a view could well be held to be consistent with the Kilbrandon philosophy. In practice, however, panel members appear to be less influenced by such arguments than by a belief in the advantages of minimal intervention.

The number of siblings in the child's family was quite unrelated to the decision reached when a child appeared before a hearing for the first time. A series of aspects of the child's personal and family circumstances were however associated with the decision to impose social work supervision rather than to discharge the referral. The relevant information was derived from routine reports and not from any research instruments. It is important to emphasize that our concern was exclusively with the descriptions, judgments and inferences that were presented to panel members: we did not undertake or commission any comprehensive independent assessment of the children in question. Very few of the areas of information to which we refer were recorded in all instances, and the fact that – say – psychiatric symptoms were not mentioned in a particular case does not necessarily mean that they were absent but may merely mean that they had not been observed by the writer of the report, or had been observed but not deemed relevant.

Children described as difficult or troublesome at home fared very differently from those referred to in positive terms, or even from those in whose case behaviour at home received no mention at all. Similarly, the child described as having leisure interests – whatever they were, apart from delinquency – was more likely to be discharged, as was the child with good or fair school attendance, or normal – by which was presumably meant unremarkable – behaviour in school. Children placed on supervision tended to be those with irregular school attendance, whose behaviour in school was characterized as either 'apathetic' or 'antisocial', and who were said to have poor relations with teachers. Those of above average intelligence and of average or above average educational attainment seem more often to have been discharged, but the numbers in these categories are distinctly small. Psychiatric symptoms were mentioned in only 12 instances, and in each such case some measure of supervision or control was imposed. A reference in the reports to undetected delinquency was also associated with an increase in the supervision rate, though of not nearly the same scale.

The last two examples illustrate the incompleteness of social background reports. Numerous studies have shown that delinquent acts are very much more widespread than the statistics of arrests and charges would suggest. Belson's study of 1,400 English boys of secondary school age (1975)[5] is reasonably typical of enquiries based on self-reported delinquency, showing that between one-third and one-half of the boys had committed property offences of various types. There is also evidence to suggest that 'official' delinquents tend in general to have committed more offences and more serious offences than those who remain undetected. One must react with some scepticism therefore to the implication of the social background reports in these cases, that undetected delinquent acts had been committed by only one in five of a series of children most of whom were known to have at least one non-trivial delinquent act on their record.

The recorded frequency of psychiatric symptoms is also of interest. There is no statistic that authoritatively defines the relationship between two such imprecise and problematic concepts as delinquency and maladjustment. Most psychiatrists would probably agree that the lives of a large proportion of delinquents are uncomplicated by emotional disturbance, but would claim that there was a minority whose anti-social behaviour was a reaction to inner conflicts or tensions of a seriousness that warranted psychiatric intervention. Epidemiological studies of general population samples have identified signs of psychiatric disorder in 12 per cent of 10-year-olds in a largely rural area and 25 per cent of those in an inner London borough (Rutter *et al.*, 1975).[6] It seems very improbable that the corresponding proportion among children appearing before hearings would be lower than these estimates, and the 6 per cent described as having psychiatric symptoms is almost certainly an under-estimate. What is important here is not the comprehensiveness or otherwise of the records as such, but simply the illustration of the power of the word; in general, it was only that which was observed and reported that influenced the decision.

Some aspects of the child's social situation seem to have had a bearing on the decision. The child living with a single parent or in some other non-conventional family structure was more likely to be placed on supervision; so was a child in a household the head of which was for any reason not gainfully employed. If the family was already known to the social work department or any similar agencies, the percentage of discharges was halved. The social class of the family, as assessed by the head of household's occupation, had an influence

TABLE 11.3

FACTORS ASSOCIATED WITH DECISIONS
(*Children at their second or subsequent hearing*)

	Decision				
	Discharge %	*Supervision* %	*List D* %	*In case* %	N
Grounds of referral					
Offence(s)	18	53	25	2	88
Truancy	15	77	8	—	13
Offence(s)+truancy	20	70	10	—	10
Others	—	—	(50)	(50)	2
Number of offences established					
1	21	60	19	4	48
2, 3	20	46	34	—	35
4+	(11)	(56)	(33)	—	9
Most serious offence established					
Theft	21	52	24	2	42
Housebreaking	12	73	12	4	26
Assault	—	(67)	(33)	—	3
Others	27	23	45	5	22

TABLE 11.3—*contd.*

	Decision				
	Discharge %	*Supervision* %	*List D* %	*In case* %	N
Age of child					
Under 12	—	(70)	(10)	(20)	10
12–13	4	56	35	4	23
14 or over	24	55	21	—	80
Number of siblings					
0, 1, 2	13	52	32	3	31
3, 4	24	49	22	4	45
5 or more	14	70	16	—	37
Child's behaviour at home					
Helpful	25	69	6	—	16
Difficult	11	46	39	4	28
Not mentioned	19	58	20	3	69
Child's leisure interests					
Mentioned	27	55	16	2	55
Not mentioned	9	59	29	3	58
School attendance					
Good/reasonable	9	82	9	—	11
Irregular	18	53	31	2	83
Not mentioned	21	58	16	5	19
Behaviour at school					
Normal	29	52	14	6	35
Anti-social	15	70	15	—	40
Easily led	8	46	46	—	13
Apathetic	8	58	33	—	12
Not mentioned	15	39	39	8	13
Relations with teachers					
Good	29	47	25	—	28
Poor	15	64	21	—	33
Not mentioned	14	58	23	6	52
Relations with peers					
Good/leader	24	51	19	5	37
Easily led	13	56	31	—	16
Unpopular	18	59	24	—	17
Not mentioned	14	61	23	2	43
Intelligence level					
Below average	15	63	20	2	60
Average	14	61	25	—	28
Above average	(11)	(33)	(56)	—	9
Not mentioned	38	38	12	12	16

TABLE 11.3—*contd.*

	Decision				
	Discharge %	*Supervision* %	*List D* %	*In case* %	N
Educational achievement					
Below average	21	51	25	4	53
Average	15	59	26	—	27
Above average	(40)	(60)	—	—	5
Not mentioned	11	64	21	4	28
History of serious illness					
Mentioned	17	71	13	—	24
Not mentioned	18	53	26	3	89
Psychiatric symptoms					
Mentioned	(11)	(56)	(33)	—	9
Not mentioned	18	57	22	3	104
Undetected delinquency					
Mentioned	10	45	45	—	20
Not mentioned	19	59	18	3	93
Child normally lives with					
Both parents	27	52	21	—	56
Mother alone	9	64	27	—	22
Other combinations	9	60	23	9	35
Employment status, head of household					
Employed	20	58	18	4	55
Housewife, not employed	6	61	28	4	18
Unemployed, sick	20	53	28	—	40
Social class					
Non-manual	(14)	(29)	(57)	—	7
Skilled	15	75	5	5	20
Semi-skilled	25	70	5	—	20
Unskilled	46	27	27	—	11
Not applicable, not known	11	55	31	4	55
Family known to agencies					
Mentioned	16	65	16	3	31
Not mentioned	18	54	26	2	82
Social worker's recommendation					
Discharge	73	27	—	—	15
Supervision	3	92	5	—	37
Residential	—	18	64	11	28
Assessment/other	(20)	(50)	(30)	—	23
No recommendation	26	61	13	—	23

that might be described as capricious rather than obvious. Children from white-collar families were placed on supervision *more* often than the children of skilled manual workers, though it was those from unskilled manual workers who had the highest supervision rate. However, the very small numbers involved and the high proportion of cases which either were not or could not be classified are warnings against easy generalization.

The factors associated with decisions in the case of those children in our sample who had appeared at at least one hearing prior to that which we observed are summarized in Table 11.3. Because of the limited sample size we have combined them, irrespective of whether the number of previous hearings was one or six. Even so, the series of 113 thus created produces some extremely small cell sizes in some of our cross-tabulations. As indicated earlier in this chapter, residential disposals were made a good deal more frequently with 'repeaters'. Only 20 of the 113 children were discharged, 64 were placed or continued on supervision, 26 (or 23 per cent) were sent to List D schools and 3 were placed in children's homes.

The table in question could be summed up by saying that those factors associated with the decision to place a child on supervision on his first appearance before a hearing are also those associated with the decision to make a residential order on a later appearance. Although broadly true however this would be an over-simplification; there are some exceptions to such a generalization.

The grounds of referral, for example, are influential in a different way. Truancy was less common at second or later hearings, but when it did arise it very commonly led to a home supervision order, rarely to a residential one. Family size, previously unrelated to outcome, was associated with decisions in respect of repeaters in a slightly surprising way; children from small families were twice as likely to be put into List D schools as those with five or more siblings. Anti-social behaviour in school and poor relations with teachers did not seem to indicate residential outcomes, although among first appearances they were likely to be associated with supervision orders. Above average intelligence tended to be associated with a residential decision, but not above average attainment; the numbers however are so small that it is really unwise to generalize.

In other respects the parallelism of the two patterns is sustained. The number of offences established continues to influence decisions while the seriousness of the offence does not – or, if it does, influences it in a somewhat unexpected fashion, with housebreaking leading to a List D commitment less often than simple theft. Children of primary school age were very unlikely to be sent away from home, though never discharged. Reputedly difficult behaviour at home, an apparent lack of leisure interests, irregular school attendance and a report of undetected delinquency, all tend to indicate a higher than average risk of a residential disposal, just as with children at their first hearing they were predictive of a home supervision order.

Children in non-conventional family situations account for fully half of the repeaters, compared to 42 per cent of first appearances; all of these children were very unlikely to be discharged when they had a previous history, and those living with mother alone seemed more likely to find themselves in a List D school. So were children from a household whose head was not gainfully employed – a category overlapping but much larger than this latter group of mothers alone. Social class of those employed and classifiable continues to exert an apparently bizarre influence, with an above average frequency of residential orders for the children of unskilled manual workers and an even higher percentage where the parent was middle class. The numbers are small however and no reliable conclusions can be drawn.

The role of the events of the hearing

In contrast to the many strong associations between items of information derived from reports and the decisions reached at hearings, the subject matter and stylistic patterns of the hearings seem to have few discernible effects upon the outcome. Discharge was more common at first hearings when positive aspects of the child were discussed, whereas advice to a parent was significantly more likely to precede the making of a supervision requirement. The use of a shocked style by panel members was associated with an above average discharge rate; the expression of shock in these cases was not unlike a reference to positive features – a statement of shocked surprise that a child with a previously good record or good home background should have committed an offence. At second or subsequent hearings a reference to positive features of the child was associated with a high home supervision rate and a low frequency of both discharge and residential orders. Some stylistic devices that on the face of it seem negative or hostile, the use of sarcasm and 'exhorts, threatens' were linked with a high proportion of discharges and a low rate of List D placements. In these cases the modes of speech thus identified were in the nature of warnings about the child's likely fate if he failed to mend his ways. The expression of shock at second or subsequent hearings tended to contain more of a sense of outrage than at first hearings, and was associated with a fairly low rate of discharge.

The content items correlated with below-average discharge rates at first hearings were drawn mainly from material in social background reports indicative of problems in the home situation – family stresses, drugs or alcohol and contact with social worker, as topics of conversation all led on to more than the customary proportion of supervision requirements. At second or subsequent hearings discussion of social worker contacts, and to a more marked extent consideration of drug or alcohol problems, tended to be predictive of residential disposals. Reference to the child's future plans, on the other hand, was quite likely to be a precursor to discharge.

Most of the associations between style and content items and the outcome of the hearing are not very strong and the fact that the content items at any rate derived largely from information and assessments contained in reports leads to some reluctance to impute independent causal influence to them. The two dimensions of the hearing that seem to have consistently significant relationships with outcome are the level of participation by family members and their recorded moods.

These relationships are most marked when we consider children's responses in the hearing. Among those attending their first hearing, silence or a monosyllabic response was noted in one-quarter of those placed on supervision and in only one-tenth of the children discharged. The distinction between answering questions fully and asking questions or speaking out freely was of less significance as a discriminant. There was however nothing resembling a corresponding differentiation of mood between these two groups of young people. Those discharged were slightly more often rated 'nervous, anxious' than those subsequently placed on supervision, and less often 'comfortable, at ease'. Children who had experienced at least one previous hearing, on the other hand, displayed a well-defined relationship between mood and outcome. Only one in twenty of those discharged had expressed anger or opposition in the course of the hearing, compared to almost one-sixth of the youngsters placed on supervision and three-tenths of those placed in a residential establishment.

TABLE 11.4

DECISIONS, IN RELATION TO PANEL MEMBERS' STYLES

	Decisions				
	Discharge %	*Supervision* %	*List D* %	*In care* %	N
	(children at first hearing)				
Style					
Encouraging	39	57	2	2	171
Sympathetic	40	57	2	1	93
Positive aspects	44	53	2	—	45
Interrogating	38	60	2	1	84
Sarcastic	33	67	—	—	39
Shocked	46	53	2	—	68
Exhorts	40	60	—	—	68
Interrupts	40	60	—	—	20
Advises parent	30	67	3	—	33
All children	40	57	2	2	186
	(children at second or subsequent hearing)				
Encouraging	20	56	22	3	102
Sympathetic	18	57	20	6	51
Positive aspects	12	76	8	4	25
Interrogating	18	57	20	4	49
Sarcastic	23	65	12	—	26
Shocked	10	65	25	—	40
Exhorts	27	62	11	—	37
Interrupts	43	29	29	—	14
Advises parent	(22)	(67)	(11)	—	9
All children	18	57	23	3	113

Almost none of those in the latter category were classed as 'comfortable' during the hearing, although more than one-third of both discharged and supervised children came into that category. 'Serious, attentive' was the recorded mood of more than half of the children who were to be discharged, as against 30 per cent of all others. The frequencies of 'passive, withdrawn' and 'nervous, anxious' moods resemble the distribution of angry and opposed moods – very rare among those who were eventually discharged, more common in those for whom a supervision decision was to be reached, and most common in the children destined for a List D school.

Level of participation in second or subsequent hearings is particularly closely correlated with the decision reached. Half of the small group of children

TABLE 11.5

DECISIONS IN RELATION TO CONTENT OF HEARINGS

	Decisions				
	Discharge %	*Supervision* %	*List D* %	*In care* %	N
	(children at first hearing)				
Content					
Grounds of referral	41	57	1	2	170
Prior record	49	52	—	—	66
School	40	57	2	1	175
Home behaviour	37	59	2	2	100
Peers	41	56	2	2	133
Family stresses	26	69	1	3	72
Family attitude	37	60	2	2	128
Contact with social worker	24	70	3	3	103
Drugs, alcohol	30	70	—	—	27
Future plans	46	54	—	—	59
Miscellaneous	32	64	—	4	53
All children	40	57	2	2	186
	(children at second or subsequent hearing)				
Grounds of referral	23	57	16	4	74
Prior record	19	63	16	2	43
School	16	55	21	3	99
Home behaviour	20	48	30	2	54
Peers	21	63	13	3	70
Family stresses	26	58	17	—	31
Family attitude	13	62	21	4	77
Contact with social worker	15	53	29	3	72
Drugs, alcohol	10	48	38	5	21
Future plans	36	60	4	—	42
Miscellaneous	11	64	19	6	36
All children	18	57	23	3	113

who were discharged had spoken out openly and almost as many had answered questions fully; only two of the youngsters in this small group of 20 had been silent or had answered only 'Yes' or 'No' throughout the hearing. The proportion answering questions more fully remained fairly constant in the groups of young people placed on home supervision or sent to residential schools. But the frequencies of the other two response categories fluctuated markedly. Minimal participation was noted in one in five of those for whom a supervision order was made and nearly one-half of those who found their way to a List D school. On the other hand, the proportion speaking out or asking questions was only one-third of the former group and one-ninth of the latter. This strong relationship can be expressed in an alternative fashion: of 36 children who at second or subsequent hearings participated actively, only three had residential orders made; of 29 who were silent throughout or gave only monosyllabic replies, 12 were required to leave home for a residential establishment.

The participation levels of mothers at first hearings seem to be largely unrelated to outcome, but this is not the case when they are more experienced. In spite of small numbers, a clear pattern of association is apparent. None of the mothers of discharged children was silent and 10 out of a total of 14 participated actively. Active participation was noted in 47 per cent of the children placed on supervision and 41 per cent of those sent to List D schools. In both of these disposal groups, the proportion in the middle category ('answers questions') was exactly the same as the proportion speaking freely. The per-

TABLE 11.6

CHILD'S PARTICIPATION IN RELATION TO DECISION

	Participation			
Decision	*Silent or Yes/No only* %	*Answers questions* %	*Asks, speaks out* %	N
		(child at first hearing)		
Discharge	10	62	29	73
Supervision	25	51	24	103
List D	(67)	—	(33)	3
In care	—	(100)	—	2
All children	19	55	26	181
		(child at second or subsequent hearing)		
Discharge	10	40	50	20
Supervision	20	45	34	64
List D	46	42	12	26
In care	(67)	—	(33)	3
All children	26	43	32	113

centage silent or replying only minimally increased to 6 per cent in the 'supervision' group and 18 per cent in the 'residential' group. When we examine mothers' moods, we again find a sharp contrast between the patterns of relationship established at first and at subsequent hearings. In the former series there seems to be a slightly greater polarization of responses among the mothers of children to be discharged than those placed on supervision; more were reported 'comfortable, at ease' and slightly more as 'nervous, anxious', with correspondingly fewer in the 'serious, attentive' category. In cases where the child had appeared on at least one previous occasion, moods of anger or opposition were more common; but only one mother of the 14 whose children were discharged came into this category, compared to more than one in seven of those whose children were put on supervision and more than one in four of the mothers of List D children. Not one of this last group of mothers was rated 'comfortable', unlike nearly one-quarter of the mothers of the 'supervision' children and more than one-half of the discharged. An 'attentive, serious' mood was more frequent when a supervision order resulted, but differed little as between the home and residential types of supervision order. 'Passive, withdrawn' and 'nervous, anxious' moods did not appear among the 'discharge' mothers, but they together account for 11 per cent of the mood-responses of mothers whose children were subsequently placed on home supervision and 23 per cent where the child was sent to a residential establishment.

Fathers present something of a contrast. They tended to be fairly active

TABLE 11.7

CHILD'S MOOD IN RELATION TO DECISION

Decision	*Negative* %	*Comfortable* %	*Attentive* %	*Passive* %	*Nervous* %	N
			(child at first hearing)			
Discharge	8	15	48	13	16	73
Supervision	9	21	41	16	14	103
List D	(33)	—	—	(67)	—	3
In care	—	—	(100)	—	—	2
All children	9	18	44	15	14	181
			(child at second or subsequent hearing)			
Discharge	5	35	55	5	—	20
Supervision	16	34	30	13	8	64
List D	31	4	31	23	12	26
In care	—	(67)	(33)	—	—	3
All children	17	28	35	13	7	113

participants in hearings whatever the outcome and there is nothing in our data to suggest any relationship between their levels of involvement and the decision finally reached, either at first or subsequent hearings. Paternal moods however follow a pattern not dissimilar to that of mothers. At first hearings a 'comfortable' mood was observed more frequently in those fathers whose children were subsequently discharged. The number of fathers involved in second or subsequent hearings in our sample was small (57), and generalization must be very tentative; but the absence of 'comfortable, at ease' observations and the increased number of those seen as 'passive, withdrawn' in the little group of fathers whose children were at the end of the hearing consigned to residential schools are certainly reminiscent of the distribution of moods noted in the comparable group of mothers.

These findings are open to more than one interpretation. It is possible for example that although the decision came after those activities of the hearing from which the level of participation was assessed, it was nevertheless the decision – or to be more precise, the expectation of the decision – that was responsible for the level of participation. This would imply that the decision in particular to impose a residential supervision order may have been formed at least tentatively before the commencement of the hearing on the basis of reports and recommendations, and that whether or not it had been so formed, it was recognized as a possibility by the child and his parents, having been conveyed to them perhaps by the social worker in the case. Our own

TABLE 11.8

MOTHER'S PARTICIPATION IN RELATION TO DECISION

Decision	*Participation* Silent or Yes/No only %	*Answers questions* %	*Asks, speaks out* %	N
	(child at first hearing)			
Discharge	11	39	50	62
Supervision	7	38	55	95
List D	—	(50)	(50)	2
In care	—	(100)	—	3
All mothers	9	40	52	162
	(child at second or subsequent hearing)			
Discharge	—	29	71	14
Supervision	6	47	47	53
List D	18	41	41	22
In care	—	(100)	—	2
All mothers	8	44	48	91

subjective impression as observers at hearings was that children seemed rarely to be surprised when a decision to impose a supervision order with a residential requirement was announced. As *Chapter 12* indicates, the more severe the decision, the more likely are the children concerned to believe that it was made *before* the hearing. The possibility of a painful outcome, on this theory, dominates the hearing and has a generally inhibiting effect on participation.

However, this hypothesis would not so easily explain the relationships observed between levels of communication and the decision to discharge the child instead of placing him under the supervision of a social worker. An alternative theory would suggest that the child's degree of involvement did indeed exert a direct influence on the outcome of the hearing. This would imply that children's panel members on the whole prefer to intervene minimally, and that they are particularly reluctant to impose residential orders. We know from our own research material that the number of 'discharge' decisions made at the end of the hearings that we observed was greater than the number of 'discharge' recommendations made by social workers, and that the number of residential orders made was less than the number of recommendations to that effect. Even though the information and recommendations contained in reports pointed towards a home supervision order rather than a discharge, or a residential requirement rather than home supervision, as the most probable outcome, panel members would on this theory still be anxious to find a justification for a lesser degree of intervention. Expressions by the child of regret

TABLE 11.9

MOTHER'S MOOD IN RELATION TO DECISION

Decision	*Mood*					N
	Negative %	*Comfortable* %	*Attentive* %	*Passive* %	*Nervous* %	
			(child at first hearing)			
Discharge	3	24	50	3	19	62
Supervision	5	16	62	3	14	95
List D	—	—	(50)	—	(50)	2
In care	(33)	—	(33)	—	(33)	3
All mothers	5	19	57	3	17	162
			(child at second or subsequent hearing)			
Discharge	7	57	36	—	—	14
Supervision	13	23	53	4	8	53
List D	27	—	50	9	14	22
In care	—	—	(50)	(50)	—	2
All mothers	15	21	50	6	9	91

TABLE 11.10

FATHER'S PARTICIPATION IN RELATION TO DECISION

Decision	Participation			N
	Silent or Yes/No only %	*Answers questions* %	*Asks, speaks out* %	
	(child at first hearing)			
Discharge	6	33	61	49
Supervision	8	25	67	61
List D	—	(67)	(33)	3
In care	—	(67)	(33)	3
All fathers	8	30	63	116
	(child at second or subsequent hearing)			
Discharge	—	(22)	(78)	9
Supervision	9	41	50	32
List D	7	36	57	14
In care	—	(50)	(50)	2
All fathers	7	37	56	57

TABLE 11.11

FATHER'S MOOD IN RELATION TO DECISION

Decision	Mood					N
	Negative %	*Comfortable* %	*Attentive* %	*Passive* %	*Nervous* %	
	(child at first hearing)					
Discharge	2	29	63	4	2	49
Supervision	8	20	59	8	5	61
List D	—	—	(67)	—	(33)	3
In care	—	(33)	(67)	—	—	3
All fathers	5	23	61	6	4	116
	(child at second or subsequent hearing)					
Discharge	—	(33)	(67)	—	—	9
Supervision	3	28	56	9	3	32
List D	7	—	71	21	—	14
In care	—	—	(100)	—	—	2
All fathers	4	21	63	11	2	57

for the offence or other occurrences that had brought him before the hearing, of concern for his or her own future, of a readiness to organize his life more constructively would therefore be looked for eagerly, as would comparable assurances on the part of the parents. The various techniques for encouraging family participation that are employed by panel members have this, according to the hypothesis we are examining, as at least part of their aim. When panel member skills are inadequate, or when family resistances seem intractable, it is more likely that 'compulsory measures of care' will be seen as unavoidable. We are not in a position to adjudicate between the two theories outlined here, and indeed we see no reason why they should be regarded as mutually exclusive. It seems more plausible that both processes play some part in explaining the relationships that we have identified, and that in many instances the two interact, with the expectation of an unfavourable outcome leading to withdrawal and silence, and thereby unwittingly increasing the likelihood of that very outcome.

Identifying independent influences

The obvious problem of interpreting the causal influence of the many items of information derived from reports is that they are not of course wholly independent of one another. The social ills referred to '. . . come not single spies, but in battalions'. Children in one-parent families are on average more likely to have a non-earning head of household *and* to have poor school attendance records *and* to have below-average educational attainment, and so on. However, although markedly intercorrelated they are not interchangeable; there is significant overlap between them but not total congruence. It should in principle therefore be possible to ascertain the effect of any one of these variables, independently of the influence of the others associated with it; from this it should be possible to add these discrete influences to obtain a measure of the summated effect of several independent factors. Several techniques of multivariate analysis have been developed for tasks of this kind; we have made use of multiple classification analysis for this purpose as well as for the basically similar analysis of reporters' decisions discussed in *Chapter 5*.

Table 11.12 summarizes data relating to three types of decision choice: to place on supervision *or* discharge at first hearings, to place on supervision *or* discharge at second and subsequent hearings, and to place on residential *or* on home supervision, all hearings combined. In the first two columns the grand mean indicates the probability of a supervision order and in the third it indicates the probability of a residential supervision order. The entries corresponding to each of the independent variables show the extent to which the given probability is increased or reduced by the value in question. All these entries have been adjusted to allow for the influence of other variables – that is to say, they are the best estimates obtainable of the independent effects of the factors listed.

Many of the influences on hearings decisions that are identified in the analysis of single factors clearly continue to have a significant role even after multivariate analysis, though the weight of their contribution is sometimes changed. At first hearings the probability of a home supervision order being made is greatly strengthened if the head of the household is not in employment, if the family is known to other agencies, if the child's behaviour at home is reported as difficult, and if he comes from either an unskilled or a white collar background. Information contained in school reports has relatively less independent influence on the decision to recommend supervision, except that a record of good school attendance markedly increases the probability of discharge. Similarly, the child who is living with both parents or whose behaviour at home is described as helpful is more likely than most to be discharged. The independent influence on the decision of such factors as leisure interests and reported levels of intelligence and educational attainment is comparatively slight.

At second or subsequent hearings, where the overall chances of a supervision requirement are significantly greater, the fact of living in a family situation other than a two-parent one increases the probability of supervision to a near-certainty. Parental employment status is almost as strong an influence on the decision, and difficult behaviour at home, lack of leisure interests and below average attainment in school each exert some independent weight on the decision. School attendance and being known to other agencies are of less importance than at first hearings. The ways in which social class differences are associated with decision-making appear quite inexplicable, and the same must be said of intelligence level. Some allowance must be made for the

---

TABLE 11.12

FACTORS ASSOCIATED WITH DECISIONS: APPLICATION OF MULTIPLE CLASSIFICATION ANALYSIS

Deviations from grand mean, adjusted for other variables

Decision:	*Discharge/place on supervision (first hearings)*		*Discharge/place on supervision (subseq. hearings)*		*Home/residential supervision (all hearings)*	
Grand mean:	0·59 (= *p. supervise*)		0·76 (= *p. supervise*)		0·15 (= *p. supervise*)	
Prior record						
No					−0·12	
Yes					+0·14	
effect						0·37
Child normally lives with						
both parents	−0·13		−0·15		+0·01	
not both parents	+0·05		+0·17		−0·01	
effect		0·08		0·37		0·03
Head of household						
employed	−0·09		−0·14		0·00	
not employed	+0·12		+0·13		0·00	
effect		0·21		0·33		0·01

TABLE 11.12—*contd.*

Decision:	*Discharge/place on supervision (first hearings)*		*Discharge/place on supervision (subseq. hearings)*		*Home/residential supervision (all hearings)*	
Grand mean:	0·59 (= *p. supervise*)		0·76 (= *p. supervise*)		0·15 (= *p. supervise*)	
Leisure interests						
some	−0·05		−0·08		−0·04	
none	+0·02		+0·09		+0·05	
effect		0·03		0·20		0·13
Family known to other agencies						
No	−0·04		−0·02		+0·01	
Yes	+0·11		+0·05		−0·03	
effect		0·13		0·07		0·06
Social class						
non-manual	+0·16		+0·04		+0·12	
skilled	+0·04		+0·10		−0·12	
semi-skilled	+0·10		−0·05		−0·07	
unskilled	+0·12		−0·29		+0·07	
not known	−0·09		+0·04		+0·04	
effect		0·17		0·25		0·22
Home behaviour						
helpful	−0·11		0·00		−0·06	
difficult	+0·15		−0·11		+0·03	
not known	+0·02		−0·03		+0·12	
effect		0·15		0·15		0·19
Educational achievement						
above average	−0·04		−0·05		−0·09	
average	−0·08		−0·02		+0·04	
below average	+0·02		−0·08		+0·03	
not known	+0·04		+0·13		+0·04	
effect		0·09		0·20		0·11
IQ level						
above average	−0·04		−0·26		+0·13	
average	0·00		−0·02		+0·04	
below average	+0·03		+0·13		+0·03	
not known	−0·05		−0·40		0·00	
effect		0·04		0·44		0·14
School attendance						
adequate	−0·12		−0·03		−0·05	
irregular	+0·06		+0·07		+0·02	
effect		0·17		0·11		0·09
Multiple R.	0·466		0·59		0·51	
N	180		84		199	

vagaries of small numbers; the IQ categories 'above average' and 'not known', for example, contain nine and 16 children respectively. It is clear however that supervision decisions at both first and subsequent hearings can be predicted with a high degree of accuracy. If we were minded to construct guide-lines for decision-making for future children's hearings with the object of ensuring that the pattern of influences remained consistent over time, there would be no difficulty in calculating a scoring system that would guarantee the continuity of the criteria implicitly contained in the decisions that we observed.

It would be a considerably more difficult task however to provide reliable guidelines for the List D decision. The initial probability is of course low (0·15) and is markedly affected only by the fact of having or not having previously appeared at a hearing. Whether the child lives with both parents or in some other home situation and whether or not the head of the household is employed, both significant factors in relation to the supervision decision in general, exercise no influence on the decision to order residential supervision. Leisure interests matter very little, and agency knowledge of the family carries virtually no weight either way. Neither school attendance nor level of achievement at school is very influential, except that 'above average' achievement strongly reduces the probability of a residential order. If a child is of above average intelligence or has a white-collar background his chances of going to a List D school are noticeably increased; though relevant direct evidence is not available, one may speculate that continued delinquency in such children is more often interpreted as a sign of some relatively serious underlying pathology and as therefore requiring some form of residential supervision. But in general it seems that the most far-reaching decision that children's hearings can make involves a larger element of idiosyncratic judgment than the less weighty decision to bring a child under the supervision of a social worker.

Central to the interpretation of the factors referred to in background reports is of course the recommendation with which the reports usually conclude. These are set out, in relation to the hearings' decision, in the final sections of Tables 11.2 and 11.3.

If we take only those reports which included a recommendation corresponding to one or other of the formal decision outcomes, we find that these corresponded with the actual disposal by the hearing in 81 or 82 per cent of cases. There were however 19 first hearings and 23 subsequent hearings where the reports did not include a recommendation, as well as 5 and 10 respectively where the social worker had recommended some further assessment, the outcomes of which were available to the hearing. If we look at *all* decisions, therefore, the proportion which conforms to specific recommendations by social workers is reduced to 71 per cent in the case of first hearings and 66 per cent where the child was appearing on the second or subsequent occasion. Although there have been numerous studies of the influence of probation officers' and social workers' reports on sentencing decisions in courts, few comparative data are available for the disposals of children's hearings. Morris (1978)[7] says of the two areas of Scotland that she studied in the early seventies that social workers' recommendations were followed in 88 per cent of all cases.

If this refers literally to all cases, it would seem that panel members' dependence on recommendations has decreased quite considerably. If however it refers only to those cases where a recommendation was made – or if, as seems improbable, a recommendation was made in every instance – the propensity to follow recommendations has declined only slightly. Comparisons with the influence of social enquiry reports on court decisions are less strictly relevant, and the conclusions of published studies are not always directly comparable with one another. Priestley, Fears and Fuller (1967)[8] showed in a study of juvenile courts in the west of England that magistrates accepted 90 per cent of supervision recommendations but only two-thirds of care recommendations. Curran (1981),[9] studying social enquiry reports to the courts in two Scottish regions, indicated that firm recommendations were made in only 68 per cent of the reports, and that these were taken up in two out of three instances. Thorpe and Pease (1976)[10] reported of two English areas that a recommendation was made in 83 per cent of cases, with a take-up rate of 78 per cent. The degree of correspondence between recommendations and decisions in our sample thus seems to be broadly in line with that established in other studies. It is perhaps marginally higher than the average for magistrates' or sheriffs' sentences, but the wider range of disposals available to the courts would automatically tend to reduce the degree of concordance.

To the extent that there is a discrepancy between the recommendations submitted by social workers and the disposals made at the conclusion of hearings, it is interesting to note its nature. At first hearings approximately one in six of the cases where the recommendation was a home supervision order in fact ended in a decision to discharge, and a corresponding proportion of children for whom discharge was recommended were placed on supervision. Of the nine recommendations for residential disposals, only four were implemented and the remainder converted by the hearing to home supervision orders. At second hearings there was a very high take-up of supervision recommendations, while a small proportion of those recommended for residential disposals were assigned to home supervision. Overall, the number of residential decisions made by the hearings (29) was significantly lower than the number of recommendations to that effect made by social workers (37).

The information about various aspects of children's lives that influences panel members is of course also the information relied upon by social workers when formulating their recommendations. How far the factual and evaluative statements serve to shape decisions independently of the extent to which they are incorporated into recommendations is an intriguing methodological question. It is doubtful whether the issue can be satisfactorily resolved without an experiment in which social workers and perhaps other authors of reports deliberately refrained from including any recommendations. Even without these the influence of reports would still be considerable, for, as we have seen, they also provide points of departure for discussion in the hearing. It is the more regrettable therefore that such a high proportion of the professional reports received by panel members are fragmented, lacking in internal cohesion and theoretical structure.

NOTES

1. R. Hood and R. Sparks, *Key Issues in Criminology*, Weidenfeld and Nicholson, 1970, Ch. 5.
2. S. Wheeler *et al.*, 'Agents of delinquency control: a comparative analysis'. In: S. Wheeler (ed.) *Controlling Delinquents*. Wiley & Sons, 1968.
3. R. M. Carter and L. T. Wilkins, 'Some factors in sentencing policy', *Journal of Criminal Law, Criminology and Police Science*, 1967, 58.
4. J. Hogarth, *Sentencing as a human process*. University of Toronto Press, 1971.
5. W. Belson, *Juvenile Theft, the causal factors*. Harper & Row, London, 1975.
6. M. L. Rutter, A. Cox, C. Tupling, M. Berger and W. Yule, 'Attainment and adjustment in two geographical areas: I. The prevalence of psychiatric disorder', *British Journal of Psychiatry*, 1975, Vol. 126.
7. Allison Morris in collaboration with Mary McIsaac, *Juvenile Justice?* Heinemann, London, 1978.
8. P. Priestley, Denise Fears and Roger Fuller, *Justice for Juveniles*. Routledge & Kegan Paul, 1977.
9. J. Curran, *Social Inquiry Reports in Scotland*. HMSO, Edinburgh, 1981.
10. J. Thorpe and K. Pease, 'The relationship between recommendations made to the court and sentences passed', *British Journal of Criminology*, 1976, Vol. 16.

12

THE CHILD'S RESPONSE

ALTHOUGH MANY THEORETICAL FORMULATIONS and critiques of juvenile justice have involved important assumptions about the way in which the young people concerned actually experience their encounter with the decision-making authority and are subsequently affected by it, there have been relatively few attempts to evaluate such theories by means of direct study of the human beings who are the subject-matter of the confident generalizations. Recent commentators on the English system of juvenile justice concluded that 'the children we talked to saw the juvenile court as a confusing, remote and primarily punitive agency' (Morris and Giller, 1977)[1], and that the situation had changed little from that described much earlier by Scott (1958)[2]. Impressions gathered in other locales about the ways of dealing with children in conflict with the law would not be at variance with this interpretation. A number of studies of young people processed through North American juvenile courts, reviewed by Catton and Erickson (1975)[3], have generally revealed many shortcomings in children's comprehension of and involvement in court proceedings. These have suggested that children are particularly susceptible to efforts to change their behaviour at this climactic stage of appearing before the judge, and that the confusing, impersonal, bureaucratic approaches of traditional courts fail to capitalize on this heightened motivation for improvement on the part of the child. It is possible therefore that a more favourable experience for the child at the proceeding might enhance the likelihood of his refraining from future delinquent behaviour, as well as providing a more humane environment in keeping with the 'best interests' philosophy of juvenile justice.

In the Scottish context, the study of children's responses to the juvenile justice system takes on an added dimension in that an explicit goal of the system is to promote the involvement of the child and parents in the hearing's discussion. Perhaps in part because the architects of the Scottish system were concerned to achieve humane goals within a child welfare framework rather than to follow a strict judicial model, the participation of clients was intended as an essential feature of the hearings. The formal court organization has been replaced in Scotland by what is intended to be a less intimidating forum where understanding of the process, contributing to it and even accepting its outcome have been specified as desirable aims. Moreover the Scottish hearings are supposed to be conducted within a legal framework that also requires standards of fairness and justice to be met. What has not so far been considered is the extent, if any, to which such objectives are achieved from the juvenile client's point of view.

This chapter presents findings based on interviews with 105 juveniles whose cases were disposed of by hearings. All those interviewed were aged 12 to 15 years and had appeared on offence grounds of referral; they represented a 57 per cent sample of all such eligible children. Details of sample selection, the interview method, the personal and case characteristics of the juveniles and analysis for non-response bias are presented in *Chapter 4*. Topics to be discussed include children's perception of the hearing event, their views on the various participants and their sense of stigma and self-labelling.

Comprehension

Comprehension of the hearing experience was examined in several ways. First, subjects were asked why they had to attend a children's hearing. For most (70 per cent) the reason given was the illegal behaviour that was the basis for the offence grounds of referral. Respondents more often expressed this in terms of a charge, such as 'stealing', 'breaking into houses', than more generally as 'getting into trouble', 'what I did'. Another 3 per cent mentioned truancy only and 8 per cent an offence in conjunction with truancy (11 per cent did actually have grounds of both established). While 3 per cent responded 'don't know' to this question, 16 per cent gave a variety of responses that were not grounds-specific, such as, 'find out what they were going to do', 'police had lifted me because I was there', 'they were trying to help me', 'to see if I was guilty or not guilty', 'glue sniffing'. In keeping with the emphasis on the offence dimension of delinquency proceedings reported in other research (Morris and Giller, 1977; Langley *et al.*, 1978)[4] the large majority of children in our sample seemed to recognize the basis for the proceeding as that of illegal acts charged against them. Although this finding runs counter to a view of the child as being there to receive help, it should be borne in mind that the purpose of the hearing was often not explained; when it was, the explanation usually ran in legalistic terms that made reference to the grounds of referral that were to be put. A consideration of the need for compulsory measures of care appeared to be largely absent in the initial communications with the child and parents.

Hearings commence with the introduction to the family of all those present in some official capacity by both name and title. To learn if the child retains this information, we asked what the other people at the hearing were called, and probed with questions such as 'which person was the chairman?', 'which was the reporter?'. The social worker, if present, was always identified correctly and usually by name as well. Over half the children (53 per cent) correctly identified all participants and 10 per cent could not specify any. In between, some could attach a title to the chairman, the panel members, or both, but not the reporter, while others could identify only the reporter. These findings indicate considerably less confusion as to the identity of the various officials at hearings than has been found in studies at court settings (Scott, 1958; Baum and Wheeler, 1968).[5]

In reply to another question which asked who made the disposal decision, the panel members singly or together were designated in this role by 84 per cent (broken down as 36 per cent by the chairman, 16 per cent by one of the other panel members and 32 per cent by all three). In addition, 4 per cent saw the panel members in conjunction with the social worker or assessment staff as the decision-makers. Five per cent saw the social worker alone performing this function and the balance said they did not know or made some other response. This is in contrast to the finding that over half the juveniles before English magistrates could not say who had made the disposition decision (Morris and Giller, 1977).[6] The children at Scottish hearings generally appeared to have quite a clear idea of who was there and what their roles were, with the reporter being the most obscure of the participants.

Similarly, the actual decision seemed to be well understood, at least in the sense that almost all children could name it or describe its immediate implications for them. Those placed on residential supervision at List D schools were more likely to describe this as being 'sent away', 'keep me there', or 'being put away'. The time period involved in the residential supervision order was not well grasped, however, with most expecting to stay up to three months initially. Those given discharges were also more likely to use colloquial expressions, such as, 'let me off', 'forget about it', 'drop the charges' many of which imply some confusion of the implications of having grounds established as opposed to their being withdrawn. The term 'supervision' was often used correctly to describe home supervision decisions, though the term 'probation' came up quite often, as did 'seeing a social worker'. Of the three respondents who said they did not know the decision, one who was discharged said he could not hear the panel members (a difficulty shared by the observer). Another could not say what had happened other than that he was not being sent to an approved school; the third, with home supervision, did not want to answer. Generally, while most children understood what was to happen to them next as a result of their hearing, the implications of a discharge, and the time projected for a residential supervision order seemed less clear than what was involved in a home supervision outcome.

The questions relating to comprehension discussed thus far have dealt with tangible aspects of every hearing process – why the child is there, who else is present and what is decided. A more general question was directed at the totality of the experience, namely did the child 'find any parts hard to understand'. More than three quarters responded that they did not. Nearly one quarter who responded affirmatively were asked to recall these aspects. Responses varied, but could be grouped into four main areas of difficulty. The most frequent complaints focussed on the panel members' deficient communication skills. More specifically, children referred to lack of clarity in the way members put questions and made comments (11 cases). The process was described by one respondent as a 'muddle' when they 'talk about one thing and then another'. Sometimes a particular panel member was seen as the source of confusion:

'she was asking questions and answering them herself – I couldn't understand anything she said'. A second group of similar responses (six cases) made reference to difficulty with the language employed in the hearing, summed up by this child: 'they used big words, that older people use. I didn't know what they meant.' A third problem area that was identified (by four subjects) casts doubts on whether the grounds had been legally established. One child commented 'I thought when he said do you accept that, he meant did I know about it and was it true, not did *I* do it'. Another elaborated that, 'first they said you were there but not involved, and then you were involved just by being there'. Finally, a fourth group of three cases referred to learning at the end that what was to happen was different from what they had thought at an earlier point in the hearing would be the outcome. Thus, while three-quarters of the sample responded that they had not found any parts hard to understand, some difficulty was experienced by the rest, related primarily to panel member communication involving questions or comments, vocabulary, legal aspects of the grounds and details of the outcome.

Participation

The majority of children seemed satisfied with their level of participation at the hearing: 82 per cent felt that the panel members wanted to hear their story, 85 per cent indicated they had said all they wanted and 94 per cent had not said anything they regretted. Twice the proportion of children thought the panel members were more interested in hearing from them than from their parents (59 per cent compared to 29 per cent), 10 per cent thought both equally and only 3 per cent neither. Indeed, when these responses are related to observed participation, it is apparent that those with low levels did not differ markedly from those with medium or high levels in their expressions of satisfaction (see Table 12.1*a*, *b*, *c*, *d*). Whatever the cause of the minority of negative responses, it is at least not rooted in simply not having taken part in the discussion.

The respondents did discriminate among the three panel members in ease of communication with them. While 42 per cent found them all quite easy to talk to, and 11 per cent perceived them as uniformly difficult in this regard, 47 per cent identified some as easier or harder than others. In relating this perception to actual participation levels, a mild tendency was displayed from those with low levels to find panel members all hard to talk to: 20 per cent compared with 10 per cent and 8 per cent of those with medium and high levels respectively (see Table 12.1*d*).

When asked who they thought was the best person to tell their story to the hearing, nearly half the children named themselves (45 per cent) or themselves plus the social worker (2 per cent). Another 13 per cent said their parents were the best representatives, 26 per cent chose the social worker alone and 2 per cent the parent and social worker together. Four per cent named some other figure such as a lawyer or family friend, one said 'no-one' and 8 per cent answered they 'didn't know' who was the best person. These figures are quite similar to those recorded in a Canadian study of 22 juveniles who had attended court proceedings: 41 per cent named themselves, 18 per cent specified their parents, 18 per cent the legal aid duty counsel, 14 per cent other figures and 9 per cent said no-one (Catton and Erickson, 1975).[7]

In relation to *actual* participation levels, children who were observed to

TABLE 12.1

CHILDREN'S PERCEPTION OF ASPECTS OF PARTICIPATION BY OBSERVED LEVELS

Perception of aspects of participation	*Observed level of participation*					
	Low %		*Medium* %		*High* %	
a Want to hear your story?						
No	21		15		21	
Yes	79		85		79	
(N = 100%)		(19)		(47)		(34)
b Say all you wanted?						
No	10		18		14	
Yes	90		82		86	
(N = 100%)		(20)		(50)		(35)
c Say anything you wished you hadn't?						
No	95		94		94	
Yes	5		6		6	
(N = 100%)		(20)		(50)		(35)
d Easy or hard to talk to?						
All same/easy	35		42		46	
All same/hard	20		10		8	
Some easy/some hard	45		48		46	
(N = 100%)		(20)		(50)		(35)
e Who best to tell story?						
Me	37		45		67	
Other	63		55		33	
(N = 100%)		(16)		(47)		(33)
f Interested in hearing from most?						
Me	63		48		71	
Parent	26		34		23	
Both the same	11		14		3	
Neither	0		4		3	
(N = 100%)		(19)		(50)		(35)

Low = Silent/Yes/No/DK
Medium = Answers questions
High = Speaks out/Elaborates/Asks questions

'Don't know' responses excluded from totals.

take the most active part in the hearing were much more likely to consider themselves the best person to tell their story than those with minimal participation (see Table 12.1*e*). A strong, direct relationship was displayed, with 67 per cent of the high participators, 45 per cent of the medium and 37 per cent of the low choosing themselves in this role. In conjunction with the earlier findings about general satisfaction with their involvement, it would appear that a significant proportion of the children preferred that others took part on their behalf, and satisfaction with a hearing was not directly affected by how much was said by the child himself. It is perhaps worth emphasizing that, while many children apparently did wish to put their views across and often did so, 'getting their say' may be more important than any absolute amount of participation. It seems possible to over-estimate the importance, from the child's point of view, of his or her level of verbal involvement. Too great an emphasis on this factor may reflect the adult's, not the child's values.

Alignment

Questions about the perceived alignment of those present at the hearing reflect the extent to which a juvenile feels the process was fair and balanced, that his interests were being considered, and that his case received the attention it deserved. In an effort to distinguish between feelings of being part of an adversarial procedure and those associated with a helping effort, two separate questions were put. One pertained to the child's view as to whether anyone present was 'on your side' and the other asked whether anyone was 'there to help you'. If an affirmative reply was received, a supplementary query, 'who most' was added. Responses are shown in Table 12.2.

In comparing the two sets of responses, it is evident that juveniles were more likely to consider 'no-one' was on their side (24 per cent) than that 'no-one' was there to help them (9 per cent). Conversely, 13 per cent thought 'everyone' was on their side and 20 per cent believed 'everyone' was there to help them. For both questions, similar proportions of other participants were identified in reply to 'who most?', with parents and/or social workers more likely to be named (38-40 per cent) than panel member-reporter combinations (21–25 per cent). The less frequent attenders at hearings, such as teachers, List D school staff and assessment personnel, were specified by 3 per cent of children as being most on their side and by 7 per cent as the person most likely to help them. These findings suggest that the vast majority of respondents did not feel completely unsupported at hearings, and that they tended to perceive a helping orientation more often than an adversarial one. Nevertheless, a minority did convey a sense of isolation and rejection within the hearing context.

Interesting Scottish-Canadian comparisons may be drawn in this area of alignment. The same questions, put to children in the Catton and Erickson (1975)[8] court study, elicited quite different responses. Three times the proportion of children answered that 'no-one' was there to help them than did so in our study (27 per cent as opposed to 9 per cent). Conversely, a somewhat smaller proportion of Canadian juveniles (18 per cent) expressed a view that 'no-one' was on their side than was found with our Scottish respondents (24 per cent). In Canada, the legal aid duty counsel was the person most often identified in both the aligned and helping roles, in nearly a third of cases, and rarely was 'everyone' associated with either function (5 per cent in each). These cross-national perceptual differences displayed by juveniles exposed to each system would appear to reflect their essential organizational contrasts; in the Canadian court setting, juveniles seem more attuned to an adversarial proceeding than to a helping one, while the opposite seems to apply for the Scottish sample.

Children were also asked directly whether the hearing 'generally was for you or against you'. Excluding 10 'don't know' responses, a majority of 55 per cent said the hearing was for them, and another 14 per cent considered it to be neutral, that is not to have taken sides. Eight per cent thought the hearing was divided, with some members for them and others against them, and 23 per cent responded that all the panel members were against them. Thus for nearly a third of the children who gave a clear response to this question, a positive sense of fairness in the process was lacking, while for 69 per cent it was present. This perception was linked rather inconsistently to outcome, in that 57 per cent of those sent to List D schools, 22 per cent receiving home supervision and 38 per cent of those discharged considered the hearing to be balanced in whole or in part against them.

When children's opinions were sought as to whether a lawyer might have

TABLE 12.2

CHILDREN'S PERCEPTIONS OF ALIGNMENT OF OTHERS AT HEARING

Others at Hearing	*On your side?* (N)	*Most?* %	*There to help you?* (N)	*Most?* %
No-one	24	24	9	9
Parent	7		11	
Social worker	23		21	
Social worker and parent	7		8	
Subtotal %		38		40
All panel members	2		8	
One panel member	13		9	
Panel member(s) and social worker	2		5	
Panel member(s) and reporter	2		1	
Reporter	2		2	
Subtotal %		21		25
Teacher/List D/Assessment	3	3	7	7
Everyone	13	13	20	20
Total (= 100%)	98		101	
Don't know	7		4	

helped them, quite a few (13 per cent) were unable to answer beyond 'don't know'. While the majority of the others responded 'no', the 22 per cent who answered affirmatively were more likely to give a qualified response than a strongly positive one. This seemed to be because so few of the children, as they themselves commented, had ever spoken to a lawyer or had much idea of what to expect of one. (Again, this limited perception is not confined to a system that operates without lawyers, see Catton and Erickson, 1975).[9] The sample members' hesitancy about the need for legal representation was also conveyed in their responses to another question which asked whether they would have liked anyone else there to speak for them. Only 3 per cent of the children specifically mentioned a lawyer. Nearly 80 per cent indicated they did not desire the presence of anyone else at their hearing. Others when named included parent, other relative, teacher, social worker, List D staff and witnesses.

Decision-making

Virtually all studies that have sought the views of delinquents claim that the outcome of the proceeding is the most crucial aspect from their point of view. We have seen that most children understood what the decision was (at least in terms of its immediate implications) and who had made it. We now consider the children's perception of the fairness of the decision and how it was reached. The reasons of the hearing, as discerned by the children, and their own sense of appropriate reasons for the disposition awarded, will also be described.

We wanted to know whether the hearings system could be said to be operating justly on the criterion that children perceived the decision as fair in their case. Nearly four out of five children (78 per cent) did think the decision was fair. Seven per cent reported mixed views, 9 per cent did not consider it fair and the balance did not comment. The sample members' sense of fairness was unrelated to prior record at hearings or to being on supervision. Some association between perception of fairness and severity of outcome was displayed, in that 67 per cent of those sent to List D schools thought the decision was fair compared to 86 per cent of those discharged or placed on supervision.

These findings are in general accord with studies in other jurisdictions which show that the bulk of processed delinquents assign legitimacy to the disposition and to the system in general. Although some of this research did not probe beyond an assessment of 'justice' or 'fairness' (Scott, 1968; Snyder, 1971; Stapleton and Teitelbaum, 1972:)[10], others sought client response to the actual decision. Thus, Morris and Giller (1977)[11] reported that 63 per cent of their English sample considered the decision fair; this sentiment was shared by 68 per cent in the Baum and Wheeler (1968)[12] study of institutionalized juveniles. This latter figure echoes the 67 per cent of children sent to List D schools in our sample who accepted this decision as fair.

As Catton and Erickson (1975)[13] have cautioned, children may acknowledge the fairness of their being brought to account for their offences and the disposition they receive, but still feel that aspects of the proceedings are unfair.

We therefore elicited views on the decision-making process in more detail. One concern was their perception of the timing of the actual decision in relation to the hearing as a whole. Their responses as to what point in the hearing the decision was made were strongly related to disposition (see Table 12.3*a*, $p<0{\cdot}01$).

Only 7 per cent of those getting a discharge thought this was decided *before* the hearing, compared to 24 per cent of those placed on home supervision and 64 per cent of those sent to List D schools. The decision was reached *during* the hearing, according to the client's interpretation, for 59 per cent of those discharged, 43 per cent with compulsory supervision and 29 per cent with a residential outcome. Those sent to List D schools were least likely to see the decision as made at the *end* of the hearing, 7 per cent as compared to one third of those receiving the other two dispositions. The child's perception of the timing of the decision was also significantly related to prior record (see Table 12.3*b*, $p<0{\cdot}001$). Repeaters were more than four times as likely to see the decision as made beforehand than first timers: 44 per cent *v.* 10 per cent.

The children were also asked if they felt they had any influence on the decision made by the hearing. The sample, with the exception of nine who expressed no opinion, was quite evenly divided between those who thought

TABLE 12.3

CHILDREN'S PERCEPTION OF TIMING OF DECISION

a By outcome	*Outcome*		
	Discharge %	*Supervision* %	*List D* %
When was decision made?			
Before hearing	7	24	64
During hearing	59	43	29
After hearing	34	33	7
(N = 100%)	29	59	13

b By prior record	*Prior record at hearings*	
	First appearance %	*Repeater* %
When was decision made?		
Before hearing	10	44
During hearing	52	37
After hearing	38	19
(N = 100%)	56	45

Four 'don't know' responses omitted.

they had helped the panel members make up their minds and those who believed they had had no influence. Again, this perception was significantly related to the actual decision (see Table 12.4*a*, $p < 0.05$), with affirmative responses coming from 58 per cent of those discharged, 46 per cent of those placed on home supervision and 14 per cent of children sent to List D school. The relationship was in a similar direction, though not significant, between perception of influence and prior record (54 per cent of first offenders responded positively and 33 per cent of repeaters). (See Table 12.4*b*). A stronger association was found with respect to being under supervision, with 54 per cent of those not, and 24 per cent of those who were, seeing themselves as influential. These findings seem to imply that more exposure to the hearings is accompanied by greater feelings of powerlessness, rather than increased confidence in affecting the outcome.

The underlying philosophy of the hearings system has a similarity to many traditional juvenile systems in that the 'best interests' of the child are meant to take precedence over criminal justice concerns such as protection of the community, deterrence and retribution. This in theory should encourage decisions at hearings to be taken in consideration of the child's situation and

TABLE 12.4

CHILDREN'S PERCEPTION OF OWN INFLUENCE ON DECISION

a By outcome

	Outcome		
	Discharge %	*Supervision* %	*List D* %
Influence the decision?			
No	42	54	86
Yes	58	46	14
(N = 100%)			

b By prior record

	Prior record at hearings	
	First appearance %	*Repeater* %
Influence the decision?		
No	46	67
Yes	54	33
(N = 100%)		

N excludes nine who replied 'don't know'.

needs rather than a tariff based on the seriousness and frequency of offending. An explicit procedural requirement that is perhaps unique to the Scottish system is that the reasons for the decision must be communicated to the child and family at the end of the hearing and be made available to them in writing if requested. As we learned in *Chapter 7*, this requirement was not fulfilled consistently. We were interested in exploring the extent to which the child discerned the reasons, and the extent of his or her agreement with them, as a basis for the decision.

Open-ended questions were used to elicit the child's perception of the most important reason to the hearing and what he or she considered it should have been. Answers were grouped according to the predominant factors, as shown in Table 12.5. Quite a high proportion, about one sixth of the sample, did not provide a reason in response to either question. Of those who did, the overall distribution of responses was quite similar, the notable exception being that school factors were seen as being more important to the hearing (31 per cent) than to the juveniles (19 per cent) while the emphasis was reversed for offence factors (hearing 15 per cent, children 27 per cent). Interestingly, when related to actual outcome, about 17 per cent of those with discharge or home supervision but *none* of those sent to List D thought the offence was most important to the hearing. The latter group gave a wide-ranging set of individualized responses, that though similarly varied when their own view of appropriate reasons was sought, tended to be different from the one attached to the panel members.

In fact, to examine only the distribution for each question separately is somewhat misleading, as the pairs of responses were not in close agreement in over half the cases. Not surprisingly, children tended to emphasize factors that seemed favourable to their case, such as a good school report or attendance, a

TABLE 12.5

CHILDREN'S PERCEPTIONS OF MOST IMPORTANT REASON FOR DECISION

Decision factors related to:	*Most important to hearing?* %	*Most important in your view?* %
Offence	15	27
Home	6	6
School	31	19
Combination of non-offence	12	11
Recreation/peers	11	9
Job/future/career	5	4
Likelihood of repeating or improving	7	7
Other/Miscellaneous	14	17
(N = 100%)	85	89
N's exclude 'don't know'.	20	16

caring family, involvement in spare time activities or the rather trivial nature of the offence or their contribution to it when acting with others. They often conveyed a sense of feeling that positive things about themselves got disproportionately little coverage compared to negative examples of assessments. Another common source of discrepancy was the attention paid by panel members to non-offence factors when the child thought the offence was most important.

The great variation in perceived reasons should not be surprising given the diversity of topics and approaches observed in hearing situations (*Chapter 8*). If the juveniles themselves stress a number of different factors as important considerations in decision-making, so too do the hearings appear to vary widely in what they emphasize. While it might be argued that the relatively infrequent mention of offence factors (15 per cent) as most important to the panel members shows they have conveyed consideration for the 'needs' of the child, this must be tempered by the contrasting view expressed by clients that the offence should be more important and school attendance and behaviour less important. Nevertheless, offence criteria appear to carry much less weight with our sample than the 59 per cent reported for English juveniles (Morris and Giller, 1977).[14]

A comparison of the two sets of 'reasons' also indicates that the children more often disagree than agree with the reasons they attribute to panel members. A disturbing feature of these findings is that those sent to List D schools, and thus presumably seen as having the greatest need for change in their behaviour, also have the least clear impression of the hearing's reason for this decision, seeing them as neither offence-oriented nor background-related, but highly idiosyncratic. In interpreting the responses of children who have been committed to residential care, some allowance must be made for an inevitable degree of defensiveness on their part. But even when all the young people's reactions, including the more critical ones, are taken into account, it still seems probable that the hearings system has gone further than most courts of which we have knowledge in involving the child in decision-making and encouraging a sense of fairness.

Attitudes towards panel members, social workers, reporters and police

An issue distinct from the purpose and effectiveness of the system in general is how the clients view its major representatives. We wanted to learn how the children regarded the principal agents of the hearings system and whether they discriminated among them. We attempted this by asking them to consider each of the 'official' participants in terms of a number of attributes: justice, empathy with children, helpfulness, punitiveness and power. These qualities were exemplified in specific statements.

(i) Justice

Wants you to be treated fairly. (Item *a*)

Helps give you a chance to tell your side of the story. (*d*)

(ii) Empathy

Cares what happens to kids. (*k*)
Is just doing his job and doesn't care about the people he sees. (*g*)
Doesn't have any idea of the kinds of problems kids have. (*e*)

(iii) Helpfulness

Helps you find out what's really going on. (*b*)
Tries to help kids stay out of trouble. (*h*)
Knows what's best for kids. (*m*)

(iv) Punitiveness

Enjoys punishing kids. (*c*)
Tries to confuse you. (*j*)
Is really a nice person, but acts nasty because that's his job. (*l*)

(v) Power – Other

Always knows when you're not telling the truth. (*f*)

(vi) Power – Self

Can easily be fooled if you're clever about it. (*i*)

To ensure consistency and comparability of the data, these thirteen statements adapted from an American interview study with court-processed juveniles (Stapleton and Teitelbaum, unpublished) were presented to all subjects. They were asked to indicate whether each item applied to any of the following: panel members, social worker, reporter or police. Most children had no difficulty in responding to this question. Time pressure interrupted three interviews, requiring the analysis to be based on 102 cases. We describe first the general trends in role perceptions for each of the four agents, and then examine the intercorrelations between roles.

The distribution of responses is shown in Table 12.6. For panel members the description most often applied (52 per cent) was 'helps give you a chance to tell your side of the story', followed by 'wants you to be treated fairly' (44 per cent) and by 'knows what's best for kids' (37 per cent). Items least frequently attached to panel members (11 per cent for each) were 'enjoys punishing kids' and 'can easily be fooled if you're clever about it'.

Social workers were described as 'wants you to be treated fairly' by 59 per cent, 'tries to help kids stay out of trouble' by 57 per cent and 'cares what happens to kids' by 50 per cent. The least mentioned item for social workers, by only one per cent, was 'enjoys punishing kids'.

Reporters received the fewest responses for all categories, with the proportion of subjects applying *any* statements to them never exceeding 10 per cent. Evidently children react less to the reporter than to the other key figures of the system. This was not so for the police, as most children gave well-defined responses; half believed that they 'enjoy punishing kids' and not one agreed that the police 'help give you a chance to tell your side of the story'. Indeed, of the 13 statements shown in Table 12.6 seven were more often applied to police than to any of the other three role players. (Four were linked most frequently with social workers, two with panel members and none with reporters).

Thus even at this point it is evident that the children do discriminate quite sharply among the various roles. It is also clear that the more hostile or cynical views apply principally to the police, although 41 per cent of children did concede that a police officer was 'really a nice person but acts nasty because that's his job'. Panel members and social workers were more often viewed in a favourable light, though panel members were not rated quite as highly as social workers. The reporter seemed a more neutral figure, judging by the general lack of response.

The intercorrelations for each item across roles (Table 12.7) show an interesting tendency for some 'favourable' opinions on qualities of justice and helpfulness (items *a*, *b*, *d*) to be significantly but negatively correlated for panel members and social workers. This suggests that one or the other participant is seen in these favourable terms rather than both. However, the opposite trend is found for some 'unfavourable' attitudes (*c*, *e*, *g*, *j*) which are positively

TABLE 12.6

CHILDREN'S ROLE PERCEPTIONS

	Item	*Per cent attaching statement to each agent*			
		Panel Members %	*Social Worker* %	*Reporter* %	*Police* %
a	Wants you to be treated fairly.	44	59	10	7
b	Helps you find out what's really going on.	17	46	7	3
c	Enjoys punishing kids.	11	1	1	51
d	Helps give you a chance to tell your side of the story.	52	23	1	0
e	Doesn't have any idea of the kinds of problems kids have.	16	5	7	25
f	Always knows when you're not telling the truth.	15	5	1	28
g	Is just doing his job and doesn't care about the people he sees.	14	10	10	44
h	Tries to help kids stay out of trouble.	22	57	3	13
i	Can easily be fooled if you're clever about it.	11	17	3	23
j	Tries to confuse you.	17	5	5	32
k	Cares what happens to kids.	28	50	2	3
l	Is really a nice person but acts nasty because that's his job.	15	10	4	41
m	Knows what's best for kids.	37	22	5	1
	(N = 100%)		102		

N excludes three incomplete interviews.

TABLE 12.7

INTER-CORRELATIONS BETWEEN DIFFERENT ROLES FOR EACH ATTITUDE

Attitude Statement		Role		
		Social Worker %	Reporter %	Police %
a	Panel Member	−0·19	0·24*	0·07
	Social Worker		0·13	−0·01
	Reporter			0·30**
b	Panel Member	−0·27*	−0·02	−0·08
	Social Worker		−0·17	−0·16
	Reporter			−0·05
c	Panel Member	0·29*	0·29*	−0·04
	Social Worker		†	0·10
	Reporter			0·10
d	Panel Member	−0·35**	−0·10	†
	Social Worker		−0·05	†
	Reporter			†
e	Panel Member	0·28*	0·20	0·06
	Social Worker		0·48**	0·18
	Reporter			0·11
f	Panel Member	0·16	0·24*	−0·01
	Social Worker		0·44**	0·26*
	Reporter			0·16
g	Panel Member	0·44**	0·44**	0·05
	Social Worker		0·56**	0·16
	Reporter			0·04
h	Panel Member	0·04	0·18	0·08
	Social Worker		−0·08	−0·14
	Reporter			0·12
i	Panel Member	0·27*	0·31**	0·11
	Social Worker		0·23*	0·07
	Reporter			0·18
j	Panel Member	0·14	0·14	−0·25*
	Social Worker		0·16	−0·06
	Reporter			−0·06
k	Panel Member	−0·02	0·22*	0·02
	Social Worker		0·00	−0·06
	Reporter			−0·02
l	Panel Member	0·05	0·06	−0·23*
	Social Worker		0·10	−0·21
	Reporter			−0·06
m	Panel Member	−0·07	0·11	0·13
	Social Worker		0·20	0·18
	Reporter			0·44**

* $p < 0·01$. ** $p < 0·001$.

† Numbers too small to allow calculation of *r*.

correlated at significant levels for panel members and social workers. This would mean that these two groups tend to be rather indistinguishable to children who view them as uncaring and punitive. In other words, the more favourable expressions of attitude may be quite discriminating (i.e. related more to the specific agent than the system in general) while unfavourable assessments may tend to encompass both of these representatives of the system. The police data also tend to this interpretation, but since many statements were never applied to the police by respondents, the result is less conclusive. It is also of interest to note that feelings of power *vis à vis* the other and self (*f* and *i*) were also attached quite consistently to all system agents.

As no analysis of this portion of the attitude data from the Stapleton and Teitelbaum study has been published, it is not possible to draw comparisons between the specific American and Scottish findings. As far as more general tendencies are concerned, research by Baum and Wheeler (1968), Snyder (1971) and Giordano (1974)[15] produced similar evidence that processed juveniles express little general hostility towards the specific agents of the system, although findings were mixed regarding the police, and seem to express a rather objective appraisal of these people as 'doing their job'.

Stigma and self-labelling

Having concentrated so far on children's specific reactions to and assessments of hearing events, we turn our attention to the less direct but potentially more far-reaching impact of the processing of delinquents. Several theorists have argued that the liability accrued as a result of the official intervention is at odds with the intended salutary effect of such a proceeding (Lemert, 1951; Becker, 1963; Matza, 1964).[16] This labelling perspective, as it is called, suggests that the public designation of a deviant or 'spoiled' identity may serve to reinforce rather than inhibit the socially undesirable behaviour by acting as a barrier to conventional role relationships. This is thought to occur in essentially two ways, first by negatively affecting interactions with significant others in the social milieu, and secondly by altering the individual's sense of self so that he feels an 'outsider'. We shall refer to the first instance, involving liability in relations with others as 'stigma'; the second, invoking a changed and somehow diminished or damaged sense of identity, as 'self-labelling'.

A critical and unresolved issue is the extent to which the negative, unintended consequences of official reactions to delinquency are anticipated or experienced by the individual so processed. Several studies have addressed this question, with somewhat varied conclusions. Snyder (1971)[17] reported that 'children felt that the greatest harm resulting from their court appearance was that other people knew about it'. Foster *et al.* (1972)[18] also found a concern among delinquents about adverse evaluations by others which was stronger in the more impersonal spheres of contact – police and future employers – than in more intimate circles – friends and family. Although the research of Ageton and Elliot (1974) and Jensen (1972)[19] supported the contention that formal contact with the control system heightened a delinquent orientation, susceptibility to self-labelling varied considerably according to race and class membership. In contrast, Hepburn (1977)[20] found that involvement in delinquent activities was more important than official intervention in generating a delinquent identification. Similarly, Siegal (1975)[21] did not find that self-labelling generally increased after official intervention, and concluded that the process of delinquent self-labelling was a complex, long-term one. There was also the suggestion in these studies that the impact of the court appearance diminished over time.

Given that comprehensive reviews of the evidence regarding the harmful effects of labelling in the juvenile justice system are available (Mahoney, 1974; Albrecht and Albrecht, 1978)[22] we have merely highlighted some research findings to illustrate some of the issues involved. Although they are far from resolved, most writers on this subject would agree that to assume a direct, inevitable, causal link between official intervention and stigma, self-labelling and increased commitment to deviant activities is a vast over-simplification and a disservice to the labelling perspective. A number of important contributing factors – including the personal background characteristics of juveniles, prior records, intensity of system involvement, actual extent of illegal activities (as opposed to detected), peer behaviour, and outcome of the intervention – have been identified in the complex labelling process.

A crucial aspect that has been neglected empirically is what effect variation in setting might have on this process. Thus, while many assumptions have been made concerning the degrading, intimidating impact of a court proceeding on a juvenile (e.g. Garfinkel, 1956; Matza, 1964; Emerson, 1969),[23] no attempt has been made to relate objective aspects of proceedings to the child's reaction in terms of stigma and self-labelling. We were provided with a unique opportunity to do so in this study.

Thorsell and Klemke (1972)[24] have proposed that, depending on the social setting and the interpersonal aspects, the labelling process may function as a 'positive, integrating force'. That is, instead of reinforcing deviant activities as most labelling proponents have argued, the process may serve to discourage the unacceptable behaviour and induce conformity. Some of the hypotheses put forward by these authors as conducive to the 'positive' outcome of intervention are especially suitable for investigation at delinquency hearings in Scotland. These are as follows:

(i) if the labelling is conducted in a confidential setting:
(ii) if the labelling has been carried out by an in-group member or significant other:
(iii) if the labelling results in efforts to re-integrate the deviant into the community:
(iv) if the label is favourable rather than derogatory.

Let us consider briefly how each of these general principles might apply in children's hearings as opposed to a conventional juvenile court system. First, as *Chapter 6* described, deliberate attempts have been made to remove hearings from court buildings and place them in more everyday locations. Combined with timetabling that avoids the 'crowded waiting room' phenomenon of traditional courts, this decentralization of hearings would appear potentially to increase the confidentiality of the proceedings. Secondly, the lay composition of the panels, with members drawn from the community at large, would seem to be nearer to 'in-group members' than judges or magistrates. The importance of this point is that someone with whom the 'deviant' can identify, and who is qualified by virtue of experience to make more personalized observations, may be better able to neutralize a resistant or hostile response. Thirdly, the concern for re-integration of the individual into the community, which is by no means unique to the system, may be seen as potentially more achievable in a hearing setting where alternatives may be discussed in an open forum. Of course, hearings have the power to remove the child from the home, but even in so doing are expected to convey why this is 'best' and, in theory, may supply positive and supportive rather than rejecting types of reasons for this decision. Fourthly, children's hearings avoid terms such as 'delinquent' and 'guilty' in favour of 'grounds being established', and any dissension to the charge on the part of the client is dealt with separately by a judicial figure. The hearing has the sole mandate to decide on an appropriate disposition. In the course of the wide-ranging discussion that is possible and divorced from questions of guilt or innocence, the panel members have considerable opportunity to make favourable statements about the juvenile. Again, this capacity for positive input would appear to be on the whole greater than is associated with traditional courts. This is not to say that juvenile courts do not share the potential for fulfilling these requirements, but rather to suggest that the organization of hearings may enhance the likelihood to a greater extent. At least in their potential, hearings could be characterized as 'low stigma/low labelling' organizations. What is not known is the extent to which these features are incorporated into actual hearings and how the clients respond.

Following earlier work by Foster *et al.* (1972),[25] the juveniles in our study were asked to describe their awareness and anticipation of change towards them by others in their immediate social network (friends, parents, teachers) or somewhat more distantly (police, future employers). The question of whether they thought they had 'a record' as a result of their appearance was also posed. Then a series of questions to elucidate the self evaluations of the juveniles was asked. The sense of stigma and self-labelling displayed by the children in these areas of perception will be summarized and then related to the hearing outcome, prior legal experience and the style of panel members.

A concern to keep the hearing event a secret might reflect the child's fear that revelation would be discrediting. Such a reaction was expressed by children interviewed by Snyder (1971).[26] Accordingly, subjects were asked if they had told their friends about it. Nearly two thirds said they had, often adding, 'they've been too', and indeed 80 per cent of the sample reported that friends had records at hearings. Many of the approximately one third who had not told friends qualified their response by comments such as 'they already knew', or 'word gets around'. When asked directly, if their friends would have a different attitude to them now, only one in eight thought this would happen. However, none in the study by Foster *et al.* (1972)[27] expected this.

Over half reported a change towards them from parents in a variety of forms. The largest number (27 per cent) described their parents' feelings of concern, worry, anger or mistrust over the incident. Another 16 per cent told of their parents' actions in punishing them, being stricter or even throwing them out of the house. And 13 per cent of the replies were miscellaneous, including descriptions of parents being nicer or more helpful to the child. Similar to the findings of Foster *et al.* (1972),[28] most of the changes attributed to parents by the juveniles could be considered short-run reactions to an offspring's being in trouble, rather than a shift to permanent negative expectations or assessments of the child. The exceptions seem to be the more extreme examples of distrust and expulsion from the home in a minority of cases. The projected likelihood of difficulties at school due to the official reaction was not relevant to eleven sample members who had or were about to leave regular school. Of those who could answer, one quarter expected some negative repercussions at school, three times the proportion reported by Foster *et al.* (1972)[29] for whom the question was relevant.

In considering the response of others more removed from the children's immediate lives, a greater degree of anticipation of stigmatization was displayed. Not only did 64 per cent expect the police to hold having been to a hearing against them, 77 per cent projected that future employers would. In fact, concerns about job prospects generated the most commentary of this series of questions, with remarks such as 'they won't trust me', 'they think you're not honest' volunteered frequently. The question about having a 'record' was not answered by 15 per cent of the sample. Of those who did reply, 56 per cent responded affirmatively and 44 per cent thought no record resulted from a hearing. These results are consistent with those of Foster *et al.* (1972)[30] in that a greater expectation of social liability was displayed with respect to more impersonal figures, but they differ in degree. In their sample, 54 per cent were concerned about the police and 40 per cent about future employers.

An important difference in the two samples was that not all the American juveniles had attended court, some penetrating the system only as far as police contact. All the Scottish juveniles had attended hearings. Unfortunately, Foster *et al.* do not present their results for these two groups separately, except for potential employers. In this instance, court processed boys had a greater anticipation of stigma than those whose cases were handled by the police alone. Even so, this level of response was lower than that displayed by our sample. Another possible explanation for the discrepancy in findings is the difference in cultural contexts. It is possible that in Scottish society, any trouble with the law is perceived to be 'held against you' to a greater extent than in the United States (and may in fact be, although we cannot ascertain this from our data). Since no comparative information is available from the pre-hearing era, it is not possible to determine whether Scottish court appearances were viewed as even more stigmatizing by juveniles than the present system. The possibility cannot be discounted, however, that hearings may be *more* stigmatizing and labelling than courts; this option is considered more fully later.

The development of an altered sense of identity (i.e. self-labelling) is a difficult concept to operationalize (see Siegal, 1975).[31] We opted for a single item indicator, 'think of self as criminal', drawing on Jensen (1972).[32] Another item, 'think of self as delinquent', was rejected after piloting because juveniles in Scotland did not seem familiar with the word 'delinquent'. To offer a contrast, with the hearings system's welfare orientation in mind, 'think of self as in need of help' was included. To expand the choices and de-emphasize any particular one, three other self-evaluation items were added. These were 'think of self as just like any other —— year old/picked on/unlucky'. In these five items directed at self perception, a minority of children saw themselves as either 'in need of help' (22 per cent) or 'criminal' (26 per cent). Most considered themselves as like anyone else their age (80 per cent). They were next more likely to answer affirmatively to being 'unlucky' (61 per cent) or 'picked on' (38 per cent).

The findings described thus far provide some evidence of a sense of stigmatization and self-labelling in children who have attended hearings. It remains to determine what factors are associated with these perceptions. Are they developed on the basis of what has gone before, or does the hearing experience contribute in some way?

Influences on stigma and self-labelling

Differences were slight (Table 12.8) between those receiving discharge, supervision or List D outcomes in their perceptions of stigma emanating from others. In regard to self-labelling, there was a tendency for those sent to List D schools to see themselves as less like others their age and more like criminals, and especially as being picked on ($p < 0.05$), when compared to those receiving either of the other dispositions.

No striking differences were apparent in sense of stigma between those appearing for the first time and repeaters, but some trends may be noted (Table 12.9). Those with *no* prior experience were somewhat *more* likely to report change from both friends and parents than those with a previous record. The emphasis was reversed in relation to police, with repeaters significantly more often anticipating negative police reaction than first timers (79 per cent *v.* 52 per cent, $p < 0.05$). In terms of self-perception, repeaters were significantly more likely to see themselves as being picked on than those without previous referrals to hearings (53 per cent *v.* 26 per cent, $p < 0.01$). They were also somewhat more likely to consider themselves criminals, but at non-significant levels (35 per cent *v.* 19 per cent).

Being on supervision or not at the time of the hearing did not really differentiate the respondents with respect to a sense of stigma. General trends were similar to, but less emphatic than, those noted above for the effect of the prior record variable.

The various styles adopted by panel members in the course of a hearing might in theory act to enhance or diminish some of the aspects of stigmatization. Virtually no empirical studies have been conducted in this field. Even with one decision-maker such as a judge, the objective recording of observation is a formidable task, compounded in a three member situation. One difficulty with our 'style' categories is that while each may be related discretely to perception, several are likely to have occurred at a given hearing, so that the effects related to any one style may be diluted. We would not expect strong patterns of association to emerge, and shall look in our findings at trends within a wider range of significance ($p < 0.10$).

When all the style items are related separately to each measure of stigma and self-labelling, some tendencies are apparent which will be summarized briefly before expanding the analysis: (the figures in brackets are percentages of children affirming this perception in hearings with that style recorded *v.* not recorded)

police stigma and a sarcastic/contemptuous style (77 per cent *v.* 60 per cent)
stigma from employer and a threatening/exhorting style (86 per cent *v.* 72 per cent)
self as in need of help and sympathetic/understanding style (29 per cent *v.* 15 per cent)
self as in need of help and interrogating/demanding style (15 per cent *v.* 29 per cent)
self as criminal and positive input (17 per cent *v.* 30 per cent)
self as unlucky and threatening/exhorting style (74 per cent *v.* 54 per cent)

TABLE 12.8

PROPORTION OF CHILDREN ANTICIPATING NEGATIVE CONSEQUENCES ACCORDING TO OUTCOME AT HEARING

	Outcome			
	Discharge %	*Supervision* %	*List D* %	*Total* %
From external sources				
Friends	15	11	8	12
Parents	44	61	54	56
School	25	22	50	25
Police	54	67	71	64
Employers	72	78	83	77
Record	60	55	57	56
Perceptions of self				
In need of help	17	26	15	22
Like others	90	82	62	80
As criminal	21	26	39	26
As unlucky	59	63	54	61
As picked on*	32	34	69	38

* $p < 0.05$.

As is evident from the large number of potential relationships excluded from the list, no association was displayed between any style items and the sense of stigma from friends, parents and teachers, nor in self-identification as 'like any other' and 'picked on'.

The patterns that did occur for self-perceptions are suggestive, especially when considered in conjunction. For instance, children were *more* likely to perceive themselves as in need of help when a sympathetic or understanding style was recorded, and *less* likely to do so when the panel was interrogating or demanding. Respondents also showed less self-perception as criminal when a positive aspect about them had been raised by the panel members but were *more* likely to see themselves as unlucky when an exhorting or threatening style had been used. We may speculate at this point that children are responding in the expected directions: favourably to a supportive hearing, with resistance and defensiveness to a harsher stance.

Interesting relationships were also shown for both anticipated stigma from employers and expectation of a record when threatening or exhorting behaviour by panel members was recorded. This may be considered in the light of observation findings (*Chapter 8*) that saw this style often expressed in terms of dire warnings about the child's future chances. Less explicable on first examination is the trend showing greater expectation of police stigma when the panel adopted a sarcastic or contemptuous style.

The next task is to extend this contingency analysis while taking into account some of the other factors that might affect the child's sense of stigmatization and self-labelling. We want to learn if the relationships are sustained or

TABLE 12.9

PROPORTION OF CHILDREN ANTICIPATING NEGATIVE CONSEQUENCES ACCORDING TO PRIOR RECORD AT HEARINGS

	Prior record at hearings	
	First Appearance %	*Repeater* %
From external sources		
Friends	15	7
Parents	58	43
School	21	31
Police*	52	79
Employers	78	74
Record	55	58
Perceptions of self		
In need of help	21	24
Like others	84	78
As criminal	19	35
As unlucky	57	65
As picked on**	26	53

* $p < 0{\cdot}05$.
** $p < 0{\cdot}01$.

altered by the introduction of personal and legal control variables, including age, sex, prior record, how jurisdiction was established and disposition. The establishment of jurisdiction by indicating whether the child has been to court for proof, is included to reflect the intensity of legal processing.

Self-labelling, panel member style and control variables

The inverse relationship between self-perception as criminal and a favourable aspect of the child expressed by panel members holds good for boys regardless of age, prior record and how jurisdiction was established but is somewhat reversed for girls; however, the number of female subjects was too small for such a result to attain significance. For those placed on supervision, there was virtually no difference in their sense of being criminal whether favourable aspects had been introduced or not (28 per cent and 26 per cent). However, of those discharged, none who had received positive feedback displayed a criminal self-perception, compared to 32 per cent who had not. Exactly the same pattern was shown for those sent to List D schools, although the small numbers limit its significance: none in hearings with positive remarks (two cases) showed this sense of stigma, and 45 per cent from hearings where such remarks were absent did so.

The tendency of children to be more likely to view themselves as in need of help when a sympathetic, understanding style was recorded was sustained throughout all categories of control variables. Within each breakdown, the relationship was strongest for younger juveniles, females, those appearing for the first time, those receiving a discharge, and children for whom jurisdiction was established by proof before the sheriff. In the last instance, none in whose case grounds had been established after appearance before the sheriff saw themselves as 'in need of help' if the hearing style was not identified as sympathetic, compared to half when such a style had been recorded.

Taking part in a hearing where an interrogating, demanding style was recorded was shown to be compatible with feeling *less* in need of help. When this pattern was examined according to our control measures, the same relationship emerged, and an interesting counterpoint to the findings of the preceding paragraph. That is, the association was more pronounced for older juveniles, males, and those placed on compulsory home supervision. First offenders showed a marginally stronger tendency than repeaters. In considering those back from jurisdiction established by proof, 100 per cent in interrogating style hearings did not acknowledge any need for help compared to 40 per cent where the panel had not displayed this stance.

The fourth combination of factors that are of interest regarding self-evaluation are those matching a feeling of being unlucky with an exhorting or threatening style of hearing. This response was enhanced for males, repeaters and those sent to List D schools. In cases where jurisdiction was established through a mixture of accepted and denied or discharged grounds, the relationship also tended to be stronger than for other ways of obtaining jurisdiction over the child. Age however had no apparent effect.

Stigma from others, panel member style and control variables

A more detailed investigation of areas in which the perceived sense of stigmatization from significant others and hearing style seemed to be related also involved the introduction of control variables. Again, as in the analysis of the sense of self-labelling just presented, some interaction effects were displayed.

First, it was noted earlier that children in hearings characterized by a sarcastic or contemptuous style were likely to expect police stigma (i.e. that the police will hold this against them). This pattern held for the older subjects but not the younger, and since the hearing was never recorded as sarcastic with girls, no comment can be made about sex difference in response to this style. First offenders appeared considerably more sensitive to police as a source of stigma when hearings were sarcastic than not, while repeaters showed no differentiation at all. One may speculate that these more naive children were somehow identifying the panel members with police as similar figures of authority. The method of establishing jurisdiction seemed to have little effect, except for the small number returning from court who expected significantly more police stigma when in this type of hearing. Regarding the decision, it is worth noting that those sent to List D schools showed the least reaction, expecting police stigma regardless of hearing style, in contrast to those given discharge or supervision.

The projection of stigma from potential employers was more common in hearings which were noted to have an exhorting or threatening style. This association was more marked for males and younger subjects of our interviews, but whether children had a prior record or not made no difference. Some tendency for those who had been to a proof hearing and for those placed on supervision to have a somewhat higher expectation of stigma with this type of hearing style, was also apparent. Essentially the same patterns were shown when 'perceptions of a record' and 'threatening style' were related with other factors held constant, but since there were many more missing responses (N = 27) the numbers do not justify more detailed consideration.

These findings have provided some preliminary evidence in support of the hypothesis that the hearing process may sometimes have an adverse effect on juvenile perceptions relating to stigma and self-labelling. This seemed pronounced in regard to police and future employers, least applicable to more intimate others, such as friends, parents and school associates, and less marked with respect to self-image than external expectations. Some interaction occurred between the background and legal characteristics in their effect on the stigma and self-labelling measures and hearing styles. This suggests that hearing style has a differential effect on juveniles depending in a way on where they are coming *from*. Younger and less experienced children seemed to react more to one approach, older recidivists (especially when given more severe outcomes) to another.

In summary, the questions of stigma and labelling are basically ones of whether the child will experience indirect negative consequences to his life and identity as a result of involvement in delinquency proceedings. Central to the goals of such official intervention is of course the notion of change. The avowed purpose of the proceedings is to benefit the child by altering his conduct in the desired direction, as defined by the norms of adult society. The concepts of stigmatization and self-labelling recognize that change may occur in a less favourable way for the child. In this theoretical perspective, attitudes towards the self, those perceived to be held and actually held by significant others in the social milieu and future employment prospects – all potentially may be altered by the public transformation of the child to delinquent status. In Scotland, this outcome does not seem to have been wholly eliminated, although as Siegal (1975)[33] noted, this process is complex and cannot be attributed solely to the official response.

Summary and Conclusions

This chapter has reported the results of interviews with 105 children aged 12 to 15 appearing before hearings on offence grounds of referral. Children's reactions to the specific hearing event have been compared when possible to those reported for more conventional court systems of juvenile justice. Since levels of comprehension of who was there and what had happened as well as satisfaction with their own participation were on the whole quite high, clients of hearings seemed better served than those dealt with in court settings. Interestingly, our respondents were similar to those interviewed in other jurisdictions in their recognition of the legal or offence basis of the proceedings rather than the helping or treatment role.

Children interviewed in our study were more likely than not to feel that at least some participants of the hearing were 'on their side' and there 'to help them'. A positive sense of fairness in the process, in the sense that the panel members were perceived as being either for them or neutral, was expressed by 69 per cent of subjects. Nearly three-quarters of the children received a 'better' outcome than they had expected, and most also thought the decision was fair in their case. The perceived reasons for the disposition varied widely and were quite frequently not in accord with what the children themselves viewed as appropriate considerations.

In a minority of about a fifth to a quarter of cases, respondents had less favourable views than those just described, particularly with respect to feelings of not being listened to, of difficulty in understanding some aspects of the hearing, of the panel members being against them, and of the decision being made before the hearing commenced. More negative reactions tended to be expressed by those with a prior record at hearings and those receiving residential dispositions. Thus, while it would not be a distortion to characterize the children's version of their experience at hearings as predominantly 'satisfactory', the shortcomings perceived by some should also receive notice.

The attitudes expressed by respondents towards the major agents of the system – social worker, panel, reporter and police – showed marked ability to discriminate between these roles. Panel members, and even more so social workers, were rated highly on justice and helpfulness items, while police were identified with punitive statements. The reporter seemed to elicit neutral rather than definitive opinions on his role from children.

An examination of the key issues of stigma and self-labelling indicated that some awareness or expectation of social liability as a result of attending a hearing was displayed, to a larger extent than found in a comparable U.S. study (Foster *et al.*, 1972).[34] Whether such a relatively high level of stigmatization would persist over time, away from the immediate reality of the hearing, could not be ascertained in the present study, but is certainly worthy of further investigation.

Self-identification as 'criminal' or 'in need of help' was acknowledged by about one quarter of the sample. Unlike the reactions to the hearing event, which were seen to be profoundly affected by prior record and outcome, these perceptions of stigma and self-labelling did not strongly relate to these factors. Some linkages were displayed between panel member style and 'deviant' perceptions. However, when these relationships were examined while controlling for personal and case characteristics, numerous interaction effects were displayed.

These interactions suggested that certain types of children were more sensitive to a particular style than to others. It was noted that the effect on the children may be the opposite to that intended by the hearing; when for instance an interrogating or demanding style was displayed to older boys placed on home supervision, they were inclined to feel *less* in need of help than when this stance was avoided. Conversely, all children (though especially the younger novices) were apt to accept they were in need of help when a sympathetic or understanding style had been in evidence. One important finding was that some positive input in reference to the child during the hearing appeared to counter the self perception as 'criminal', even in those sent to List D schools. The important but hitherto largely untested assumption that the setting and manner of interactions that occur in the course of delinquency proceedings can affect the juvenile's response, for better or for worse, receives support from this study.

NOTES

1. A. Morris and H. Giller, 'The client's perspective', *Criminal Law Review*, 1977.
2. P. D. Scott, 'Juvenile courts: the juvenile's point of view', *British Journal of Criminology*, 1958, 9(3).
3. K. Catton and P. G. Erickson, 'The juvenile's perception of the role of defence counsel in juvenile court'. Working paper, Centre of Criminology, University of Toronto, Toronto, 1975.
4. A. Morris and H. Giller, op. cit.
   M. Langley, B. J. Thomas and R. Parkinson, 'Youths' expectations and perceptions of their initial juvenile court experiences', *Canadian Journal of Criminology*, 1978, 20(1).
5. P. D. Scott, op. cit.
   M. Baum and S. Wheeler, 'Becoming an inmate' in: S. Wheeler (ed.), *Controlling Delinquents*. Wiley, New York, 1968.
6. A. Morris and H. Giller, op. cit.
7. K. Catton and P. G. Erickson, op. cit.

8. Ibid.
9. Ibid.
10. P. D. Scott, op. cit.
E. C. Snyder, 'The impact of the juvenile court hearing on the child', *Crime and Delinquency*, 1971.
V. Stapleton and L. E. Teitelbaum, *In Defence of Youth*. Russell Sage, New York, 1972.
11. A. Morris and H. Giller, op. cit.
12. M. Baum and S. Wheeler, op. cit.
13. K. Catton and P. G. Erickson, op. cit.
14. A. Morris and H. Giller, op. cit.
15. M. Baum and S. Wheeler, op. cit.
E. C. Snyder, op. cit.
P. C. Giordano, 'The juvenile justice system: the client perspective', Ph.D. Thesis, University of Minnesota, 1974.
16. E. M. Lemert, *Social Pathology*. McGraw-Hill, New York, 1951.
H. S. Becker, *Outsiders*. Free Press, New York, 1963.
D. Matza, *Delinquency and Drift*. Wiley, New York, 1964.
17. E. C. Snyder, op. cit.
18. J. D. Foster, S. Dinitz and W. C. Reckless, 'Perceptions of stigma following public intervention for delinquent behaviour', *Social Problems*, 1972, 20(2).
19. S. S. Ageton and D. S. Elliott, 'The effects of legal processing on delinquent orientations', *Social Problems*, 1974, 22(1).
G. F. Jensen, 'Delinquency and adolescent self-conceptions: a study of the personal relevance of infraction, *Social Problems*, 1972, 20(1).
20. J. R. Hepburn, 'The impact of police intervention upon juvenile delinquents', *Criminology*, 1977, 15(2).
21. L. J. Siegal, 'The effect of juvenile justice processing on the self-labelling of juvenile offenders', Ph.D. Thesis, State University of New York at Albany, 1975.
22. A. R. Mahoney, 'The effect of labelling upon youths in the juvenile justice system: a review of the evidence', *Law and Society Review*, 1974, 8(4).
G. L. Albrecht and M. H. Albrecht, 'A critical assessment of labelling in the juvenile justice system', *The Justice System Journal*, 1978, 4.
23. H. Garfinkel, 'Conditions of successful degradation ceremonies', *American Journal of Sociology*, 1956, 61.
D. Matza, op. cit.
R. M. Emerson, *Judging Delinquents*, Aldine, Chicago, 1969.
24. B. A. Thorsell and L. W. Klemke, 'The labelling process: reinforcement and deterrent?', *Law and Society Review*, 1972, 6.
25. J. D. Foster, *et al.*, op. cit.
26. E. C. Snyder, op. cit.
27. J. D. Foster, *et al.*, op. cit.
28. Ibid.
29. Ibid.
30. Ibid.
31. L. J. Siegal, op. cit.
32. G. F. Jensen, op. cit.
33. L. J. Siegal, op. cit.
34. J. D. Foster *et al.*, op. cit.

13

THE PARENTS' RESPONSE

ALTHOUGH THE POWERS OF HEARINGS do not extend beyond the children who appear before them, there is an obligation on parents to be present, and failure to do so may constitute an offence (1968 Act, S.41(3)). The view that youthful misbehaviour stems from parental shortcomings of one kind or another – a view shared by the overwhelming majority of members of children's panels – constitutes a powerful argument for the presence of parents at the hearing. If there is to be any hope of initiating change on that occasion, the involvement of parents in the discussion and their acceptance of a measure of responsibility for co-operation in the future might well be considered essential prerequisites.

How adequately parents understand the procedure of the hearings, how far they feel caught up in its deliberations, whether they respond positively or negatively to its events, and what they judge to be the aims of panel members are therefore questions of practical significance as well as theoretical interest; questions moreover which can be answered only by direct enquiry among a sample of parents who have taken part in a children's hearing. Our own study, as explained in *Chapter 4*, embraced the parents of only 36 of the 105 children interviewed. The small scale and the uneven geographical distribution of the sample would not justify any more substantial claim than that the findings of the interviews are a very tentative indication of parental attitudes and opinions. At this level however they are not without interest, while the striking similarities observed among the opinions elicited suggest that the resulting picture may not be totally unrepresentative.

Parents were approached at the same time as children and in the same way. All of the interviews were conducted immediately after the hearing. In 13 cases the mother alone was interviewed, in eight cases the father alone, in 14 cases both parents and in one case a mother, father and grandfather. The parents of 31 boys and five girls were interviewed, including parents of two 12-year-olds, ten 13-year-olds, nine 14-year-olds and fifteen 15-year-olds. Exactly half the sample were attending their first hearing.

The grounds of referral included the commonest categories of offence – theft, theft by shoplifting, housebreaking, breach of the peace, malicious mischief, obstruction. There were no unusual grounds of referral in terms of quality or quantity apart from one child referred on 14 separate grounds of theft, all committed within a two-week period and involving almost the entire stock of one shop on each occasion. Three children were simultaneously referred for truancy as well as offences. Twenty-seven of the cases were initial hearings and nine were precipitated reviews. The decisions reached by the hearing were as follows: 18 home supervision orders, 14 discharges and four residential supervision orders which included one child received into care.

The pattern of the interview was essentially similar to that administered to children, with the exception of the sections on role perception and identification; these were omitted on the grounds that, while useful in assisting children to identify roles, the style was inappropriate for adult respondents.

Expectations

Those parents of the 18 children who were attending a hearing for the first time were asked whether the hearing was as they had expected it to be, and in what ways it was the same or different from what they had expected. Of the 18, eight had expected a more formal experience and that panel members would take an authoritarian approach.

> 'It was more relaxing than expected. We thought it would be more like a court'
>
> 'The panel chairman's attitude: I was expecting him to put him away. He was so understanding'.

One father thought the hearing had been too sympathetic and had

> 'Expected it to be more authoritative – it wasn't hard enough'.

Half of the first-time parents, therefore, gave a positive response to the question of expectations, mostly in terms of the informality, sympathy and understanding they experienced on the part of panel members. The parents of five children attending for the first time expressed no surprise at their experience and it is likely that these parents were well briefed by the social worker beforehand.

> 'We knew there would be three panel members and we would get help'.

Interestingly four of the five children in these cases had very different expectations of the hearing, including anticipating a court-room atmosphere, more questions being asked and many more people being present. Two parents answered the question solely in terms of expecting a different decision at the end of the hearing.

Those parents who had attended a hearing previously were asked if this last one differed from the one before. Ten of the 18 parents concerned did not see any qualitative difference between the two. Five parents thought that the most recent occasion had been more agreeable, and one mother who had attended 10 previous hearings with her son commented that each occasion became more informal and less stressful than the last.

'Each one becomes a little more informal. We were worried the first time'
'This panel was far nicer. Maybe the social worker had something to do with it. The report was better than they expected'.

Two parents contrasted this experience with the previous hearing which had clearly ended in a continuation, and one expressed pleasure that a decision had been reached.

'This time they made a decision. In the past they dithered about'.

One mother only felt that this hearing had been harsher than on the previous occasion.

"Our son was built up to go home. His hopes were dashed'.

Overall only one parent expressed very negative feelings in response to the question on expectations, although there were several partially critical responses. It should also be noted that almost half the total number of respondents who felt that their expectations had not been met by the hearing did not elaborate on their response and simply answered that the hearing had proceeded as they had anticipated or else had not seemed qualitatively different from previous hearings. It would not be justifiable therefore to assume from the data collected in response to this question that every parent but one had a wholly positive experience.

Comprehension

Asked why they and their child were at the hearing, 25 parents mentioned a specific charge or offence and five mentioned an offence together with truancy. (Only three children were actually referred on grounds of truancy together with offences and only one parent of those children also gave truancy as a reason for the child's appearance). In the four cases where parents mentioned truancy as a reason for attending the hearing in addition to offences, although truancy had not figured in the grounds of referral, there had been a good deal of discussion in the hearing about school attendance; it is perhaps not surprising therefore that non-attendance was emphasized by parents. What is perhaps more significant is that two parents whose children *were* referred for truancy did not mention it at all as a reason for being at the hearing, although again there had been a good deal of discussion in the hearing about school attendance. In addition, in the nine precipitated review cases in the sample, only two parents mentioned that their child's supervision was being reviewed in addition to the consideration of new offences.

Altogether the parents of 32 of the children spoke of the grounds of referral as the reason for the family's presence, giving an essentially legalistic response. Two parents interpreted the question more in terms of one of the cardinal principles of the system – that of the child's 'best interests':

'We came to find the best thing for 'B''
'We were interested in our son's welfare'.

One father responded accurately if rather literally:

> 'We received a summons and both parents had to come to see if we agreed to the grounds so we could have a discussion'.

The remaining respondent (the same mother who had attended 10 previous hearings with her son) commented rather wearily:

> 'It was a continuation – they've been waiting for a place for him'.

Parents did not tend towards a 'treatment' perspective in their responses to this section of the interview, perhaps not surprisingly in view of the fact that the form of words employed in the notification of the hearing that families receive tends to emphasize the grounds rather than the welfare aspect of the hearing. In addition, at the hearing itself the purpose of the hearing had been explained in only 22 of these cases; those explanations that were given had tended to a 'legalistic' or 'procedural' emphasis in 17 instances:

> 'I've got something to read out to you and you will say whether you understand and then whether you did it'.

The overwhelming majority of parents felt that they had understood everything that had happened. Three of the four dissenters were confused over 'legal' matters. In two cases the grounds were not understood and in one case the decision had not been clarified.

> 'The actual details of the charge. We couldn't understand the legal parts about the charge – the wording was wrong'.
> 'The panel confuse you. They didn't seem to understand – they kept asking 'T' if he agreed, when it was already proved in the sheriff court. The panel members use words we don't understand'.
> 'The length of supervision – they told me six months and told the social worker three months'.

One parent clearly had different expectations of the manner in which panel members would deal with the child and had expected some kind of verbal chastisement.

> 'The panel didn't talk straight – didn't tell him off enough'.

These four respondents were, however, the only parents who found any part of the hearing difficult to comprehend, and the ease with which most parents seemed to understand the process was perhaps assisted by the fact that all the respondents found at least one or two panel members easy to talk to. In addition all but one of the parents found that they were listened to. Even the one parent who disagreed with this statement commented that the social worker had already given the parents' views quite adequately and did not appear to be commenting unfavourably on panel members' receptivity.

Participation

All of the parents had found it easy to talk to panel members, although four felt that their child had found some difficulty in communicating,

'I felt that the questions weren't appropriate for his level of thinking'.
'The child doesn't talk easily'.

Several of the parents who thought that their child had no difficulties in this respect commented on the efforts panel members had made in encouraging their child to talk. One father added that although both he and his child found it easy to speak, he was unsure

'whether the child should be in when those very personal things are being discussed'.

There were three parents, however, who felt that they had not said everything they wanted to say in the hearing. One mother wished, for example, she had made the panel members aware of her feelings that

'it was an unfair decision to bring him before the panel because another boy committed the same offence but got off the hearing'.

Three parents also remarked that there were things they wished they had not said in the hearing. One mother expressed her feelings thus:

'I don't like to talk in front of my son about him. I wished for five minutes with him being outside the room'.

Another mother regretted that she had told the hearing of her doubts about whether her son would go to school in the next few weeks as she felt this had affected their attitude. In another case a father felt he had made his wife 'feel stupid' after divulging information about his son's school attendance of which she had been unaware.

Parents were asked who, in their opinion, was the best person to put their point of view in the hearing. Exactly half the respondents felt that they, the parents, were the best people to do this. Ten felt that the social worker was best suited for the task. Interestingly, three parents believed that the reporter should put their point of view, although it was not our impression that the reporter had played a particularly active role in the hearings concerned. One father thought that a lawyer would have made a useful contribution in addition to his own, and commented that had a lawyer been present

'there never would have been a case'.

(This father asserted throughout the interview that his son should not have come before the hearing because in his opinion there was no legal case to answer. The same respondent also noted that the social worker 'never said much'.)

Twenty-eight parents came away from the hearing feeling that the panel members were more interested in the child than in themselves. The remaining eight parents thought that the members of the hearing were equally interested in both child and parents.

Proceedings

Questions related to the notion of culpability produced a remarkable response. Parents were asked –

'Do you think the panel thought that there was anyone to blame?'.

Not one parent came away from the hearing thinking that he or she was being blamed. Half of the parents felt that panel members were not blaming anyone at all.

'They gave their views generally but didn't blame anyone'
'No, there was no blame. 'D' was stupid. They knew it was just a prank'.

The remainder divided almost equally between those who thought the panel blamed the child and those who felt that friends, peers or siblings were to blame.

'The child himself'
'Three other boys'
'Her big sister led her into it'
'The company he's keeping'.

The reaction of parents to this question is particularly interesting in view of the personal opinions of panel members (*Chapter 14*). However in spite of these opinions reference to parental shortcomings is rarely made in discussion during hearings. In the sample as a whole advice was given to parents on how to handle the child in only 14 per cent of cases (*Chapter 8*).

When parents were asked to comment on the amount of time the hearing spent discussing the case, the majority thought that it had been adequate. There were some who thought the hearing had been too short:

'They should have spent more time discussing the details of the charge'
'They didn't spend much time discussing anything'.

One lone father thought the hearing had been too long:

'They shouldn't have spent any time on it. She shouldn't have been there. I already punished her – that should have been enough'.

In answer to the question

'Did you think that there was anyone in the room to help you?'

we received varied but very definite responses: eight of the 36 parents felt that no-one in the room had been there to help –

'No, 'T' will need to help himself'.

'They were just passing the buck on to social work who are understaffed'.

Ten parents came away feeling that panel members, singly or in combination, were there to help, and of those 10, five singled out an individual panel member for praise:

'The chairman and the man on the left with the beard'
'The chairman – he was very partial to the accused'.

Three parents thought that the reporter was most helpful (but not the same three parents who felt that the reporter was best able to present their case). Six parents thought the social worker was the most helpful, and in one case a school teacher was singled out. Overall, 28 of our sample of 36 thought that there was at least one helpful person in the room, although all had found that the hearing was an easy setting in which to talk and that at least one or two members of the panel were easy to talk to.

One parent alone felt that the hearing was against the child but her comment was a qualified one:

'They were for him earlier but now they're tired of all this hanging over him for so long'.

The majority of parents thought the hearing was for the child and the family. Some parents came away with mixed or neutral feelings:

'In a way they're for – I hope, anyway. But there's no-one to supervise the case'
'They were for his interests but against him for what he'd done'.

Outcome

Asked what the hearing had decided in their child's case, 30 out of 36 parents accurately described the decision, using the correct terminology, and a further five accurately described the decision, using colloquial terminology:

'He was admonished' (discharge)
'He's to attend school and attend the social worker, then there'll be a review on supervision' (compulsory home supervision order).

One father had not absorbed the supervision decision and thought that his son's case would simply be reviewed in 'three to six months'.

Parents were then asked why they thought the decision had been made. This was a question which could be cross-checked with the reasons given by the chairman in the hearing and noted in our observations. In 18 cases the chairmen gave no reasons at all for the decision, and so it is perhaps not surprising that in only eight out of the 36 cases did the reasons given by parents and hearing concur. (In the total sample reasons for the decision were not stated in 42 per cent of cases; see *Chapter 7*.) However, apart from three parents who had no idea, all gave some reason. Two of the three 'Don't know' responses came from the group of 18 parents who had been given no reasons by the hearing.

The eight cases where the reasons given by panel members and parents concur fall into two categories, the first of which is family centred and has to do with parental care and control. In these five cases it was adequate parental care which was stressed:

'Because we were keeping him back from children that were a bad influence'
'They thought we could manage him'
'They put the responsibility on us'
'The parents had everything in hand'
'Good home support'.

In the remaining three cases the reasons related to education:

'They were worried about her school and her age'
'Because he had a good school report and is behaving better'
'Educational reasons. He has missed so much'.

There were nine cases where the reasons given by panel members and parents differed, and in most cases differed quite radically in more than just wording:

'First offence'
('You are well enough looked after at home' – Chairman)
'Because he had only one previous conviction'
('This will help you to steady down and lead a steady life instead of committing offences' – Chairman)
'Probably because he played such a small part in the offence'
('We feel he has grown up. You are caring parents and communicate with him' – Chairman)
'Not a serious charge'
('You don't require any help at the moment' – Chairman)

In these cases parents emphasized either the minor nature of the offence or the child's previous record. In a further two cases parents gave 'deterrent' reasons for the decision:

'Because it might be too easy to do it again if discharged'
('He has impressed the panel with his new found interest in fish, and his mother thinks that a social worker would help him' – Chairman)
'They thought he didn't need a residential placement. It'll teach him a lesson'.
('This is to help you to keep out of trouble until you are working' – Chairman).

In two further cases in this category parents gave pragmatic reasons for the panel's decision:

'Because they have not got a place available at List D'
('We've tried everything. If you come back we will have to consider List D' – Chairman)

'The social worker recommended it'.

('This is to help you. The things you did were stupid' – Chairman).

In those cases where panel members' and parents' reasons differ, the former tended towards the category of 'care and control', and there is a significant contrast between their emphasis and parents' emphasis on the offence and notions of general deterrence.

In the cases where panel members gave no reasons at all for the decision, some parents again put forward offence-orientated reasons for the decision:

'They realised he was innocent'
'Because he's never been in trouble before'
'First offence. It was to keep an eye on him'
'Because he didn't intend to steal'.

There were several responses which fell into the category of 'pragmatic' reasons:

'Because I suggested it'
'Nothing else they can do with him'.

In addition, there were some interesting responses which could be categorised as overtly concerned with control:

'To watch us'
'I think they want to check on him'.

There was only one 'care' orientated response:

'They want to help her health because she's addicted to glue'.

One striking feature of this section of the interview is the fact that in half of the cases no reasons had been given to the family. In the sample as a whole the percentage of such cases is slightly smaller but nevertheless quite substantial. Thus, in half the sample of parent interviews, respondents were relying on the discussion in the hearing to guide their comments. When the large number of offence-orientated reasons is considered, it seems probable that the discussion of offences in the hearing (which was noted in our observations of the total sample as occurring on 81 per cent of occasions in terms of the current grounds and 36 per cent of the time in terms of prior record) is accorded a fair amount of significance by parents. It is certainly important to panel members irrespective of their expressed reasons for their decisions. It would, therefore, be a reasonable deduction on the part of parents that consideration of the offence is an influential element in panel members' thinking on the question of disposition. In addition, the fact that the offence itself is a self-sufficient ground of referral, and may indicate a need for compulsory measures of care, may reinforce parents' thinking on this question. It is also probable that in cases where both the offence and the child's needs are discussed, the former tends to outweigh the latter in the opinions of parents.

The point that is being laboured here is undoubtedly a very obvious one –

if the child had not committed an offence he or she would not be at the hearing, and so of course it is singularly significant to everyone involved. Where parents and panel members part company is over the interpretation of the importance of the offence; the panel members' view that offending demonstrates a potential need for care is not one clearly shared by many parents.

Twenty-eight parents expressed general satisfaction when asked about their personal feelings concerning the decision. There were a few who had mixed or very negative feelings:

> 'It was the best of a doubtful deal. I wouldn't want him to go to List D'
> 'Too soft'.
> 'It was fair but it's not enough. They don't give me enough help. I've to go home now and worry myself sick about him'.
> 'Alright because someone can come and talk to 'S', but then it won't happen. There's no social workers'
> 'Panels are a waste of time. They're not qualified to judge'.

Parents of 33 of the children thought that the decision was fair. In one case a mother felt a decision to continue a List D school requirement was unfair. In another case a father thought a home supervision decision was 'too soft', and the mother and father of a boy who was placed on a compulsory residential supervision order felt that 'there was nothing else they could do'.

In 27 of the cases parents believed that the panel members had made the decision either during the hearing or at the end. Only seven parents thought that the decision had been made beforehand.

> 'Yes, the decision is already made before you go in. It's based on the reports'
> 'I think they had gone by the reports and decided beforehand'
> 'One panel member had decided as soon as we walked in the door'.

Some of the parents who felt that the members' minds were made up before the hearing started made very definite statements. They emphasized the influence of the reports and the recommendations of the social worker. There were others who thought this might be the case but were not absolutely certain:

> 'Hard to say. They'd read the reports so you ken (know) yourself you might make up your mind beforehand'.

On the question of parental influence on the decision, the respondents were again fairly evenly divided. Nineteen parents thought they had had some influence and 13 felt very definitely that they had not. There were in addition four parents who could not answer this question:

> 'The background definitely influenced them so I suppose we as people did'
> 'Yes, something to do with it but not much. It's the same as court. They make up their minds before they even see you'.

Nineteen parents felt that they had participated fully in the decision-making process together with their child, and 14 thought that the panel members alone had made up their minds. The remainder of the sample believed that the panel members and the social worker had made the decision.

We asked parents to tell us what if anything had helped panel members in coming to their decision and received very varied answers. There were far fewer offence-orientated responses to this question than to the question on reasons. In six cases the nature of the offence was put forward as being influential. Parents of 11 children clearly felt that personal factors pertaining to the child had been helpful to the hearing. Some comments related to the child's record of behaviour:

'Glue sniffing'
'No-one had followed it up but he still stayed out of bother'

and others to the child's self-presentation at the hearing:

'The boy speaking up for himself'
'He showed a positive attitude when he was asked about his interests and his ambition to be a jockey'.

Equally, eight parents laid great emphasis on the family background, particularly their own influence on panel members:

'The interest shown by us'
'The parents' attitude'
'That we were keeping him back from children who were a bad influence'
'I think they liked the family outings – we go together to the skating'
'The fact of a good home'.

We also asked parents what *they* felt should have been the most important influence on the hearing and again received comments relating mainly to the child and the family background:

'The boy's honesty'
'Family background – if the mother cares about the child'
'If a whole family is caring – that's important'
'The child's relationship with his parents. Whether they communicate with the child and are interested in him'
'The panel could see the parents have control over the child'.

In nine cases educational factors figure in answer to this question, perhaps not surprisingly in view of our observations that school was discussed in more than 90 per cent of all cases observed and in all but two of the cases included in this sample of parents.

One interesting factor emerging from the responses to this section of the interview is the emphasis on 'personal' rather than 'criminal' characteristics. This contrasts with the offence-orientated comments we received when we asked for the panel members' reasons for the decision. It would be easy to conclude from the data that while parents felt that school reports, personal behaviour and parental concern were influential, ultimately the degree of seriousness of the offence tipped the balance as far as the disposition was concerned. Equally it is clear that while the offence was considered important, parents thought that personal characteristics coloured the panel members' attitude towards the 'event'.

The balance between 'legalistic' and 'personal' factors is important. Indeed it has figured largely in controversy over the principles on which the hearing system is based. It is in the circumstances quite striking that parents concluded that a lawyer would have been of little assistance in the hearing. Only three parents had spoken to a lawyer and only two had felt a lawyer would have been of any assistance at all.

Stigma

As far as their assessment of the stigmatizing effect of the hearings experience was concerned, parents were in general more optimistic than their children. Asked if they would prefer it if neighbours and friends did not find out about the hearing and whether they believed people would think any differently about them if they were made aware of it, 23 parents expressed indifference while 13 felt some kind of potential stigma. There were more parents of 'repeaters' in the 'indifferent' category and more parents of 'first timers' in the 'stigma' category – 15 of the 23 'indifferent' responses were parents of repeaters, and nine of the 13 'stigma' responses were parents of first timers. Overall 19 parents had chosen not to tell friends about the appearance, coinciding very closely with the 17 parents who had no friends with children who had been to a hearing.

Twenty-two parents thought that their child would not have a criminal record but there was a relatively large number of 'don't know' responses in this section of the interview. Further questions related to expected future difficulties with school, the police and employers. Again around two-thirds of the sample of parents felt that there would be no difficulties at school but only just over one-third thought that the police would not hold the offence against the child. Some of the responses in this category were very forthright:

'It'll no do him any good'
'Yes, we have evidence of this from our other son. There's a lot of police harassment in the area. They're just stopped for nothing'
'Yes, the police are doing their utmost to get 'M' away'
'Yes – it depends on the environment, the area they stay. Police that work in areas of delinquency are apt to be vindictive'.

In terms of future employment parents were more hopeful, 24 believing that employers would not be influenced by the child's record.

How parents see their children is a peculiarly sensitive question and perhaps not easily addressed even in a carefully planned research interview. It is worth recording however that 22 parents did not see their child as being in need of help and that 30 thought he or she was just like any other child. Almost all the parents in the sample (34 out of 36) did not think of their child as criminal; a majority (21) thought that their child was unlucky, but most

(26) rejected the idea that he had been picked on. While these responses resemble the pattern of the replies given by the corresponding children, they are not identical. Children were more likely to see themselves as criminals, decidedly more likely to see themselves as unfairly singled out, and less inclined than their parents to see themselves as in need of help.

Some general principles

Parents' views on the main purpose of children's hearings in general reveal an interesting variety of assumptions. Nearly half (15) of the parents interviewed gave an essentially treatment oriented response:

'To understand the background and environment of the boy and to help him'
'Panels draw the family together'
'A panel is more able to get to the root of the trouble. They find out about the family background and consider it'
'To try and find out why children behave like this'
'To try and sift out family problems as the cause of the child's problems'.

Two parents who gave this category of response commented on two of the avowed aims of the hearings system:

'(Panel members are) people who come from the same sort of background. More understanding – you get a chance to speak'
'It's fair – they aim to help children more than a court'.

There were 10 responses which might broadly be defined as implying a deterrent view though without an emphasis on punishment:

'It's to try and make them realise the wrong they cause without putting them away'
'To try and bring them to their senses before they go really bad'.

Two parents thought the children's panels served no useful purpose:

'I think they're a waste of time. There's no amenities and no social workers'
'A waste of time'.

There were other comments which contrasted the hearing with the court experience:

'It's a softening up of the juvenile court system'
'It's so they don't have to take them to court'
'A more relaxed, easy atmosphere. In court they don't want to know'
'So it's more intimate and you can speak easier than standing in a court room where you can't speak at all'.

Describing the purpose of hearings, a few parents had spontaneously compared them with the courts. A further question was designed expressly to elicit just such comparisons. Twenty-nine parents felt that hearings were less 'official' and more sympathetic than the court:

> 'You get a chance to talk. Court is frightening'
> 'Yes, at a panel you can speak. You don't get a chance at court'
> 'The courts don't consider the parents' point of view. Panels do'
> 'It's less official (at the hearing). More like schoolteachers talking to you'.

One parent commented on the separation of the finding of guilt or innocence from the disposition:

> 'Court is really to decide right or wrong. The panel is for the discussion of problems'.

Another parent mentioned the welfare principle involved in the hearings system:

> 'I think a court would condemn a boy at that age. They should treat them differently, not as adults'.

Two parents talked about the different disposals open to the court:

> 'It's harder in court. There would have been a fine for the child which could have meant financial hardship'
> 'In court you get charged, then fined, and then they're doing it again in no time. You can't punish them. It doesn't work'.

Although the majority of respondents compared the hearing very favourably with the court there were two parents who thought there was little difference between the two systems:

> 'They're about the same'
> 'The same, except talking is easier at the panel. But they do the same job'.

and one lone dissenter who felt that

> 'The panel is much too lackadaisical'.

There was, therefore, an overall favourable response to these questions, with most parents making reference to the informality of the setting and the ease of communication. The hearings in which these families were involved do seem in the main to have achieved the system's avowed aim of a setting enabling families to feel relatively at ease and to discuss fully any relevant problems.

However, the opinions of these parents as to the main reasons why children get into trouble contrast strikingly with the views expressed in general terms by panel members. Twenty parents felt that boredom and lack of leisure facilities were the major cause followed by five who mentioned peer group influence. Two parents thought that overwhelming temptation caused children to get into trouble. One parent laconically stated that 'The police need to fill their books', and only one mentioned lack of parental care as a root cause of children ending up in trouble. Nevertheless, 28 of the 36 sets of parents believed that panel members understood the reasons why children committed offences.

In a reply to a final question whether they thought children's hearings were the best way of dealing with young people in trouble, 21 parents expressed an affirmative view, while a further 10 thought that they were effective for younger children and first offenders. Only one parent thought that court was probably better:

'They're not strict enough – too nice on the panel'.

Conclusions

In general parental response to the hearing was extremely favourable in certain key respects. In terms of perceived informality and ease of communication, the majority of parents spoke very positively of their experiences. Most parents also felt that they had understood everything that had happened; this was confirmed by their responses to the question on the nature of the decision, which the majority described accurately.

In addition most parents came away from the hearing feeling that they had been listened to and that generally the hearing was on their and their child's side. However there was a significant minority of parents who felt the need for some kind of advocacy on their behalf, be it by a social worker, the reporter or, in one case, a lawyer.

It seems that in other areas parents differ in their views from panel members. Parents tend to be distinctly offence oriented in response to questions on why they were at the hearing. Given that of the 36 cases in the sample the purpose of the hearing was explained in only 22 instances and that the explanation when it was given tended to emphasize the 'legal' aspect of the proceedings, parental concentration on the offence is scarcely surprising.

On the question of 'blame' parents' views are again at variance with those of panel members. In our sample not one parent felt that his or her own shortcomings were considered relevant by the hearing. Much of the discussion in children's hearings tends to be child-centred in any case (*Chapter 6*) and references to parenting as such are uncommon.

The reasons for the decision as perceived by parents again tended to emphasize the offence and/or the child, apart from five cases where the grounds were discharged and the hearing chairman emphasized *good* parental support. However, there was again a good deal of laxity in hearing chairmen in the matter of giving reasons; this common omission may have been a factor in accounting for these views.

Factors perceived by parents as influencing the hearing were varied. Parents of 17 children emphasized either the offence, the child's record of behaviour, his behaviour at school or his self-presentation at the hearing. Eight parents stressed their own influence. On the question of influence there was, therefore, a shift from the offence towards personal characteristics which is further emphasized by parents' comments on what they felt should have been influential on the hearing. Here many more parents stressed the family background, but as a compensating or extenuating factor rather than in the sense of being to blame for the child's behaviour. On the question of the causes of delinquency most parents cited boredom, peer group influence and temptation, and only one parent suggested lack of parental care. The majority of parents also thought their child was quite ordinary, neither criminal nor in need of help.

There are on the face of it some internal contradictions in the account that parents characteristically give of children's hearings, and it is arguable that to some extent these reflect ambiguities which are inherent within the system itself. Thus, most parents emphasize the offence as the reason for the child being called before a hearing, see the decision as related principally to the offence, and do not view their children – or presumably themselves – as anything out of the ordinary. At the same time, nearly half the parents in our sample gave a 'treatment' type of response to a question on the general purpose of children's hearings; others contrasted the hearing and the court experience, commenting that the former provided an atmosphere where potential problems could be discussed.

To accept the validity of a general principle, while simultaneously denying or at least failing to acknowledge the applicability of the principle to oneself, is a fairly widespread human weakness, at any rate in circumstances where a full acceptance at the personal level would involve significant changes in one's way of life or in one's view of oneself. In the particular case of children's hearings this common frailty may be given further encouragement by weaknesses in the conduct of the hearing and by the reluctance of most panel members to embark on discussion of sensitive family matters. Typically, the dialogue of the hearing oscillates between factors immediately associated with the offence, and the child's school attendance and his behaviour at home; an explicit focus on parental responsibility is rare.

Yet even if parents do not openly concede the applicability of the hearings' 'welfare' function to themselves, the extent of their recognition of the general principle is not without significance. It has been suggested that parents accord legitimacy to the juvenile court on the basis of its judicial properties (Morris & Giller, 1977)[1], but it is clear that the positive reaction to children's hearings of almost all the parents in our sample is not in any way diminished by their perception of the differences between hearings and courts. Indeed, when comparisons are made they are almost never to the advantage of the system that formerly prevailed in Scotland. Perhaps the most notable feature of the parental attitudes expressed is the feeling that their own opinions were valued and that they had participated in the process in a way which would not have been possible in another setting. Bearing in mind our own at times critical response to some aspects of the conduct of children's hearings, it might be thought that parents are if anything over-generous in their judgments; obviously, basic courtesy and recognition as individuals are highly valued. One can only speculate on how often these elementary requirements of civilised interaction may have been lacking in other agencies with which these parents may previously have been in contact.

NOTE

1. A. Morris and H. Giller, 'The client's perspective', *Criminal Law Review*, 1977.

14

PANEL MEMBERS' AND SOCIAL WORKERS' VIEWS

I. DELINQUENCY AND ITS MANAGEMENT

Studying panel members

The maintenance of the system of children's hearings is dependent upon its ability to attract a flow of new recruits, adequate both numerically and qualitatively, to the membership of children's panels. The original panels established in 1970–1971 were, as reported in *Chapter 1*, over-supplied with volunteers. Membership is not static however. Participants give up their membership because their work takes them or their husbands to another town, or because they develop new enthusiasms or find the work of the panel too painful or too frustrating. It has been estimated that in the city of Glasgow approximately 50 of every 100 newly-recruited panel members withdraw within the space of three years, and that the greater part of this loss is associated with change of domicile. New recruitment is therefore essential; in Scotland as a whole about 400 members of the public are drawn each year into a form of voluntary service that carries little if any publicly recognized status and of course attracts no tangible rewards. Their motives for joining are not at all well understood, and we ourselves have made no attempt to penetrate that mystery. Recognizing however that voluntary movements, like political parties, are composed of persons who in the aggregate are in some psychological or sociological sense distinguishable from the general population, it seemed to us essential to illuminate so far as our methods permitted some of the key characteristics of those who make up the membership of children's panels. The characteristics to which we attached particular importance were their ideas about the system itself – its aims, the disposals open to it, the desirability of changes in powers or jurisdiction – and about the causal factors that were ultimately responsible for the law-breaking or other behaviour of the children who appear before hearings.

It may be argued that the system incorporates a formal philosophy of decision-making, an acceptance of which is incumbent on all panel members. But that philosophy is open to interpretation, and no one can say in what form it is held by those who become members of children's panels or in what direction it may change as a consequence of continued exposure to delinquency and social pathology. Nor can one say *ab initio* what is involved in giving concrete operational expression to general principles. A key requirement of the system is the individualization of decision-making, and all panel members are enjoined to have regard for the best interests of the child. But how these best interests are construed, and what actions are deemed appropriate to promoting them, cannot be determined without direct examination both of decisions and of the specific principles claimed to underlie them. Earlier chapters have identified some of the dimensions of decision-making in hearings. It remains to describe the beliefs and opinions that panel members bring to bear on that complex task.

Some writers have approached the question of panel members' values and attitudes, but only inferentially. A fair amount of attention has been given to the occupational class composition of panel membership, and the wholly unastonishing finding that white collar occupations were numerically predominant has generated a variety of reactions and interpretations.[1] The lack of congruence between the social composition of children's panels and that of the communities they serve has been put forward as implying a departure from the intentions of the system's architects. But Kilbrandon[2] had seen panels as made up mainly of people with specialized experience of children, while the 1966 White Paper,[3] in departing from that view, had emphasized the desirability of panels being drawn from a wide range of occupational groups but without any suggestion that they should constitute a perfect microcosm either of particular local communities or of Scottish society as a whole. However, what has underlain much of the reactions to these findings – whether by Children's Panel Advisory Committees, searching out new ways to attract working class members, or by serving panel members, incensed by what many of them have interpreted as a critical reflection on their suitability – has been the belief that middle class status was being identified with a distinctive set of values, hopelessly at odds with those of the hearing system's clients and unsympathetic to their predicaments. Yet the presumed value correlates of social class have been casually inferred and never directly investigated. For reasons set out in *Chapter 4*, we ourselves made no attempt to study more fundamental and generalized attitudes such as conservatism or punitiveness. We did however gather material on a variety of beliefs directly associated with the practice of hearings.

The study of opinions and beliefs should not be seen as an easily accessible alternative to the study of behaviour in social situations. The relations between the two are complex and each has its own validity. The former should not be studied – and rarely are – with any assumption that they enable the latter to be neatly predicted. They form however one component in our understanding of social reality, and an important if elusive one. In the specific context of the study of children's hearings, the degree of compatibility between the expressed beliefs and opinions of panel members and both observed patterns of practice in hearings and the experience as perceived by children or parents, is itself a matter of great interest and a potentially valuable guide to ambiguities or contradictions within the system.

Studying social workers

The children's hearings system has from its beginning been wholly dependent on the social work services of local authorities to meet some of its most important requirements. As earlier chapters have shown, reporters to children's panels make extensive use of preliminary social background reports in deciding whether or not to bring a referred child before a hearing, while the hearings themselves draw heavily on social workers' reports as signposts to topics of discussion with families, as warnings of areas of danger to be avoided and as influential guides to decision-making. In addition, social workers are responsible for carrying out the several thousand home supervision orders made each year by children's hearings. Yet in spite of the fact that the local authority social work departments and the children's hearings were brought into being by the same legislation, they have remained organizationally independent and their brief history has not been wholly free from tension.

In the early days, complaints by panel members and reporters about delayed and inadequate reports were commonplace, and doubts about the quality of social work supervision are still widely held. These surface disagreements reflect a difference in scales of priorities and possibly in values. To panel members, it seems self-evident that the supervision needs of the children before them call for an immediate and sustained professional response by social workers. For social workers, however, burdened by excessive case-loads, new supervision orders or new requests for reports must be weighed against competing demands on their time by a multiplicity of clients with needs that seem no less pressing. The fact that the child who reaches the social worker through the hearings system is an involuntary client may in itself create some reservations on the social worker's part.

Before the introduction of children's hearings, work with delinquents was the responsibility of the probation service.[4] Its officers had specialized responsibilities, and dealt almost exclusively with 'statutory' cases. Building up and sustaining a relationship with clients within a framework of compulsory powers was the normal expectation of entrants to the probation service. But the generic social workers who are now responsible for work with children's hearings – and for social work with the courts – have a more varied range of attitudes to the use of authority. For many social workers, the notion of voluntary entry into and voluntary withdrawal from a client–social worker relationship is of central importance; so that, although the demands of a supervision order cannot well be ignored, they are not infrequently approached with a certain ambivalence.

How far social workers in fact share the perspectives of panel members and how far they differ – in respect of the general aims of the hearings system, the objectives of supervision or other decisions, or the supposed causes of delinquent behaviour – has been a matter for speculation, but is susceptible to empirical enquiry. In order to gather information on similarities and differences between the views of members of these two key groups, our study of panel members' opinions was repeated, in a modified form, with a sample of social workers.

Some sample characteristics

The distribution by region of both samples was summarized in *Chapter 4*. In view of the fact that the response rate in both postal enquiries was not very much in excess of one-half, a few notes on other defining characteristics of the samples may also be useful; in particular, having regard to the recurrence of class-related themes in discussions of the recruitment of panel members, some indication of the social class composition of one group of respondents is called for. Table 14.1 sets out the relevant information.

As the questionnaire did not press for information about husband's occupation or about previous occupation if no longer gainfully employed, the returns included a substantial number who described themselves simply as 'housewives' (197 or 43 per cent of all females). There were also 29 persons who gave no information at all under this heading and 51 who gave job titles too vague ('civil servant', for example, or 'engineer') to be classified accurately. The remainder, half the female panel members and 88 per cent of the males, were allocated to one of the Registrar-General's social classes. For each of these, and separately for each sex, two percentages are shown, indicating their contribution to the entire sample of that sex and (in brackets) the proportion that they make up of those male or female panel members who can be placed in one or other of the formal categories. The outstanding feature of the distri-

TABLE 14.1

PANEL MEMBERS BY SEX AND OCCUPATIONAL CLASS

Registrar-General's class	*Males* %	*Females* %
I	19 (22)	5 (11)
II	40 (45)	29 (56)
III NM	11 (13)	12 (25)
III M	11 (13)	1 (1)
IV+V	7 (8)	4 (6)
Not classified		
Housewives	—	43
Retired	2	—
Unemployed	1	*
Unclassifiable	9	6
(N = 100%)	449	457

Sex of respondent not indicated in 15 cases

* = Less than 1 per cent.

bution is of course the numerical predominance of the Registrar-General's 'intermediate' occupations, a category including teachers, librarians, and many social service occupations; these account for about half the 'classified' sample. The 'professional' group (architects, medical and dental practitioners, university teachers, for example), though very much smaller than the 'intermediate' category, still contributes substantially to panel membership if one bears in mind that it accounts for perhaps five per cent of the general Scottish population. By contrast, just over one in five of the male panel members and a considerably smaller proportion of employed females follow manual occupations, although the latter account for well over half the general population. Although precise comparisons with other enquiries are not possible, it does not seem that there has been any very far reaching change in the social make-up of panel membership since the first recruitment of members (*Chapter 2*), with the possible exception of a modest increase in the proportion of manual workers. What we cannot exclude however (any more than we can confirm it) is the possibility that there may have been a quite substantial increase in working class panel membership which is not apparent in our figures because of a low response rate among those in manual occupations.

The median age of those panel members who answered our questions was a little over 40. Exactly one-third fell in the age-group 35–44, with one-quarter younger than 35 and just over two-fifths aged 45 or above. Among the younger panel members very few (1 per cent of all members) were less than 25 years old, while at the other end of the age scale members aged 55 or more were fairly uncommon (12 per cent of the total). The comparative shortage of elderly panel members is of course a reflection of deliberate recruitment policy. There is an interesting interaction between age and social class: panel membership seems to attract younger professional people and older manual workers. Twenty-eight per cent of middle-class members are aged less than 35, compared to 15 per cent of working-class panel members.

As far as length of service as a panel member is concerned, the sample represented all possible durations, from 99 respondents who were still at the time in their first year of service to 97 who had the maximum of eight years' service to their credit. On the whole, the sample was weighted towards more recent recruits. Forty-five per cent had been panel members for less than three years; this proportion did not vary with social class. It is not possible to say whether there is any element of selectivity in the response rate associated with length of service, but what is known about turnover suggests that the 60 per cent of all panel members who replied to the questionnaire were fairly typical in this respect.

The profession of social work, unlike the role of children's panel member, was not created by the 1968 Act; nevertheless, the growth of professional social work since the implementation of the Act has been so rapid that only a minority of present-day practitioners have experience going back before 1969. Forty-nine per cent of our sample of social workers had had less than five years' professional experience, an accurate reflection of the doubling of local authority field social work staff during the four or five years preceding our enquiry. Almost one-third had been in practice for between five and nine years, and just under one-fifth of the sample had experience that went back before the formation in 1969 of general purpose social work departments in Scotland. The median age of field social workers might be expected to be ten years or so lower than that of children's panel members.

Theories of delinquency

An open-ended question was presented to panel members and social workers in the following terms:

> 'In view ot your experience in dealing with offence cases and reading (*for social workers* preparing) social background reports, what do you consider to be the main factors which contribute to delinquent behaviour?'

Respondents were asked to write not more than four brief statements. The majority in fact gave three or four answers; the mean number of statements was 3·4 for panel members and 3·5 for social workers. It proved possible to allocate almost all the statements put forward into one or other of eight broad categories of factors that were believed to contribute to delinquent behaviour. Table 14.2 shows, for each of these categories, how frequently it was put forward by panel members as the first factor among their statements, how often it occurred among *all* the responses of panel members, and how often among *all* the statements offered by social workers.

'Lack of parental care and control' was considered to be by far the most common factor in the child's background associated with delinquency. Under that general theme panel members identified the following detrimental influences:

> 'the parents' physical, emotional or intellectual neglect of the child',
> 'the parents' personal attitudes, behaviour and moral outlook',
> 'the parents' lack of respect for authority, property and education',
> 'inadequate, feckless, worthless parents'.

The range of statements contained in the category described above conform with the notion expressed by the Kilbrandon Committee that delinquency is primarily a family issue and, more precisely, due to inadequacies in the 'bringing up process'. In this category panel members described almost all possible areas where parents are likely to go wrong in bringing up their children, referring both to indirect influences by means of their example or their attitudes, and to direct neglect to nurture the child adequately at the physical, emotional or intellectual level. The use of one-word derogatory statements about the parents of delinquents such as 'feckless' or 'worthless' was quite common and suggested that, for many respondents, parental inadequacy was not likely to be confined to certain crucial aspects of the parent–child relationship, but was rather an expression of a total inability on the part of the parents to offer the child adequate care at any level. Half of all panel members put forward as their first statement an item that fell under this heading. When *all* panel member responses are considered, lack of parental care and control remains the most frequent response, accounting for 28 per cent of all answers. Among social worker responses, on the other hand, it amounts to 20 per cent of the total, and is equalled in frequency by one other factor and surpassed by a third.

Panel members produced one other purely family-centred theme as an associated factor in delinquent behaviour which, though similar to 'lack of parental care and control', is less directly pointed at parental inadequacy as such and is more concerned with circumstances of family life. The category was labelled 'family instability' and included such statements as the following:

'breakdown of marriage',
'mental illness',
'death of a parent',
'one-parent families',
'co-habiting parents',
'poor relationship in general, and lack of communication'.

The statements in this category usually referred to these or other events or states as giving rise to stress or causing the disruption of the family as a unit, the statements listed above being the most common. A causal relation between these factors and delinquency is certainly more difficult to interpret than in the previous category, which seemed to emphasize the link between delinquency and an upbringing which fails to teach acceptable values and behaviour. In statements referring to 'family instability' the assumption is made that delin-

TABLE 14.2

VIEWS ON CAUSAL FACTORS IN DELINQUENCY

	Frequency with which cited among:		
Factors identified	*Panel members' first responses* %	*Panel members' combined responses* %	*Social workers' combined responses* %
Lack of parental care and control	50	28	20
Family instability	27	17	13
Environmental deprivation	12	16	20
Delinquent sub-culture	4	12	22
Educational maladjustment	2	11	10
Emotional maladjustment	2	5	12
Alcohol or drug abuse (child or parent)	1	4	1
Low intelligence (child or parent)	1	3	*
Miscellaneous responses	1	4	2
(N = 100%)	912	3112	601

* Less than 1 per cent.

quency is symptomatic of stress and unhappiness. Admittedly, panel members may feel that difficulties in the family circumstances are not conducive to good parenting and therefore give rise to delinquency, but the issue of family instability was not stated in the context of parental shortcomings and was quite clearly seen as a separate matter. It might be said that this category is more sympathetic than the former, since it takes into account the circumstances within the family which are partially or totally beyond its control. More than one quarter of panel members gave prior place to a statement of this kind. This is the second most common type of causal factor identified by panel members, though in social workers' explanations it falls only in fourth place.

Although the two notions of defective parenting and family instability may be distinct in acknowledging different problem areas, both may be incorporated in the concept of 'shortcomings in the family environment' and are in line with the Kilbrandon Committee's theories of delinquency.

Problems associated with the school environment are also present in panel members' thinking, though they are rarely put into first place and account for only one-ninth of all panel members' causal statements. Under the general theme of 'educational maladjustment' the following factors were mentioned:

'inadequate discipline at school',
'the child's lack of achievement',
'truancy from school',
'poor or inappropriate education'.

These factors were usually referred to as 'pressures' which might lead directly or indirectly to delinquency; responsibility for the child's difficulties seems to be attributed at different levels. Truancy itself as a causal factor might suggest that the child is partly responsible for ensuing delinquency, but the greater part of the blame is seen to reside with the educational system itself for failing to provide adequate discipline or appropriate education for certain children. The minimal support for the notion that school life, or the lack of it, may in some cases cause a child to become delinquent was in one sense unexpected, since in 91 per cent of 301 hearings observed, school was a major discussion topic. It is difficult to see how the relevance of the topic can be otherwise justified if panel members do not believe it to be in some way associated with the child's behavioural problems whether these take the form of offences or not. In comparison to inadequate parenting, school life and school attendance which might of course be dependent in many ways upon parental control, do not appear to have high priority as factors contributing to delinquency in the view of panel members.

It is of great interest that what might be considered normally child-focused concepts receive little support from panel members as important factors contributing to delinquency. A theme did emerge entitled 'emotional maladjustment' which included references to the following:

'the child's personal problems of adjustment',
'adolescent problems, failure to mature',
'feelings of isolation, inferiority'.

Statements in this category were quite uncommon and on many occasions seemed to be added as an afterthought. The majority of panel members favour the view that something outside the child is most likely to be responsible for his or her delinquent behaviour. This approach is not inconsistent with the Kilbrandon philosophy as we understand it, with its pervasive belief that the 'personal difficulties' which give rise to delinquency would not normally emerge without there being some detrimental external force in the child's immediate environment. The rarity of references to psychopathology does however run counter to the belief, encountered from time to time, that care oriented systems necessarily entail a view of delinquency as in the nature of a disease, to be eradicated by treatment.

Of the four remaining categories, two expand the notion of 'environmental' causes and two refer to highly specific shortcomings in parents and children. Of the four, the most frequently subscribed to was the notion of 'environmental deprivation', which sees connections between circumstances which impose hardship on family life and delinquency. In this category references were made to:

'poor living conditions',
'overcrowding, large families, inadequate housing',
'unemployment, poverty, lack of leisure facilities'.

Although unusual among panel members' first responses, it ranks fourth when all their answers are considered. Social workers however differ and put this factor into their accounts as often as they refer to lack of parental care.

The second category, relating to the environment, does so at the psychological level, and was rather loosely entitled 'delinquent subculture'. This category included some references to rather more general trends towards greater permissiveness in society:

'living in areas of high delinquency',
'peer group influences',
'a family's criminal activities',
'lack of effective deterrents in a permissive society',
'a reduction in social values'.

Both of these categories concentrate less on the immediate shortcomings of the family or the child than on the conditions in which panel members believe families and children with shortcomings tend to live. These wider referents associated with delinquency certainly incorporate much more distancing from the immediate family or school environment as the root cause of behavioural problems. Both these categories were surprisingly well represented given that the hearings system is geared in the first instance to the problems of the individual child and his family and not to finding solutions to general social problems. Those panel members who feel that much wider social circumstances have an immediate effect on family function and cohesion and on the child's values and behaviour, no doubt base their conviction on the observation that hearings deal repeatedly with families who have very similar circumstances and come from areas described as deprived. They believe the family environment is embedded in a much wider environmental field, whose influences cause problems to emerge at family level. Those taking the view that delinquency begins in society outside the individual family might be expected to experience more dissatisfaction with the methods pursued by the hearings system since these have an individualistic application and are clearly limited in their ability to bring about the more radical changes which a large number of panel members imply are necessary for relief from delinquency and other 'family' problems. For social workers, sub-cultural explanations rank highest and explanations in terms of environmental deprivation are only slightly less common. Can there still be any support for the belief that social workers are dedicated to a psychoanalytic view of man?

The remaining two categories were 'child's or parents' low intelligence' and 'the abuse of alcohol or drugs by child or parents'. Low intelligence was invariably mentioned as such and was distinct from difficulties at school or low academic achievement. No specific mention was made of low intelligence as the outcome baldly of either genetic or environmental influences, and when mentioned it was stated as being a contributing factor in delinquency. The suggestion seemed to be that intellectual shortcomings facilitate delinquent behaviour because the child or parent is unable to grasp the consequences of such behaviour or to learn acceptable behaviour in the first place. Similarly 'abuse of alcohol or drugs' is open to interpretation. The references to this are fairly infrequent but we can speculate that alcohol and drugs, if taken by children, blur perception and cause alterations in behaviour, and that drinking, especially as a group pursuit, might lead to loss of self-control and consequent delinquency. When associated with parents, abuse of alcohol or drugs seemed an aspect of poor parenting. Likewise in children, the misuse of alcohol or drugs (notably glue) might be taken as a personal inadequacy or an aspect of environment. These two highly specific factors can perhaps be seen as concrete examples of environmental or personal shortcomings applying to parents and children which, if our analysis of the material had been less detailed, might not have emerged as separate factors and might have been placed appropriately in other categories.

Neither these, nor indeed any of the categories included, attempts to explain specifically how these environmental or personal factors might function in association with delinquency. In this, of course, panel members do not differ from the members of the Kilbrandon Committee whose theories had little real explanatory value but did have a definite appeal to liberal common sense. Overall, panel members' views about the causes of delinquency are generally consistent with the original thinking on which the system was based.

It would seem that inadequate parenting and a family's external circumstances both material and cultural are the major factors which panel members associate with delinquent behaviour. The instability of family life, particularly when unstable or unusual marital relations are involved, produces delinquency via stress factors affecting the child's sense of security. Emotional problems in the parents' lives however are generally felt to be of less significance in the child's development than parental neglect or inappropriate parenting. It was not usually stated that parental neglect might have had mitigating circumstances and it was more often presented as the result of ignorance and a failure to assume parental responsibility. There was a definite note of hostility in some answers when referring to parents which strongly suggested that parents were 'blameworthy'. This was much less frequently observed when children's inadequacies were mentioned, though a few panel members did express the notion that 'inherent badness' and 'wickedness' were at the root of some delinquent behaviour; the term 'psychopath' was never used but would seem to convey the tone of these answers.

It is obvious that the form of the questionnaire is somewhat restricting and it would be naive to come to the conclusion that panel members do not recognize an interaction of circumstances in the delinquent's background. Looking across all categories of statements a pattern of deprivation emerges. Panel members produce a picture of the delinquent child living in a materially deprived environment subject to parental shortcomings and stress, and learning inappropriate values from peers, parents and the media. Parental shortcomings might be offset in view of the weight of opinion favouring material and social deprivation in a wider sense as contributing to delinquency. However further analysis of the material reveals that environmental deprivation or cultural factors is rarely given as a first answer. Panel members were not asked to rank their answers in importance but, given the trend to place 'parental shortcomings' first, it does not seem justified to assume that wider factors are generally thought to produce parental shortcomings.

It is clear from our observations of discussions at hearings that panel members do not assume that children who commit offences or absent themselves from school are merely giving expression to an uncomplicated defiance of authority. Instead, they are inclined to interpret such behaviour as a product of a number of interlocking and detrimental forces. Analysis of the frequency with which various topics were discussed at hearings demonstrates the large part played by subjects relating to the child and his immediate environment. 'Behaviour at home' was an item recorded in half of all hearings, the child's peers in two-thirds, family stresses on one-third of all occasions and family attitudes on two-thirds. However, in only 14 per cent of hearings did panel members find it necessary to advise parents on care and control of the child. This is a surprising disparity, considering that parental inadequacy is the dominant issue in panel members' thinking about delinquency.

Panel members have no jurisdiction over parents, and it is possible that in the circumstances there is a reluctance openly to challenge them. Our own findings however indicate a tendency not only to avoid direct criticism of parents at hearings with offence or truancy grounds, but also to allay any fears parents may have that they are blameworthy. Of the 36 parents interviewed after offence hearings none felt that panel members held them responsible for their child's actions, and 28 believed that the hearing had been focussed particularly on the child's character and behaviour. Either the child himself or his peer group or no-one at all was culpable, so parents thought, in the eyes of the panel members. Our impressions as observers coincide with the views of both children and parents in describing the hearing as a predominantly child-centred event. Inherent flaws in children's personalities are not identified as important factors in the opinions expressed by panel members as to the causes of delinquent behaviour; it is certainly not an assumption that parents are helpless that explains the style of hearings.

It is possible that the hearing situation itself, coupled with a lack of powers over parents, encourages the emphases that we noted, and that this may work against the parents' realization that treatment measures are intended to benefit the whole family. It was originally hoped that by persuasion and co-operation parents might be encouraged to change their approach to child management. But in the hearing parents tend to react defensively to criticism, and panel members are usually extremely reluctant to risk provoking a confrontation. Children on the other hand present little or no threat. Given both an absence of legal powers and inhibitions at the interpersonal level, it is a good deal easier for panel members to convey the impression that either the child or his absent friends – if anyone – is held responsible for the situation. Parents are not antagonized; but neither, on the other hand, are they led to believe that measures to be imposed by the hearing have relevance for them as well as to the child.

Social class differences among panel members are not associated with any important variations in their theories of delinquency. Sixteen per cent of manual worker panel members gave environmental deprivation as their first explanatory statement, compared to only 12 per cent of white collar panel members, while on the other hand the concept of a delinquent sub-culture was evident in four per cent of middle-class 'first' explanations, as against only one per cent of the corresponding working-class statements. But lack of parental care and family instability are cited with equal frequency in all social groups.

The views of social workers on the causes of delinquency are interestingly and significantly different from those of children's panel members. The latter cite lack of parental care and control in one form or another more frequently than any other single factor (28 per cent of all statements), followed by environmental deprivation and family instability (17 and 16 per cent respectively); a delinquent subculture is referred to as a causal element in only 12 per cent of their statements. In spite of the rather widespread belief that social workers are preoccupied with the formative significance of parent-child relationships, those in our sample were very conscious of the role of environmental influences of different kinds. Although far from disregarding the role of family influences, social workers do not place them in such a dominant position as do panel members. Lack of parental care and family instability together accounted for 33 per cent of all the causal statements made by social workers, compared to 44 per cent of panel members' statements. A delinquent subculture was the most commonly selected item, and this and environmental deprivation accounted for 42 per cent of social workers' statements; among the opinions put forward by panel members these together made up only 29 per cent. Perhaps surprisingly, statements which involved some negative evaluation of the delinquent child's personal make-up, though they added up to only one in eight of the judgments of social workers, were still noticeably more frequently put forward than in the opinions offered by panel members; only one in 20 of the latter statements referred to the child's own inadequacies.

Responding to delinquency

The generally prevalent view that environmental factors, usually in the family background and in the type of parental care experienced by the child, are responsible for delinquent behaviour might lead to the supposition that treatment measures will be directed in the majority of cases at resolving a child's problems, with an emphasis on ensuring adequate parental care. It is nevertheless a fact that any decision made about a young offender in the hearing system will centre upon the subsequent behaviour of the child and not of the parents. It is the child who becomes legally responsible under the conditions of a home supervision requirement or a List D placement. Parents are not subject to the conditions imposed by these orders. It is not therefore immediately obvious, given panel members' beliefs about delinquency, what purpose they have in mind when the decision is made to impose supervision upon a young offender. As far as the parents are concerned, a panel member is unable to do more than involve them in establishing grounds and in the hearing discussion, meanwhile making the assumption that the family as a whole will benefit from a child's compulsory contact with the prescribed agencies.

This 'child-centred' structure of hearing jurisdiction hinders the recognition that the measures decided upon will affect the family as a unit, despite the original claim that there are likely to be problems in a child's background which are at the root of his unsatisfactory behaviour. For this reason the questions concerning purposes of treatment, both general and specific, which were presented to panel members refer only to the child. Moreover, panel members were asked only to consider children who had committed offences when giving their answers, in order to ascertain how far objectives other than those which are clearly welfare-oriented are intended by panel members when establishing supervision over young offenders. An identical question was given to social workers.

As shown in Table 14.3, four statements were set out, each of which summed up a different objective in responding to young offenders: reform or rehabilitation, retribution, deterrence of others and deterrence of the individual concerned. They were not put forward as mutually exclusive, and respondents were invited to indicate their degree of agreement or disagreement with each statement on a five-point scale. The table describes the distribution of responses to each statement by panel members and social workers respectively.

Panel members were more likely to 'strongly agree' with every statement than were social workers, although their general patterns of preference were similar. The former overwhelmingly endorsed the 'reform and rehabilitation' objective; it was accepted with virtually no dissentients, and for the most part accepted unreservedly. The notion of deterrence of the individual offender, with its clear reference to the imposition of penalties, was nevertheless also accepted by nearly two-fifths of all panel members, though only one member in eleven felt able to express strong agreement. Retribution and general public deterrence were the least attractive theme, evoking agreement from only one-fifth of panel members. The retributivist objective rarely led to an 'indifferent' response; disagreement or strong disagreement was the reaction of nearly three-quarters of the panel sample.

Social workers generally tended to be a little more sceptical about all the statements of objectives. Their rejection of retribution and deterrence as appropriate aims for the hearings system was even more pronounced than that of panel members. Although they endorsed the rehabilitation objective almost as frequently as did panel members, they did so less unreservedly; they were more likely to 'agree' (52 per cent) than to 'strongly agree' (39 per cent), while panel members expressed 'strong agreement' in 71 per cent of cases and 'agreement' in only 27 per cent. Thus in both groups we find a minority – in the case of panel members, a by no means insignificant minority – identifying deterrent punishment as an appropriate objective, a general rejection of retribution, and a high degree of endorsement of that objective, rehabilitation, which corresponds most closely to the Kilbrandon philosophy.

The question of objectives was pursued in more specific contexts; panel members were asked what aims they had in mind when placing a child on

TABLE 14.3

OBJECTIVES IN DEALING WITH YOUNG OFFENDERS

Statement of objectives		*Response frequency*					
		Strongly Agree %	*Agree* %	*Indifferent* %	*Disagree* %	*Strongly Disagree* %	N (= 100%)
1. To attempt to change the offender's behaviour by the treatment and corrective measures available.	P.M.	71	27	*	*	*	921
	S.W.	39	52	3	4	2	170
2. To impose a just punishment which fits the severity of the offence.	P.M.	5	14	8	35	38	921
	S.W.	1	12	6	29	52	170
3. To use the measures available mainly as an example to potential offenders.	P.M.	5	16	13	39	27	921
	S.W.	1	11	18	32	38	170
4. To impose a penalty so that the offender will refrain from committing offences for fear of further penalties	P.M.	9	29	13	33	16	921
	S.W.	1	22	19	29	29	170

* = Less than 1 per cent. P.M. = Panel members. S.W. = Social workers.

home supervision, when making a supervision order with a residential requirement (List D school) and when placing a child in a local authority children's home. Social workers were correspondingly asked their opinions on the objectives of these disposals. Respondents were not invited to agree or disagree with proferred statements, but were asked to generate ideas of their own; not more than three statements concerning the objectives of each measure were requested, and analysis was again based on the identification of themes. In addition, panel members and social workers were asked to describe the kinds of children they thought most suitable for each disposition. Tables 14.4, 14.5 and 14.6 summarize respectively the views expressed concerning the objectives of each measure.

TABLE 14.4

OBJECTIVES OF HOME SUPERVISION

*Statement of objectives**	*Response frequency*	
	Panel Members %	*Social Workers* %
To help the child 'Providing the child with general support, help and guidance'.	13	15
To control the child 'Controlling the child's anti-social behaviour'. 'Providing discipline otherwise lacking'. 'Influencing child's school attendance and the company he keeps'. 'Generally monitoring or watching over him'.	19	10
Communication and protection 'The social worker becomes a friend and confidant who provides the child with a base in the community, helping him find alternative leisure pursuits, friends'. The social worker protects the child from inadequate parenting and helps counter isolation and stress'.	14	3
Involvement with the parents or family 'The social worker encourages a sense of parental responsibility, guiding, advising and instructing parents on handling the child'. 'Helping the whole family with problems, especially those which affect the child'. 'Assessing the domestic situation, monitoring family life'.	42	65
Maintaining the family as a unit 'Avoiding removal of the child from home to prevent disruption of family life, trauma to the child/parents and institutionalization of the child'.	10	7
Miscellaneous answers Those not contributing to any of the above broad categories.	2	—

* Quotations indicate the type of answer placed in each category.

All of the measures listed produced a wide-ranging array of objectives. As the table shows home supervision was seen to have the following possible aims; 'helping the child and giving him support and guidance', 'controlling the child's anti-social behaviour and instilling discipline', 'providing the child with a confidant primarily to counteract poor parenting and provide reliable friendship', 'encouraging parental responsibility through instructing and guiding parents in handling children' and 'maintaining the family as a unit – i.e. to avoid the distress caused by removing a child from home'. The most frequently occurring of these objectives was the guidance and instruction of parents. This is not surprising considering the conviction among panel members that parents of children in need of compulsory measures of care are usually slow to adopt

TABLE 14.5

OBJECTIVES OF RESIDENTIAL SUPERVISION

Statement of objectives	*Response frequency*	
	Panel Members %	*Social Workers* %
To provide a structured environment 'Providing a child with an environment offering stability, reliability and predictability'. 'Consistent care, a solid routine, caring adults'. 'Helping child with his problems, giving him the rudiments of an alternative life style'. 'Providing remedial or special education, vocational guidance or help, general support'.	30	36
Punishment for offences 'Remove the child's freedom and impose discipline'. 'Punish the child for offences'. 'Secure'. 'Confine'. 'Contain'.	6	3
Protection for society and the community 'Remove the child from the community to prevent further misdemeanours and with a view to protecting society'. 'To protect other children from his or her influence'.	3	3
Induce social conformity and rehabilitate 'Teach the child to conform to expected social standards'. 'Instil discipline'. 'Teach or enforce correct behaviour'. 'Change the child's attitude to society, authority, other people'. 'Enforce education'.	43	34
Protect the child 'Protect the child at risk from family, peers, or any detrimental influences'. 'Remove the child who is beyond parental control and who may need a cooling off period'.	13	24
Miscellaneous answers	5	—

correct parental responsibility, and strengthens the view that emphasis of hearings' jurisdiction over the child alone, at least as far as those children who are placed on home supervision are concerned, is not easily reconciled with the aims of the hearings system. It seems that the social worker is seen by panel members not so much as a substitute parent for the child but as someone who will act in the child's best interests by influencing the parents; considering the limited degree of engagement with parents, the expectation is a demanding one. Family problems and family stresses which might include a probing of parental practices towards the child were discussed in only 34 per cent of hearings and yet, as we have seen, panel members feel that home supervision ought to be directed at just this area and not only to be designed to act upon the child.

Social workers' views were notably more concentrated than those of panel members. There was less emphasis on control of the child and more on working with the family; two-thirds of the social worker respondents saw this as an objective of home supervision. They had however a less explicit conception of the types of children for whom home supervision would be particularly suitable, with fully one-third not attempting to list characteristics. Those replies that were given emphasized early and potentially remediable

TABLE 14.6

OBJECTIVES OF PLACEMENT IN CHILDREN'S HOME

Statement of objectives	*Response frequency*	
	Panel Members %	*Social Workers* %
The child's protection 'Protecting the child by removing him from a home where he is being actively harmed'. 'Protect the child from neglect, physical or emotional'.	13	23
Providing a substitute home 'Removing the child from a home which falls short of the basic requirements'. 'Compensate for material or emotional short-comings and provide a normal home life'. (Active cruelty or neglect was not emphasised in these statements.)	70	55
Social or educational training 'Encouraging or teaching acceptable social behaviour where the parental home does not provide adequate example'. 'To allow adequate schooling where, for any reason, this is not being achieved at home'.	14	9
Miscellaneous answers	3	9
No response	—	4

delinquency, while panel members placed a heavier emphasis on the existence of positive aspects of the family, commenting particularly on parental or relationship qualities which made the resolution of problems possible.

The objectives given by panel members for a List D placement indicate a strong shift in emphasis; the objectives now become largely child-centred. Few respondents mentioned parents in the context of List D objectives and the majority referred to the residential school as a place where rehabilitation or re-training of the child is the aim. The educative process can be seen as a constant theme across the two types of disposition, except that now the child becomes the centre of the educative process as against the parents or family. Parents are mentioned only as having constituted some risk to the child or as having been unable to control the child.

In the case of residential placements, a typical child who might benefit was seen most commonly as a habitual offender for whom home supervision had been ineffective, and less frequently as a child who had been subject to 'poor influences in the home', that is, inadequately controlled and cared for. The child benefiting from home supervision had been most often described as a first or occasional offender whose parents, though reasonably caring, did not provide adequate control. Social workers' views of residential objectives differed in some respects from those of panel members. Providing the child with a structured and supportive environment plays a larger part, as does protecting the child from adverse influences, while the emphasis on inducing social conformity is appreciably reduced. Lack of parental care and control and the demonstrated failure of home supervision are most commonly put forward by social workers as indications for a residential requirement, rather than habitual offending as such.

Placement in children's homes was considered appropriate for very young offenders or for children thought to be in need of discipline and social education by only a minority of respondents. On the whole, the children's home is seen to provide substitute parenting and home life, either long or short term, where parents are considered unfit or unable for a variety of reasons to offer the child adequate care. Social workers gave greater priority than did panel members to the positive protection of children from harm or neglect, but even so most of their responses were in terms of the provision of substitute homes.

According to the views expressed by panel members home supervision and List D placements are in general designed to bring about some change in the child's behaviour and attitudes. Where supervision in the community is concerned there is ideally some attempt to advise parents on the control of the child, and the general approach towards the child himself has elements of control and discipline as well as help and support. The objective of residential schools is to provide a more intensely structured treatment in the absence of the parents, and here respondents place more emphasis upon aspects of control directed at rehabilitating the child for a return to the community. Parental behaviour is a key determining factor in whether or not a particular measure is right for a particular child and in the opinion of respondents, plays a large part in the success or failure of supervision in the community and in necessitating the removal of a child from home. The assessment of a child's needs and whether or not these are being met seems to depend largely upon the panel members' estimation of parents presumably on the basis of reports or their behaviour at hearings. The extent to which parents are considered to be caring and capable is important in the choice of measures for a particular child, almost as important as the issue of the child's behaviour past and present. Panel members' views on the objectives of the various measures emphasize once again the discrepancy between the impression which parents, children and observers received from panel members concerning the nature of the hearings system (an impression which does not incorporate the system's views of parental responsibility or liability for a child's behaviour) and the actual beliefs of panel members.

In spite of their more generous recognition of the role of environmental and sub-cultural factors in delinquency, social workers when answering questions concerning objectives of measures and the characteristics of children suited to these measures, tended to adhere throughout to the ideology of the system in expressing the view that the life-style of the clients and the child's experience of his parents were the central issues. Panel members, however, invited to describe the types of children for whom particular measures were appropriate, were inclined to give greater weight to offence-related factors or to the child's behaviour, thus expressing views which were basically consistent with their opinions about the general objectives of treatment measures.

NOTES

1. *See*, for example, David May and Gilbert Smith, 'The appointment of the Aberdeen city children's panel', *British Journal of Social Work*, 1971 1(1).
   Elizabeth Mapstone, 'The selection of the children's panel for the county of Fife', *British Journal of Social Work*, 1973, 2(4).
2. Report of the Committee on Children and Young Persons (Scotland) Cmnd. 2306, HMSO, 1964 (*Kilbrandon Report*).
3. *Social Work and the Community*. Cmnd. 3065, HMSO, 1966.
4. For a full account of the work of the probation service see David Haxby, *Probation, a Changing Service*. Constable, London, 1978.

15

PANEL MEMBERS' AND SOCIAL WORKERS' VIEWS

II. THE HEARING AND ITS PARTICIPANTS

Emphases in the hearing

In addition to offering their views on factors related to delinquent behaviour and the objectives of the disposals open to children's hearings, members of both groups of respondents to the questionnaires discussed in *Chapter 14* were invited to express opinions on the characteristics of a 'good' hearing and of 'good' panel members, as well as on a number of specific aspects of the present and future of children's hearings. The information provided in this way helps to throw light on similarities and differences in the ideologies of the two groups concerned, with respect to some central features of the system of children's hearings.

Both groups, for example, were presented with a list of eight objectives that might be emphasized in a hearing, and asked to select three which in their opinion should be stressed in what they would consider to be an 'ideal' hearing. Replies, summarized in Table 15.1, indicate a striking degree of agreement between panel members and social workers in the objectives to which they assign priority.

The table clearly confirms the emphasis placed by both groups on the informal and participative aspects of the hearing. The full involvement of the child and parents and family comprehension of all that transpires within the hearing are objectives endorsed by the overwhelming majority of panel members and social workers alike. No other characteristic of an ideal hearing is identified by even half of either sample. Little importance seems to be attached to procedural requirements; only 6 per cent of panel members and even fewer social workers see precise observance of procedural rules as an essential part of an excellent hearing. The conveying of 'legal and technical information' is also assigned a generally low priority in the opinion of members of both samples.

Seen alongside our observations of the actual conduct of hearings, these responses indicate a consistency between the relatively low level of procedural compliance that characterizes the average hearing and a tendency to attach over-riding importance to communication and comprehension, even at the expense of the formal rules of procedure. Indeed, it seems likely that the latter are sometimes seen as potentially inhibiting to full involvement; it is worth repeating that our own evidence does not in any way confirm the notion that adherence to legal requirements hampers communication, and points if anything to a positive relationship between the two. But while generalized opinion and specific practice are here – perhaps regrettably – in harmony, there seems to be a distinct contrast between the very heavy emphasis placed on the family's understanding of everything that takes place at the hearing and the failure of panel members in the majority of observed hearings to ask the child whether he understood the decision of the hearing or agreed with it. It is no doubt assumed that an understanding of the issues raised in discussion will lead automatically to the family's grasping clearly the reasons for the decision reached; yet our evidence from interviews suggests that reasons are imputed to panel members which may not always accurately reflect the latter's scale of values.

Certain other aspects of the hearing – the manifest seriousness of the event, an atmosphere of equality and the difference between a hearing and a court appearance – are identified as of major importance by between one-fifth and two-fifths of panel members and social workers alike. Two of these three considerations also point clearly to an informal atmosphere; the first is obviously seen as attainable in an informal setting. This latter appears to be an accurate

TABLE 15.1

ASPECTS OF AN IDEAL HEARING

	Percentage selecting given attribute	
	Panel members %	*Social workers* %
The full participation of the child and parents in the discussion.	85	94
The parents' and the child's understanding of *all* that takes place at hearings.	86	89
The hearing's impact on the child and parents as a serious event.	43	40
An atmosphere of communality and equality between family and other hearings members.	38	30
The difference between the hearing and the court.	19	22
The hearing as a body of authority with powers over the family.	13	9
The observance of all procedural requirements.	6	4
Conveying legal and technical information to the family.	4	9
(N = 100%)	921	170

assessment; certainly none of the children or parents interviewed gave the impression of having taken the hearing anything but seriously.

Although virtually all panel members see the presence of at least one parent as essential to the success of a children's hearing (98 per cent, to be precise, expressed that opinion), and although family participation is seen as a defining characteristic of a good hearing, there is a diversity of views as to the principal objective of parental involvement. Asked (perhaps unfairly) to select one of four proffered reasons for the participation of parents, panel members most commonly referred to involvement in decision-making, less often to the provision of information and to support for the treatment process. The lesser weight attached to the latter objective is perhaps surprising, given the views on parental responsibility expressed by panel members elsewhere in the same questionnaire, but it is not inconsistent with the rather widespread reluctance of panel members to engage in discussion with parents on potentially sensitive matters. The views of social workers are broadly similar, except that they assign lower priority to the provision of information, seeing this no doubt as primarily their own responsibility (Table 15.2).

The ideal panel member

What attributes do panel members themselves believe are particularly valuable in those conducting children's hearings? And how far do these opinions coincide with perhaps slightly more disinterested views expressed by social workers on the same subject? Eleven varied statements were presented, and respondents in both categories were asked to say of each whether or not they believed it important that a panel member should possess the quality in question.

TABLE 15.2

REASONS FOR PARENTAL INVOLVEMENT IN THE HEARING DISCUSSION

	Percentage selecting given reason	
Statement of reasons	*Panel members* %	*Social workers* %
To allow parents to take part in the decision-making and thereby avoid the impression that they are being judged by other members of the community.	41	48
In order to give information about the child and family background which will help in decision-making.	27	13
In order to help support the treatment process.	25	28
To put forward their own point of view.	4	9
Question not answered.	3	2
(N = 100%)	921	170

Table 15.3 indicates both major areas of agreement and some minor but revealing differences in outlook.

An understanding approach to others and the ability to appreciate the circumstances of another's life were the two most highly desirable and important characteristics of panel members. These were endorsed by virtually every respondent in both groups. Being socially skilled, with the ability to allow others easy communication was considered to be almost as important as the first two attributes, being rated important by more than nine out of ten in each category. It is noteworthy that these three most important factors can be seen almost as personality traits and at the very least as attitudes to others which are highly personal. It would seem, given the considerably lesser importance attributed by panel members to more concrete factors such as actually living in the child's and parents' local community or having lived in an area which produces high rates of delinquency, that empathy for the typical family's circumstances is thought of as not necessarily to be gained from direct personal experience. The implication is that the ability of panel members to inspire confidence in the family far outweighs any benefit that might be gained from the family's identifying panel members as having backgrounds similar to their own. Being a parent was considered by the majority to be an important consideration, though once again the actual life experience of panel members was not judged to be as overwhelmingly important as the more personal attributes. The 46 per cent agreement with the notion that panel members require a firm,

TABLE 15.3

CHARACTERISTICS THOUGHT TO BE DESIRABLE IN PANEL MEMBERS

	Percentage judging characteristic important	
Statement of characteristics	*Panel members* %	*Social workers* %
Sympathy for and understanding of others.	99	100
Experience of living in an area of high delinquency.	34	44
Being a parent.	71	62
Having a firm, authoritative approach.	46	39
Knowledge of aspects of the law relevant to the hearings.	60	64
Being a representative of the clients' local community.	37	61
Specialized or professional knowledge of children.	51	64
High intellectual ability.	15	11
Socially skilled and easy to talk to.	93	94
Firm religious convictions.	17	6
Ability and experience to empathize with another's life situation.	98	98
(N = 100%)	921	170

authoritative approach is perhaps an expression of the belief that this inspires confidence and trust if combined with the correct level of understanding. Intelligence of a high order, which might be considered to be an aspect of personality, was not thought of as an important contributor to a panel member's success. Knowledge of relevant aspects of the law was desirable according to the majority of panel members, though not of major importance. Similarly, specialized or professional knowledge of children was judged to be of less importance than being a parent, and was not seen as of outstanding significance. Religious convictions were not commonly seen to have a great deal to contribute to the panel member's effective discharge of his role.

Overall, panel members place more importance upon the personality attributes and on the ease with which a member can allow communication to take place at hearings. There is relatively little emphasis upon aspects which might be described as special qualifications, knowledge or experience. Panel members tend to minimise the importance of having experienced environmental circumstances similar to those of the majority of the families that they see. The skill of the panel member is deemed to lie in highly personal and interpersonal areas. Sincerity, helpfulness and reliability are the qualities that it is important for the client to perceive, but panel members see themselves ideally as operating on the basis of deeply-rooted personal qualities, and not as mere specialists in impression management.

Analysis of the various styles adopted by panel members at the hearings observed indicates that an encouraging approach was adopted by panel members far more frequently than any other style. Exhortations, sarcasm, interrogations without expression of patience or understanding and the tendency to convey shock and distaste to the family all occurred, not insignificantly but much less frequently. In general, panel members adopt a style which reflects their judgment of the importance of certain personal characteristics. Interviews with parents confirm that panel members are seen, in the majority of cases, to be unexpectedly pleasant and understanding.

Social workers' views on the most desirable characteristics of panel members are generally similar, particularly in emphasizing the importance of sympathy and understanding for others and of being socially skilled and approachable. Ability to grasp and appreciate the circumstances of another's life is also considered relatively important by both groups. Social workers, however, seem distinctly more in agreement with the idea of 'representativeness', one of the debated aspects of panel membership. Sixty-one per cent of social workers as opposed to 37 per cent of panel members considered that the panel member ought to be representative of local communities which he served, and slightly more, proportionately, of social workers agreed with the usefulness of actually experiencing life in an area of high juvenile delinquency – 44 per cent of social workers compared to 34 per cent of panel members. Only one other statement in this question produced a slight shift of emphasis between the views of the two groups; social workers gave slightly more support to the idea that panel members ought to possess specialized or professional knowledge of children. It will be recalled that in its original conception of the 'juvenile panel' the

Kilbrandon Committee had thought of the members of the panel as people with specialized knowledge of children and their problems. From the drafting of the 1966 White Paper onwards this proposal had given way to a more 'democratic' definition of panel membership; this, it was recommended, should be drawn from a wide range of social and occupational groups. On the face of it, the concept of community representativeness and that of specialist composition are not easily reconciled. Social workers seem to be expressing the feeling that in some sense panel members ought to have rather more in common with the families appearing before them, and that at the same time, considering the nature of the decisions they make, they ought to have more specialist expertise in matters of child development and its problems. It would be of great interest to know by what means our social worker respondents believe that these equally desired but largely incompatible objectives might both be achieved.

The social worker's functions

While virtually all panel members agree that the presence of the social worker in the case is essential for a satisfactory hearing, there is room for some variety of opinion as to the role which the social worker should play. The

TABLE 15.4

SOCIAL WORKERS' VIEWS ON THEIR OWN ROLE AT HEARINGS

	Response percentage				
Statement of role	*Strongly Agree* %	*Agree* %	*Indifferent* %	*Disagree* %	*Strongly Disagree* %
To recommend and implement panel decisions so as to comply as far as possible with the aims of the system.	17	62	11	7	3
To provide the hearing with objective information about the clients and an independent evaluation of the child's needs.	63	37	—	—	—
To protect the welfare of the community by attempting to ensure that the best standards of the community are met in the clients.	4	26	22	39	9
To represent the clients at the hearing to ensure that any action taken is in the child's best interests and to offer help and support to the family.	52	40	4	4	—
(N = 100%)			170		

questionnaire addressed to social workers listed four statements summarizing alternative emphases in the social worker's function. Respondents were not asked to choose between these, but rather to express their degree of agreement or disagreement with each. As Table 15.4 shows, the major commitment of respondents was to the individual child or family. Few rated protection of the general welfare of the community as central to their role. The provision of objective information and evaluation of needs produced the highest level of agreement overall, while the statement implying a protective and supportive role towards clients at the hearings also produced very high agreement. To what extent social workers fulfil either of these roles at hearings was not a question this study attempted to answer. It is, however, of interest that despite the fact that 92 per cent of social workers feel that they have a function at hearings which can be described as 'representative of the client', the oral contribution by social workers at observed hearings was usually slight, and certainly substantially and consistently lower than that of other participants. It seems possible that there may be a measure of conflict in the social workers' role; the substance of background reports prepared for hearings quite often carries negative implications about the character and behaviour of the clients, making it difficult for social workers to undertake without ambiguity a purely representative and supportive role in all cases. It may also be the case that social workers are not clear about the extent to which oral participation is expected of them at hearings nor about the extent to which they may direct or challenge the style and content of discussions.

Our questions about the qualities desirable in panel members were not matched by any enquiry into the attributes of the ideal social worker. Panel members were however asked whether they had in general found social background reports useful in helping them to understand a child and his or her particular circumstances; they were also questioned specifically about the recommendations provided in the reports. The responses summarized in Table 15.5 indicate a fairly high level of satisfaction on the part of panel members; there are very few who do not see social background reports as useful guides

TABLE 15.5

PANEL MEMBERS' VIEWS ON THE USEFULNESS OF SOCIAL WORKERS' REPORTS AND RECOMMENDATIONS

	Percentage expressing given opinion	
Statement of views	*Reports* %	*Recommendations* %
Very useful	24	21
Useful	68	74
Not useful	6	4
Question not answered	2	1
(N = 100%)	170	

to understanding and to decision-making. Nevertheless, the general tendency to judge reports and recommendations as 'useful' rather than 'very useful' implies an attitude which, though distinctly positive perhaps stops short of the enthusiastic; given these responses alone, one might predict a rather more limited relationship between recommendations and hearings decisions than we have found to obtain.

Difficulties and criticisms

On the assumption that the complexity of the hearings system can potentially give rise to a wide range of operational problems for its participants, social workers and panel members were questioned as to whether they had experienced difficulty in a number of specified areas. Table 15.6 shows the

TABLE 15.6
AREAS OF DIFFICULTY

	Percentage reporting 'some difficulty' %
Panel members	
Working within the limits of available treatment resources.	92
Following the progress of children who attend hearings.	82
Having confidence in the effectiveness of hearings.	66
Meeting all the procedural requirements of the hearings.	38
Communicating effectively with the family.	38
Working with other panel members.	18
(N = 100%)	921
Social workers	
Achieving your aims with children assigned to you under home supervision orders.	92
Making recommendations within the range of available alternatives.	77
Working with other hearing members, i.e. panel members and reporters.	51
Working within the compulsory framework of the hearings system.	40
Gaining access to related professional services.	39
Gaining co-operation of families in preparing social background reports.	21
(N = 100%)	170

proportions in the two groups who agreed that they had encountered particular difficulties.

The most striking feature of the table is its indication of a high level of frustration among panel members at the limitations of available treatment resources. In the context of a system which justifies intervention on the basis of its potential to achieve beneficial changes, the limited range of disposals available to hearings and the unpredictable quality of the services available have been a constant target of criticism among panel members; very few indeed do not identify this as a source of difficulty in their work. Interestingly related to this is the problem of confidence in the effectiveness of the system. Two panel members in three say that they have had some difficulty in maintaining a satisfying sense of confidence. The mention of effectiveness clearly relates this to outcome and suggests a fairly critical awareness of the limitations of existing arrangements for supervision. Knowledge of results is obviously crucial. This can be obtained from research studies of the follow-up type or, less systematically but no doubt more satisfactorily from the standpoint of practitioners, from observation of the subsequent history of individual children who have appeared at a hearing. In spite of the fact that in most regions it is customary for review hearings to include at least one of the members who made the original supervision order, more than four-fifths of panel members say that they have had difficulty in following the progress of children who have passed through the system. What might be termed practice skills are much less often seen as presenting difficulty. Communicating effectively with families and meeting procedural requirements are acknowledged as difficulties by minorities of panel members, though our own findings imply that there is ample opportunity for the improvement of skills.

The two problems that most frequently trouble social workers are closely allied to the leading concerns of panel members. Three out of four have had difficulties in making recommendations within the range of available alternatives, and fully nine-tenths report difficulty in achieving their aims with children assigned to them under supervision orders. If panel members are critical, social workers are clearly not complacent. This may reflect inadequate access to supportive services or insufficient time or a combination of these. There are also signs however that a proportion of social workers are not fully attuned to work within the hearings system. Some 40 per cent have found difficulty in working within a framework of compulsion, and half the sample have had problems in working with panel members or reporters.

We know from replies to other questions that social workers are conscious of uncertainties about some aspects of their role. Although three-quarters of the social workers questioned believed that there was a clear understanding of what was expected of them in the preparation of social background reports, only one in three thought that the nature of their role in the hearing itself had been adequately clarified. Given these substantial areas of doubt, it is scarcely surprising to have found evidence of both reservations by panel members and difficulties in working relationships.

It is encouraging that social workers on the whole see themselves as inadequately prepared for work in the hearings system, and do not place upon others all the responsibility for their own dilemmas. Some of the problems associated with the growth of the generic principle in social work education and practice have been indicated in earlier chapters. Table 15.7 shows the distribution of social workers' replies to a question concerning the best way of allocating social work responsibility for practice in the hearings system. Only 11 per cent supported what is in effect the status quo, namely the inclusion of work with hearings in a mixed case-load with no change in training. This does not mean that the generic principle was rejected. Well over half preferred the idea of the involvement of all area-based social workers, but with the proviso that relevant training should be improved and extended. There was minority support for the notion of specialization however. Only a handful favoured the principle of a small corps of specialists working exclusively in the hearings system, but nearly one in four was attracted to the notion of a group of specialist social workers concerned with a wide range of problems affecting children and young people.

Further powers for children's hearings

While improved training would no doubt make for more efficient practice within the hearings system, it would obviously not be regarded as a panacea by those who have doubts about the overall effectiveness of the system and are conscious of the limited range of dispositions available. While two-thirds of social workers and more than three-quarters of panel members are in general satisfied with the effectiveness of the system, only small minorities express

TABLE 15.7

SOCIAL WORKERS' VIEWS ON SOCIAL WORK RESPONSIBILITY FOR PRACTICE WITH CHILDREN'S HEARINGS

Statement of views	*Percentage endorsing alternative statements* %
All area-based social workers as part of a mixed case-load, with no change in training.	11
All area-based social workers as part of a mixed case-load, with improved and extended training in this field of work.	57
A limited number of specialist social workers working exclusively with the children's hearings system.	4
A limited number of specialist social workers working with the children's hearings system but also dealing with a wider range of problems of children and young people.	23
No answer given.	5
(N = 100%)	170

themselves as 'very satisfied' – 3 per cent in the former and ten per cent in the latter group. Those who select the proffered category 'satisfied' rather than 'very satisfied' seem to acknowledge the possibility of improvement (Table 15.8).

In the light of the widespread recognition of the difficulties of working within the limits of existing treatment resources, it is of interest to consider the reactions of both samples to a number of new powers which might conceivably be added to the disposals currently available to children's hearings. We omitted to ask respondents to give reasons for their choice of new powers, and can therefore only speculate about the purposes they had in mind. Table 15.9 indicates varying degrees of support for each power suggested, with noticeably lower levels of enthusiasm among social workers in each instance.

Eighty-nine per cent of panel members agreed that the power to order

TABLE 15.8

PERCEIVED EFFECTIVENESS OF HEARINGS SYSTEM

	Percentage expressing satisfaction with effectiveness	
	Panel members %	*Social workers* %
Very satisfied	10	3
Satisfied	68	62
Not satisfied	19	33
Question not answered	3	2
(N = 100%)	921	170

TABLE 15.9

VIEWS ON EXTENDED POWERS FOR HEARINGS SYSTEM

	Percentage supporting given extension of powers	
Statement of views	*Panel members* %	*Social workers* %
Defer decision	66	65
Fine parents	41	25
Confiscate weapons	63	48
Order reparation or community service	89	75
Reclaim stolen goods or money	58	38
Order corporal punishment	11	5
Refer to sheriff	74	59
(N = 100%)	921	170

reparation from the child would be advantageous despite the practical difficulties this would entail. It was assumed that reparation would apply only to the child and that the idea was not to be interpreted in purely financial terms; some form of compensatory action, whether directly associated with damage done by a child or not, was seen to be appropriate. Panel members have frequently been observed at hearings to make suggestions to both child and parents that some form of compensation to offended parties or to the community in general would be desirable, both as a form of discipline for the child and as a way of regaining a lost reputation in the immediate community. These suggestions usually occurred in hearings involving theft or damage to property, and the idea seemed to meet with the approval of parents perhaps because it appeared pertinent to the grounds of referral. The possibility of fining parents received less general approval as a possible function of hearings than did reparation. The pros and cons of fining as a hearing practice was dealt with in detail by the Kilbrandon Committee, which discussed both the legal constraints on fining parents for actions committed by children and the incompatibility of applying statutory powers to parents in a system which advocates the treatment of the individual child. The system in its present form maintains the judgment of the Kilbrandon Report that while parental shortcomings are probably the factor most consistently associated with delinquency, punitive action against parents was not an appropriate response. Panel members, whose views on parental responsibility are clear, do not always agree that intervention against parents is undesirable. Forty-one per cent believe that the right to fine parents would be a power worth having.

The majority of panel members would be in favour of making more use of their discretion in referring certain cases to the sheriff. At present denial, or partial denial of grounds may involve a referral for proof or discharge of the grounds, while appeals against hearings decisions are automatically taken to the sheriff court. It is widely believed, however, that certain cases dealt with in the hearings system might be more appropriately handled by the sheriff court, and it is suggested that the system might be improved by widening panel members' discretion to allow the transfer of these cases.

The powers to reclaim stolen goods and confiscate offensive weapons were also seen as desirable by the majority of respondents. It seems likely that many panel members feel in need of more tangible powers than they have at present. They perhaps feel that the psychological impact of reclaiming stolen goods or confiscating offensive weapons might lend weight to subsequent action taken on behalf of the child's best interests and emphasize the serious intentions of the hearings system. It is interesting to note that, in spite of the wish to be able to refer certain cases to the sheriff court, the acquisition of the power to confiscate weapons would probably have the effect of transferring cases in the opposite direction.

Corporal punishment was discussed and emphatically rejected by the Kilbrandon Committee. In principle its efficacy was in doubt; at a practical level it was thought that no agency would care to administer it as a public treatment measure, and objectively it was seen to negate parental responsibility.

The latter objection does not seem powerful, since a supervision order must be seen as supplementary if not supplanting parental responsibility. It is clear however that physical punishment is a very improbable means of altering the behaviour of a child on a long-term basis, given the belief that that behaviour reflects wider difficulties. It is surprising, therefore, that as many as 11 per cent of panel members believed that corporal punishment would be a valuable treatment measure. How corporal punishment might be the outcome of discussion centred on issues concerned with family background and behaviour at home and school is not easy to imagine. Nevertheless, experience has apparently led some panel members to the conclusion that certain children would benefit from the shock of corporal punishment; the not insubstantial ghost of a belief in the efficacy of the crime-punishment approach to delinquency still lingers.

Postponing the hearing decision gained the agreement of two panel members in three, who saw it as an appropriate power for the hearings. The practice has developed naturally in some regions and differs from the normal practice of continuing the hearing for reports, proof or other reasons, in that the delay before making a decision has a function in itself. Normally, that purpose is to allow the child an opportunity to change his or her behaviour without formal intervention and to allow panel members greater scope to decide whether or not the child is in need of such measures. Postponing the decision may be to some extent an attempt to minimize pressure on supervision resources and might also be seen as utilizing the hearing itself as an educative experience for the child.

With the exception of the deferred decision, there was markedly less support by social workers than by panel members for each new power suggested. The power to order some form of reparation was widely supported, and a majority of social workers favoured the power to refer cases to the sheriff. But fining, confiscating weapons and reclaiming stolen property were all endorsed only by minorities among the social workers studied. The idea of introducing corporal punishment was rejected by 19 social workers out of 20.

Panel members were also questioned about possible extensions to their present jurisdiction. There was little support for any proposal to enlarge the system's responsibility to include all young people up to the age of 18. The welfare approach, incorporating concepts of prevention, reformation and protection, may be judged superfluous for young adults whose formative years are over or almost over and for whom parental control has become unnecessary. Older offenders are perhaps considered to be 'set in their ways' and too cynical for a system which does not adopt a crime-responsibility-punishment approach. The frustration felt by panel members in dealing with older children was obvious in a number of cases observed and was evident in panel members' attempts to point out that those children who had failed to absorb the educational message of the hearings system would soon as a result be subject to a more direct approach. These children who had usually been under the system's jurisdiction for some time were seen as representing something of a lost cause; panel members were heard to state at hearings that the child had gone beyond the scope of the system and should now accept full responsibility for his actions.

By contrast, there was strong support for any proposal to extend the jurisdiction of hearings to cover children requiring custody arrangements after the divorce or separation of parents (67 per cent)[1] or children requiring decisions in respect of adoption or fostering arrangements (57 per cent). Panel members thus accurately reflect the assumption inherent in the hearings system that children who offend and children who are in need of protection or basic care constitute compatible groups in terms of the provisions made in both the process and the resources of the system. The system functions in the belief that all action taken is directed to the welfare of the child and that there is no need for a radical change of approach in dealing with the juvenile offender or the child in need of care arrangements.

The hearings system depends upon complex and quite subtle relationships between its lay and its professional personnel. Because they bring to their separate but interlocking tasks both general values and specific expectations which may differ, perhaps quite substantially, from one group to another, a degree of tension in those relationships is inevitable. It is clear from our findings that although social workers and children's panel members do not display identical patterns of opinion and belief, there is no suggestion that their positions are polarized. The differences are essentially differences of emphasis: in particular, social workers tend to be a little more sceptical, a little less wholeheartedly committed to the ideology of the hearings system. Their differences from panel members do not however take them in the direction of a more conventional approach to law and order; their rejection of punitive attitudes is even more sharply decisive. These and similar variations in outlook do not present any threat to the stability of the system; they might indeed provide material for creative debate, though rarely if ever has that developed. What is harder to justify is the continuation, after several years of children's hearings, of serious uncertainty in the minds of social workers as to their own role in the hearing and in relation to supervision. There is little in the attitudes expressed in response to our enquiries which might prove a serious impediment to a shared understanding of roles and responsibilities, but much to be gained from attempting such a resolution.

NOTE

1. The Royal Commission on Legal Services in Scotland has since recommended that both reporters to children's panels and children's hearings should have a role in decisions about custody subsequent to divorce.

16

IMPLICATIONS FOR CHANGE IN SCOTLAND

IN OUR FINAL CHAPTERS we stand back from the presentation of research findings in order to consider their significance and their implications. First, we ask whether there are failings or imperfections indicated by the data which are capable of being remedied by changes in organization, practice or training. In reviewing the research material in this way we try not to adopt any personal evaluative or ideological stance, but seek rather to identify areas where the criteria for change follow from the hearings system's own assumptions and priorities. The next chapter takes as its point of departure those issues relevant to the American debate on juvenile justice that were discussed in Chapter 2, and examines the essential differences between a hearings system and a court system in the American context. Finally, we place the Scottish system in a wider context, discussing its 'performance' in relation to a number of aspects or dimensions of juvenile justice systems in general.

In considering whether there is need for change in the domestic scene, and if so how this might be accomplished, we take account of the activities of children's panel members, the responsibilities of reporters and the adequacy of the information available to children's hearings, and finally ask whether it would be advantageous to restrict in some way the discretion currently exercised by reporters and panel members.

The work of children's panel members

If this section of our report is largely concerned with areas of weakness, it is not because we fail to recognize or adequately to appreciate the impressive strengths displayed by the majority of panel members. To the contrary; we draw attention to the need for improvement and suggest ways in which it might be achieved, precisely because we believe that the commitment of its lay participants is one of the hearings system's principal advantages and that it provides a foundation upon which higher standards of practice can be built.

Problems were observed to arise in carrying out procedural requirements in hearings, in an occasional tendency to block family participation by the use of particular modes of speech, and in a widespread avoidance of serious engagement with parents. All of these observations raise fairly controversial issues and carry implications for change.

There is very strong evidence that a significant proportion of children's hearings fall short of the by no means excessively demanding standards laid down in the 1968 Act and the Hearings Rules. We have no evidence to suggest that the procedural failings which we observed contributed to specific decisions of an unjust or inappropriate nature, but this does not in any way justify the widespread laxity. It reflects unfavourably on both panel members and reporters, and it is also needless. We can show clearly that those hearings which are impeccable with respect to procedure tend to fall above the average of the sample as far as family participation is concerned.

However humane the motives of those panel members who sometimes neglect this aspect of their obligations, these failings are capable of bringing the hearings system into disrepute unless they are honestly acknowledged and reformed. For all we know, children's hearings are no more lax than many long-established minor courts; the possibility is discussed in *Chapter 18*. But the fact remains that the hearings system is new, unconventional, threatens many cherished assumptions and is therefore vulnerable. Failure on the part of panel members and reporters to put their own house in order might lead not merely to criticism but to attempts to introduce changes that might affect features that they positively value.

The creation and maintenance of an informal atmosphere, in the interests of which much procedural propriety is sacrificed, is seen by panel members as the principal means towards open communication and an honest examination of the child's behaviour. The goal that panel members set for themselves is, we have no doubt, extremely difficult to attain, given the lack of previous personal familiarity in most cases and the inescapable asymmetry of relationships in the hearing situation. We conclude from our observations that the actual performance of panel members in this regard is extremely variable in quality. At one extreme we find examples of hearings characterized by the use of sarcasm and sermonizing, with minimal opportunities for family involvement. Equally, we find hearings which approximate very closely indeed to the ideal that panel members hold up, marked by empathy, understanding and genuine dialogue. In terms of their ability to elicit active participation and attitudes that are free from excesses of defensiveness or hostility, most hearings seem to occupy intermediate positions, falling somewhere short of their own ideal but nevertheless containing a number of positive features.

Our own conclusion that, in spite of many imperfections, performance should, considering all the circumstances, be judged distinctly creditable is confirmed by the response of the system's clients. Indeed, the verdict of children and parents who have passed through the system is more positive than ours as observers, reflecting no doubt a lower level of expectation. There is no suggestion that the young people and their parents found the hearing anything other than a serious experience. Although their comments are not free from criticism, we find a high degree of agreement on those questions that relate to participation. There is a sense of having been listened to, a sense of having been allowed to express themselves, a belief that panel members were genuinely interested in the views expressed and were helpful in their intentions. It seems clear that the measure of informality achieved is generally greater than the family members had expected and that they respond to this appreciatively, even though we as detached observers are conscious of some discrepancies between aspiration and achievement.

In almost all the hearings observed a conscious effort was made to evoke participation by the use of an encouraging and non-directive style. This does not mean however that panel members were consistently non-judgmental or non-directive. It is clear from our evidence that the style we have called 'encouraging' not infrequently co-existed with approaches that were potentially more inhibiting. But although some ways of conducting a hearing are rather more or rather less likely to bring an active response from clients, there are no simple or clear-cut relationships. Conversational styles that are effective with children may have a negative impact upon parents, and vice versa.

Some of the styles adopted by panel members, however, seem to have little to commend them. The use of sarcasm, a tendency to interrupt, the use of the imperative and the practice of exhortation all serve in varying degrees to induce silence or monosyllabic speech, or anger or opposition, particularly in children and their mothers; fathers are on the whole more resilient and less affected by the styles adopted by panel members. But even if they do not have a discernible impact on the level of participation, the use of essentially aggressive styles can rarely be justified in terms of the hearings system's own philosophy.

A special aspect of the communication problem is implied by the contrast between the views expressed by panel members as to the causes of delinquency and the attitudes that they adopt within the hearing itself. To an overwhelming extent, panel members see young offenders as victims of social and economic circumstances, but most commonly of the inadequacies of their parents. There is a very widespread belief that if children are in trouble it is because their parents have failed them; they had it in their power to have acted differently, had they so chosen. So panel members argue, and there is no reason to doubt their sincerity; such views are, after all, wholly in keeping with the underlying principles of the Kilbrandon Report, though many panel members express them more vehemently. Yet observers at hearings would rarely come to the conclusion that panel members hold views of this kind. Certainly the parents themselves would be astonished. Of 36 parents interviewed after hearings, not one believed that the panel members had held him or her responsible for the child's delinquency; the child himself, or his associates, or no-one in particular might have been thought culpable, but never mother or father.

Another perspective on the reluctance of panel members to engage in discussion of potentially sensitive issues is provided by a comparison between the topics included in social background and other professional reports and the subjects discussed at the relevant hearings. In general, we find that topics introduced into reports act as springboards for conversation in the hearing.

But when social workers comment in unfavourable terms on specific features of the parents, the statements tend to act as danger signals, warning panel members to avoid thin ice.

No-one who is aware of the skill and self-confidence required to initiate and sustain a dialogue in which one participant is confronted with his own shortcomings can fail to sympathise with panel members if they shrink from such a task, settle for superficial and 'safe' topics of conversation, and sometimes even appear to collude with parents against the child. Yet in doing so they are contradicting their own beliefs. Perhaps more importantly, they may be missing an opportunity to prepare the way for the supervision process. Most social workers see supervision as requiring work with the whole family and not merely with the delinquent child, but few parents would imagine that the supervision process has any connection with them.

To raise standards in these areas of performance cannot be simple, but should not be written off as an unattainable objective. The fact that very high levels of practice were in fact observed in a substantial proportion of hearings clearly demonstrates that both excellent procedure and an impressive command of communication skills are within the grasp of panel members. To bring all or most practice to the level of the best involves the re-examination of both selection and training.

It is often argued that the ability to create in others a sense of confidence, to put them at their ease, to encourage an honest expression of feelings as well as statements of fact, derives essentially from qualities of the individual personality; and that these qualities, if not innate, are sufficiently well developed and integrated in the mature adult for training to be either unnecessary or useless. The argument is, of course, not restricted to the tasks of children's panel members but is frequently raised in discussing selection and training for any profession in which the abilities to communicate and to form effective personal relationships play important parts: teaching and social work are obvious examples. To the extent that the argument is valid, the responsibility of those who select (in this instance, would-be panel members) is a heavy one. We referred in an earlier chapter to the serious attention given to this aspect of the selection process by Children's Panel Advisory Committees. But we are not aware of any procedure actually in use that has more than face validity – any, that is to say, in which the judgments made at the time of selection have subsequently been examined in relation to measures of performance in the hearing itself. Given present knowledge, it might not prove exceptionally difficult to develop relevant criterion measures by means of which the effectiveness of existing selection procedures would be estimated and possibilities of improvement, if this seemed desirable, could be considered. We think it is important for relevant studies to be set in train at an early date.

But it would be neither just nor realistic to impose upon selectors the entire responsibility for ensuring that all the work of children's hearings is carried out by panel members equipped with all the skills needed to ensure a high level of participation. In the first place, there is no reason to believe that there is any selection process without a margin of error; methods can be improved, often greatly improved, but rarely if ever perfected. Secondly, if selectors were determined to minimize errors, they might well set standards so high that they excluded any applicant about whom there was any shadow of uncertainty and thus reduced the flow of new entrants to the hearings system to a mere trickle of paragons. Some risks are unavoidable, and a share of the responsibility for creating and maintaining standards must therefore be allocated to the training function. As far as skill in observing all the procedural requirements of the hearing are concerned, training must obviously carry by far the greater part of that responsibility. We cannot help wondering however whether the emphasis that some regions in their recruitment publicity place upon the common-sensical nature of the panel member's work may not encourage an under-estimation of the more formal, procedural aspects of the role from the very beginning.

There are no natural forces at work within the system which will bring about improved standards without a deliberate drive, and training must we believe be at the heart of that drive. The training demands at present made on panel members are extremely modest. In-service training is not obligatory, and the weight given to legal and procedural matters during preliminary training is very light indeed in some regions. Because of the voluntary nature of panel members' commitments, there is something of a tendency to keep demands on them to a minimum – a tendency which does less than justice to the seriousness of their obligations. And while we may need new research before we can significantly improve the selection of panel members, we know enough to proceed without delay to a marked improvement in their training.

The form and content of training

The recent shift – presumably on grounds of administrative economy – to an initial period of appointment for panel members of five years would in itself justify a re-examination of current training provisions even if there were no direct evidence of remediable weakness in performance.

It cannot be assumed that a single course of training, however sophisticated, will polish skills so that they can never be tarnished in subsequent use. The effects of experience as a panel member are widely believed to be wholly beneficial, but this may be a serious over-simplification. In the other scale of the balance we may need to set the danger of a loss of freshness and a gradual decline into routine as well as the hazard, perhaps peculiar to this field of work, that long-continued exposure to delinquency and family disturbance may erode an initial idealism and blunt sensitivities. What is required in the longer term is not merely training in a formal sense but more importantly the means and the opportunity for panel members to monitor their own performance, and the encouragement to use that opportunity in a climate that stimulates self-awareness and self-criticism rather than defensiveness and denial.

While current practice tends to emphasize preparatory training and to assign relatively little importance to in-service training, it is far from certain that the former has or can be expected to have a profound impact. Members are at this stage preoccupied with their expectations of practice and uncertainty about their ability to cope with the human encounters awaiting them. Observing at hearings is the part of training most valued by new members, not least because of the relief at actually being in a situation where they can identify with those conducting the hearing, work through some of their own responses and reactions and weigh up their own potential for successful performance. Formal teaching about social services, about human growth and development, even about communications is unlikely to achieve a great deal in the face of these personal anxieties. The aims of pre-service training must therefore be modest. It should provide new members with a broad outline of the main features of their role, detailed information on procedures and powers, and, through role play and discussion with experienced panel members, sufficient confidence to conduct their first hearing. A well-developed understanding of the task and of the social skills required to carry it through are more likely to be acquired within the context of practical experience.

Two complementary approaches are suggested: the introduction of a probationary year and the provision of a refresher course around the end of the third year. After completing initial training panel members would commence service on hearings and would be required during their first year of office to attend further training on specific topics. These should include

a course on procedure and practice;
a course on communication, with an emphasis on the development of personal skills relevant to the specific circumstances of children's hearings;
a course on chairmanship.

In the fullest sense a probationary year would end with a personal assessment on the strength of which a decision about future service would be made. Such a far-reaching move is not anticipated at present if only because of the lack of assessment techniques of agreed reliability and validity. The probationary year even in the more limited sense implied here would provide members with an opportunity to consolidate their learning and to make new advances in understanding the task, and to share systematically with tutors and others their early experience at hearings.

But it is not only during the first year of service that panel members' skills need to be sharpened and their knowledge of the task developed. Experience alone does not guarantee a steady improvement of standards; indeed, it is arguable that unless a panel member has the opportunity to examine his own experience critically, he may well fall into stereotyped patterns of response and fail to recognize where improvement is called for or how it may be achieved. A refresher course during the third year of office would help to avoid the danger of practice deteriorating. Members could be withdrawn from service on hearings for a period of three or four months in order to allow time for attendance at training. The third year seems an appropriate time to require further participation in training. The strength of the initial commitment might be expected to become weaker by this time, fresh approaches to practice are less likely to be tried, the distance from the probationary year is sufficient to allow bad habits to settle, the system itself may have undergone some changes and new services may have developed since panel members had an opportunity to look closely at provisions.

The refresher course would aim to fill gaps in knowledge and to strengthen competence in those areas of practice that are particularly demanding and difficult. As far as possible the training content would relate to the needs identified in the individual panel member. This process of review needs to be carried out carefully and sensitively. Selected experienced panel members acting as tutors on a local basis may be able to take a 'monitoring' role, and individual panel members could contribute to their own assessment by the use of a self-evaluation instrument.

These proposals imply some reorientation of existing training arrangements, but no new staff and minimal additional cost. Much of the executive responsibility would fall on panel member tutors, a group already actively and productively engaged in pre-service training. Carefully selected and prepared, working in association with professional contributors and making use of well-designed training material, they are capable of contributing to both probationary and refresher training and could become a powerful influence in the development of improved standards of practice. Existing regional training organizers would plan, co-ordinate and oversee all training activities in their respective regions, while the Panel Training Resource Centre[1] (initiated as a Scotland-wide service in 1980) would be available to create appropriate training and evaluation materials and to contribute to specialized tasks such as the training of tutors. It is assumed that new training initiatives should be followed at a suitable interval by a sample study designed to measure change in standards of practice in children's hearings, using the findings reported here as baseline data.

The role of the chairman

A pattern of work has evolved in the practice of children's hearings which places an exceptionally heavy burden on the member who acts as chairman. Not only does he or she carry the formal responsibilities discussed above, but is also constantly, sometimes almost continuously, involved in the verbal interchange of the hearing. Of 301 hearings observed, there were only ten in which the chairman's level of participation was coded as 'slight'. This is not to say that the chairman wholly dominated the proceedings; one or both of the other panel members was judged to be actively involved at three out of every four hearings. But members other than the chairman are not obliged to do more than take part in the discussion as much or as little as they see fit, so that there is a clear contrast between the complexity of their tasks and that of the chairman.

In principle, all panel members are equal and all may be called upon to chair a hearing. In some regions the practice is to designate in advance the member who is to chair each session, with the possibility (although this is never stated openly) that some may be called upon more frequently than others. Elsewhere this practice is avoided, and no decision is reached about chairmanship until the panel members assemble. Our own sample was divided evenly (150 : 151) between those in which the chairman had and had not been pre-selected.

We do not advocate the creation of two classes of panel member, but we think it essential that the particular demands of the role of chairman should be clearly acknowledged. We believe therefore that no new panel member should chair hearings before completing the special course in chairmanship referred to above, and that any member should feel free to indicate that he or she would prefer not to assume the role of chairman, without any sense that they were thereby failing in their responsibilities as panel members. We suggest also that there is a strong case for the role of the chairman in the hearing to be more narrowly defined. Instead of acting as the hearing's principal spokesman, he should stand back slightly from the proceedings, encourage the active participation of the other panel members, and sum up at the end. This is, of course, the way in which the chairman is expected to function in many deliberative bodies, where an important aspect of his role is to draw out other members but where constant active involvement on his part would be frowned upon. Above all, the chairman of the hearing would then be free to give that close attention to ensuring procedural propriety which is required by statute and essential if justice is to be seen to be done.

The work of reporters

We take quite different views of the work done by reporters to children's panels when they are functioning as intake officials and of their role in the course of the hearing itself. In the former capacity their discretionary powers are exercised on a very considerable scale. About half of all offenders referred to reporters do not find their way to a hearing. As a consequence of this and of some reduction in the number of children entering the system, the total appearances before hearings and courts combined is less than half the number proceeded against in the various courts ten years earlier.

Diversion by reporters does not for the most part involve the provision of either compulsory or voluntary alternatives. The proportions for whom informal supervision is arranged with the social work department or who are referred back to the police for a formal warning are small. Four-fifths of all those offence cases diverted from hearings were not brought to the notice of any agency. Reporters always notified the families concerned of their decision to take no formal action, and a few reporters interviewed children and parents and attempted to exert some moral pressure. The sum of their activities in respect of non-referred cases however could be described quite precisely as 'minimal intervention'.

Guided by no formal rules or agreed criteria, reporters require information from social work, school and other sources, and their decisions to divert are in practice influenced by a combination of known prior record, seriousness of current offence and awareness of 'problems' in the domestic background. The ability to identify cases where a relatively low risk of subsequent delinquency justified non-referral seems to have been developed to quite a high degree. Something in the region of three quarters of all the new referrals thus dealt with in the early months of 1976 did not come to the reporter's notice on any later occasion.

We are not convinced that closer regulation of the activities of reporters when exercising their referring functions would have significant advantages; the uses and limitations of offering decision 'guidelines' to reporters and to hearings are discussed later in this chapter, where the drawbacks, it is suggested, are likely to outweigh any gains. But while we would not favour a large apparatus of control, we believe there is a case, on general grounds of public policy, for greater accountability in the work of reporters. When decisions are made, reasons – of a non-tautological character – should be expressed in writing. Some record-keeping in reporters' offices is not of the highest quality, and a standard pattern of recording and summarizing basic information would be advantageous. Some reporters produce valuable annual reports on their work; all reporters should be expected to follow this pattern. Finally, we think there is a case for one person with advisory functions to be attached to the appropriate central department to ensure a degree of oversight, encouragement and where necessary criticism of the work of reporters. But we would not wish to see any development that would inhibit the useful and conscientious work done by reporters in their role as intake officials. The hearings system, we believe, has through this role achieved a substantial measure of diversion, with many advantages and few if any visible costs.

The skill displayed by reporters in dealing with referrals at the pre-hearing stage cannot be said to be matched within the hearing itself. The fairly modest contribution made by reporters to the maintenance of procedural standards is on the face of it surprising. There is of course no doubt that the formal responsibility for conducting the hearing in accordance with the rules of procedure rests with the hearing chairman. But the reporter is always present. According to Finlayson[2], '. . . he acts in some quasi-legal advisory role to the hearing members and also in a clerical role to record minutes of proceedings of the actual hearing'. This view of the reporter's function is echoed by many chairmen when they perform introductions at the beginning of the hearing: 'Mr. X is here to keep us right on any legal matters'. But the 'quasi-legal advisory role' has no statutory basis, and is certainly not seen as incumbent upon them by all reporters. Some quite explicitly disclaim any responsibility in this area, while some others, confronted with research findings, have been known to comment cheerfully that they were only too familiar with the procedural errors of panel members. We do not see this as a very satisfactory state of affairs. While we are not in favour of any reduction in the responsibilities of panel members, we would strongly recommend that a directive be issued to regional reporters by the central department, placing a clear obligation upon them and their assistants to advise hearing chairmen on all matters of procedure.

How advice should be conveyed is not a question that can be dealt with by statutory instruments. Our impression from observation – though we cannot confirm this by precise evidence – was that for some reporters the problem was not that they did not have a statutory responsibility to ensure procedural conformity but that they lacked the social skills necessary to contribute to the proceedings appropriately, without obtrusiveness and without creating embarrassment. This points to a need for a particular type of training, focussed upon the skills involved in the interaction processes of the hearing, such as is not generally associated with the professional preparation of those whose duties are largely administrative and legal. But in relation to the training of reporters we are speaking not of infiltrating some unconventional new element into an established pattern but of a design yet to be undertaken.

One of the more surprising features of the Scottish system of children's hearings is that although the Secretary of State has powers to determine the qualifications of reporters, he has not so far chosen to do so. There were initial uncertainties within the professional group, and when these were resolved an era of financial stringency had begun and very many new developments in the public sector were postponed indefinitely. The training of reporters may become a reality sooner than many other projects. Precisely what form that training should take is a matter to be decided between the reporters themselves, central government and the university establishment concerned. The only conviction we would express in the present context is that the programme should be specifically constructed around the role and responsibilities of the reporter, and not be a collage made up of extracts from existing courses in law and social work. In advocating an early beginning for this unusually challenging venture into professional training, we are not arguing that the most important task is to raise standards of practice above an unacceptably low level. Most of our judgments of the work of reporters are very positive. We see specialist training as a means towards defining and maintaining the highest standards, of safeguarding against possible destructive criticism and of giving added strength to a relatively small group with extremely important responsibilities.

Professional reports

The analyses reported in *Chapter 11* demonstrate the substantial influence that the reports received by panel members have both on the focus of the hearing and on the decision reached. They also suggest that the reliance placed upon them implies a more generous compliment to their professional quality and relevance than is invariably merited. We have made no attempt to grade or classify social work reports according to a number of formal criteria, and are therefore not in a position to say what proportion exhibit varying degrees of excellence. Our very strong impression, as indicated in *Chapter 10*, is that although it would be possible to identify reports which are clearly written, free from jargon, coherently organized, skilled in their presentation of a recognizable individual and linking their recommendations for supervision with an estimate of the personal objectives that might realistically be pursued if the recommendations were accepted, such reports would not account for the majority of those submitted to children's hearings. Too few reports are compiled with the specific needs of panel members as decision-makers in mind; too many are in the nature of 'general purpose' reports, lacking sharpness of focus and with a recommendation added like a postscript.

In considering how change might be effected we are conscious of the fact that the provision of background reports is only one of the social worker's responsibilities in relation to the children's hearings system; he is also obliged to carry out any supervision requirements that the hearing may impose. That major component of his work has not come within the scope of our studies, and it is not easy to make recommendations without taking account of the social worker's task as a whole. There are nevertheless implications for training and for experiment even in the more restricted present context.

Social work training courses in Scotland, both graduate and non-graduate, are planned to meet the requirements of a United Kingdom qualification. While there are powerful arguments against any change that would restrict the movement of social workers between Scotland and England, there is a case for giving more emphatic recognition to the distinctive features of social work practice in Scotland than is at present afforded in some courses. Work with the hearings system is one of the most important of these, and it is essential for every social work student not merely to understand the structure and operation of the system but to acquire skill in – among other things – the preparation of reports designed to be of maximum value to panel members. Practising social workers are strikingly aware of the limitations of the training they have received, and our evidence suggests that they might welcome additional preparation for work with the hearings. New ventures in training should go hand in hand with experiments to devise more effective approaches to the construction of reports. No authoritative guidelines for use in the preparation of reports are at present available to social workers. Notes of guidance could now be prepared, perhaps using alternative forms, and evaluated in terms of their perceived utility to social workers and panel members.

In the longer term, there may be questions about a degree of specialization in area social work teams, with work for the hearings system forming a major part of a special emphasis on social work with older children. It would be improper however to claim that the findings presented in this volume in themselves provide a sufficient basis for such a proposal.

Schools are the other major source of information. Although there is not a comparable statutory obligation on the education authorities to produce reports for children's hearings, it seems to be uniformly accepted throughout Scotland that this is a proper responsibility for guidance teachers.[3] It would be hard to discover any further uniformity. Teachers are for the most part a good deal more distant from the hearings system than are social workers, and are often poorly informed about its requirements. Regional reporters, no doubt recognizing this, issue standard forms for each child on whom a report is requested. Each reporter uses a different form. These vary in length from half a small sheet to one which, with very full notes of guidance, runs to six pages. They ask for different information, and also ask for the same information in different ways. There is no particular merit in uniformity, but it does seem likely that some of these forms are better than others. And the very close attention that, as we have seen, panel members pay to school performance and behaviour would justify more systematic thought than has so far been applied in this area. We would favour two moves. First, the preparation of an explanatory booklet for guidance and other teachers. Secondly, a series of experiments with existing and possibly also new forms for educational reports, with a view to determining the format, breadth and depth of coverage which comes closest to meeting the needs of panel members, while remaining compatible with the working methods and time constraints of guidance teachers and with the range of information available to them.

The management of discretion

Proposals for change that have been put forward in this chapter have been largely limited to matters of training and organization. They have taken for granted the maintenance of the existing broad structure and *modus operandi* of the hearings system and do not involve any radical departures; their objective is to make the system work better within its own terms of reference, not to alter the terms of reference. Before concluding the chapter we must take account of a particular line of criticism which has potential relevance to children's hearings as well as to many other legal and welfare systems. This is the criticism of the discretionary powers given to 'professionals' and 'officials' especially in bureaucratic agencies, and an associated pressure for conformity to rules or what is sometimes referred to as a 'return to legality'. Gross disparities in sentencing are, of course, one example of what many hold to be an abuse of discretionary powers. Clearly, the wide discretion enjoyed by reporters might also be subject to criticism under this heading. A generalized suspicion of and even hostility towards 'professionals' is an integral part of the critique of discretion, and is nowhere more powerfully articulated than by professional academics. However, the fact that panel members are laymen by no means exempts them from scrutiny, especially when it is apparent that the advice of social workers substantially influences their judgments.

The substantial American literature on discretion has more recently been joined by a considerable and growing body of British writing. From a sustained encounter with the latter one emerges with the sensation of having lived for some time on a diet made up almost entirely of soufflés. The contributions are whipped up, for the most part, from intellectual ingredients of high quality. While some fall flat in the making, most emerge as light, airy, even elegant confections. But their lack of bulk and body leaves the reader hungry for even a few morsels of factual protein. Thus, most writers on the subject maintain, no doubt with justification, that the exercise of discretionary powers in the public services tends to operate to the disadvantage of clients and claimants. But how many clients of which systems are disadvantaged in what ways and to what extent, and whether any of the as yet unmeasured damage done by discretionary decisions is counterbalanced by discretionary processes operating to the advantage of clients, remain questions which have scarcely begun to be formulated, let alone put to the test. Few contributors to the debate would wish to see the complete abolition of discretionary powers and the substitution of inflexible rules, but to what degree and by what means such powers might most effectively and constructively be restricted, remain matters for further exploration.

In fairness to British writings on this subject, it must be said that many are explicitly of the nature of prolegomena, designed to stimulate interest in the possibilities of research. Consideration of the issue of discretion in the United States on the other hand has reached a stage in which specific proposals for change are being produced; and whereas British discussion has most commonly taken as its starting point the income maintenance system, American arguments and proposals have more often arisen from a consideration of the problem of variation in judicial sentencing. The heavy criticism evoked by disparities in sentencing has led to an interest in mandatory sentencing policies as well as to considerable discussion of the possibility of a middle road, the structuring of judicial discretion by the use of 'sentencing guidelines' – with the latter seen not as gentle advice but interpreted in a fairly strict and formal sense. Such work as that of Wilkins *et al.* (1978)[4] on the development of guidelines is of particular interest in the present context, for it is in principle easily applicable to the decision-making of both reporters and panel members.

The approach outlined and recommended in this report derives from Wilkins' earlier work on parole recommendations. Basically the project involves (1) trying to identify the implicit sentencing policy of judges by calculating the predictive value of various items of information available to them at the time of sentencing, and ultimately combining the most powerful of these into a multiple regression equation which gives the best estimate of sentencing decisions; (2) on the basis of the latter findings, establishing a series of grids or matrices which can be used to read off the 'most probable' sentence in any given case; (3) testing these models against a further series of judicial decisions made independently, in order to see how many decisions would have been correctly predicted from the matrices; (4) recommending one or more of such models as a guide to sentencing practice, with the further recommendation that decisions falling outside the guidelines should require a written justification.

In this study, up to 205 items of information were extracted from the records of 200 randomly selected cases that had passed through the District Courts of Denver, Colorado, and a similar number from the District Courts of Vermont. Only six items of information made a statistically significant contribution to explaining variations in sentencing decisions in the former jurisdiction, and only four in the latter. Five different models of sentencing guidelines were developed, three in Denver and two in Vermont, each using a grid system designed to predict sentencing decisions. Basically, each model involves two axes, one indicating the seriousness of the offence and the other certain summarized and weighted characteristics of the offender; the appropriate sentence depends on the location of any individual in relation to the two axes.

The five models, differing principally in the complexity of the weighting system applied, were tested in terms of their ability to predict judicial decisions in the two jurisdictions concerned. It should be noted however that the criterion was successful prediction of 'in/out' – i.e., the decision whether or not to imprison, with no reference to length of sentence. The relatively crude nature of the test is referred to only in passing and its implications are not discussed; these might, however, be quite significant, especially if much of the argument about sentencing disparities revolves round duration of imprisonment. Within these limits, the models proved able to predict between 73 and 83 per cent of decisions. The narrow range is interesting, suggesting that the statistically more refined models offered very little gain in accuracy. Analysis of subjective estimates by judges indicated that they believed offender variables (e.g. prior criminal history) to have a greater influence on their sentences than offence seriousness variables, except in those cases which they deemed to be of a very serious nature (e.g. one involving serious personal injury), when the relative perceived influence of the two sets of factors was reversed. After discussions with judges and further analyses a synthesis model was designed. On this, the offence score was the sum of the intraclass rank of the offence at conviction plus the harm/loss modifier.* The offender score was the sum of the offender's prior conviction, legal status, revocation and incarceration scores, minus his social stability score (full-time or part-time employment, weighted for duration). This proved capable of predicting 85–90 per cent of decisions on an 'in/out' basis, and 80–85 per cent when the more stringent criterion of 'sentence imposed not more than 1 year ± that indicated by guidelines' was applied.

An implementation phase appears to have been under way when the present report was prepared. For each criminal case arising, Denver judges were notified (before sentencing) of the sentence that the guidelines would indicate in that case. This would normally be calculated by probation officers. It is stressed that judges are not obliged to confirm the disposition emerging from the application of guidelines, but they are encouraged to write a reasoned justification of any sentencing decision that departs from the indicated sentence. These are expected to amount to 10–20 per cent of all sentences. The guidelines, the authors emphasize, are intended only to keep judges informed of the characteristic sentencing practice of the generality of judges in a given jurisdiction, in relation to a case with a particular combination of offence and offender characteristics.

The first part of this project, with its attempt to identify the factors correlated with sentencing decisions, is methodologically indistinguishable from our own work on decisions by reporters and disposals by hearings, and is of obvious interest and relevance. However, the transformation of regression analyses into the components of a tool for operational use raises both technical and philosophical issues of considerable importance – issues which appear not to be addressed at all by the authors of this report.

One puzzling feature is their failure to relate this work to any systematic examination – or indeed any examination at all – of the initiating problem of sentencing disparities. If we are not clear what disparities occur, how frequently, and for what reasons, how can we estimate the likely effectiveness of this

* This is a weighting intended to bring out the 'real' seriousness of the offence as distinct from its statutory classification. In practice it ranged from 0 (no victim) to + 5 (caused death).

technique for reducing them? Common sense suggests that the impact is unlikely to be great. First, it is assumed that each jurisdiction (in practice, it would seem, each county except in the case of very small states) will be encouraged to develop its own system of guidelines. The method can do nothing, therefore, to reduce disparities between jurisdictions, which may well be more striking. Secondly, the fairly high predictive ability of the guidelines suggests that a considerable measure of consistency in sentencing already prevails within jurisdictions. (In the hypothetical limiting case, when guidelines can accurately predict 100 per cent of judicial decisions, we have no need of guidelines because all judges are implicitly working within them already.) In the minority of cases when sentences do not conform with guidelines few judges should have much difficulty in providing an acceptable explanation of their statistically deviant decisions. No doubt the authors believe that judges who are regularly reminded of any discrepancies between their own and 'standard' sentencing practices will gradually be encouraged to move towards a 'mainstream' position, but this may be very optimistic. Common sense, however, is what we fall back on when we lack knowledge; and the empirical vacuum in which this project was carried out makes any systematic evaluation virtually impossible.

There are other potentially difficult problems which might be created in the transition from regression coefficients to guidelines. There is an area where the boundary between neutral calculations and personal value-based judgment can rapidly become blurred. There is no single route which takes us unambiguously from descriptive statistical relationships to operational rules. As the number of different models indicates, there are many different ways of selecting, combining and weighting variables. Some of these combinations may have the effect, perhaps quite unwittingly, of weighting the scales for or against offenders with certain characteristics. For example, the use of employment stability as a mitigating factor, as in some of the Wilkins models, is likely to be to the detriment of blacks and some other minority groups. The use in some models of both number of prior arrests and number of prior convictions might be held to involve too great a negative loading for previous criminal record. The chances of statistical sleight of hand cannot be ignored.

But how great is 'too great'? Here we touch upon what is perhaps the most serious weakness of this study. It was carried out not merely in an empirical but in a philosophical vacuum. By proposing to resolve the problem of sentencing discrepancies through an emphasis on consistency or continuity, it tends to impart permanence to current judicial practice and to accept the determinants of that practice as given. Any debate on the objectives of punishment is foreclosed, although the theories of punishment implicit in the judicial decisions studied do not seem to accord neatly with any one philosophy. If we chose explicitly to embody alternative assumptions about the objectives of punishment in separate guidelines, we would give very different weightings to different offences and offender variables and open up the possibility of quite different sentences for the same offender. Perhaps much or some disparity in sentencing flows from conflicting but unexpressed assumptions about the nature and object of punishment. Should not these be made explicit and their practical implications discussed, on the basis of data which the Wilkins method could go a long way to generate? In the end, the philosophical limitations and the empirical limitations of this study turn out to be closely related.

For reasons that arise in part from these limitations and in part from our judgment of the hearings system, we conclude that statistically-derived guidelines do not have a useful contribution to make within the Scottish context. A belief in the principle of individualized decision-making is central to the way in which both reporters and panel members see their work, and would create serious resistance to any suggestion of formal decision-rules; before advocating such a change, one would need to be powerfully convinced of the distinctive advantages of the latter. It is important to recall that the discretion exercised by reporters and by children's hearings, though by no means insignificant, is extremely limited compared to that of most adult courts, including those studied by Wilkins. For all practical purposes, only two choices are available to reporters and three to members of children's hearings; the most severe custodial decision is a supervision order with a life not exceeding one year. In the Denver/Vermont study, a sentence was judged to be successfully predicted if it fell within the limits of one year more and one year less than that indicated by the guidelines. Again, Wilkins and his colleagues recommend that sentences 'outside' the guidelines should have a written justification. Reasons for decisions are supposed to be given both orally and in writing after *every* disposal by a children's hearing. The quality of practice is not at present uniformly high and needs to be improved sharply, but the obligation is clear. There is not at present a corresponding requirement for reporters to give reasons for their decisions; we have already recommended that this should be changed.

It is, however, a basic philosophical inconsistency in the use of guidelines of this type to manage discretion that makes them peculiarly inappropriate in the Scottish system. The authors are insistent that they are not concerned with 'what ought to be', but only with 'what is' – that is to say, they seek only to ascertain how decisions are made, not how they ought to be made. But the act of incorporating the determinants of decisions into a set of guidelines for future practice inevitably makes assumptions of a prescriptive kind. The object of the guidelines is not merely to reduce sentencing inconsistency but to maintain continuity of practice over time; in effect, the factors that have shaped decisions should continue to do so in the future. For the hearings system at any rate, to embrace a principle of historical continuity could not be reconciled with its commitment to pursuing the best interests of children. To perpetuate a set of decision rules derived from past practice would imply that the decision-making criteria that they embodied were indeed maximally effective in promoting those interests. Few panel members would be so complacent as to make such an assumption. The philosophy of decision-making to which they are committed should entail not merely the rejection of unchanging criteria, but a positive search for information on the consequences of disposals which could be incorporated in a feedback process and used to increase the effectiveness of decisions. That outcomes are still so poorly understood is a significant weakness of the system as a whole. We return to this theme in *Chapter 18*.

NOTES

1. The Panel Training Resource Centre is an independent and privately funded service which was established in 1980 at the University of Glasgow. Its function is to create audio and audio visual materials for use in the training of children's panel members throughout Scotland. For further information see *The Hearing*, bulletin of the panel training resource centre, issue 1, November 1980.
2. A. F. Finlayson, 'The Reporter': in F. M. Martin and K. Murray (eds.), *Children's Hearings*, Scottish Academic Press, 1976.
3. For a full discussion of the role of the school guidance teacher, see Patricia Thomas, 'School Guidance': ibid.
4. L. Wilkins, J. Kress, D. Gottfredson, J. Calpin and A. Gelman, *Sentencing guidelines: structuring judicial discretion*, National Institute of Law Enforcement and Criminal Justice Law Enforcement Assistance Administration, U.S. Department of Justice, February 1978.

17

THE PLACE OF CHILDREN'S HEARINGS IN THE REFORM OF AMERICAN JUVENILE JUSTICE

The end of an era

It has recently been noted by the National Task Force to Develop Standards and Goals for Juvenile Justice and Delinquency Prevention that, 'Since there is virtually no experience in the United States with other than judicially determined and imposed dispositions, there is no data upon which to draw either to support or detract from the call for lay or expert panels.'[1] This is fortunately no longer true, at least as to lay panels. Although admittedly not from American experience, the data presented in earlier chapters is nonetheless highly relevant to the issue addressed by the Task Force – a re-evaluation of whether juvenile courts in America should continue to be the sole authority to make disposition decisions. In this chapter we conclude that they should not and that it would constitute significant progress in the evolution of American juvenile justice to institute a children's hearings system patterned on the Scottish model.

Discussion of the significance of our research for the American juvenile justice system is complicated, however, by three factors. The first arises from the required recognition that there are, in fact, 57 separate and independent American juvenile justice systems: 50 states, the District of Columbia, the national government, Puerto Rico, the Virgin Islands, Guam, American Samoa and the Trust Territories. While not all of these are of equal import, it is obvious that generalization concerning 'America' can be undertaken only with great trepidation. In addition, although change, trial and error, innovation and such have been a constant feature of American juvenile justice, the past decade has witnessed shifts that appear to be of such a fundamental character that there is demanded more than the usual caution required in assessing a system in near perpetual flux. Finally, it is not to be expected that changes in the juvenile justice system proceed in a single direction since reform has traditionally been largely an adversary process, pitting against those who see the problem of children's criminal behaviour as presenting primarily a question of what to do for children, others who perceive the policy issues focussing on what to do about crime. Juvenile justice has been and continues to be a shifting set of compromises in which the interests of both public safety and child welfare could be served: children could be taken off the street and restrained so long as they would be provided with the things they need – religious instruction, moral education, vocational training, psychotherapy, reinforcement of behaviour, – while under restraint; vast discretion could be exercised so long as decision-makers lost sight of neither side's interests. The results of the adversary reform process appear either as a series of trade-offs, with public safety provisions and child welfare changes maintained in some mutually acceptable proportion, or as provisions which simultaneously support both sides. Reforms that have been proposed and adopted within the past few years have concentrated on the latter type, manifested primarily in the application of criminal jurisprudence to the juvenile justice process.

The tenure of most of these compromises and trade-offs has proved limited, however, and their replacement with new ones has been a prominent feature of juvenile justice history. It took most of the 19th century for it to be acknowledged by children's advocates, for example, that child welfare and confinement in a secure corrections institution were wholly incompatible. Following that acknowledgment, the 20th century's juvenile court then became the major vehicle for making the accommodation between public safety and child welfare. Juvenile correctional institutions stayed on, no longer as a compromise, but mostly as a major instrument of crime suppression. One of the fundamental changes that appears currently to be under way involves the disappearance of the juvenile court as a unique institution for requisitioning and administering child welfare services, and its emergence as a court administering criminal justice for children.

To observe that until about a decade ago there had been an unrealistic overemphasis on the court's commitment to promoting child welfare and to dealing with children in a way that did not involve punishment for crime is to understate the history. For most of its tenure the court was normally described as more of a social agency than a court of law. Its supporters (nearly everyone) accepted it as an authoritative means for expressing society's concern for its wayward children. With the development of more and more knowledge about the well-springs of human behaviour the court took on an expert function as well, applying science to the problem of delinquency. It was to make dispositions on the basis of information that would help the child and identify the course of action most likely to prevent further misbehaviour, thereby serving both the child's and the public's interest. But the unravelling of this prevention-oriented child welfare system of justice is now widely accepted. Scientific claims to changing children's behaviour have either lost credibility or, as in the case of drug therapies, become morally unacceptable. The cost of even trying to implement a child welfare philosophy, measured in terms of abuses in the corrections programmes perpetuated from earlier days with only cosmetic changes or in overreaching in the courtroom, has been proving too high. Prevention of juvenile delinquency, the rallying point of all reformers since the 1820s that received its last significant sponsorship with the report of the 1967

Presidential Crime Commission, is now barely mentioned as a function of the juvenile court or the juvenile justice system. The long-accepted postulate that what serves the developmental and individualized interests of the child similarly serves the interests of the public is no longer believable, and with the dissolution of this key linkage there is acceptance of the long-denied view that the delinquent and the state are adversaries. With that we seem to have the beginnings of a third major set of compromises and trade-offs in American juvenile justice, following the creation of juvenile corrections and the appearance of the juvenile court. This latest homeostasis appears to involve a strong emphasis on formal social control, replicating the criminal justice system's balancing of public and private interests in which the public's interest continues to be in crime control but the child's interest comes to focus on a citizen's liberty and freedom from restraint rather than on a young person's interest in proper development, a supportive family environment, reassurance of public confidence in his future and other child-centred concerns which the juvenile court was traditionally thought to secure for him.

It is unnecessary, however, that these traditional concerns for children be entirely put aside. Delinquents and the state are not always adversaries and what we lack is an effective means for expressing the view that in many, perhaps most, instances of delinquent behaviour the interests of the state and those of children are still linked. Many of our findings suggest that by integrating a children's hearings system into the current criminal justice type reforms many child-centred interests can be preserved and public safety protected, without at the same time reintroducing the abuses of an earlier era. Prior to identifying the findings and describing this sort of integration it is first necessary to outline the basis for believing that criminal justice concerns are coming to dominate and structure American juvenile justice.

The directions of reform

Several sources highlight the directions being taken, among which legislation is of prime importance. As part of the current round of juvenile justice reform several of the states have rewritten their entire juvenile justice legislation.[2] Others have amended key provisions, such as those dealing with jurisdiction, dispositions and corrections.[3] A more comprehensive view of the changes that are afoot can be obtained from the work of the nearly completed Juvenile Justice Standards Project; twenty volumes of proposed reforms have been approved by the American Bar Association in 1979 and 1980 while consideration of two additional volumes has been deferred.[4] These sources constitute the central material from which our sense of direction has been culled. Although the new statutes to be discussed account for virtually all of the recent legislative changes of any major proportions, it needs to be reiterated that they still describe activity in only a minority of American jurisdictions.

Little discussion is required, for example, of what has happened to the adjudication process, the trial that follows a child's denial of the delinquency charges. Here the developments have been fairly uniform. As far as the law is concerned the procedures of a criminal trial are to be observed in the juvenile court. The Supreme Court's refusal to require jury trials in the juvenile court is an unsignificant exception.[5] Proposed changes are in the direction of still more legal rights in this process and toward an emphasis on assuring that children, because they are children, are not denied the protection of criminal procedures. As the ABA puts it:

> 'The unique features of the juvenile process – those characteristics that distinguish it from the criminal process and justify its existence as a separate system of social control – ought to be emphasized, in general, in phases of the process other than adjudication. This is not to say that juvenile court adjudication should merely be a junior criminal trial, although many of the constitutional protections associated with criminal adjudication proceedings must be recognized in juvenile adjudications. The fact of immaturity of the subject of the proceedings is recognized throughout these standards and, accordingly, greater protections are frequently provided juveniles than would be required in the case of the trial of an adult for a criminal offence'.[6]

Other key parts of recent developments appear with less uniformity than the criminalization of adjudication procedures, although they are among the most recent revisions of juvenile justice law. Two are of particular importance: statutory criteria for making dispositions and legislative statements of the purposes of juvenile justice. Taken together these provisions suggest that: (1) juvenile justice reform continues to articulate the views of both child welfare advocates and public safety advocates; (2) the public safety factor is receiving unprecedented statutory expression and prominence; and (3) child welfare interests are primarily promoted, as in the A.B.A.'s Adjudication Standards, by obtaining for the child the protections against abuse and over-reaching afforded by the criminal justice process, either as it presently provides them or as it can be refined to take account of the immaturity of defendants. Judicial acknowledgments of these developments and their meaning are already appearing. In a recent opinion the Supreme Court of West Virginia, for example, not only recognized the evolution toward a punitive juvenile justice philosophy of this sort, but indicated as well its awareness of the dual roots of juvenile justice reform.

> 'In reaching the conclusion that rehabilitation alone does not exhaust the goals of a juvenile disposition, and that responsibility and deterrence are also important elements in our juvenile philosophy, we

> have not simply embraced a conservative theory that juvenile delinquents need to be punished. Liberals and conservatives alike may find solace in this opinion because we acknowledge what has been an unspoken conclusion: our treatment looks a lot like punishment. At first glance an agreement among commentators at both philosophic poles may appear strange; however, both share the conclusion that treatment is often disguised punishment. Liberals are pleased that juvenile courts must exercise restraint in resorting to questionable 'treatments' at the dispositional stage and conservatives are pleased that it has been admitted that punishment can be a viable goal of any given juvenile disposition.
>
> While conservatives talk about punishment as 'retribution' and the cornerstone of 'responsibility', the liberal child advocates speak in terms of the 'right to punishment.' Once the rehabilitative model is accepted, the next fight is always to show that 'treatment' is often a caricature – something worthy of a story of Kafka or a Soviet mental hospital. Therefore, while the conservatives throw up their hands because they believe punishment works better than treatment, the juvenile advocates return increasingly to punishment on the grounds that punishment is much less punishing than 'treatment.'[7]

The ensuing examination of disposition criteria and legislative statements of purpose illustrates the developments alluded to by the West Virginia court.

Disposition criteria

Juvenile court philosophy is often articulated in criteria that are to guide the disposition decision, expressing what it is that society hopes to accomplish with its young offenders. The traditional child-centred view of this is expressed in Section 31 of the Uniform Juvenile Court Act, 1968 which single-mindedly declares: 'If the child is found to be a delinquent child the court may make any of the following orders of disposition best suited to his treatment, rehabilitation, and welfare.'[8] Two years earlier the United States Children's Bureau had taken the same position.

> 'The essential philosophy of the court handling children's cases has been called "individualized

> justice." This in essence means that the court selects a disposition through which the needs of the child can best be met, that it is a "legal tribunal where law and science, especially the science of medicine and those sciences which deal with human behaviour, such as biology, sociology, and psychology, work side by side" and that its purpose is remedial and to a degree preventive, rather than punitive.'[9]

A comparison of these with the Iowa Juvenile Justice Act, 1978, indicates the nature of the change that had been wrought by the late nineteen-seventies. That state's legislature has enjoined the juvenile court to 'enter the least restrictive dispositional order appropriate in view of the seriousness of the delinquent act, the child's culpability as indicated by the circumstances of the particular case, the age of the child and the child's prior record.'[10] The American Bar Association, too, recommends that dispositions be controlled by offence, responsibility and prior record. Standard 2.1 of its Standards Relating to Dispositions provides:

> 'In choosing among statutorily permissible dispositions, the court should employ the least restrictive category and duration of disposition that is appropriate to the seriousness of the offence, as modified by the degree of culpability indicated by circumstances of the particular case and by the age and prior record of the juvenile.'[11]

These references to 'least restrictive' are important. They function in the same way as do the references to the various aspects of the seriousness of the child's offending, and need to be interpreted in the context of a child welfare reform position that sees dispositions based on needs of the child as being often more restrictive than they would have been if only offence seriousness had been the basic consideration. An offence that would warrant only a few months incarceration for an adult, because the damage done or threatened was of a minor nature, might lead to a commitment for several years by a court that saw a delinquent child in need of a 'warm and structured environment' that could influence his habits, attitudes and skills. The Iowa and A.B.A. provisions are, therefore, a liberty-promoting codification of a *lex talionis* in the form of a rule '*no more than* an eye for an eye.' For advocates of public safety reform, concerned that the seriousness of the child's offending was receiving *inadequate* consideration, the new disposition criteria are equally welcomed.

The same joint children's freedom and public safety sponsorship can be seen in policies of the 1978 Juvenile Code of the state of Maine, in provisions that have been borrowed directly from the Maine Criminal Code and the Model Penal Code of the American Law Institute, that restrict (and thereby authorize) locking up delinquent children only when called for by protection of the public considerations. Section 3313 (1) provides:

> 'The court shall enter an order of disposition for a juvenile who has been adjudicated as having committed a juvenile crime without imposing placement in a secure institution as disposition unless, having regard to the nature and circumstances of the crime and the history, character and condition of the juvenile, it finds that his confinement is necessary for protection of the public because:
>
> A. There is undue risk that, during the period of a suspended sentence, the juvenile will commit another crime;
>
> B. The juvenile is in need of correctional treatment that can be provided most effectively by his commitment to an institution; or
>
> C. A lesser sentence will depreciate the seriousness of the juvenile's conduct.'[12]

The Florida Juvenile Justice Act, 1978 has no similar presumption against a secure commitment, but it is in the same vein as its northern neighbour in authorizing and limiting commitments to cases where the public's protection demands it. That commitment decision is to turn on:

> '1. The seriousness of the offence to the community.
> 2. Whether protection of the community required adjudication and commitment to the department.
> 3. Whether the offence was committed in an aggressive, violent, premeditated, or wilful manner.
> 4. Whether the offence was against persons or against property, greater weight being given to offences against persons, especially if personal injury resulted.
> 5. The sophistication and maturity of the child, as determined by consideration of his home, environmental situation, emotional attitude, and pattern of living.
> 6. The child (*sic*) record and previous criminal history of the child, including without limitations:
>   a. Previous contacts with the department, the Department of Corrections, other law enforcement agencies, and courts,
>   b. Prior periods of probation or community control,
>   c. Prior adjudications of delinquency, and
>   d. Prior commitments to institutions.
> 7. The prospects for adequate protection of the public and the likelihood of reasonable rehabilitation of the child if he is committed to a community services programme or facility.'[13]

Purposes of juvenile justice

If the disposition criteria discussed above suggest that the problem of delinquency is increasingly coming to be primarily a problem of crime control, the suggestion is corroborated by an examination of statutory statements of the purposes to be served in the juvenile justice system. In place of the traditional purpose of providing for the best interests of children coming before the court there are appearing statements that identify juvenile justice as a system of social control barely different from the criminal justice system. In the state of Washington, for example, 1977 legislation declares the purposes to include a design to '(a) Protect the citizenry from criminal behaviour; (b) Provide for determining whether accused juveniles have committed offences; (c) Make the juvenile offender accountable for his or her criminal behaviour; (d) Provide punishment commensurate with age, crime, and criminal history of the juvenile offender; (e) Provide due process for juveniles alleged to have committed an offence.'[14]

California too, long known for its announced devotion to child welfare principles in the administration of its juvenile justice system, has added to the avowed purposes of its system the aim '(a) . . . to protect the public from criminal conduct of minors, to impose on the minor a sense of responsibility for his own acts; . . .' The revised purposes continue: '(b) The purpose of this chapter also includes protection of the public from the consequences of criminal activity, and to such purpose probation officers, peace officers, and juvenile courts shall take into account such protection of the public in their determinations under this chapter.'[15] In Florida there is an outright acknowledgment that retributive punishment has a role to play in the juvenile court. That state's 1978 revisions include: 'The purposes of this chapter are: (a) To protect society more effectively by substituting for retributive punishment, whenever possible, methods of offender rehabilitation and rehabilitative restitution, recognizing that the application of sanctions which are consistent with the seriousness of the offences is appropriate in all cases.'[16] The American Bar Association's statement of purposes highlights the essential values of criminal justice, declaring the purposes of a juvenile delinquency code to include: 'A. to forbid conduct that unjustifiably and without excuse inflicts or risks substantial harm to individual or public interests; B. to safeguard conduct that is without fault or culpability from condemnation as delinquent; C. to give fair warning of what conduct is prohibited and of the consequences of violation.'[17] These references to fundamental penal law policies are not surprising for the introduction to this volume informs us that: 'The following recommendations . . . are intended to be viewed within a criminal law matrix that resembles, in essential features, the Model Penal Code.'[18]

There is, therefore, in an examination of emerging statements of purpose a reiteration of what seems to be inferrable from the juvenile court disposition criteria, namely, a reliance on principles of criminal jurisprudence and an acceptance that what ought to constitute the general aims of a modern criminal court ought similarly to define the goals of a modern juvenile court.

Other adaptations from criminal justice

In a system centrally concerned with the best interests of the child there is little need for a public prosecutor. But as a direct consequence of the recognized adversary relationship between the child and the state his appearance and role are expanding. There is, moreover, little doubt on where his priorities lie. The American Bar Association, for example, declares that 'The primary duty of the juvenile prosecutor is to seek justice: to fully and faithfully represent the interest of the state, without losing sight of the philosophy and purpose of the family court.'[19] Public prosecutors have also been given increasingly important responsibilities through enactment of statutes granting them discretion to have a child tried in the criminal court rather than the juvenile court. Several states and the national government have legislated in this direction, relying on the prosecutor being part of the law enforcement process rather than an official in the child welfare machinery, one whose primary obligation therefore can be counted on to be the assurance of public safety and secondarily, if at all, the best interests of children.[20]

The dispositions that legislatures have lately been authorizing have a similar cast of criminal justice and contain little that child welfare advocates could have supported except as a trade-off for something else in a legislative package that elsewhere promoted children's interests. In 1977, for example, Colorado created a classification of 'repeat juvenile offender' and 'violent juvenile offender' both of whom must be committed by the juvenile court.[21] New York's authorization of harsh sentences for children is notorious.[22] Mandatory sentencing schemes have also been enacted in Delaware and Washington.[23] The Washington system represents the greatest departure from tradition. It requires commitment for those whose offending is high on a scale of seriousness and conversely forbids commitment of those whose offending is not serious. 'Seriousness' for these purposes is numerically computed on the basis of the child's age, prior history of offending and the scaling of offence seriousness already established in the state penal code. For example, a fifteen-year-old who has been found guilty of the offence of rape is first given 250 points on the basis of a grid with the offence on one axis and the age of the child on the other. If it has been, let us say, 6 to 12 months since his last offence, the 250 is multiplied by a factor of 1·8, a figure also derived from a grid with offence and criminal history axis. The resulting figure of 450 is then entered into another table which then produces for the juvenile court judge the decision that the child must be confined for a period of from 40 to 50 months, followed by a maximum parole period of an additional 18 months. This is the mandated result in the ordinary case. The judge can impose a different sentence provided he puts in writing his reasons for considering the case before him not to be ordinary.[24] This method of determining dispositions closely parallels the system of sentencing guidelines that has been at the heart of the proposed revision of the Federal criminal laws.[25]

Child welfare in the new directions

Alongside the newly appearing indications that the state proposes to deal with the delinquent child as a problem of public protection, there curiously persist the more traditional commitments to look after and care for him. The Maine law, for example, declares that any child subject to the Juvenile Code is to receive 'such care and guidance, preferably in his own home, as will best serve his welfare and the interests of society.'[26] Even in Washington where the tradition of individualized justice has been most subdued, the recitation of goals includes a purpose to: 'Provide necessary treatment, supervision, and custody for juvenile offenders.'[27] California, too, still speaks of serving 'the spiritual, emotional, mental and physical welfare of the minor.'[28] The American Bar Association's disposition criteria remind the juvenile court judge that 'Once the category and duration of the disposition have been determined, the choice of a particular programme within the category should include consideration of the needs and desires of the juvenile.'[29] In fact, no state that has recently reformulated its statement of juvenile justice purposes has expelled a commitment to the best interests of the child from its restatement.

The meaning of these commitments is far from clear, however, despite the achievements of child welfare proponents in the new penal law oriented legislation and standards, achievements which include authorization of penalties that are significantly less severe than those that may be imposed on adults found guilty of the same offences, as in Washington and under the A.B.A.'s standards;[30] continued reliance on diversion programmes;[31] subjecting plea bargaining to legislative guidelines;[32] withholding the handicaps of a criminal conviction;[33] not permitting waiver of the right to counsel without first consulting an attorney;[34] minimizing the damage to the child's good name by the privacy extended to juvenile court hearings and records;[35] and defences to criminal prosecutions derived from the Model Penal Code and creatively applied to juvenile court proceedings by the A.B.A.'s Standards Relating to Juvenile Delinquency and Sanctions.[36]

These are all elements of child welfare in the sense that they serve to minimize some of the unnecessarily destructive aspects of being prosecuted, dictating that the state pursue its interest in crime suppression by taking no more from the child than that purpose justly requires. The clearest statement of this as a matter of principle can be seen in the frequently appearing provision that the least restrictive alternative be chosen. They also enhance the fairness of the proceedings by invoking and refining the rules of criminal procedure developed by a tradition of adversary judicial battle where the stakes involve a stigmatizing loss of freedom. It would, in fact, be fair to characterize the evolution of juvenile justice in the past few years as the development of, if not an ideal, at least a vastly improved system of criminal justice. The alternative to the traditional juvenile court is proving not to be the ill-reputed lower criminal courts of the country, as the President's Crime Commission feared in 1967;[37] the heir is rather a greatly strengthened and modernized criminal court, specializing in the criminal trials of children. And, as the widespread borrowings from what is considered progressive in adult criminal justice indicates, the metamorphosis of juvenile justice into an ideal system of criminal justice needs hardly to be viewed as inadvertent.

In a sense, therefore, there *is* a manifest concern for child welfare; the child's interests are served by providing him with this sort of criminal justice system. There is little room to doubt that it is an improvement over the former system that purported to be centrally occupied with providing him cures and rehabilitation. But it is a system predicated on the assumption that the state's primary reaction to every delinquent act must be self-defence, so that every delinquent child's critical interest is in resisting the control sought to be exercised over him. Both sides, however, more often share the same interest – that the child outgrow his delinquent behaviour.

Protecting growth

A hearings system has a unique contribution to make to the critical and widely accepted policy of restraint in reactions to delinquency. Among the most difficult tasks for juvenile justice reform is to find appropriate vehicles to control overreacting to youthful crime. On the one hand, the commission of crime demands some reaction, regardless of the age of the criminal, otherwise the law's commands become simple requests and compliance a matter of individual choice in lieu of a universally applicable demand. In the case of adolescent crime, moreover, the reaction must be sufficient to insure that experience does not sow the belief that what the law forbids may be entered upon with impunity. On the other hand, youthful offending also appears to be generally transient and seldom the invariable harbinger of adult criminal careers as was proclaimed by the early juvenile justice reformers. Time and maturation appear to be our most reliable allies in bringing children's criminal behaviour to an end. From this perspective the problem of overreacting becomes an issue of not interfering with that maturation process more than is necessary to preserve the integrity of the law by reaffirming that its requirements are binding upon children. This is not a matter of making the child grow by administering curative programmes of one sort or another. It is rather a question of letting him grow in the expectation that his delinquencies will go the way of his soprano voice. In Zimring's phrase, the task is to provide the delinquent 'room to reform,' to give him the opportunity to transit to adulthood without being isolated and rejected and without a permanent stigma from involvement with the justice system.[38] Clearly this bit of wisdom is not new and is already adopted in a scaled-down set of penalties and requirements for least restrictive choices. But it would be difficult to identify a vehicle that is organizationally and philosophically more ill-suited for this policy of granting room to reform and protecting normal growth than a criminal (or criminalized) court, the institution whose esoteric formalisms and dramatic encounters we rely on to assess criminal responsibility, to administer condemnation and to isolate the offender from the law-abiding. The overpowering emphasis is on adversary battle, the identification of winner and loser. Protection of growth is neither a significant purpose there nor an expected outcome. By opting for a criminal jurisprudence the new system of justice for children sacrifices the long-term interest of the public and of children themselves in normal maturation, to the short-term public need for law enforcement and the child's short-term need for the limits of penal law. That is an eminently sensible trade-off that is called for in some cases, namely, when the offending is serious, immediate public protection interests are paramount, and the child is at risk of arbitrary and severe deprivations. But it is merely a gratuitous loss when the offending is trivial and the stakes for the child under proportionality rules are relatively inconsequential; then the immediate issue is a reiteration of social values, so that protecting normal growth can and should be a central policy goal.

Our research provides encouraging indications that a children's hearings system is, by contrast to a criminalized court, well-suited to the task of providing room to reform and protecting growth in a humane environment while at the same time upholding the values of the law. As to the last of these, the findings reported in *Chapter 8* demonstrate the capacity of the hearings to dwell on the child's offence and his motivation. In 81% of the observed hearings the discussion included the grounds of referral in an effort to bring home to the child his responsibility not only to society and to his future, but to his family as well. The centrality of this sort of limit-setting was not, moreover, lost on the children. To the overwhelming majority of those whom we interviewed the reason why they were at a hearing was to account for their misbehaviour (*Chapter 12*). These findings, and the quotations from hearings included in *Chapter 8* make it wholly inaccurate to characterize the hearings system as being based on a medical model that is unconcerned with responsibility and devoid of strenuous exhortations to improve behaviour. Reiteration of values is a major activity of the hearings.

It is also clear that the hearings system minimizes isolating the child, and protects growth in at least two significant ways. Despite their awareness of the central significance of their offending to their appearance before a hearing, most of the children reported not finding themselves in a hostile environment. Less than one in ten told us there was no one at the hearing to help them, while less than a *fourth* of them found no one on their side (*Chapter 12*). Importantly, the same question about whether anyone was there to help produced three times as many 'no-one' responses in a [Canadian] court setting even when defence counsel could have been nominated as a helper. Children may intuitively appreciate what some research is indicating – that having a lawyer may make things worse.[39] But even when defence lawyers are wholly absent the hearings seem to succeed in having the young offenders understand that their offending is the reason d'être of their appearance but without at the same time requiring of them an experience of isolation, rejection and hostility.

The second manifestation of growth protection is that the hearings sustain and support the social setting in which the child will mature. The direct and immediate involvement of the child's parents in the hearing serves to emphasize the child's position in his family, an important counterweight to his *de facto* role as defendant. Rather than having the child in the dock with his parents placed among the spectators, the hearings array the family together on one side of the table, confronting the members of the panel on the other. And, of course, more than formal seating arrangements demonstrate that the hearing is an event in which all participate as a consequence of the delinquency. *Chapter 9* reports the high degree of parental participation in the dialogue of hearings, with only about one parent in 12 sitting through the hearing without making any significant contribution to the discussions. Tables 9.4 and 9.5 suggest further that the intensity of parental involvement does not depend on whether they are comfortable and at ease or angry and hostile. In *Chapter 13* we reported that nearly all parents understood what had happened at the hearing and that all of them found it easy to take part in the discussion. Yet no parent felt he or she was being blamed, despite the evidence that family issues are often discussed in the hearing (*Chapter 8*). It should not be surprising in this context, however, that with no formal jurisdiction over parents, we also found that the panel offered advice to them in child-rearing in only 14% of the hearings observed.

On the whole, the evidence cogently indicates that the hearing is very much a family affair and consequently a significant undertaking to avoid isolating the child from those on whom he most depends for support on making it to adulthood. Just how significant this is can be appreciated by comparing these proceedings to those of the criminalized juvenile court which is commanded to focus in pleading, adjudication and disposition on the child's offence, on *his* responsibility, on *his* prior record, on the threat *he* poses to society. There is little of significance his family can contribute to a resolution of such issues. The great lack of concern for parental involvement in the present movement for reform in American juvenile justice is illustrated by the A.B.A.'s standards relating to disposition procedures which go no further than to require that the judge, in the disposition hearing, 'afford the . . . juvenile's parents or legal guardian an opportunity to address the court.'[40] There is no expectation that the judge will engage them in meaningful and extensive discussion, and no assumption that they have a substantial role to play in the judicial experience of their child; there is everything in the formality and impersonal atmosphere to inhibit such a candid exchange. This is as it must be in a criminal prosecution that is highly individualistic, focuses on culpability and admits of little shared responsibility. The parents participate in the disposition decision as advocates, 'addressing the court;' prepared speeches are invited, most likely those that are prepared by counsel. It may be anomalous that families participate so little even in a place called a *family* court, but that is the view of at least some observers.

> 'Family court now provides procedural safeguards
> and it is assumed that the dignity of the courtroom
> has been improved. If so, it has been at high cost.
> The combination of decorum and legal formality,
> coupled with adversary presentations, has made
> many a courtroom an intimidating place – a place
> where lawyers are comfortable and families are not.
> Instead of a place where parents and children can be

> heard and understood, and where wounds can begin to heal, it is now a place where the family is stage-managed to step through certain squares in the dance of the adversaries.'[41]

None of this should be unexpected, however, since 'family' court refers primarily to court jurisdiction – power to hear offences by one family member against another and a range of domestic affairs that may be wide or narrow. There is little, if anything, that a family court is to do by way of informal and intimate involvement of family members in decision-making. The family court is still a court and the opportunity to preserve and enhance the child's status as a family member, to avoid an unnecessary degree of isolation from those whose respect and involvement are crucial for his normal growth, is largely ignored in a court setting. This shortcoming is partly a consequence of criminalization and formality, but it also derives from present-day reformers adopting a view that long plagued empiric research into delinquency, the acceptance of delinquency as a monolithic concept, disregarding that although it is sometimes seriously disrupting criminal behaviour, it is mostly a matter of minor nuisances. Prior to the present round of reform, the juvenile justice system avoided reflecting this fallacy by providing two systems of justice, one in the criminal court and one in the juvenile court. Public protection and child welfare were the accepted philosophical distinctions between them. Although there is still afoot in the statutes a child welfare philosophy – one that is different from a concern for legal rights – it has no institutional expression as a result of the merger of the juvenile court with the criminal court. The position formally occupied by the juvenile court where the social welfare of children was to be given priority over public safety is vacant. A children's hearings system can fill that vacancy, but the question is whether this can be done without re-introducing the abuses that we now acknowledge to be associated with traditional juvenile courts.

A fair trial

Attention is first directed to the issue of providing a satisfactory hearing for children who plead not guilty. One of the major shortcomings claimed against the traditional juvenile court was that a child could not get a fair trial on the charges before a judge who was responsible not only for determining the child's guilt or innocence but also for making decisions in the child's best interests. The desire to help infected the duty to adjudicate so that cases of weak and questionable evidence would be decided *against* the child in order to permit the court to order a disposition that would accomplish things *for* the child. Interestingly enough, this may still be a problem in the newly criminalized juvenile court if juvenile court judges continue to cling to the idea that they are responsible for child welfare. The temptation is no less powerful today to avoid turning loose a needy child on a legal or evidentiary 'technicality'.

The Scottish system maintains the integrity of the trial process by not assigning child welfare responsibilities to the Sheriff Court where contested cases are tried. When the child or his parents deny the charges, the hearing can then discharge the referral, but if it decides the case should be retained, it must be sent to the Sheriff Court for adjudication; the hearing itself has no authority to weigh the evidence on the charge or determine guilt or innocence. In the case of a child who has been prosecuted in the Sheriff Court initially, it is open to the sheriff to request the advice of a hearing as to his sentence, or to assign the case definitively to a hearing for its disposal. These latter provisions are a necessary consequence of recognizing that even when the serious nature of the charge requires a criminal-type trial, there needs to be flexibility to recognize further that the seriousness may be only superficial. A charge of robbery may entail beating an old woman in order to get her purse; but it may also be no more than a school-yard fight over possession of a football.

American arrangements could similarly protect the integrity of trials by providing the criminal or criminalized court with the power to try cases that involved denials before a children's hearing and, if guilt is established, referral back to the panel for its procedures and dispositions. So too with cases that would, on account of their seriousness, be statutorily within the original jurisdiction of the criminal or criminalized court; there could be discretion to remand them to the children's hearing for final disposition. These procedures would assure that trials are exclusively concerned with trial procedures, and perhaps would assure this better than do many of the reformed juvenile courts that continue to lodge trial and disposition authority in a single judge whose remit may be to look after child welfare as well as public safety.

But in both Scotland and America contested trials are unusual. The great majority of children admit to having engaged in the behaviour charged against them; for them fairness in the adjudication process is essentially a matter of the quality of procedures relied on in determining whether they voluntarily admit the charges. While our observations at hearings did not include an attempt to evaluate tone of voice, facial expressions or other such sources of possible intimidation by the chairman in putting the grounds to the child for his acceptance or denial, we do have indirect evidence suggesting the magnitude of this problem. Comments by four of the 105 interviewed children indicated that their acceptance may have been taken improperly, largely due to misunderstanding on their part of what the chairman was talking about (*Chapter 12*). While it will be recalled that these interviews were only from hearings that reached a final decision, there is no apparent reason why these figures should grossly misrepresent what would be learned from children at all hearings and they provide a useful estimate. Whether this estimate is better or worse than the proportion of improper guilty pleas in juvenile courts cannot be determined; but an estimate of less than 4 per cent illegality is not unacceptable, especially in a dynamic system that admits of improvement; and the hearings system can be improved in this regard by having the child consult with an attorney prior to his appearance at the hearing, and by having the reporter at the hearing, who should himself be legally qualified, responsible for guarding against intimidation and for assuring the hearing that the facts admitted by the child do amount to an offence. There is no reason, in other words, why the hearings cannot administer pleading arrangements that are at least as fair as those found in a court.

Treatment abuses and children's hearings

American experience with a therapeutic juvenile justice system has produced much of the agenda for reform, with the idea of coerced cures and the conceptual assimilation of criminal conduct to a need for treatment being the prime targets for change. The so-called medical model that focuses on personal social facts rather than characteristics of the criminal offending is being replaced by one in which a nearly exclusive emphasis is placed on offence-related factors. The clinician's judgment implicit in the therapeutic orientation is being excised in favour of judicial evaluations of culpability, deterrence and the like. What do our findings indicate about whether the children's hearings system has adopted or avoided these discredited rehabilitative dogmas? Here we need to take account of decisions reached by both reporters and by hearings.

It must first be pointed out that the structure of the system itself provides important safeguards against capture by an ideology, at least in the conduct of hearings. The performance of panel members is subject to monitoring from several sources: the chairman of the sitting panel, the chairmen of the area and regional panels, and informal observations by the reporter and fellow panel members. Information from these sources can be employed by chairmen to suspend assignments of any panel member who appears committed to a view that all delinquent children need to be cured (or that they all need to be punished), the Secretary of State may drop from the panel roster entirely any such dogmatist, or refuse to reappoint him. Unlike judges, whose performance can hardly be subject to ongoing evaluation except for a narrow range of misconduct, the lapse of skills or the lapse into dogmatism of children's panel members need not go unattended by persons responsible for maintaining the technical and philosophical integrity of the system. In addition to this sort of supervision, account must also be taken of the obligation that can be imposed on panel members to undergo both pre-service and in-service training that can strengthen their skills and sophistication.

The hearings system does not, however, allow for such controls and compulsory training of the reporters. They can only be removed by the Secretary of State and although he also has authority to require particular credentials for initially taking the post of reporter and can make participation in in-service training a condition of the appointment, no such action has yet been taken. Our research into decision-making by reporters, therefore, tells us of the informal norms that seem to have developed in the discharge of their responsibilities.

Chapter 5 reports our findings on reporters' decisions concerning referral to a hearing. These tell us, first, that the reporters have not adopted the view that the commission of an offence is a symptom looking for a cure. Table 5.9 shows that only 45 per cent of the boys and 36 per cent of the girls who are referred to reporters on offence grounds are sent on to a hearing. Altogether, only about 4 out of 10 children who commit offences are seen by reporters as requiring evaluation by a hearing for possible use of its compulsory power (Table 5.5). The hearing itself does not control its own intake, but does it see an offence that is referred to it as a cry for help and the need for some sort of supervision? Clearly not with first offenders whom the hearings discharge 49 per cent of the time (Table 11.2). When only one offence is charged the first time the discharge rate rises to 55 per cent, and when there are four or more offences on this occasion the discharge rate falls to 24 per cent. Seriousness of offending is obviously important. Similarly indicating a lack of commitment to a therapeutic justice is the finding that the hearings often discharge the youngest children who come before them for the first time (46 per cent of those under 12) suggesting as we noted in *Chapter 11*, that the panel members are more influenced by 'a belief in the advantages of minimal intervention,' than they are of the child saving virtues of early intervention.

On the other hand, factors not associated with seriousness or recidivism also play a powerful role. For example, Table 5.20 indicates that a child referred to the reporter for the first time who is reported to have family problems, has a record of irregular attendance at school and is reported to display behaviour problems at school is almost certainly to be referred to a hearing. The hearings similarly rely on social factors in reaching decisions. For example, a child who has already appeared before a hearing and who comes from other than a two-parent family has a better than 9 out of 10 chance of being placed on supervision rather than discharged; at his first hearing, the unemployed status of the head of the child's household significantly influences the decision.

The impression emerges from an examination of what influences decision-making in the children's hearings system that it is neither a medical model nor a just-deserts model. The system proceeds pragmatically, as we concluded in regard to reporters in *Chapter 5*, 'to balance, in offence cases, the seriousness of the offence or offences committed against an inevitably subjective and indirect estimate of the strengths and weaknesses of the child's home and school situation.' It appears to be, in this respect, the captive of no ideology, a result perhaps of the pivotal responsibilities discharged by laymen who do not see themselves as experts in the rehabilitation of children. As Table 15.3 demonstrates, the hearings are conducted by people who see it as far more important that they possess the ability to understand and empathise with others and have the quality of being easy to talk to than it is to be a highly intelligent specialist in children's affairs. These are not opinions to be unexpected from laymen, but they do corroborate the impression that reliance on a pseudo-expertise for the rehabilitation of delinquent children does not play a significant role in the system.

Legality

The question of the capacity of the children's hearings to function in an atmosphere of legality is of major importance in light of American experience that associates informality and an expressed priority for the best interest of delinquent children with a blatant disregard of children's legal rights. No matter what its other virtues, any addition to the juvenile justice system must observe both the fairness standard demanded by due process of law and the procedural rules that structure the proceedings. In *Chapter 7* we reported our findings concerning the degree of compliance with procedural rules in the hearings we observed. Our finding that some of the required procedures were frequently disregarded (Table 7.1) prompts two sorts of comments. One is that some of the deficiencies are serious and central to the professed purpose of the hearings to promote communication and invite participation. Failure to refer to the social background report not only handicaps accomplishment of these goals but denies the parents and children the opportunity to challenge and dispute the information and judgments that are conveyed to the panel members by the reports, creating thereby an unnecessary risk that the decision may turn on faulty data. That the hearings neglect to ask the child and his parents if they understand and agree with the decision reached is similarly disturbing, especially in light of the findings in *Chapter 12* that the children's perceptions of the reasons are often at variance with those relied on by the panel.

The second comment is one of frustration, for there is no way of telling whether the legality and illegality we have observed is different from or the same as that which might be observed in a juvenile court. While it would be tempting to venture that the presence of defence counsel in juvenile courts strongly suggests a high degree of legality and observance of applicable rules of law, there is much room to doubt the validity of that sort of comparison, doubt that arises from research studies indicating that juvenile court judges manage to avoid appointing defence counsel altogether in some cases and in others can effectively neutralize his zeal in advocating enforcement of his client's rights.[42] Furthermore, it appears from our observations that procedural regularity is, in part, a function of the amount of time devoted to the hearing. Shorter hearings have more procedural faults than longer ones. If that finding can be generalized then the notoriously hurried nature of juvenile court hearings casts further doubt on their procedural purity.

One of the most critical findings in *Chapter 9* directly disputes the American experience that links informality with disregard for legal requirements. In Table 9.6 we report that informality, measured by the intense participation of children and parents, does not occur more often in hearings that are below average in their observance of the rules. Quite to the contrary, participation is higher in those hearings that do best in conforming to the rules, expecially by mothers, with the difference on the part of children and fathers being marginal. While the figures do not prove that participation increases with procedural regularity, they do clearly demonstrate that in the hearings system participation does not require sacrifice of procedural legality.

A new system

A children's hearings system in America would in some ways resemble and in some ways differ from the Scottish model. It would function in conjunction with a court system having exclusive jurisdiction over children charged with the most serious offences. Whether this is a criminalized juvenile court, the regular adult court, or some combination of the two involves important policy choices, but since the system proposed depends very little on what choice is made the issues raised are not pursued and it is assumed that a criminal court system is in place. The remainder of this section constitutes only a broad outline of possible arrangements, some of which have already been suggested in this chapter.

The new system would utilize panels of lay volunteers and an executive official with responsibilities similar to those held by the reporter in Scotland but who would, in America, always be a lawyer. The panels would have compulsory powers, deal with children who acknowledged their culpability, or had denied charges that were subsequently proved against them or who had been remanded to the panel by a criminal court in which prosecution had been initiated. As in Scotland, they would be directed to engage in informal discussions with these children and their families concerning how the powers should be exercised. Children who denied that they had committed the offence charged against them would be tried in the criminal court under rules that apply to all criminal trials subject to modification to take account of their immaturity, perhaps as recommended by the A.B.A. If found guilty, the child would be returned to the panel for the same proceedings that follow an acknowledgment of culpability initially. Thus far the recommendation follows the Scottish model closely. A major difference is that the child would be required to reach a decision on how to plead at the hearing only after he had discussed the case with an attorney (not the reporter). He would be entitled to the assistance of counsel again only if he chose to appeal the decision of the panel. The compulsory powers would include a process for compelling the attendance of children and their parents, enforceable by a court, and power to make orders concerning the child; the hearings would not, however, have the power of commitment. Included would be the authority to order that the child submit to supervision, that he attend programmes in his leisure time, that he make restitution to the victim of his offence, that he provide community service, or that he be discharged.

To which children would this apply? To those under the age of 16, but not all of those. Children charged with the most serious offences, defined legislatively with the same irreducible degree of subjectivity that attends any drawing of lines where the differences are mostly of degree, would be excluded. The public prosecutor could, in collaboration with the reporter, authorize the reporter to consider the case of any child brought to the prosecutor's attention (mostly by the police) for commission of a serious offence. Serious offenders would be tried in the court of criminal jurisdiction. If found guilty of an offence not within the court's original jurisdiction they would have to be remanded to the panel for disposition; if found guilty of the offence charged such a remand would be discretionary, and would follow a hearing on the remand issue.

The panel system would retain jurisdiction over children under 16 regardless of the number of times they reappeared, so long as their offences did not progress into the serious class that would bring them within jurisdiction of the criminal court. Chronicity would not be treated equally with the seriousness of the offence for jurisdictional purposes. No transfer or waiver power from panel to court should be provided; continued offending is better met by a policy of restraint and efforts to 'talk it out' rather than by one that may irreversibly and unnecessarily abort unusually slow maturation.

The reporter would receive cases from all sources, including the prosecutor, and would have power to divert any of them out of the system. This would be unconditional, however, – as it is in Scotland – with no opportunity to reassert jurisdiction on the same facts. The standard he would employ for this would be one formulated on the principle of protecting growth within the child's family. For making this decision the reporter could make only a limited investigation. The purpose of the hearing before the panel would be to identify through discussion with child and parents what might be done to strengthen family ties and to keep the child out of further trouble with the law, recognizing that some of the panel's powers – community service – are punitive in nature. When the reporter expects that the panel might want to discuss restitution, an option not officially available in Scotland, or he determines that it might otherwise be useful, he could invite the victim of the child's offence to participate in the discussion, subject to the power of the panel to limit this participation or to forgo it entirely.

In these circumstances the panel would need mediation skills, but it should be required to deal with the victim only *pro se* and not through his attorney. The reporter would also be responsible for having prepared and made available to the panel in advance of the hearing background information about the child, unless the reporter determined that the child, after consultation with an attorney, intends to deny the charge. Both the child and the parents would be invited, but not required, to provide written information about themselves which they would like the panel to consider and the resources of the reporter's office would be available to assist them to articulate this information. This is not included within current Scottish practice. The reporter would also be responsible for communicating to the child and parents the substance of the background report he had caused to be made, subject to withholding information which it would be detrimental to the child or the parent to disclose.

The setting of the hearing would be informal in the sense of being dissociated from any court or school facilities and without the displays of authority represented by the presence of flags or seals. It should be sufficiently formal, however, to reflect that the panel speaks on behalf of the community in its concern for law-breaking and for children's growth. At the outset of the hearing the chairman of the panel would explain the charges to the child and parents, verify that they had spoken with an attorney, and determine whether the child denies or accepts what is alleged against him. The reporter would be responsible for determining and certifying for the record that what the child agrees to does constitute an offence under the law. The chairman would then explain the purpose of the hearing and describe the powers that might be exercised by the panel. Following the discussions, the decision would be reached by the panel in the presence of the family and the reasons for it announced. The family would be provided a written statement of the decision and reasons before they left the facility in which the hearing is held. Special care would be taken by the reporter to identify for the family reasons that relied on factual assumptions that had been disputed by the family so that an appeal could be taken in an effort to establish the family's version of material facts.

The reporter and the panel members are obviously key officials in this scheme. In addition to being legally trained the reporter would have to possess considerable administrative skill. Recruitment and training of reporters and panel members would be a major priority in organizing a hearings system. Although our research did not extend to this matter, there is much to learn from the Scottish experience in recruitment and training even though the emphasis there on responsibility for legal matters is significantly less than is proposed here. American panels should, moreover, be designed to reflect as closely as possible the racial and ethnic mix of the population that appears before them.

No mention has yet been made of the supporting service that is essential to carrying out a panel system. Kilbrandon proposed that education authorities be given responsibility for investigation and supervision, while in the end these tasks fell to the newly-created generic social work departments of local government. The obvious candidates in America for these jobs are existing juvenile court probation officers. Whether they would be available depends in large part on what happens to the juvenile court. If enough of them would be freed of juvenile court responsibilities, an account of the contraction or abolition of its jurisdiction, it would remain to be resolved whether they would be administratively absorbed into executive probation departments, organized as an independent children's hearing service, or, in light of the sense it would make to give the hearings jurisdiction in care and protection cases as well as delinquency, to create a new service by merging the probation staff with the child protection service.

Many issues remain unexamined, including whether a guidelines system similar to that used in Washington would be a useful feature of a hearings system, whether the separation of powers doctrine would limit the functions that could be assigned to a children's hearings system, and the extent to which the movement toward neighbourhood justice centres and alternative dispute resolution vehicles has already established some parts of a children's hearings system. For these and other questions our reported findings provide relevant data.

NOTES

1. National Institute for Juvenile Justice and Delinquency Prevention, A Comparative Analysis of Standards and State Practices, vol. IX, Juvenile Dispositions and Corrections, Working Papers of the National Task Force to Develop Standards and Goals for Juvenile Justice and Delinquency Prevention, p. 22, 1977.
2. For example, Florida Stat. Ann. §§ 39.001–39.337, 1977; Iowa Code, ch. 232 (1978); Maine Rev. Stat. tit. 15 §§ 3001–3602, 1977; Washington Rev. Code ch. 13.OY, 1977. The Florida law includes provisions for a community arbitration programme

which, although not obligatory on the child or his parents and in many other ways significantly different from a children's hearings system, is a step in the direction of such a system. See Florida Stat. Ann. §§ 39.331–39.337. See also Alaska Stat. § 47.10.075 (providing for panel of high school students who, with consent of the child, may 'hear the case and advise the court of a recommended judgment and order.')
3. For example, California Welfare and Institutions Code §§ 707,726, 1977; Colorado Rev. Stat. §§ 19–01–103(23.5), 19–01–103(28), 1977; Delaware Rev. Stat. tit. 10 § 937(c); New York Family Court Act § 712(b); Penal Law § 70.05(2), (3), 1978.
4. The approved volumes contain standards relating to Adjudication, Appeals and Collateral Review, Architecture of Facilities, Counsel for Private Parties, Court Organization and Administration, Prosecution, Dispositional Procedures, Dispositions, Corrections Administration, Interim Status, Juvenile Delinquency and Sanctions, Juvenile Records and Information Systems, Monitoring, Planning for Juvenile Justice, Police Handling of Juvenile Problems, Pre-trial Court Proceedings, Rights of Minors, the Juvenile Probation Function, Transfer Between Courts and Youth Services Agencies. Standards relating to Abuse and Neglect and to Non-criminal Misbehaviour have not been considered.
5. *McKeiver v. Pennsylvania*, 403 U.S. 528, 1971.
6. Standards Relating to Adjudication, p. 2, 1979.
7. *State ex rel. D.D.H. v. Dostert*, 269 S.E. 2d 401, 415–16, W. Va., 1980.
8. National Conference of Commissioners Uniform State Laws, Uniform Juvenile Court Act § 31, 1968.
9. U.S. Department of Health, Education and Welfare, Children's Bureau, Standards for Juvenile and Family Courts, p. 1, 1966.
10. Iowa Code § 232.52(1) (1980–81 Supp.).
11. Standards Relating to Dispositions, p. 6, 1979.
12. Maine Rev. Stat. tit. 15 § 3313(1).
13. Florida Stat. Ann. § 39.09(3)(d) (1980 Supp.).
14. Washington Rev. Code § 13.40.010(2)(a)–(e) (1980–81 Supp.).
15. California Welfare and Institutions Code § 202, 1977.
16. Florida Stat. Ann. § 39.001(2)(a) (1980 Supp.).
17. Standards Relating to Juvenile Delinquency and Sanctions, p. 3, 1980.
18. Ibid., p. 2.
19. Standards Relating to Prosecution, p. 13, 1979.
20. See, for example, Nebraska Rev. Stat. §§ 43–202(3)(b), (c); 43–202.01(a).
21. Colorado Rev. Stat. §§ 19–01–103(23.5), (28), 1977.
22. New York Criminal Procedure Law § 1.20(42); Penal Law §§ 10.00(18), 30.00(2).
23. Delaware Rev. Stat. tit. 10 § 937(c); Washington Rev. Code § 13.40.030(b).
24. Washington Rev. Code §§ 13.40.160(1), (2), 4(c).
25. F. Kennedy, Toward a New System of Criminal Sentencing: Law With Order, *American Criminal Law Review*, vol. 16, pp. 353–382, 1979.
26. Maine Rev. Stat. tit. 15 § 3002(1) (A).
27. Washington Rev. Code § 13.YO.010(2) (f).
28. California Welfare and Institutions Code § 202(a).
29. Standards Relating to Dispositions, p. 6, 1979.
30. See U.S. Office of Juvenile Justice and Delinquency Prevention, Reports of the National Juvenile Justice Centers, A National Assessment of Serious Crime and the Juvenile Justice System: The Need for a Rational Response, vol. III. Legislation, Jurisdiction, Program Interventions, and Confidentiality of Juvenile Records, pp. 46–50, 1980; Standards Relating to Juvenile Delinquency and Sanctions, pp. 41–44, 1980.
31. Iowa Code § 232.46 (1980–81 Supp.).
32. Iowa Code § 232.43 (1980–81 Supp.).
33. Standards Relating to Adjudication, p. 11, 1979.
34. Alaska Stat. § 47.10.050(b) (if charged with a felony).
35. Standards Relating to Juvenile Records and Information Systems, 1979.

36. Standards Relating to Juvenile Delinquency and Sanctions, pp. 5–6, 1980.
37. President's Commission on Law Enforcement and Administration of Justice, 1967.
38. Franklin E. Zimring, Background Paper in Confronting Youth Crime, Report of the Twentieth-Century Fund Task Force on Sentencing Policy Toward Young Offenders, pp. 79–80, 1978.
39. See Stevens H. Clarke and Gary G. Koch, Juvenile Court: Therapy or Crime Control, and Do Lawyers Make A Difference? *Law & Society Review*, vol. 14, 1980.
40. Standards Relating to Disposition Procedures, p. 20, 1979.
41. Phyllis R. Snyder and Lawrence H. Martin, Leaving the Family Out of Family Court: Criminalizing the Juvenile Justice System, *American Journal of Orthopsychiatry*, 48(3), 1978.
42. Clarke and Koch, op. cit., note 39.

18

IN PERSPECTIVE

IN THE COURSE OF A STUDY employing a variety of methodological approaches we have attempted to define and analyse those features of the Scottish juvenile justice system that in our opinion may have particular significance for policy-makers and practitioners both in our own country and in other jurisdictions where considerations of change and reform serve to direct attention to foreign experience. A large part of the debate over the processing of young offenders, certainly in the United Kingdom and no doubt in some degree elsewhere, has been conducted in an empirical vacuum. Assertions based on ideological prejudgments have to a striking extent taken the place of systematic observation and measured examination of social and legal realities. While we know of little in the history of political decision-making – especially in areas such as this where expressed attitudes and proposals often reflect deep emotionally-based concerns – to suggest that research findings have some special power to shape events, it seemed to us essential to redress the balance by building up a substantial body of data derived from systematic studies.

At the outset, we disclaimed any intention to submit the children's hearings system to some definitive global evaluation. This was partly because we recognized that the scope of our enquiries, though broad, was still limited in certain crucial respects. The strong emphasis in our studies on decision-making within the system and on the factors directly and indirectly associated with these processes, led us to exclude not only the selective practices that precede the involvement of the reporter to the children's panel, but also, more significantly from the standpoint of evaluation, any study at the individual level of the subsequent histories of children who had passed through the hearings system. But a more powerful reason for our conviction that we were not in a position to pass any final judgment in terms of success or failure was the lack of any agreed criteria by which judgments should be made. If those who designed the system had made an unambiguous statement of its central objective, it might have been possible to assess empirically with what degree of success this objective had been attained. But no such formulation is available, and in its absence the search for evaluative criteria has no pre-defined path to follow.

In *Chapter 16* we made a number of judgments on the operation in practice of the children's hearings system, and suggested some ways in which higher standards might be achieved. These were not judgments which involved the identification of an over-riding objective, but rather constituted an attempt to assess the reality of practice against advanced, perhaps even ideal standards which we and other writers on the hearings system have derived from its formal philosophy. We next looked at current trends in the re-shaping of juvenile justice in the U.S.A. and asked whether in the light of our research findings it seemed that something in the nature of a hearings system had a part to play, and if so in what ways the Scottish pattern might need to be modified. In this final chapter we try to set that pattern in a wider perspective, identifying certain aspects or dimensions of juvenile systems in general and commenting on the 'performance' of the Scottish system in relation to each.

We are struck by the number of writers on juvenile and other justice systems whose own values (frequently unacknowledged) lead them to make categorical judgments (often of a highly critical nature) and who seem never to question the universal acceptability of those values, writing rather as if the latter had some transcendent validity; the phenomenon has its parallels in many other fields of social policy. We are conscious of the fact that features of the children's hearings system as revealed in our research material which we would judge more or less favourably, unfavourably or neutrally might be quite differently evaluated by other observers whose personal values differed in some significant respects from our own. For example, we would tend to judge rather favourably the fact that children usually emerge from the experience of a hearing without acquiring a deep conviction that they are wicked people; we recognize, however, that some of our fellow-citizens would see this as reflecting critically on the hearings system, since they believe it is morally right (and presumably socially expedient) for young delinquents forcefully to be made aware of their own turpitude. The diversity of prevailing value-systems is in itself of great importance as constituting a key feature of the environment of any juvenile justice system in a democratic society.

Formality

Traditionally, the dispensing of justice tends to be associated with very formal – sometimes, indeed, awe-inspiring – settings, in which the various participants are clearly identified and segregated, and with a high degree of formality in procedure. Juvenile courts in many countries are now often a good deal less elaborate architecturally than their adult counterparts and their procedure somewhat simplified, no doubt because of the belief that to expose the young to the full panoply of the law is less likely to evoke awe and respect than mere bewilderment. Nevertheless, it is not generally considered appropriate to eliminate all resemblance between juvenile and adult courts. Thus Priestley *et al.*,[1] having observed juvenile courts in the West of England, comment:

> 'Despite the simplification of procedures, the juvenile court in action still retains the look and the feel of some of the dramatic ritual which dignifies adult justice. The drama, it was suggested earlier, is

> that of making manifest the otherwise disembodied values of justice, social control and welfare. The power of the State is often symbolized in the Royal Crest, set high up in a central position behind the bench. The bench itself is raised a step or two above the level of the courtroom and the front of it is almost always totally enclosed, in contrast to the tables behind which other servants of the court sit. Defendants and their parents have no such aids to social ease within the courtroom. They sit on straightforward chairs or have to stand whilst being addressed by the court. The dramatic elements in this physical setting are sometimes heightened by the abrupt entries and departures of the magistrates, to the accompaniment of loud commands to rise or "be seated".'

The Scottish system has deliberately aimed for, and seems to have achieved, a high degree of informality, using unpretentious buildings in commonplace surroundings and hearing rooms laid out, with few exceptions, with extreme simplicity and in such a way as to minimize rather than exaggerate social distance between family members and decision makers. Those settings of which we were critical were if anything too casual. The desire to locate hearings within the local community has led, in the case of some smaller areas where the volume of work does not justify the use of separate accommodation, to a choice of premises where either unsuitable design factors or simultaneous usage might reduce the degree of privacy.

Members of children's panels attach the highest importance to the reduction of formality not merely in the physical setting of children's hearings but also in the proceedings that take place there. The simplicity of the milieu is seen as a means of reducing the tension felt by the child and his parents and thus of facilitating a more natural conversational exchange. That the way in which panel members approach their task, no less than the informality of the surroundings, yields a considerable measure of success has been amply demonstrated. In this respect, the comments of the system's clients provide rather convincing evidence. Although we are aware of shortcomings and have suggested means by which these might be made good, we have little doubt that in terms of its capacity to achieve informal communication the Scottish system should be judged distinctly successful.

We are acutely conscious however of the high price paid for a lack of formality by way of a casual attitude to procedural requirements. There is, of course, a familiar argument that a lack of concern for legal safeguards is an inevitable corollary of a welfare-oriented approach to juvenile justice. According to this viewpoint, the temptation to assume control of young offenders' destinies, doubtless with benevolent intentions, is so powerful that legal protections are perceived as irritating and irrelevant obstacles, to be ignored or circumvented whenever it seems necessary. Only the substitution of a fully judicial system would suffice, given this interpretation, to ensure adequate standards of procedural propriety. Our data do not however support the conclusion that so far as its ability to maintain the legal rights of children are concerned, the Scottish system is flawed beyond redemption. Encouraged by the finding that the price paid for informality is not an inescapable one, we have argued that those responsible for the conduct of children's hearings should be apprised of their shortcomings and given new opportunities for learning and for the reform of practice. Present standards should not be judged incapable of improvement unless and until it can be demonstrated that a significant new investment in relevant training has failed to accomplish a substantial measure of change.

We must be careful, even so, that the comparisons we make between alternative systems are comparisons of like with like. There is perhaps a danger that we may observe children's hearings in considerable detail, take note of their procedural imperfections and as a result compare them unfavourably, not with a similar study of an alternative system in action, but with an ideal formulation of an alternative system. Thus, Cavenagh (1980)[2] writes of the English juvenile courts:

> 'But the fundamental legal basis of the juvenile court is the same as that of the adult court. There are the same procedural safeguards for the accused juvenile as for the adult, for example specific definition of charges, proof beyond a reasonable doubt in criminal cases, eligibility for legal aid at public expense, hearsay and involuntary admissions inadmissible as evidence, the rules relating to bias, the court's duty to help an unrepresented defendant, the right of the press to be present, the tradition of the criminal jurisdiction that the weight of the sentence should be in proportion to the gravity of the offence and record, the special sentencing provisions for offenders aged under 21, rights of appeal, convictions becoming spent with the passage of time.'

It would be of the very greatest interest to know how frequently all rights and safeguards are actually observed in practice – how many juvenile courts in reality live up to their own high ideals. Relevant comparative documentation is sadly lacking, and there is very little research evidence of an even broadly comparable nature. What little research material there is tends to be of a qualitative and ethnographic nature, and limited to one or two courts whose representativeness it is impossible to determine. For example, Parker, Casburn and Turnbull (1980)[3] describe a juvenile court near Liverpool in which the thinnest façade of legalism covers socially-biased magisterial attitudes and vindictive sentencing practices. It is, of course, possible that the court in question is unique in England; perhaps, however, it represents an end-point on a continuum towards which some other courts approximate in greater or lesser degree; we have at present no means of knowing. The approach of Parker and his colleagues is admittedly a polemical one, as is that of Carlen (1976)[4] in her highly critical study of (adult) magistrates' courts. Her comment that:

> '. . . judicial violation of the mundane expectations which usually enable fully adult people to cope with unfamiliar situations, judicial tolerance of flawed communication systems, and a judicial perversion of the accepted modes of conventional practice, realise a structure of tacit coercion . . .'

may or may not be a balanced appraisal, but it should at least warn us against any easy assumption that a judicial system in practice necessarily fulfils the promise that its model holds out, any more than a system based on welfare considerations.

Punitiveness

The notion of punishment plays a central part in almost all criminal codes, although they may differ greatly in their conceptions of the types and degrees of punishment appropriate to given offences and in the objectives that they openly or implicitly attribute to punishment. In general, punishment involves the infliction of suffering or deprivation, whether mild or severe and whether deterrent, incapacitative or retributive in intention. The children's hearings system, on the other hand, does not employ the rhetoric of punishment. Assuming that the degree of responsibility of children and young people referred to the system is at best a limited one, its stance is paternalistic rather than punitive. Children may be 'in need of compulsory measures of care'; that is to say, their activities and their circumstances, considered in combination, suggest a need for a degree of education, guidance, control or treatment which could not be achieved without a measure of compulsory intervention. Compulsion is rarely an attractive prospect for the person to whom it is applied, especially if it involves the requirement to live for a period in an institutional setting away from the family home. But the compulsory application of supervision does not, in the formal philosophy of the hearings system, carry the connotation of punishment.

That formal philosophy is endorsed by a large majority of children's panel members. There are exceptions. The notion of retributive punishment is accepted by one panel member in five, as is the idea that the measures available should be used to deter other potential offenders, while as many as 38 per cent believe that penalties should be imposed with the object of deterring the offender. These are not insignificant proportions, but not of the same order as the acceptance by more than nine-tenths of all panel members that the purpose of the available measures is to bring about changes in behaviour. Again, about one-fifth see the objective of home supervision as the exercise of control and

9 per cent see the aim of residential supervision as either punishment or incapacitation; but substantial majorities believe that social work supervision involves the provision of help, guidance and support and that confinement to a List D school should mean (fairly strict) social education in a stable environment. One panel member in nine even favours the use of corporal punishment, though the overwhelming majority reject any such proposal. Concepts of punitiveness thus play some part in the thinking of a minority of panel members, though they seem to be capable of co-existing with what many hold to be a logically incompatible welfare philosophy. Most panel members in our sample, however, appear to recognize neither conflict not ambivalence.

The opinions of panel members as to the causes of delinquency are wholly consistent with a non-punitive approach to decision-making. The theme of personal responsibility for delinquent acts, central to the moral justification of punishment, has virtually no place in the wide array of opinions presented. In one form or another, the delinquent child is invariably portrayed as victim: victim sometimes of an impoverished environment, most commonly of inadequate parenting or a seriously unstable family situation. That is not to say that the concept of responsibility is entirely alien to panel members. Underlying attitudes to parents are often harshly critical; if they are seen as the source of their children's problems and difficulties, it is usually with the fairly clear implication that they (the parents) can be held responsible for circumstances which they have created and that they had it in their power to have acted or lived differently had they so chosen. This is not an invariable response; sometimes there emerges from the recorded opinions of panel members a sense of the pitiable futility and hopelessness of the lives of the parents themselves. It is also clear from our own findings that in their encounters with individual children in the course of hearings, panel members do not relate to them as if they were wholly without responsibility for their acts. Commonly, however, the reader is conscious of a sharp distinction between the degrees of responsibility imputed to the two generations.

We have cited a differentiation between punishment and compulsory care that is based principally upon intentions. This view allows for the possibility that paternalistic measures may sometimes be experienced as painful or restrictive by the recipient, but argues that this is fortuitous, unintended and essentially undesirable; such occurrences, it is held, do not contradict the non-punitive nature of the measures. We are conscious that this distinction places an immense premium on good faith; indeed, it might even be said that it contains a temptation to hypocrisy. Because most of us prefer to impute benevolent motives to ourselves, it is comparatively easy to believe that the pain we inflict is an unfortunate by-product of our essentially helpful intentions. But if what we were doing consistently feels like punishment to those at the receiving end and looks like punishment to thoughtful and disinterested observers, there may come a time when the sincerity of our motives is called in question. Punitiveness unconvincingly disguised as welfare has, after all, been a frequent target of criticism; and some writers on the Scottish hearings system have no doubt of its basic dishonesty:

> 'There (Scotland), high levels of intervention in the lives of children and their families occurred through the re-emergence of the principle of the offence as the primary criterion of intervention supplemented and reinforced by a subjective and stereotypical image of the delinquent. Although treatment was the *official* goal priority, control of the child's behaviour became the *operational* goal priority. . . . What is promoted, therefore, as a welfare jurisdiction is no more than a replication of the practice south of the border.' (Morris *et al.*, 1980).[5]

The authors of this criticism are formidable in battle; their undocumented assertions have a lethal aim. Before the intellectual obituary of the Scottish system passes into history, however, we should be certain that what appears to be its crumpled corpse is not in reality a sack of straw. If we are prepared to reject the explicit principles of the system as irrelevant and the personal beliefs of those who put the system into operation as mere self-deception, we might still perhaps suspend judgment on the issues of intrusiveness and punitiveness until we have accurately reviewed the kinds of disposal that are actually made.

The powers of hearings have been listed earlier in this report, but it is worth drawing attention to some of the exclusions. Children's hearings in Scotland have no power to send anyone under 16 to a prison, to a borstal establishment or to a detention centre. They are not permitted to impose any financial penalty. Of the limited number of options available to them, only the supervision order with a residential requirement, involving as it does removal from home, enforced intimacy with strangers and a more or less disciplined regime, could be regarded as having punitive possibilities by a decision-maker intent on imposing punishments. This was the decision reached in between 9 and 10 per cent of the hearings we observed, a proportion corresponding very closely to the national frequency. It is worth recalling that more than four times as many children were discharged, not conditionally but absolutely, and that half of all offenders coming to the notice of reporters did not even reach the hearing stage.

The power to commit children to residential establishments is always employed with reluctance. As we have seen, it is used very rarely indeed with children making their first appearance before a hearing and with only one in three of those who have previously appeared on at least six previous occasions. Expressions of concern or remorse or undertakings for the future are eagerly elicited as justifications for an alternative disposal. The fact that offence history and offence seriousness alone do not allow us to forecast precisely who will be the subject of a residential supervision order tends to lend support to the essentially non-punitive role ascribed to List D schools by most panel members. Perhaps most importantly, the use being made of residential supervision is on the decline. At the end of 1973 1,617 children were resident in List D schools under a current supervision order; at the time of writing (late 1980) the resident population had been reduced to 1,200. There is now a surplus of List D places and the probability that at least three schools will close in the near future. This is due in part to falling referral rates, in part to the growth of community-based schemes of intermediate treatment.

This steadily downward trend is the more noteworthy because it contrasts strikingly with the position in England and Wales, where legislation intended to reduce the punishment-orientation of the juvenile courts appears to have led to a marked increase in the number of residential commitments.

We suspect (though without any systematic evidence) that most panel members would welcome the further growth of alternatives to residential care, but that few would be in favour of the entire abolition of the List D schools which they believe to have a continuing function, not as punishment centres for incorrigible rogues but as structured environments providing social education and rehabilitation.

A definitive comment on punitiveness would require a detailed analysis of List D regimes and of their effect on the young people entrusted to them. Our studies did not touch on these questions, and our extremely subjective impressions of wide variation in their environments, of withdrawal in varying degrees from the norm of the 'total institution' and of concomitant attempts to create something in the nature of a therapeutic environment have no scientific status. We do, however, tentatively conclude that the children's hearings system cannot accurately be characterized as punitive, in intent or in performance.

Individualization

Individualized decision-making is a central element in the image of the ideal children's hearing. Professional reports that provide a detailed assessment of the child's circumstances and needs prepare the way for full discussion with the family, leading in its turn to a decision particularly appropriate to the individual. Critics on the other hand have been known to claim that in spite of a rhetoric of individualization children's hearings in practice operate a simple tariff system. The reality, we think, does not justify either the very optimistic view or the more cynical interpretation.

It would be easier to comment fully on the claim that a tariff system of disposals guides children's hearings if those who make the claim were explicit about what they believed the nature of the tariff to be. We believe the condition would be met if it could be shown that decisions and disposals were related directly and exclusively to the characteristics of the offence, in particular the degree of recidivism it represents or to some measure of the seriousness of the offence. Thus, a well-defined tariff system would be in operation if, for example, we found that:

> all first referrals led to the reporter taking no
> further action; all second referrals came to a
> hearing but were dismissed; all third referrals led to

a home supervision order; and all fourth referrals
led to a residential supervision order.

What we discover in fact is that while decisions by reporters and disposals by hearings are significantly influenced both by the number of prior referrals and by considerations of the seriousness of the current offence, a variety of aspects of personal and domestic circumstances also help to shape decision-making. It has been argued (Asquith, 1979)[6] that when panel members are influenced by the number of previous referrals the significant element in their subjective consideration is not the offence history as such but rather the indication that this provides of the child's degree of disturbance and need for help. This is an interesting interpretation, but a refutation of the claim that a simple tariff system is in operation does not depend upon its accuracy. It is perfectly true that the number of previous referrals significantly affects the *probability* of any given outcome, as within certain limits do some aspects of offence seriousness, but they do not uniquely or even overwhelmingly determine it. That probability is also affected by other considerations which reflect a recognition of personal and environmental difficulties. A combination of these enables decisions to be predicted with a fair measure of accuracy; neither previous record not offence seriousness alone does so.

Our analysis of non-offence influences on decision-making brings out an important negative finding. The scales are not weighed against children of low socio-economic status or those in single-parent families. When reports indicate difficulties for the child in these households, the chances of referral to a hearing are increased, as are the chances of a hearing terminating in a supervision requirement; but when 'perceived problems' is held constant, there is no substantial influence on decision-making. Simple stereotypes do not seem to be used as indicators of need and justifications for intervention.

All of this is, however, a long way from saying that decisions are truly individualized. For two major reasons, the hearings system fails to reach the standard it has set itself. First, the quality of the information available to panel members in individual cases though sometimes high is often disappointing. Professional reports tend to reflect the preoccupations of those who compile them rather than the needs of those who use them. The powerful influence of their recommendations is not matched by the skill with which they are formulated or the cogency with which they are argued. Recommendations usually have the appearance of having been grafted on at the end of a somewhat discursive description rather than of flowing logically from an incisive review. Panel members in their turn are often less conscientious than they might be in following up in the hearing information and suggestions contained in reports. These findings have important implications for training, discussed earlier. Social workers, conscious of the limitations of the preparation they have received, may require not merely specific guidance in the construction of reports, but a deeper awareness of the underlying principles of assessment and evaluation. Experiments with alternative approaches to report-writing could make a valuable contribution to the development of more effective documentation for hearings. Panel members in their turn need greater skill in interpreting information and in opening up sensitive and less superficial areas in the course of the hearing though they are perhaps less aware of their limitations.

Secondly – and this is no doubt a consideration inhibiting social workers and other authors of reports as well as constraining panel members – we must recognize the limited range of disposals formally available to hearings. It is unrealistic to expect decision-making to be highly individualized when there are so few decisions that can be made. No doubt one or other of the options available must sometimes seem truly the most appropriate course, having regard to the needs of a particular child, but often the choice may mean little more than that it is the least unsuitable of the possibilities open.

The possibility of additional powers for children's hearings has recently been raised in a 'Consultative Memorandum' issued on behalf of the Secretary of State (Social Work Services Group, 1980).[7] The document in question, although claiming that its object is to strengthen the hearings system and not to make any change in its underlying principles, in fact proposes a number of powers, some of an explicitly punitive nature; these include the imposition of fines, the ordering of compulsory reparation and the right to refer unco-operative parents to the sheriff court with a view to the imposition of 'caution' (i.e. the deposit of a sum of money which is forfeit if their child offends again). These proposals stem from the unargued assumption – discussed earlier in this chapter – that since all compulsory measures tend to be unpopular, they are therefore indistinguishable from punishment, so that the creation of additional measures which do not claim to be anything other than punitive would not affect the essential nature of the system.

That this assumption is clearly debatable has been pointed out by some of those who responded to the government invitation to comment on the consultative memorandum (Murray, 1980).[8] This latter analysis of responses makes it clear that rejoinders to the proposed changes were on balance strongly negative. In particular, the observations submitted by regional children's panels and by the representative body of panel members were unanimous in their rejection of powers of a punitive nature. In this respect, the ideas put forward on behalf of panel members are to some degree at variance with those expressed by panel members when approached as individuals. It is clear from our own findings (see *Chapter 15*) that the power to order reparation would be welcomed by a very large majority of panel members, while the power to fine parents receives the approval of a substantial minority. Our questions were circulated at least a year earlier than the Government's consultative document, and the possible additional powers listed are not identical. But the data seem to suggest a wish for a wider range of disposals, greater than might have been supposed from a consideration of formal responses to the Secretaty of State. It is at least possible that the consultative memorandum's emphasis on punishment, and its demonstrably superficial grasp of the hearings system's principles, may have served to alert panel members to the potential hazards of the proposed changes. Their reactions to the political document indicates a closer adherence to their basic philosophy when the context of the proposals makes their implications clearer. At the time of writing it is still uncertain whether the proposed changes will be implemented or withdrawn; but whether, if brought into effect, they would indeed permit a more effective individualization of decisions is questionable.

Yet if expressly punitive powers are to be excluded, the problem of how to respond more flexibly to the need for measures of care will continue to confront panel members. Above all, there is a case for greater inventiveness in the use of those powers that now exist. Home supervision in particular is too frequently identified in only the most general terms; it should often be possible to consider with the social worker in the case the specific objectives to be pursued and styles of supervision to be employed. 'Intermediate treatment' covers a bewildering variety of group activities, and panel members should have sufficient knowledge of the provisions available to be able to recommend types of programme that they believe will be helpful in the individual case. Residential establishments should offer, and be known to offer, a wide range of environments and opportunities, and be selected for their specific appropriateness. Such disposals are not unknown at present, but they tend to be the exception rather than the rule.

Of course, no juvenile justice system, however sincere its commitment to welfare principles, can possibly meet all the needs of the children who come before it. Panel members cannot make poor children rich or substitute caring and competent for inadequate and neglectful parents. But they should at least be able to exert pressure on other public services outside the limited area in which they have direct powers, by expressing forceful recommendations concerning needs that their clients may have for special educational services or for medical or psychological care, or for social services of different kinds for their parents. For such an approach to be effective, we should need to see a network of services more open and more flexible than any we are now familiar with.

Unintended consequences

Judges have been known to remark that the results of the sentences that they passed were of no concern to them. Such an opinion is consistent with a wholly retributivist approach to punishment; but actions have consequences whether those responsible for the actions take heed of them or not, and from the viewpoint of public policy in general, as distinct from that of the individual decision-maker, it is doubtful whether the sum-total of consequences can properly be ignored. There is abundant evidence in many spheres that the outcomes of social action may be quite different from, or additional to, those that were consciously intended, and there is correspondingly a growing recognition that the study of policies in action should also take account of these unintended effects, so far as they can be identified. The study of penal policies and practices has been markedly influenced by a body of writing that has drawn attention to a variety of damaging effects that, it is claimed, can flow from the processing of offenders. Such concepts as degradation, labelling and stigma have been the subject of a forceful and colourful sociological literature, which has helped to stimulate interest in ideas of minimal intervention. Much of the writing in question is, we believe, somewhat naive and over-simplified. Nevertheless, it cannot be brushed aside in the examination of a system committed to a consequentialist justification for intervention. The possibility that the procedures and decisions of children's hearings may have unintentionally damaging effects must be given serious consideration.

The informality of children's hearings and the simplicity of the settings in which almost all of them are conducted are intended, among other things, to avoid humiliating and degrading young offenders and their families. We noted examples of sarcasm, interrogation and interruption (not very frequently but not very rarely) on the part of some panel members, which might tend to work against this objective. Nevertheless, interviews with children and parents make it clear that the participants did not see the experience as confusing, remote or hurtful. The reduction of ritual, the comparative intimacy of the setting and the use of more or less plain language all seem to contribute to this.

The term labelling is often used indiscriminately to refer both to changes in the sense of identity of a person who has been designated as deviant, and to changes in the attitudes of others towards that person. We have thought it more useful to refer to only the former as a labelling effect and to employ the term stigma to indicate the latter, while recognizing the possibility that the two effects may interact. To what extent children who have appeared before hearings are in fact regarded by others in a more hostile or critical manner, and whether they are indeed disadvantaged as a result of their contacts with the system are not matters on which we have any evidence. What we do know is that the expectation of stigma is quite strong. A substantial majority believe that they would be handicapped in their future relations with the police and with potential employers as a result of their experience. Although the proportions so reporting varied according to the outcome of their hearing, it is striking that more than half of those who had been discharged expected the police to react negatively towards them in the future, while nearly three-quarters of those discharged thought that an employer would mistrust them. We do not know how far these expectations are soundly based, and it would be of considerable interest and importance to examine this as well as other aspects of the after-histories of the clients of the hearings system. This whole area might have important implications for reintegration and rehabilitation. Meanwhile the fact that such beliefs are quite prevalent cannot be lightly ignored.

The labelling issue, on the other hand, seems to present few problems. The great majority of children who have been through hearings see themselves as little different from other youngsters – unlucky, no doubt, and perhaps unfairly singled out for attention, but not often as criminal and even less often (in spite of the terminology of children's hearings) as in need of help. The sense of identity seems fairly sturdy and in most instances not easily damaged by the hearing experience. Labelling theory has been promoted a good deal more vigorously than the research evidence justifies, and for all we know juvenile courts and comparable bodies in other jurisdictions have no greater tendency to implant or reinforce a delinquent sense of identity. All we can say with confidence is that the large majority of hearings clients do not appear to be negatively affected in this particular way.

There remains the final possibility that the life experiences that lead from the hearing decision may have unintended harmful consequences. Opinions may be divided as to whether social work supervision serves any useful purpose, but at least we know of no serious evidence to suggest that it actually does any damage. The focus of concern must be the residential supervision order, for there is a good deal in the literature to indicate that correctional institutions take on some of the features of a delinquent sub-culture and provide informal preparation for more advanced stages in a delinquent career. None of the literature relates to Scottish List D schools, and some of it does not take account of recent developments in residential services. Our study did not extend to an examination of institutional life, and we can do no more than remain alert to the possibility that such placements may have deleterious effects that counteract their intended, rehabilitative functions. Of course, they may not. That possibility can be neither dismissed nor confirmed without further careful study. If such a study were to be undertaken, it might well embrace the whole range of residential provision for children and young people in Scotland and consider not merely present variations in the quality of services offered but also what reforms or innovations may be desirable. For a system that justifies intervention in paternalistic terms, *primum non nocere* is a good starting principle. Beyond that, it might even be possible to shake off some of the widespread contemporary nihilism about prevention and change. As Nigel Walker[9] has remarked, we have not been conspicuously more successful in finding ways to prevent war or poverty or to cure cancer than to prevent delinquency; but this strengthens rather than removes our obligation to maintain our efforts.

NOTES

1. Philip Priestley, Denise Fears and Roger Fuller, *Justice for juveniles*, Routledge and Kegan Paul, 1977.
2. W. E. Cavenagh, 'Children in trouble and troublesome children', in: V. Lorne Stewart, *Troubled children around the world*. New York University Press, 1981.
3. Howard Parker, Maggie Casburn and David Turnbull, 'The production of punitive juvenile justice', *British Journal of Criminology*, 20(3), 1980.
4. Pat Carlen, *Magistrates' justice*. Martin Robertson, 1976.
5. Allison Morris, Henri Giller, Elizabeth Szwed and Hugh Geach, *Justice for children*. Macmillan, 1980.
6. Stewart Asquith, 'Frames of relevance and decision-making in children's hearings and juvenile courts: a comparative study', Ph.D. thesis, University of Edinburgh, 1979.
7. Social Work Services Group, 'Children's hearings: consultative memorandum on Part III of the Social Work (Scotland) Act 1968', April 1980.
8. Kathleen Murray, 'Attitudes to change in the children's hearings system', *The Hearing*, 1, 1980.
9. Nigel Walker, *Punishment, danger and stigma*. Basil Blackwell, 1980.

BIBLIOGRAPHY OF THE CHILDREN'S HEARINGS SYSTEM

ASQUITH, S. 1977 Relevance and lay participation in juvenile justice
British Journal of Law and Society 4, 1

BROWN, P. & BLOOMFIELD, T., eds. 1979 *Legality and community*
Aberdeen Peoples Press

BRUCE, N. 1975 Children's hearings: a retrospect
British Journal of Criminology 15, 4

BRUCE, N. 1978 Scottish children's panels and their critics
Journal of Adolescence 1, 3

BRUCE, N. & SPENCER, J. 1974 Children's hearings and the Scottish courts
In: JONES, K., ed., *Yearbook of social policy in Britain 1973*
Routledge and Kegan Paul

BRUCE, N. & SPENCER, J. 1976 *Face to face with families*
McDonald

CAMPAIGN FOR THE CARE OF DEPRIVED CHILDREN 1974 Justice for children: the Scottish system and its application to Ireland
Care Discussion Paper 2

CLARK, D. 1977 Personality characteristics of applicants and members of children's panels
British Journal of Criminology 17, 3

CURRAN, J. 1977 *The children's hearing system: a review of research*
A Scottish Office Social Research Study, Edinburgh: HMSO

FINLAYSON, A. 1978 Social work and the court
In: CCETSW *Good enough parenting*

FOX, S. 1974 Juvenile justice reform: innovations in Scotland
American Criminal Law Review 12, 1

FOX, S. 1974 Evaluation of the system by an American observer
International Journal of Offender Therapy and Comparative Criminology 18, 3

FOX, S. 1975 The Scottish panels: an American viewpoint on children's right to punishment
Journal of the Law Society of Scotland 20, 3

GORDON, G. 1972 Provisions relating to children
Renton and Brown's Criminal procedure according to the law of Scotland 4th ed.
Edinburgh: W. Green & Son

GORDON, G. 1973 Prosecuting children: an assessment of the situation in the light of the 1968 Act
Journal of the Law Society of Scotland 18, 11

GRANT, J. 1971 Juvenile justice: Part III of the Social Work (Scotland) Act, 1968
Juridical Review 2

GRANT, J. 1975 The legal safeguards for the rights of the child and parents in the children's hearing system
Juridical Review 3

GRANT, J. 1975 The children's hearing system in Scotland: its strength and weaknesses
Irish Jurist 10

GRANT, J. 1975 The Rehabilitation of Offenders Act, 1974, and children's hearings
Journal of the Law Society of Scotland 20, 4

GRANT, J. 1976 Legal United 1, Reporters' Association 2
Journal of the Law Society of Scotland 21, 3

KELLY, A. 1974 Children's hearings
International Journal of Offender Therapy and Comparative Criminology 18, 3

McISAAC, M. & McCLINTOCK, F. 1976 The juvenile justice system in Scotland
In: United Nations Social Defence Research Institute, *Juvenile justice: an international survey*

MACK, J. & RITCHIE, M. 1974 *Police warnings*
University of Glasgow

MAPSTONE, E. 1972 The selection of the children's panels for the county of Fife
British Journal of Social Work 2, 4

MARTIN, F. 1978 The future of juvenile justice: English courts and Scottish hearings
Howard Journal of Penology and Crime Prevention 17, 2

MARTIN, F. & MURRAY, K., eds. 1976 *Children's hearings*
Scottish Academic Press

MARTIN, F. & MURRAY, K. 1981 Juvenile justice in Scotland
In: Lorne Stewart, V., ed., *Troubled children around the world*
New York University Press

MAY, D. 1971 Delinquency control and the treatment model: some implications of recent legislation
British Journal of Criminology 11, 4

MAY, D. 1977 Rhetoric and reality: the consequence of unacknowledged ambiguity in the children's panel system
British Journal of Criminology 17, 3

MAY, D. 1979 The children's hearing system: Part 1 The limits to legislative action, Part 2 The limits to social work influence
Journal of Social Welfare Law

MAY, D. & SMITH, G. 1970 Policy interpretation and the children's panels
Journal of Applied Social Studies 2

MORRIS, A. 1972 Children's hearings in Scotland
Criminal Law Review 693

MORRIS, A. 1974 Scottish juvenile justice: a critique
In: HOOD, R., ed., *Crime, criminology and public policy*
Heinemann

MORRIS, A. 1976 Juvenile justice, where next? *Howard Journal of Penology and Crime Prevention* 18

MORRIS, A. & MCISAAC, M. 1978 *Juvenile justice?* Heinemann

MURRAY, K. 1974 Children's panel training: learning to change *Scottish Journal of Adult Education* 1, 2

MURRAY, K. 1979 Juvenile justice and children's hearings In: ENGLISH, J. & MARTIN, F., eds., *Social services in Scotland* Scottish Academic Press

MURRAY, G. & ROWE, A. 1973 Children's panels: implications for the future *Policy and Politics* 1, 4

PARSLOE, P. 1976 Social work and the justice model *British Journal of Social Work* 6, 1

PARSLOE, P. 1978 *Juvenile justice in Britain and the United States* Routledge and Kegan Paul

ROWE, A. 1972 *Initial selection for children's panels in Scotland* Bookstall Publications, London

RUSHFORTH, M. 1978 *Committal to residential care: a case study in juvenile justice* A Scottish Office Social Research Study, HMSO, Edinburgh

SMITH, G. 1977 The place of 'professional ideology' in the analysis of 'social policy': some theoretical conclusions from a pilot study of the children's panels *The Sociological Review* 25, 12

SMITH, G. 1978 'Little kiddies' and 'criminal acts': the role of social work in the children's hearings *British Journal of Social Work* 7, 4

SMITH, G. 1978 The meaning of 'success' in social policy *Public Administration* 56

SMITH, G. & MAY, D. 1971 The appointment of the Aberdeen city children's panel *British Journal of Social Work* 1, 1

SMITH, G. & MAY, D. 1980 Executing 'decisions' in the children's hearings *Sociology* 14, 4

WHALLEY, L. *et al.* 1978 Psychiatric referrals from Scottish children's hearings *Journal of Child Psychology and Psychiatry* 19

INDEX

NAME INDEX